Paul Fox (ed.)

Decadences

Morality and Aesthetics in British Literature

STUDIES IN ENGLISH LITERATURES

Edited by Koray Melikoğlu and Özden Sözalan
ISSN 1614-4651

1   *Özden Sözalan*
     The Staged Encounter: Contemporary Feminism and Women's Drama
     ISBN 3-89821-367-6

2   *Paul Fox (ed.)*
     Decadences: Morality and Aesthetics in British Literature
     ISBN 3-89821-573-3

FORTHCOMING (MANUSCRIPT WORKING TITLES)

Daniel Shea
James Joyce and the Mythology of Modernism
ISBN 3-89821-574-1

David Ellis
Black Writing in Britain since 1945
ISBN 3-89821-591-1

Paul Fox (ed.)
Victorian Detective and Mystery Fiction
ISBN 3-89821-593-8

Paul Fox (ed.)

DECADENCES

Morality and Aesthetics in British Literature

ibidem-Verlag
Stuttgart

Bibliografische Information Der Deutschen Bibliothek

Die Deutsche Bibliothek verzeichnet diese Publikation in der Deutschen
Nationalbibliografie; detaillierte bibliografische Daten sind im Internet
über <http://dnb.ddb.de> abrufbar.

Cover illustration:
Edward Tennyson Reed: "Britannia à la Beardsley".
(By Our "Yellow" Decadent.)
From Punch's Almanack for 1895.

A CIP catalogue record for this book is available from:
Die Deutsche Bibliothek
http://dnb.ddb.de

∞

Gedruckt auf alterungsbeständigem, säurefreien Papier
Printed on acid-free paper

ISSN 1614-4651

ISBN 3-89821-573-3

© *ibidem*-Verlag
Stuttgart 2006
Alle Rechte vorbehalten

Contents

Preface

This collection seeks to examine the intersections of aesthetics and morality, of what Decadence means to art and society at various moments in British literature. The inclination toward either the artistic or social perspective in each essay has been rendered more straightforwardly by employing capitalization for aesthetic Decadence, and the lower-case to illustrate moral decadence.

Both artistic and social values are inflected by their histories, and, as time passes, so the definition of what it means to be D/decadent alters. The very ideas of the decline from a higher standard, of social malaise, of aesthetic ennui, all presume certain facts about the past, the present, and the linear nature of time itself. To reject the past as a given, and to relish the subtleties of present nuance, is the beginning of Decadence.

Purportedly decadent artists focused upon the fleeting present, ascribed value to experiencing the aesthetic moment in its purest form, and it was precisely due to this focus upon living in, and for, the moment that society often responded by expressing moral contempt for the perceived hedonism of art. The aesthetic rejection of contemporary value added to the conflict between the literary and social inflections of Decadent interpretation. The *truly* decadent was condemned by artists as the stranglehold society maintained on individual interpretation and the interpretation of oneself. This conflict underlies the range of essays in the collection.

Decadent artists would perhaps argue that it is precisely in the emphasis upon the value of the present moment that a higher system of evaluating life is produced. It adds a greater import to every action, to every perception of the world. It provides an ethical standard of interaction between the individual and society, a communion that aesthetes found lacking in the strictures of conventional morality. The reinterpretation of these restrictions upon the individual, favoring an ethical interaction between the artist and the world, becomes the counterpoint to society's moral condemnation.

The Decadent artist encouraged reading the world as a text written for each individual. The first essay in this collection suggests how one might read as a Decadent, to reconstitute the textual in personal terms and for the present. As the reader moves between the points charted by the several contributors, it is hoped that suggestions will be presented that both revise what it means to be Decadent and that afford a new and valuable means to perceiving our present.

Paul Fox

Containing the Poisonous Text: Decadent Readers, Reading Decadence[1]

Shafquat Towheed

Institute of English Studies, University of London

Abstract: In re-reading representative texts by Huysmans, Lee, Pater and Wilde, in this essay I will aim to demonstrate that the history of Decadent writing is inseparable from a concept of decadent reading, and specifically, from a socially constructed, aesthetically self-conscious, and fictionally mediated practice of reading: a practice of reading that offers a possible epistemology of Decadence.

Reading Petronius' *Satyricon* in the blue and orange hued safety of his asylum and ancestral library room, Des Esseintes, the aristocratic anti-hero of Joris-Karl Huysmans' book without a plot, *À rebours* (1884), responds to the fragmentary Latin narrative from the age of Nero with a heady mixture of desire, disgust, and dispassionate analysis. Observing the "extraordinary vigour and precise colouring" of Petronius' narrative, a "realistic novel" of "Roman life in the raw," he applauds the episodic nature of "this story with no plot or action in it" and "no need to fake a conclusion or point a moral" that relates in a "style that makes free of every dialect" and "makes every man talk in his own idiom" the "erotic adventures of certain sons of Sodom" (43). Reading synchronically rather than diachronically, Des Esseintes' partial, focalised re-reading of a familiar (perhaps even, over-familiar) narrative problematises extant classical paradigms of reading practice.

The emotional impact of Des Esseintes' bravura act of reading Petronius and re-imagining the decadent past is intriguing. This particular reading act, potentially both intensive and extensive, is an

---

[1] I am grateful to Josephine Guy and Adrian Poole for reading and commenting on drafts of this paper.

example of the logocentrism of Decadence, its determination, as Sharon Bassett (261-62) has noted, to "live its bookish education" through its reading of the classics. Such an approach is not without risk. Filled with disgust at the state of modern literature, Des Esseintes' reading experience rapidly degenerates into a tactile and bibliophilic handling of his "superb copy" of the text, an "octavo edition of 1585 printed by J. Dousa at Leyden" and glossed with marginalia and a commentary on the text; Des Esseintes' most prized Latin work is explicitly intertextual (44).[2] The influence of the *Satyricon* is manifold. It excites Des Esseintes' imagination with images of the "minor events," "bestial incidents" and "obscene antics" of "everyday life of Rome" while at the same time, it fuels his disgust at the majority of contemporary French literature, which unlike the *Satyricon*, has failed in his judgment to depict "in a splendidly wrought style" the "vices of a decrepit civilization, a crumbling Empire" without a "word of approval or condemnation" (42, 44).

This solipsistic reading experience provokes both intimacy with an irretrievable classical (and decadent) past, and alienation from an inexorably more remote and unpalatable present. Increasingly, Des Esseintes defines himself, and the experiential world around him through his reading from within the secluded asylum of his library, but the reading experience itself, while facilitating self-identification with Decadent writers and their readers past and present, does not offer any form of emotional consolation; after reading the *Satyricon* for example, Des Esseintes can only take tactile pleas-

---

[2] Petronii Arbitri Viri Consularis *Satyricon* and Iani Dousae Nordovicis *Pro Satyrico Petronii Arbitri Viri Consularis* (Lugduni Batavorum, 1585). Bound together in an octavo volume, first part dated 1585, the second part, which is a commentary on the text, dated 1583. The handsome text is glossed throughout with marginal comments and decorated woodcut capitals; British Library call mark 1607/4687.

ure from his reverent handling of the handsome volume, not from reading the text.[3] Indeed, Des Esseintes' re-reading (or perhaps, mis-reading?) fails even to match the tone of Petronius' anarchic, optimistic and episodic narrative.

Des Esseintes' reading practice is invariably fugitive, desultory, unsystematic, fragmentary, inchoate, unmediated, impressionistic, phenomenological and without any semblance of a system of pedagogy; it is a truant re-reading of literature for its own sake, with the entirety of the text subordinated to the individual part that he chooses to read, exemplified by his deliberately perverse reading of seventh- and eighth-century hagiography, "dipping at odd moments into the works" (50), and his constantly interrupted attention to whatever "old quarto" is at hand (78, 83). Des Esseintes' reading practice, clearly a decadent reading practice, recapitulates Paul Bourget's theory of the regressive decomposition of literature from the whole text to the individual word and anticipates Havelock Ellis' (175) designation of Decadence as a "heterogeneous" aesthetic style, a style which is "beautiful because the whole is subordinated to the parts," and one which he affirms, can only exist "in relation to a classic style." Des Esseintes' desultory re-reading fractures established hermeneutic practice, which as Matei Calinescu (168) points out, depends upon interpreting the "significance of each part" in the "light of the whole and that of the whole in the light of each part." By consistently privileging the part over the whole, decadent reading, and more to the point, decadent *re-reading*, conspicuously disrupts this dialectic of hermeneutic exchange.

---

[3] Des Esseintes' inability to derive emotional consolation from any reading within Huysmans' anti-naturalist narrative is a repeated and intensifying motif in *À rebours*; see his responses to reading maritime timetables (34), St. Augustine (48), Poe (73), Lacordaire (87), Schopenhauer (92-95), Dickens (132), profane literature (179), Balzac (180) and Flaubert and Gautier (189).

Des Esseintes' truncated reading experience, where part of the text dominates the volume, or even the author's entire oeuvre, invariably results in renewed disappointment, and often precludes, rather than facilitates, an actual reading, or re-reading, of the book at hand. Indeed, by the end of *À rebours*, the emotionally and psychologically exhausted Des Esseintes is almost incapable of reading, for he finds that none of his books are "sufficiently hardened to go through the next process, the reading mill" (179), a comment which is more apposite when applied to the reader than to the text. Sometimes the ostensibly synchronic reading experience itself is fetishised and cathected; examining the binding of an edition of *L'après-midi d'un faune*, with its covering of "Japanese felt as white as curdled milk" for example, precludes the act of reading (aloud or otherwise) the brief lines of Mallarmé's exquisite verse (197-98). Des Esseintes' apparent surfeit of reading and anxiety of re-reading provokes exhaustion and ennui, and in this he prefigures the intertextual dilemma (what to read? when to stop reading?) that has plagued the modern and post-modern reader. This paradox is all the more apposite when we consider the inherently bibliographic nature of the Decadent novel.[4] At once a parataxis and a reader, Decadent fiction is defined through the hinterland of texts it draws upon, inviting the reader to scrutinise named volumes, while at the same time repudiating the effects of those very acts of extensive reading.

What is clear is that Des Esseintes' decadent reading practice has destroyed the much desired nineteenth-century ideal of the "intellectual communion between a hieratic writer and an ideal reader," a communion that he believes can only be re-established through the decomposition and concentration of the novel into a prose-poem of a "page or two" (199). The idea of the dialogic relationship between the writer and the ideal reader was ubiquitous at the time; in Eng-

---

[4] See, for example, Schoolfield.

land, Vernon Lee, Walter Pater and Oscar Wilde all addressed this issue repeatedly in both fiction and criticism. Far from inducing appetite or producing satiety, Des Esseintes' reading practice has instead resulted in literary dyspepsia and a closed list; his "anthology" is to be the "last book in his library" (199), a list of titles that will never be read again (within the narrative, he has no heirs, literary or otherwise). Paradoxically, Des Esseintes' repeated re-reading of his library promulgates and enforces the end of his own reading. Corralling his volumes into the *cordon sanitaire* of his literary asylum/mausoleum, Des Esseintes ironically both anticipates the failed attempts at the policing of literature deemed "decadent" – "poisonous texts"– as well as confirming the potentially debilitating influence, what Jankélévitch (339) describes as the "fever of proliferation" of these titles on their putative readers.[5] Indeed, Des Esseintes' insistence upon constantly selecting, organising and eliminating titles from his library, and his increasing inability to read his favourite texts without a concomitant detrimental physical or psychological effect – even reading his favourite, Poe, leaves him "trembling" (192) – validates the untrammelled, disruptive, potent and unpredictable influence of books, even when confined in the temporal and physical space of a private library. While it articulated an entire school of late nineteenth-century critical thinking that celebrated Decadent literature *and* the decadence of literary culture, Huysmans' "breviary of decadence" also suggested that the direct impact of the

---

[5] Almost all the contemporary French titles in Des Esseintes' collection were cited for prosecution for obscenity by the National Vigilance Association in their 1888 campaign against Vizetelly's English translation and distribution of Zola in Britain, including Flaubert's *Madame Bovary* and *Salammbô*, the Goncourts' *Germinie Lacertaux* and *Renée Mauperin*, Gautier's *Mademoiselle de Maupin*, Murger's *Vie de bohême*, Maupassant's *Bel-ami* and *Une vie*, Daudet's *Sapho*, and Bourget's *Crime d'amour* and *Cruelle énigme*; see Decker, 93-94.

written word upon the consciousness and identity formation of the individual reader was spectacularly undiminished. In a demonstrative act of decadent disavowal, a narrative that delineates the psychological and emotional exhaustion of re-reading itself establishes the potency of the influence of the book on prospective (and presumably, new) readers.

Petronius' humorous and worldly narrative is not the only influential, potentially "poisonous" text in Des Esseintes' Decadent library, described as "one of the most significant collections of books in the entire history of literature" (Cevasco, *Breviary* 6), in the villa at Fontenay-aux-Roses, but it is remarkable for offering an extended ironic commentary on the reason for literary decadence. In "Eumolpus in the Art Gallery," Petronius satirises the complacent and widespread assumption of literary decline by placing a simplistic analysis in the mouth of Eumolpus, a poet of remarkable unpopularity and ineptitude, who blames the current state of the arts on the "lust for money" and obsession with "wine and the women of the street" and a disrespect for the past: "we censure the old ways, but teach and learn nothing but vices" (Petronius 75).[6] As an example of a Roman work that interrogates the notion of cultural decadence, Huysmans' deployment of Petronius is doubly ironic; Eumolpus' stale opinions anticipate those of many contemporary reviewers, while Petronius' own place in posterity is vindicated by the survival and re-amplification of the *Satyricon* through Huysmans' novel and beyond. Des Esseintes', and the reader's, literary taste and judgment is negotiated through the filter of the *Satyricon*, a narrative in which the determinedly synchronic nineteenth-century reader can observe "subtle style, acute observation, and solid construction" and a "curious similarity" with the "modern French novels" of contemporary decadent fiction (44).

---

[6] See Beck.

At the earliest stages of the conception of the work, Huysmans had insisted upon defining Des Esseintes and his sensibility through his reading; writing to Stéphane Mallarmé in October 1882, he noted that his character enjoyed reading "the writers of the exquisite and penetrating period of Roman decadence," the "barbarous and delicious poems of Orientius, Veranius of Gévaudan, Baudonivia," the French of "Poe, Baudelaire, the second part of *La Faustin*," adding that he was "using the word decadence so as to be intelligible" to his readers (Beaumont 44-45). Huysmans' repeated use of the term "decadence" attached a pre-existing "intelligible" context to his relentless use of metafictional strategies to define his novel. Writing to Edmond de Goncourt to express his admiration for *La Faustin* (1882), Huysmans praised the author's ability to write in the same style and register as Petronius, a language he described as being "nerveux, élégant, déprave, cet éréthisme savant que les Latins de la décadence ont eu aussi et qui a été décrit par Pétrone" (Lambert 71). Goncourt's resurrection of the Latin decadence of Petronius is brought to bear upon his own "breviary of the decadence," for Des Esseintes insistently compares Petronius (and to a lesser extent, Apuleius) to the contemporary *décadents* whose work he has amassed in creating his definitive bibliographic catalogue of French literature, which includes Mallarmé, Goncourt, Baudelaire, Verlaine and Gautier (180-200).

Writing to Émile Zola after the publication of *À rebours* in the spring of 1884, and wary of offending the master of Naturalism with his relentlessly heterodox text, Huysmans misleadingly insisted upon the medico-scientific realism of his case study. "I took trouble throughout the book, in a desire for perfect accuracy," he declared, by following "step by step Bouchut and Axenfeld's books on neurosis" (Beaumont, 54-55).[7] In attempting to defend the realism of his work, Huysmans' rhetoric mimicked the discourse of anti-decadent critics who insisted upon reading Decadent literature as testamentary clinical evidence for mental and physical illness, as a diseased text emanating from a diseased body, as language that had deviated "from the established norms in an attempt to reproduce pathology on a textual level" (Hustvedt 23).[8] Yet while Huysmans presented the novel to Zola as a realist text that illustrated Des Esseintes' psychopathology, the individual acts of reading that he articulated within the work suggested something altogether different: a work defined intertextually through specific acts of desultory, decadent reading, and the interpretative strategies in which its readers would be forced to engage. Huysmans' description of the novel to Zola betrays his own anxiety about how *À rebours* would be read and interpreted, but it also displays his awareness of the potential of the book for influencing, and radically destabilising its readers.

The belief in the direct, determining influence of the Decadent text upon its readers was accepted in equal measure by both the champions and the detractors of Decadent literature. Havelock Ellis, possibly the most sensitive of *fin de siècle* commentators on Decadent writing, observed that the formative effect of Des Esseintes' fictional reading practice was a synecdoche for his creator's self-identification as the leading *décadent* of his age, and that both were

---

[7] Huysmans' alleged source texts were Eugène Bouchut's *De l'état nerveux aigu et chronique, ou nervosisme appelé névropathie aiguë cérebro-pneumo-gastrique etc* (Paris, 1860) and Alexandre Axenfeld's *Traité des névroses* (Paris, 1882).

[8] See Lang, Laurent, Nordau. For a recent medico-scientific reading, see Jordanova; for a Kleinian reading of Des Esseintes' orality and regression, see Ziegler.

"moulded" (185) by their reading. "Des Esseintes' predilections in literature," Ellis (181) notes, are "without question" faithfully reflected in "his creator's impressions." For Ellis, the reading experience that took place within Des Esseintes' asylum/library proved the determining influence of books in shaping Huysmans' Decadent literary style *and* defining the self-identification of the decadent through his or her individual reading practice. "The three chapters [. . .] which describe Des Esseintes' library," Ellis (185) observes, "may serve at once both to indicate the chief moulding influence on Huysmans' own style" and to define the "precise nature of decadence in art and the fundamental part it plays". Ellis is unequivocal about the ability of individual books to shape, influence, and even define, their readers. "The final value of any book," he observes, "is in its power to reveal to us our own real selves" (vii). In the potential parallax offered through the filter of the "poisonous book," Ellis' interpretation of decadent identity is unambiguous: you read what you are, but more importantly, *you are what you read.*

The increasingly clamorous debate over the perceived influence of the decadent book, an influence mediated through a reading practice that was invariably fugitive, fragmentary, impressionistic, antinomian and self-consciously reflected in the text itself, was widely articulated in late nineteenth-century public discourse. These anxieties of both influence *and* dissemination were amplified by new developments in psychology, such as the concept of subliminal influence. The parapsychologist F. W. H. Myers (200-01) suggested that the effect of the subliminal on the individual would render "the ordinary senses more acute," and even more disturbingly for the moral censors of the age, claimed that "we seldom give the name of genius to any piece of work into which some uprush of subliminal faculty has not entered." The potentially uncontrollable nature of decadent reading, as both a practice and a subject, brought out the moralist in Vernon Lee. Drawing upon the importance of a moral economy of reading, Lee's homologue Baldwin (*Baldwin* 228) warned against the danger of Decadent literature: "I would rather that the English novel were reduced to the condition of Sunday reading for girls of twelve," he declared, "than that such a novel as Maupassant's *Une Vie* or Gautier's *Mademoiselle de Maupin* should be written in this country."[9]

The immediate effect of an inappropriate reader's inappropriate reading was depicted with some comic relish by the popular novelist William John Locke in his *Stella Maris* (1913). Picking up her uncle's copy of an unnamed French novel which her aunt describes as unsuitable for "young girls" as it deals with "a certain side of life that is not wholesome for young girls to dwell upon," Stella decides to read the book regardless. Stella's reading practice is furtive, fugitive, spontaneous and unsystematic – in other words – decadent; smuggling the book "up to her bedroom," she "opened it in the middle," but "after a few pages her cheeks grew hot and her heart cold, and she threw the book out of the window" (255). For contemporary observers, Stella's reading and the specific neuropathology of her response, a response that echoed and amplified previous anxieties about spasmodic poetry and sensation fiction, was only too common. "The scene is entirely typical" of the period, observed Amy Cruse (68), adding that it was the result of "the younger generation having claimed its right to read what it pleased" from "beginning to end" – something that Stella, despite being a virgin reader, rather than a decadent re-reader of this specific text, consciously does not do.[10] And yet, even while mainstream popular fiction attempted to proscribe Decadent literature by dramatising the allegedly deleterious effect that it had upon its readers, thereby presenting in short-

---

[9] For Lee's theories of reading, see Towheed.

[10] It is debatable whether Stella's fictionalised reading practice is randomly phenomenological or is informed by knowledge of where to look in the specific text.

hand a titillating simulacrum of reading, it depended upon the very existence of Decadent writing in order to define its own wholesomeness; Locke's popular satirical novel, for example, was published by John Lane, the chief publisher in the 1890s of Decadent literature.[11] Anti-decadent writing depended upon a hinterland of Decadent literature in order to define itself; it also required a reading practice that could be identified and ostensibly contained. As Liz Constable (306-07) has observed, the "strategy of *naming* decadence" was "ineffective in pre-empting truant readings" because when the "supposed decadence in question" was the "practice of *reading*" itself it could not be "quarantined by its naming"; indeed, naming only rendered the "phenomenon more contagious."

In the ostensibly ordered domesticity of Victorian bourgeois life, the Decadent text threatened to destabilize the established, policed norms of reading. At a time when the two most "clearly contested areas" (Flint 103) in the home between the sexes – the library and the bedroom – were also the main loci of individual reading, the circulation of the Decadent text and with it, its fugitive and potentially emotionally bewildering, arousing and exhausting experience of reading, threatened to undermine the policed harmony of bourgeois domestic life, wholesomely symbolized through the domestic pedagogical model: family reading conducted under the gaze of the ever-vigilant *pater familias*. The difficulty of containing an often inchoate and evasive Decadent text within the confines of a private library room, a space that by its very existence, represented male, ostensibly impervious patriarchal domestic authority, was widely noted; despite the strictures of the Victorian home, "once admitted to the house it was difficult, almost impossible, to keep the children" from reading such literature (Cruse 60). Nor did parents often know

---

[11] See Nelson and Stetz. At twenty-two, Stella is still subject to a debate over her reading, drawing attention to the *perceived* influence of the Decadent book upon readers of all ages.

how to police the reading of minors, with all French literature assumed to be potentially dangerous; "a respectable father of a family," Cruse (58-59) notes, "would have been as shocked to see his daughter reading *François le Champis* as to see her reading *Mademoiselle de Maupin*." The only form of acceptable containment was vigilant exclusion from the home, and in order to maintain this, the householder needed to know the reading habits of the governess who supervised the children's education. In one of her advice books, the novelist and journalist Jane Ellen Panton (321-22) stipulated her criteria for the reading habits of the ideal governess: "she should not understand what 'decadent' and *fin-de-siècle* mean," adding that "if such information is not imported into one area of the house, its contamination cannot spread." The widespread epidemiological discourse about containing the perceived contaminating influence of Decadent literature in the British domestic arena clearly mirrored the wider public debate about the censorship of obscene literature.

Relentlessly self-conscious and defining itself through the parataxis of books that have been previously read, re-read, or misread by its fictional protagonists, Decadent writing is by its very nature gripped by anxieties over the nature, extent and implications of its textual borrowings. For Huysmans, the systematic deployment of the list in *À rebours*, a method derived from naturalism, was in itself a creative problem; as Robert Ziegler (11) has pointed out, "Huysmans grappled from the outset with the problem of acknowledging the authority of his sources," while at the same time "appropriating and adapting them to his own literary art." Nor was this anxiety of influence and authority confined to Huysmans' breviary alone; Oscar Wilde, and to a lesser extent, Walter Pater both suffered from the same irremediable problem.[12] The writers of literature perceived

---

[12] Described by Pater in *Marius the Epicurean* as "a burden of precedent, laid upon every artist" (91). For Pater's use of and problems with his sources, see

as being decadent often themselves internalised the burden of literary influence and proffered the quandary to their reader, offering textual evidence for the direct influence of a specific work on the self-identification of the protagonist, while publicly disclaiming the ability of literary fiction to influence its readers. Pater's Marius, Flavian and Gaston, Wilde's Dorian Gray, Basil and Lord Henry, and Lee's Anne Brown and Madame Elaguine are, like Huysmans' Des Esseintes, all shaped and defined to differing degrees by their individual and repeated re-reading of Decadent writing, whether classical or contemporary, Latin or French, "yellow," "golden" or "poisonous."

Decadent literature was perceived as being capable of influencing and harming the reader despite his or her (and in the case of the policing of reading, it was often her) own consciousness of what was being actively read, absorbed and assimilated, and in this respect, the spectre of the "poisonous text" bolstered determinist arguments about the influence of fiction. Ellis, Lee, Locke, Myers, Panton, et al. all suggest the potential for Decadent writing – for the "poisonous text" – to shape the reader's consciousness; the reader's theoretical autonomy or putative resistance is barely articulated. Throughout this period, Decadent fiction was embedded in the discourse of multiple anxieties centred upon the act of reading: the author's anxiety of being influenced by his sources, the reader's anxiety of being influenced through the act of reading, and society's anxiety about the influence of the text upon its readers. In a British literary context, there are three writers in particular – Vernon Lee, Walter Pater and Oscar Wilde – all of them influential novelists, aesthetes and critics, who in their attempts to negotiate these looming crises in

Bloom, "Walter Pater" and *Ringers in the Tower*, Donoghue and Inman; for Wilde's, see Martin, Nassar, Riquelme and Schoolfield.

reading, offer us narrative traces replete with the problematic nature of reading (and/or re-reading) Decadent writing.

In her intemperately anti-aesthetic first novel *Miss Brown* (1884), Vernon Lee makes an uncomplicated case for the determining influence of the Decadent novel. A physically imposing and morally uncorrupted Scottish-Italian servant girl, Anne Brown is taken up by the aesthete, artist and pre-Raphaelite poet Arthur Hamlin; in a reprise of the Pygmalion story, he decides to offer her a literary education so that she can "become worthy of him" (1: 208). Taken out of the guardianship of the Perry household in Florence, where despite the loose literary morals of the "Sapphic" Mrs Perry, Anne reads only "Dante" and "Italian grammar" (1: 65), she is soon exposed to the bewildering variety of literature circulating in late Victorian England, including the *Vita Nuova*, Petrarch, and Hamlin's own suggestive verses, poetry which Mr Perry describes unequivocally as "sad trash" but permissible; "all poetry isn't fit for women to read," he observes (1: 136). Despite the risqué nature of his own "fleshy" verse, Hamlin insists upon policing Anne's reading; nothing "save the very best should ever be read by you," he ironically informs her (1: 226).

Introduced to Hamlin's aesthetic set, Anne soon encounters Decadent writing and its proponents. The aesthetic poet Cosmo Chough, whose verse is described by Hamlin's aunt as being "perfectly indecent" (1: 277), transgresses Anne Brown's carefully demarcated and policed territory of reading by "discussing the most striking literary obscenities, from Petronius to Walt Whitman" (2: 25). Worse follows when the artist Edmund Lewis offers her a copy of Théophile Gautier's *Mademoiselle de Maupin* (1835), itself a landmark of Decadent writing, to read. Glancing at "the page, pencil marked all round" and "then at the title," she understands the potential influence of the volume at hand. "I have never read it," she tells Lewis, "but I have often heard that it is a book which a man does not offer a woman except as an insult" (2: 149-50). "Reading" and identifying the contaminating peril of the decadent book precedes, and sometimes, precludes, a reading of it, but despite her physical revulsion at Gautier's novel, an encounter which perfectly limns contemporary anxieties about the influence of decadent books on their readers, she does in fact, possess at least one Gautier volume herself. Scanning the shelves of her library (Anne's occupation of a contained, male space) her cousin Robert Brown notes a "*Contes des Gautier*" and finds it unbecoming a lady (2: 226). Brown expresses concern about the direction of her reading; paraphrasing and misquoting Pater in an attempt to warn Anne – "the object of the wise man is to make his life consist in as many moments of thrilling impressions as possible" – he once again draws attention to the potent influence of art on life, literature on identity, the Decadent work upon its reader, the Paterian *ur*-text upon its cultural context.[13]

In fact, Anne Brown has already become both a reader of Decadence, and a decadent reader. Reading Hamlin's latest lurid offerings, and worried that she has been subliminally moulded by it, she is left "wondering whether all the impure poetry which she had lately been reading" might "not be making her imagine things which were not meant; and Anne blushed at the thought" (2: 87). The subsequent coercive plot resolution bluntly demonstrates Lee's overriding didactic message; "thrust into the midst of a demoralised school of literature which glorified in moral indifference" (3: 280), Anne's offer to marry the now terminally depraved Hamlin, despite not being in love with him, is both predictable and inevitable. Decadent reading produces a pathetically decadent outcome, even within the context of a satire against aestheticism.

---

[13] Clearly garbled from the "Conclusion" to Pater's *The Renaissance*. Ironically, Brown's argument against the influence of Pater's aestheticism is dependent upon his misreading of it.

In case we are left in any doubt about the direct, determining and apparently detrimental influence of Decadent works upon their readers, Lee offers us the haunting spectre of the "extraordinary, charming, intelligent, depraved" (3: 222) Madame Elaguine, one of the earliest depictions of the female *décadent* in English fiction. Madame Elaguine's Kensington house is "strewn with French novels" (3: 5), and her literary tastes mirror Des Esseintes'; she has "a passion for Alfred de Musset, for Gautier, for Catulle Mèndes" (2: 250), she admits to caring "too much for Baudelaire" (3: 90), and her reading habits are similarly desultory and unsystematic: she is often found "lying on a sofa, a heap of books about her, reading none, fidgety and vacant" (3: 91). Sacha Elaguine's polymorphous perversity is explained largely through the filter of a dissipated, unsupervised childhood spent reading French novels, an upbringing which has left her with an appetite for the "forbidden," the "unreal" and the "theatrical" (3: 222). As a commentary on the nexus of anxieties around morality, Decadent literature and reading practice, Lee's novel is both conventional and exemplary.

Written at the same time as Lee's didactic novel, Walter Pater's *Marius the Epicurean* (1885) offers the spectacle of a viaticum which insists upon reading as a form of moral improvement and self-development, while at the same time suggests the gratification and self-identification derived from reading for its own sake. Drawing upon the established tradition of the *Bildungsroman*, Pater's narrative is punctuated by specific, staged acts of reading, including perhaps the most famous example of "truant reading" in nineteenth-century literature, Marius and Flavian's idyllic, absorbed, antinomian reading of Apuleius' *Metamorphoses*, an exegetic reading which violates the temporal and chronological structure of the novel's narrative. Under Flavian's physical, emotional, idealistic and pedagogical influence, Marius resolves to acquire the "art" of "relieving the ideals or poetic traits, the elements of distinction, in our everyday life" by "exclusively living in them" (65), the part once again superseding the whole, and this consciousness of the aesthetic life, "a revelation in colour and form" (65-66) is roused through his reading of Apuleius. In representing a determining act of reading, Pater's Janus-like gaze casts its eyes upon future readers (glossing both Gautier and Baudelaire), as well as past ones; the identification of the author with his work and of the reader with his reading is unequivocal, for literary and personal influence are inseparable. "A book, like a person, has its fortunes with one," it is "lucky or unlucky in the precise moment of its falling in our way" (87-88), the narrator observes, and yet this fortuitous, overtly phenomenological reading experience has the potential to change the life of the reader forever. For Marius, the ideal type of the absorbed, impressionist (and decadent) reader, reading and re-reading the "Golden Book" redefines his consciousness (it has a "peculiar place in his remembrance"), his purpose, and his identity: "he felt a sort of personal gratitude to its writer," seeing in it "doubtless far more than was really there for any other reader" (88). Marius' determination to live through the text, his over-determined, over-inscribed response to reading Apuleius, accurately depicts the reading experience of the contemporary Decadent.

The pedagogical strategies (Platonic dialogues, Socratic mentoring, symposia and so on) depicted in the novel are largely systematic, institutionalised, policed, and internally interpreted, but in the example of Marius' impressionistic, overreaching "truant" reading,

Pater insistently affirms the autonomous potential for self-fashioning through the individual act of reading.[14] Despite the novel's overtly pedagogical tone and structure, the intellectually seductive, ubiquitously homoerotic subtext – the freethinking truancy of Pater's influence in Oxford at the time – lies perilously visible beneath the diaphaneitè surface of the text.[15] Pater's insistence on the fortuitous influence of the "golden book" and the vitality of the classical past, on its ability to mould the personality of the reader, as well as his potentially autonomous self-identification through his reading, left his novel open to criticism; indeed, his very investment in the determining power of literature increased anxieties of reception and dissemination, anxieties that had been widely circulating since the controversy surrounding the conclusion to *The Renaissance* (1873). While *Marius* is certainly Pater's most profound commitment to the shaping of the reader through the reading experience, "a metafictional meditation upon the act of reading, upon its own reception by a reader" and "upon its efforts to render the reader receptive" (Kaiser 200), it remains playful, even irresponsible about the outcome of that reading; under the pretext of historical realism it also invites the reader to participate in their own phenomenological, impressionistic and subjective acts of interpretation and self-identification. As Denis Donoghue has suggested, "Paterian or impressionist criticism tends to lead, after a while, an independent life" (43), and in this respect, *Marius*, part novel, part manifesto, be-

---

[14] This dichotomy between authoritarian and libertarian reading is alluded to repeatedly in the novel; see for example, Flavian's literary programme, "partly conservative or reactionary" and "partly popular and revolutionary" (88).

[15] See Dowling, Kaiser, Monsman, Potolsky and Shuter.

came its own "golden book," an open invitation to the interpretative work (and play) of its readers. Pater could not control the reading of his work or the dissemination of his ideas, nor did he consider it to be aesthetically or ideologically desirable, and in the decade following its publication, truant, decadent readings of Pater's books proliferated.[16] Haunted by the spectre of an influence it could not contain, *Marius the Epicurean* perilously negotiated a path between conflicting late nineteenth-century arguments about the nature and extent of the influence of a "decadent" book upon its readers, a path that Pater would clearly have to retrace, again and again in his literary career.

Both the allure and the danger of decadent reading is central to Oscar Wilde's only novel, *The Picture of Dorian Gray* (1890-91). The unpoliced domestic spaces (sitting rooms, salons, studios, attics, library rooms) of the novel freely circulate both classical and contemporary works of Decadent literature between consenting adult males for their own exclusive, elite consumption; parodying the distribution of censored texts through lending libraries, Wilde's circulating system disseminates Gautier's poems, *Les cent nouvelles nouvelles*, *Manon Lescaut*, and most famously, *À rebours*. Lord Henry's gift of a well-thumbed "book bound in yellow paper, the cover slightly torn and the edges soiled" (96) soon has Dorian's complete attention. Replicating Marius and Flavian's absorbed truant reading of Apuleius, Dorian's reading of "the strangest book that he had ever read," a "psychological study of a certain young Parisian" (113) arrests time and fractures the chronology of the novel; he starts reading at five o'clock, and finishes before nine, but the next chapter opens "years" later (100). As Matei Calinescu (56) has observed, reading, and particularly re-reading, with its tendency to-

---

[16] See Bassett, Dowling and Potolsky.

wards ideas of mythic and circular time, can "weaken the sense of
irresistible linearity and unidirectionality of both textual time and
biological time" within the narrative, despite remaining "subject to
the inexorable law [. . .] obviously one does not grow younger while
reading or re-reading a book." Unless of course, the reader is Dorian
Gray; Wilde's novel articulates the possibilities of an overdetermined decadent reading, where the part totally obliterates the whole,
where the freight of the intertext overwhelms the host text, and
where the linear narrative time of *Dorian Gray* is usurped by the
fictive stasis of Huysmans' novel.

Decadent fiction is explicitly intertextual, and the invasive inter-
jection of Huysmans' text upon Wilde's novel demands from the
reader a repudiation of the hermeneutics of traditional teleological
narrative. Commenting on Des Esseintes' intertextual reading of
Baudelaire's "Le Gâteau" in *À rebours*, Michael Riffaterre has noted
that what "appears ludicrous and improbable" in the narrative "disappears as soon as we stop considering it as a narrative progression
motivated in a normal fashion"; that is, if we no longer read the
novel telelogically, "but consider it instead as an antinomy overdetermined by the intertext" (Riffaterre 77), in other words, by privileging the part over the whole. In Decadent fiction, this overdetermining is represented through individual acts of reading which invite the reader to assess the narrative through the parallax of the
cited intertext(s), a "formal eccentricity" (78) which is a stylistic sta-
ple of Decadent writing, and brings with it, as Riffaterre suggests, a
responsibility to read the text with "full awareness and complete
participation" (78) rather than passive, unconscious involvement.

Unlike in Pater's novel however, Dorian's overdetermined reading
precludes rather than promotes a closer scrutiny of the text, or indeed, of the process of reading; while Flavian's reading makes him
an "ardent, indefatigable student of words" (88), Dorian's absorbed,
or rather, *involved* reading of the yellow book is perilously (and

negatively) subliminal: "the mere cadence of the sentences, the subtle monotony of their music" produces in his mind "a form of reverie, a malady of dreaming" that makes him "unconscious" (98).[17] In fact, Dorian's reading is dangerous precisely because of his lack of analytical scrutiny, context, or intellectual engagement; reading in the early evening only by the fading "wan light of a solitary star" until he "could read no more" (98), it is open to question whether in this aestheticised *mise en scène*, he even finishes reading his "yellow book."

Wilde's kaleidoscopic, harlequin text, revelling in the 'burden of precedent' of past literature from which it borrows freely and promiscuously, celebrates the impressionist, overdetermined, truant reading practice of the decadent reader; it also implicitly suggests the impossibility of its policing.[18] Dorian's fetishised collection of "nine large paper copies of the first edition" of the "yellow book," all "bound in different colours" to "suit his various moods" (98) visibly demonstrates the end result of a reading practice where the "whole is subordinated to the parts" (Ellis 175), in this case, the niceties of the binding overdetermining the interpretation of the text (like Des Esseintes, Dorian's erotic sublimation is partly bibliophilic, if not bibliomanic). Indeed, mimicking the rhetoric of re-reading, the effect of Huysmans' "prefiguring" text has left him with a "nature over which he seemed, at times to have almost entirely lost control" (98). *À rebours* is a work from whose imaginative grasp, interpretative nexus, and above all, influential example of overdetermining reading practice, Dorian Gray cannot escape. Repeatedly returning to his "ancestors in literature," and re-reading the "seventh chapter" (113) of the work – the part, rather than the whole – monomaniacally "over and over again," he sees everything mediated

---

[17] For a stimulating discussion of involved vs. absorbed reading, see Calinescu.
[18] For Wilde's borrowings (and plagiarism) see Guy and Raby.

entirely through this one work of fiction: he views "the whole of history" as "merely the record of his life" (113). Far from seeing the literary past, as Flavian in *Marius* does, as a spur to new creativity, a "burden of precedent, laid upon every artist" (91) that must be overcome, Dorian's increasingly wrought, fruitless and truncated decadent reading practice exactly replicates that of Des Esseintes, provoking dyspepsia, disgust, accidia and anomie, rather than sharpening the literary appetite. As Matei Calinescu (133) has noted, the "joys of reading intertextually dissolve in the absence of a principle of internal coherence," and Dorian's reading of Huysmans' novel is nothing if not unsystematic and incoherent. Dorian's anti-paradigm of reading practice, where the smallest particle, the Paterian *débris* (a single chapter of a Decadent novel) takes precedent over the whole corpus of imaginative literature, prompts his most infamous accusation at Lord Henry: "you poisoned me with a book once. I should not forgive that" (166). It is Dorian's reading habits, and not his morality, that have in fact been "poisoned". As George Cevasco has observed, Dorian's library is significantly less impressive than that of Des Esseintes, and as a result, his ability to read in context is undoubtedly hampered; re-reading Huysmans' novel precludes rather than encourages further reading, suggesting once again, the disproportionate, overarching, fatal influence of a single work on the untrained, ill-equipped mind.[19] In *Dorian Gray*, Wilde offers a decadent reading of a decadent reader, a fatal, truant misreading of Pater's antinomian espousal of the moral and creative benefit of aesthetic impressionism, and paradoxically, a disavowal of the all pervasive influence of literature on the informed reader; the poisonous "yellow book," despite having many readers within the fictionally limned boundaries of the novel, poisons only Dorian. Decadent writing is inextricably bound up with the question of the

---

[19] Cevasco, *Breviary*, 80.

interpretative strategies of the reader, and in this regard, Wilde's novel challenges the reader to rise to the interpretative task at which Dorian so patently fails.

While only Dorian falls prey to the "yellow book," the perceived influence of Wilde's novel on the reading public was immediate; the *Daily Chronicle* denounced *Dorian Gray* as a "poisonous book," the *St. James' Gazette* called it "corrupt" and announced that it "ought to be chucked into the fire" (*Dorian Gray* 343, 335). The impact of Wilde's novel was felt beyond the immediate controversy in the periodical press. As Gerald Monsman has demonstrated, the public debate that heralded the appearance of *Dorian Gray* forced Walter Pater back to work on his still incomplete manuscript, *Gaston de Latour* (1898); cancelling a planned trip to Italy in August 1890, he immediately set about distancing his own views from those of his wayward and truant pupil.[20] Pater's unfinished novel is unequivocal about the direct, determining influence of reading creative literature on identity formation and moral development, but unlike Wilde, he insisted open the importance of pedagogy within the confines of the text, as well as outside it. Whether Pater's final fictional work represents a retreat from the argument first articulated in *The Renaissance* or a recapitulation of it remains a matter for debate, but what is clear is that the importance of intertextual strategies of reading and interpretation are if anything, amplified even further in *Gaston*.

Like almost all Decadent novels, Pater's last piece of fiction deals with the idea of the direct influence of one text, in this case, Pierre de Ronsard's *Odes* (1553) on a historicised fictional reader, Gaston; once again, Pater privileges the synchronic process of re-reading and self-identification from a phenomenological encounter with a "golden book". Given to him by his inamorata Jasmin, as "perhaps the best of services" (26), Gaston's repeated reading of Ronsard's

---

[20] See Monsman, *Gaston de Latour* xl.

poems opens up a new imaginative world. With its "golden-green binding" and "yellow edges," the portable volume of Ronsard"s verse had "proved the key to a new world of seemingly boundless intellectual resources" (26), and Pater's espousal of a synchronic, imaginative reading is clear. "Just eighteen years old, and the work of the poet's own youth," Ronsard's *Odes* take "possession" of Gaston with the "ready intimacy of one's equal in age, fresh in every point" and the effect of this particular truant reading is one of intellectual renewal rather than anomie: Gaston "experienced what it is the function of contemporary poetry to effect anew for sensitive youth in each succeeding generation" (26). Once again, as in *The Renaissance*, Pater's analogue for the potency of poetry is taken from the plastic arts; "at best, poetry of the past could move one with no more directness than the beautiful faces of antiquity," faces which Pater reminds us, "are not here for us to see and unaffectedly love them" (27).

It is through literature and not sculpture that the "age renews itself," and Pater's claim for the influence of imaginative literature is bold; poetry "grows superb and large" in order to "fill a certain mental situation made ready in advance" (27), and if we are in any doubt about the centrality of the reading experience in defining temporality, Gaston's idyllic, spring reading of Ronsard's verse takes place in chapter three, suitably titled "Modernity." Gaston's reading practice is explicitly decadent, with the part conspicuously superseding the whole; seeing the world through "the ear, the eye, of his favourite poet" (28) leads Gaston to an aesthetic "doctrine" that insists upon seeing the "pleasantly aesthetic [. . .] elements of life at an advantage" until "they seemed to occupy the entire surface" (28-29), a disproportionate, overdetermined perspective acquired from his reading of Ronsard that he controversially considers to be an "undeniable good service" (29). And yet, in the very chapter in which Pater recapitulates the joys of truant reading first expounded in

Marius, he offers the contemporary reader a warning about the potential danger of both decadent reading and reading Decadence. Observing Gaston's own increasingly conflicted sense of the "incompatibility" between the "two rival claimants upon him" – sacred and profane love – Pater glosses Baudelaire's "flowers of evil" (37) in suggesting both the perils of Decadence, and the possible resolution of this seemingly intractable problem that it might offer: "might there be perhaps, somewhere, in some penetrative mind in this age of novelties, some scheme of truth, some science of men and things" which could "harmonise for him his earlier and later preferences" or else "establish, to his pacification, the exclusive supremacy of the latter?" (37). While Gaston is self-consciously brought back from the decadent brink, Pater's rhetorical question to his contemporary readers remains perilously unanswered.

For Pater, the potentially determining, formative influence of the "golden book" had to be mitigated, and this could only be achieved through the aesthetic and moral effort of his readers. *Gaston de Latour* is Pater's last attempt at managing the critical reception of his ideas – in effect, the afterlife of his books – through the sustained fictional depiction of an ideal paradigm of synchronic reading and its intertextual interpretation. Paradoxically, while Pater celebrated the potent, life changing influence of chance reading in *Gaston de Latour*, he consciously disavowed the possibility that truant reading alone could offer Gaston (or his readers) the aesthetic and emotional fulfilment that they sought, caught as they all were, in late Victorian England as much as in Renaissance France, between the simultaneously conflicting and revivifying "bad neighbourship of what was old and what was new" (37). It was effectively Pater's final manifesto for shaping his readers, and a prefiguring of the Modernist need to reinterpret, rehistoricise, and renew the past through the act of reading.

Long before they had been formally identified, policed or circumscribed, Decadent texts, their authors, and their readers, as I have
shown, were constructed through the very act of reading. Typically
defined by an anxiety of influence that their authors could not contain, and an anxiety of dissemination that their readers could not
deny, Decadent literature occupied a radically destabilising, interstitial space in the history of reading. As Linda Dowling (176) has
noted, the "poisonous text," the "fatal book of Victorian Decadence," itself fashioned as a simulacrum of the reading experience
embedded within the narrative, partly came to "symbolize anxiety
about the newly problematic status of written language." As the ambiguous contradictions between authorial intention and narrative
contention grew, the "poisonous text" acted as the textual marker for
the multiple misreadings that in varying degrees, Decadent narratives self-consciously and intentionally invited from their readers.[21]
The Decadent text required a decadent reader, and the decadent
reader's own uniquely differentiated and often perverse reading
practice insisted upon a self-conscious identification with the text
being scrutinised, a process which was invariably validated through
the often explicitly intertextual nature of the narrative itself. The
decadent reader was trained and not born; his or her ability to read
the implied and subliminal rather than the explicatory and seemingly didactic aspects of the narrative was usually evidence of conscious, interpretative reading and membership of an elite reading
community.[22] Whether it was through Des Esseintes' reading of

---

[21] See for example, Eichner. The perverse "misreading" that he observes is
surely intentional.

[22] All of the fictionally depicted influential books I have discussed are in Latin
or French; by implication, the self-identification (or otherwise) of the English

Petronius, Flavian's reading of Apuleius, Dorian Gray's reading of Huysmans, or Gaston's reading of Pierre de Ronsard, the self-identification of the fictional Decadent with his chosen, privately circulating text, whether "golden," "yellow," or "poisonous," defined his status, and often his personal library (the locus for the literary sublimation of desire, disgust and disappointment) became the arena for this fugitive exercise in re-reading and self-fashioning.

The history of Decadent writing is inseparable from a concept of decadent reading, and specifically, from a socially constructed, aesthetically self-conscious, and fictionally mediated practice of fugitive reading, with the "whole subordinated to the parts" that defied attempts to control it and offers us both a possible taxonomy and epistemology of Decadence. In this respect, Decadent texts consistently challenged the nineteenth-century theoretical fiction of ideal readers by formally representing self-selecting re-readers – in many senses, today's normal readers – as those who "skip, skim, swim back and forth" (Calinescu 273) in their interaction with the text. There may or may not have been anything approximating a Decadent "movement," in English literature, but there were, and potentially, still are, many decadent readers. Both the advocates of Decadent writing and their opponents in the last decades of the nineteenth century were united by one certainty: that creative literature was of central importance in anatomising and directing the cultural and social tendencies of the era. The decadent reader's reading practice became as much an object of identification and enquiry as the morphological scrutiny directed to its body, and the analytical psycho-pathology directed at its mind. Far from being at the tail-end – the twilight – of an exhausted century, the literature of the *fin de siècle* resounds with the vitality of a debate that placed the impor-

---

decadent reader with their book(s) cannot take place in the vernacular. Intertextuality is predicated by translation.

tance of the individual's intertextual re-reading of influential literature (and its policing) at the centre of an increasingly autonomous,
self-fashioned, modernist world.

Works Cited

Antosh, Ruth B. *Reality and Illusion in the Novels of J.-K. Huysmans*. Amsterdam: Rodopi, 1986.

Bassett, Sharon. "'Golden Mediocrity': Pater's Marcus Aurelius and
the Making of Decadence." Constable et al. 254-67.

Beaumont, Barbara, ed. *The Road from Decadence: From Brothel
to Cloister, Selected Letters of J. K. Huysmans*. London: Ath-
lone, 1989.

Beck, Roger. "Eumolpus *poeta*, Eumolpus *fabulator*: A Study of
Characterization in the *Satyricon*." *Phoenix* 33 (1979): 239-53.

Bloom, Harold. *Ringers in the Tower: Studies in the Romantic Tradition*. Chicago: U of Chicago P, 1971.

---. "Walter Pater: the Intoxification of Belatedness." *Yale French
Studies* 50 (1974): 163-89.

Bourget, Paul. *Essais de psychologie contemporaine*. Paris: 1883.

Calinescu, Matei. *Rereading*. London: Yale UP, 1993.

Cevasco, G. A. *The Breviary of the Decadence: J. K. Huysmans' À
Rebours and English Literature*. New York: AMS, 2001.

---. "Des Esseintes' Library." *American Book Collector* 21 (May
1971): 7-11.

Constable, Liz, Dennis Denisoff and Matthew Potolsky, ed. *Perennial Decay: On the Aesthetics and Politics of Decadence*.
Philadelphia: U of Pennsylvania P, 1999.

Cruse, Amy. *After the Victorians*. London: George Allen and Unwin, 1938.

Decker, Clarence R. *The Victorian Conscience*. New York: Twayne,
1952.

Donoghue, Denis. *The Practice of Reading*. London: Yale UP, 1998.

Dowling, Linda. "Pater, Moore and the Fatal Book." *Prose Studies* 7.2 (1984): 168-78.

Eichner, Hans. "Against the Grain: Huysmans' *À rebours*, Wilde's *Dorian Gray*, and Hoffmannsthal's *Der Tor und der Tod*." *Narrative Ironies*. Ed. Raymond A. Prier and Gerald Gillespie Amsterdam: Rodopi, 1997. 191-206.

Ellis, Havelock. *Affirmations*. London: Walter Scott, 1898.

Flint, Kate. *The Woman Reader, 1837-1914*. Oxford: Clarendon, 1991.

Guy, Josephine M. "Self-Plagiarism, Creativity and Craftsmanship in Oscar Wilde." *English Literature in Transition, 1880-1920* 41.1 (1998): 6-23.

Hustvedt, Asti, ed. *The Decadent Reader: Fiction, Fantasy and Perversion from* Fin-de-siècle *France*. New York: Urzone, 1998.

Huysmans, Joris-Karl. *Against Nature*. Trans. Robert Baldick. London: Penguin, 1959. Trans. of *À rebours*. 1884.

Inman, Billie Andrew. *Walter Pater and his Reading 1874-1877*. New York: Garland, 1990.

Jankélévitch, Vladimir. "La Décadence." *Révue de métaphysique et de morale* 55 (1950): 337-69.

Jordanova, Ludmilla. "'A Slap in the Face for Old Mother Nature': Disease, Debility and Decay in Huysmans' *A Rebours*." *Literature and Medicine* 15.1 (1996): 112-28.

Kaiser, Matthew. "Marius at Oxford: Paterian Pedagogy and the Ethics of Seduction." *Walter Pater: Transparencies of Desire*. Ed. Laurel Brake, Lesley Higgins and Carolyn Williams. Greensboro, NC: ELT, 2002. 189-200.

Lambert, Pierre, ed. *Lettres inédites à Edmond de Goncourt*. Paris: Nizet, 1956.

Lang, Andrew. "Decadence." *Critic* 37 (1900): 171-73.

Laurent, Émile. *La poésie décadent devant la science psychiatrique.* Paris: Maloine, 1897.

Lee, Vernon. *Baldwin: A Book of Dialogues.* London: T. Fisher Unwin, 1886.

---. *Belcaro: Being Essays on Sundry Aesthetical Questions.* London: W. Satchell, 1881.

---. *Miss Brown.* London: Blackwood, 1884.

Le Gallienne, Richard. *Retrospective Reviews.* London: John Lane, 1896.

Locke, William John. *Stella Maris.* London: John Lane, 1913.

Martin, Robert K. "Parody and Homage: the Presence of Pater in *Dorian Gray.*" *Victorian Newsletter* 63 (1983): 15-18.

Monsman, Gerald. "Pater and his Younger Contemporaries." *Victorian Newsletter* 48 (1975): 1-9.

Myers, F. W. H. *Journal of the Society for Psychical Research* 5 (Feb. 1892): 200-02.

Nassar, Christopher S. "On originality and influence: Oscar Wilde's Technique." *Journal of the Eighteen Nineties Society* 24 (1997): 37-47.

Nelson, James G. *The Early Nineties: A View from the Bodley Head.* Cambridge, MA: Harvard UP, 1971.

Nordau, Max. *Degeneration.* London: Heinemann, 1895.Panton, J. E. *A Gentlewoman's Home: The Whole Art of Building, Furnishing, and Beautifying the Home.* London: "The Gentlewoman" Offices, 1896.

Pater, Walter. *Gaston de Latour: The Revised Text.* Ed. Gerald Monsman. Greensboro, NC: ELT, 1995.

---. *Marius the Epicurean.* Harmondsworth: Penguin, 1985.

Petronii Arbitri Viri Consularis. *Satyricon* Leyden: J. Dousa, 1585.

Petronius. *Satyricon.* Trans. P. G. Walsh. Oxford: Clarendon, 1996.

Potolsky, Matthew. "Fear of Falling: Walter Pater's *Marius the Epicurean* as a dangerous influence." *ELH* 65.3 (1998): 701-29.

---. "Pale Imitations: Walter Pater's Decadent Historiography." Constable et al. 235-53.

Raby, Peter. *Oscar Wilde*. Cambridge: Cambridge UP, 1988.

Riffaterre, Michael. "Decadent Paradoxes." Constable et al. 65-79.

Riquelme, John Paul. "Oscar Wilde's Aesthetic Gothic: Walter Pater, Dark Enlightenment, and *The Picture of Dorian Gray*." *Modern Fiction Studies* 46.3 (2000): 609-31.

Schoolfield, George C. *A Baedeker of Decadence: Charting a Literary Fashion, 1884-1927*. London: Yale UP, 2003.

Shuter, William. "Pater, Wilde, Douglas and the Impact of 'Greats.'" *English Literature in Transition, 1880-1920* 46.3 (2002): 250-78.

Stetz, Margaret D. and Mark Samuels Lasner. *England in the 1890s: Literary Publishing at the Bodley Head*. Washington DC: Georgetown UP, 1990.

Towheed, Shafquat. "Determining 'fluctuating opinions': Vernon Lee, 'Popular' Fiction, and Theories of Reading." *Nineteenth-Century Literature* 60.2 (2005): 199-236.

Wilde, Oscar. *The Picture of Dorian Gray*. Ed. Donald L. Lawler. Norton Critical Edition. New York: Norton, 1988.

---. "The Decay of Lying." *The Artist as Critic: Critical Writings of Oscar Wilde*. Ed. Richard Ellman. Chicago: Chicago UP, 1969.

Ziegler, Robert. *The Mirror of Divinity: The World and Creation in J.-K. Huysmans*. Newark: U of Delaware P, 2004.

Arthur Symons' Decadent Aesthetics: Stéphane Mallarmé and the Dancer Revisited

Petra Dierkes-Thrun
Santa Clara University

Abstract: This essay analyzes Arthur Symons' creative reception and adaptation of Stéphane Mallarmé's Symbolist aesthetics, especially the Symbolist dancer figure, in Symons' major theoretical writings and dance poems of the 1890s. I argue that Symons interpreted Mallarmé's work through a decidedly Decadent lens, which reconfigured Symbolist themes of linguistic struggle, poetic evocation, and aesthetic dreaming, to express the sense of an acute spiritual as well as aesthetic crisis of *fin de siècle* literature and culture.

Arthur Symons is most remembered today for his role as a mediator between French and English Decadence and Symbolism, a *fin de siècle* poet and cultural theorist whose seminal work *The Symbolist Movement in Literature* (1899) introduced a generation of readers and writers (among them William Butler Yeats and T. S. Eliot) to the writings of Verlaine, Huysmans, Laforgue, and most importantly, Stéphane Mallarmé. In his biography, Karl Beckson stresses the Modernists' acknowledged debt to Symons: T. S. Eliot, for example, described *The Symbolist Movement in Literature* as a "revelation" and "an introduction to wholly new feelings," "one of those [books] which have affected the course of my life" (*Sacred Wood* 5; qtd. in Beckson, *Life* 200). Symons' work on Mallarmé and Symbolism also particularly influenced W. B. Yeats, with whom Symons shared rooms in Fountain Court from October 1895 to March 1896, and who was "always careful to acknowledge a special debt he owed his old friend and confidant, Arthur Symons," "his principal source of information regarding Mallarmé" since his own French was sadly lacking (Morris, "Form" 99-100). Symons first met the Symbolist *maître* on his 1890 visit to Paris, when he attended one of

Mallarmé's famous *mardis* in the Rue de Rome. Throughout the 1890s and continuing after Mallarmé's death in 1898, Symons would function as Mallarmé's English translator and inofficial spokesperson, who managed to adapt and explain Mallarmé's complex aesthetic so well that even Mallarmé himself was full of enthusiasm and gratitude. In a letter dated February 28, 1897, he thanked Symons for his review of the Symbolist manifesto *Divagations* in *The Saturday Review*, practically calling him his *alter ego*: "What an admirable page, yours [. . .] I can see myself as in a mirror in which I recognize my essential aesthetic [. . .] There is nothing that I wanted to say that you have not put your finger on first. I squeeze your entire hand" (Morris, "Letters" 352).

During these years Symons also studied and masterfully translated some of Mallarmé's *Hérodiade* fragments (based on the Biblical legend of the daughter of Herodias, Salome, who became the iconic dancer of *fin de siècle* literature and art).[1] In another letter from January 12, 1897, Mallarmé found lavish words of praise for the congeniality of Symons' translation:

---

[1] In his *Autobiographies*, Yeats enshrined the lasting effect Symons' translation and explanation of Mallarmé's *Hérodiade* had upon him, as a symbolic figure he found congenial to his own work as a poet:

> I can remember the day in Fountain Court when Symons first read me Herodiade's address to some Sibyl who is her nurse and, it may be, the moon also [. . .] Yet I am certain that there was something in myself compelling me to attempt creation of an art as separate from everything heterogeneous and casual, from all character and circumstance, as some Herodiade of our theatre, dancing seemingly alone in her narrow luminous circle. (247)

For important critical discussions of Yeats' debt to Symons' translations and interpretations of Mallarmé, and Yeats' reception of the Symbolist dancer figure, see Kermode (*Image*), Bruce Morris ("Form"), Haskell M. Block, Karl Beckson ("Tumbler"), Sylvia Ellis.

Yes, my dear poet, I have received and have perused, and I
am now familiar with your priceless translation of the
Hérodiade. It seems to me [. . .] that I have written it in
English myself. How could you have transposed certain
things from that *Poésie*, the very tone itself? The amusing
thing is that it's now I who am very proud. (Morris, "Letters" 350)

Privately circulated by Mallarmé's artistic entourage in Paris and
among the members of the Rhymers Club in London (which Symons had joined in 1890), *Hérodiade* already contained poetic
themes that would become the conceptual center of many of Symons' own dance writings: an emphasis on aesthetic individualism,
mirrors, dream, forgetting, and a skeptical view of the ultimate vi-
ability of a metaphysical connection through poetic language. Be-
sides providing a fundamental theoretical affinity for Symons that
lasted throughout the years of his simultaneous intellectual
collaboration with Yeats (whose mysticism was the second major
influence on Symons during the 1890s, and to whom *The Symbolist
Movement in Literature* is dedicated), Mallarmé's work thus
importantly shaped Symons' own poetic practice and thematic
interest in the 1890s. Most of Symons' poems on dance and dancers
– a popular subject of Symbolist poetry – stem from his period of
intense contact with Mallarmé from 1891 to 1898, when Symons
was keenly interested in understanding and translating Mallarmé's
aesthetic for the English cultural context, and actively sought to
infuse English literature with Decadent-Symbolist aesthetics. In
Symons' best-known dance poems written throughout the 1890s and
collected in *London Nights* (1895), *Images of Good and Evil* (1899),
and *Lesbia and Other Poems* (1920), and in his essay "The World as
Ballet" (republished in *Studies in Seven Arts*, 1906), we do not only
see Symons grapple with his own longstanding erotic obsession
with dancers (he was romantically involved with several dancers of the

Moulin Rouge, the Folies-Bergère, and the Empire), but also bring his sensual experiences and impressions at the music-hall into dialogue with Decadent and Symbolist aesthetic theory, especially his explorations of Mallarmé.

While the general role Symons played as a cultural mediator between Mallarmé and Yeats has been well explored by critics, and Symons' masterful translations of Mallarmé have been analyzed (in addition to portions of *Divagations* and *Hérodiade*, he translated 26 of Mallarmé's *Poésies*),[2] comparatively little attention has been paid to Symons' own creative interpretation of Mallarmé's Symbolism in the context of his early championship of French Decadence. Even though Symons faithfully articulated Mallarmé's major Symbolist themes and goals – as Mallarmé's personal endorsements of Symons' reviews and translations indicate – this essay argues that Symons actually showed a decided preference for certain Decadent themes and aesthetic issues within Mallarmé's work, which first appear in the 1893 essay "The Decadent Movement in Literature," and continue, with only slightly shifted yet much elaborated emphasis, in *The Symbolist Movement in Literature.* Mallarmé's recognition of the essential inadequacy of language and his symbolic use of dancers as inhuman ciphers for the *Idéal* (both the aesthetic and the metaphysical one) in such essays as "Ballets" (1886), "Les Fonds dans le Ballet" (Mallarmé's famous review of Loïe Fuller's 1893 performances), and the series of short sketches collected as "Crayonné au Théâtre" (published from 1886-1896 in *La Revue franco-américaine, La Revue indépendante*, and the *National Observer*), provided Symons with a fascinating reading foil for his own erotic and aesthetic experiences as a fan and critic of music-halls and dancers. Symons' 1897 prose piece "The World as Ballet" in

---

[2] For Symons' translations of Mallarmé's *Poésies*, see Morris' 1986 edition; cf. also Morris ("Form").

particular contains strong echoes of Mallarmé's well-known conceptualization of dance as an enigmatic, dreamlike experience and *écriture corporelle*, a superior physical form of aesthetic representation akin to the Symbolist goal of perfect evocation. But to this fascination with Mallarmé Symons added a Decadent interest that focused on metaphysical longing and dissatisfaction, the desirability of dream and forgetfulness, artifice, and a haunting awareness of death, as we shall see below. Such themes also occupied many of the other writers and artists associated with the Rhymers Club, whom Yeats called the "Tragic Generation." Yeats writes in his *Autobiographies* that, marked by metaphysical dissatisfaction and disillusion, these "strange souls [. . .] with hearts that Christianity, as shaped by history, cannot satisfy," had already lost the faith that art could produce the new "sacred book" that would emulate Mallarmé's "trembling of the veil of the Temple": "[s]ome of us thought that book near towards the end of last century, but the tide sank again" (243).[3] In order to show the influence of the context of Decadence on Symons' readings and interpretations of Symbolism and especially the Symbolist dancer, a brief excursion into Symons' understanding of Mallarmé will provide the necessary background for my argument in the first half of the essay. From this general analysis of Symons' approach to Mallarmé's Symbolism, I will then return to Symons' adaptations of the dancer, to show how they were simultaneously influenced by his theoretical understanding of Mallarmé, and his ongoing commitment to Decadent themes and concerns.

   Arthur Symons first expressed his understanding of Stéphane Mallarmé in "The Decadent Movement in Literature," the influential essay published in the November 1893 issue of *Harper's New*

---

[3] Among the artists of the "tragic generation" Yeats names are Arthur Symons, Lionel Johnson, Aubrey Beardsley, Ernest Dowson, Oscar Wilde, Henrik Ibsen, George Bernard Shaw, and others.

Monthly Magazine, and continued to develop it in *The Symbolist Movement in Literature*. In the "Decadence" essay, Mallarmé still takes a close second place behind Paul Verlaine as Symons' ideal Decadent poet (to whom he would dedicate *London Nights* in 1895), and Symbolism appears as a "branch" of Decadence side by side with Impressionism. In *The Symbolist Movement in Literature*, published three years after Verlaine's death, Symons then elevates Mallarmé to his principal figure and, in response to a changed cultural climate increasingly critical of Decadence, officially tries to put Symbolism at a safe distance from the associations with Decadence which Symons himself had helped to cement with his focus on the "spiritual and moral perversity" of this "new and beautiful and interesting disease" in "The Decadent Movement" (859).[4]

And yet, despite the title change and the apparent shift in focus from Decadence to Symbolism from the 1893 essay to the 1899 book, Symons' original conceptualization of Mallarmé's inherently Decadent themes remained essentially the same. With a skeptical metaphysical and aesthetic sensibility that would emerge fully in *The Symbolist Movement in Literature*, the "Decadence" essay already directed Symons' interpretive trajectory toward the spiritual dimension of Decadence and Symbolism, and established the basis of his approach to Mallarmé's aesthetic. In both works, Mallarmé

---

[4] By the end of the decade, in the wake of the 1895 Wilde trials and the English translation of Max Nordau's *Degeneration*, such pathological language had taken on sinister moral overtones of cultural apocalypse, and hence become untenable, as Symons realized in his function as editor of *The Savoy* (cf. Bristow [65], Munro [47-48]). In the Introduction to *The Symbolist Movement in Literature*, Symons tries hard to downplay his previous cultural association between Symbolism and Decadence, in order to salvage Symbolism from the critics of Decadence, arguing that the "interlude, half a mock-interlude, of Decadence" should only be understood as a forerunner for "something more serious," Symbolism, "in which art returns to the one pathway, leading through beautiful things to eternal beauty" (7).

appears preoccupied with a seriously-minded but skeptical spiritual search, which reflects and reacts to what Symons saw as the fundamental religious, aesthetic, and cultural crisis of the 19th century. In "The Decadent Movement" Symons explains the relation between the *"maladie fin de siècle"* of writers such as the Goncourt brothers, Verlaine, Huysmans, Maeterlinck, Mallarmé, and (somewhat surprisingly) the English poet W. E. Henley, by citing Ernest Hello's characterization of the nineteenth century as "[h]aving desire without light, curiosity without wisdom, seeking God by strange ways, by ways traced by the hands of men; offering rash incense upon the high places to an unknown God, who is the God of darkness." The *formal* experimentation of Decadence thus becomes a sincere and urgent search for *spiritual* renewal; Decadent writers, says Symons, search for "*la vérité vraie*, the very essence of truth," "the truth of appearances to the senses, of the visible world to the eyes that see it; and the truth of spiritual things to the spiritual vision." Decadent literature's "disease of form" signifies "this endeavour after a perfect truth to one's impression, one's intuition" through a "revolt from ready-made impressions and conclusions, a revolt from the ready-made of language, from the bondage of traditional form, of a form become rigid" ("Decadent Movement" 859).

In *The Symbolist Movement*, this intrinsic relation between experimental poetic language and earnest spiritual search lays the ground for Symons' large-scale characterization of Symbolism as the "spiritualising of the word" (202), and Mallarmé as a flagship figure (the "prophet and pontiff of the movement," as Symons had called him in "The Decadent Movement" [862]). Symons' tendency to present Decadence and Symbolism in religious terms becomes even more pronounced and affirmative in *The Symbolist Movement*, where it forms a recurrent and dominant theme according to which Symbolist "literature, bowed down by so many burdens, may at last attain liberty, and its authentic speech," but "accepts a heavier burden; for in speaking to us so intimately, so solemnly, as only tradition had hitherto spoken to us, it becomes itself a kind of religion, with all the duties and the responsibilities of the sacred ritual" (8). In Symons' view, Symbolism continued the Decadent reaction to the *fin de siècle* crisis of faith in even more pronounced form, dedicating itself fully, as Mallarmé did, to "the chimerical search for the virginity of language" as a new secular locus of Truth (195).

Symons clearly admires Mallarmé's search (he even calls it "heroic" [196]), but pinpoints a split impulse in Mallarmé and the Symbolist writer: an ambiguity towards language and words, as potentially liberating and dangerously precarious forces. On the one hand, according to Symons the Symbolist poet is wholly dedicated to "that perfecting of form in its capacity for allusion and suggestion, that confidence in the eternal correspondences between the visible and the invisible universe, which Mallarmé taught" (202-03). For Mallarmé, the word is "a living thing [. . .] by which the spirit is extracted from matter; takes form, perhaps assumes immortality"; "[t]o evoke, by some elaborate, instantaneous magic of language, without the formality of an after all impossible description; to be, rather than to express: that is what Mallarmé has consistently, and from the first, sought in verse and prose" (195-96). On the other hand, the picture Symons paints of Mallarmé's spiritual-linguistic search is neither a dedicated secular one that configures the aesthetic *Idéal* as a replacement for the Absolute, nor an orthodox religious one that believes it can touch and unite itself with a God through poetic representation. The word can ideally function as the magnificent "philtre [sic] of the evocation," but words are also precarious, evanescent, and sometimes altogether unattainable; one must forever struggle with their transitory and elusive nature, without being able to control them completely. Symons (188) quotes Mallarmé's telling assessment of poetry as "the language of a state of crisis," which he interprets as a sign that Mallarmé made a studied sense of linguistic emergency his own operating principle; to Symons, "all his poems" are "the evocation of a passing ecstasy, arrested in mid-flight" (195). It is important here that Symons characterizes Mallarmé's poetry as the *passing* and *arrested* (momentarily stopped), ecstatic flight of words, highlighting the fleeting and conditional quality of poetic achievement. For Symons, Mallarmé's Symbolist language and poetics thus oscillate between brief moments of powerful aesthetic ecstasy (which can perhaps provide a fleeting, maddening *glimpse* of the Absolute) and crushing disillusion and defeat – indicating a fundamental spiritual and linguistic doubt about the attainability of the very goals of Symbolist poetry.

Apparently it was precisely the intellectual honesty and urgency of Stéphane Mallarmé's conflict, his pursuit of the perfect word and image against the odds, which fascinated Symons. In fact, what Symons most responded to in Mallarmé's work in *The Symbolist Movement* was the French poet's emphasis on the inevitable flaws and incompleteness of aesthetic communication, the sense of mystery that results from his awareness that he can only ever be a partial master of poetic Truth and literary evocation. To Symons, Mallarmé appeared "always divided between an absolute aim at the absolute, that is, the unattainable, and a too logical disdain for the compromise by which, after all, literature is literature" (180), and was keenly aware of the inadequacy of words, their inability to produce an instantaneous, lasting authenticity – the *Idéal* was necessarily always a step ahead. Experiencing "an extreme discontent with even the best of [words'] service," the Mallarmé of Symons' *Symbolist Movement* finds himself not their master, but only their (perhaps ultimately unsuccessful) hunter. Symons uses an interesting metaphor of an illusive and elusive butterfly to characterize the alluring flight of the word: "[Mallarmé] has sought this wandering, illusive, beckoning butterfly, the soul of dreams, over more and more entangled ground; and it has led him into the depths of many forests, far from the sunlight" (195). Although he acknowledges Mallarmé's many "marvelous discoveries by the way," Symons characteristically keeps the actual result of the Symbolist poet's hunt an open question: "[t]o say that he has found what he sought is impossible." Both in his 1893 and 1899 remarks on Decadence and Symbolism, then, Symons displays a fundamental ambivalence toward the success of their efforts to distill a sacred essence out of language: while the goals are lofty (and Symons' deep sympathy with them is palpable throughout "The Decadent Movement" and *The Symbolist Movement in Literature*), a positive outcome is by no means assured.

Both Decadent and Symbolist literature carried essential spiritual impulses for Symons, as I have pointed out, but his presentation of Mallarmé's aesthetics throughout both works appears comparatively more secular and modern than Paul Verlaine's, more focused on language itself rather than the world of Platonic forms, for which language has traditionally been understood to provide an entryway. *The Symbolist Movement in Literature* shows us a Stéphane Mallarmé who is deeply engaged in a struggle with language, and through language, a wrestling with questions of human agency and the "immortality" of the spirit (195). In Mallarmé, self-conscious linguistic and poetic ambiguity determines the spiritual impulse of Symbolism, so that any vision of the Absolute takes the shape of always-haunting, always-escaping language, words, and poetic images. While Symons' understanding of Symbolist aesthetics continued to oscillate between intuitive hope for the possibility of the creation of quasi-metaphysical experience via poetic evocation ("mysticism," one of Yeats' key concepts, is a prominent synonym for the "spiritualising of the word" in *The Symbolist Movement*), and a lucid acknowledgment of the spiritual-linguistic limits which hindered a Stéphane Mallarmé, the dancer became an important point of symbolic reference for Symons – as it had for Mallarmé himself.

Aside from Symons' inevitable contact with the trope because of its central importance to Mallarmé's aesthetics, it was also a natural fit for the Englishman, who was an avid theatergoer and devotee of music halls in Paris and London during the most intense years of his contact with the French Symbolist and Decadent movements in the 1890s, and his tenure as the editor of *The Savoy* in London. Having frequented music-halls since the age of 17 (when he visited London for the first time), on his journeys to Paris Symons familiarized himself with French establishments such as the *Moulin Rouge* and the *Chat Noir* (Beckson 54). He also wrote reviews of new ballets and performers for such journals as the *Star* (where he was the music-hall critic), the *Monthly Review*, *Black and White*, published a regular editorial column entitled "At the Alhambra: Impressions and Sensations" for *The Savoy*, and was generally considered an expert on the contemporary London and Paris dance scene (Bargainnier 190).

During the years of his most important intellectual activity, from the early 1890s until his devastating mental breakdown in 1908, Symons' writings on dance and dancers were fundamentally shaped by both Decadent and Symbolist elements. As Symons negotiated his affiliation with Mallarmé and Verlaine in France while increasingly experiencing the spell of Yeats' mystical explorations in the 1890s, while he continued to highlight the spiritual urgency of Decadents such as Huysmans (cf. his analysis of Huysmans' *Là-Bas* in *The Symbolist Movement*), and grappled with his strange addiction to the theatrical and erotic demi-monde described in *London Nights*, his poetic representations of dancers and music-hall scenes took on a characteristically ambiguous, haunting, and often quite pessimistic metaphysical outlook, conscious of the inevitable *decadence* of aesthetic and erotic bliss.

To see Symons´ dancers accordingly as expressions of a Decadent and incipiently modern rather than a lingering Romantic sensibility, means to disagree with Frank Kermode's landmark argument about the Symbolist dancer trope in *Romantic Image* and "Poet and Dancer Before Diaghilev." Kermode famously placed Mallarmé's and Symons' dancers in the continuity of the Romantic and Idealist tradition, arguing that for Symons, Mallarmé, and Yeats, the dancer approximated and encapsulated an experience of the Sublime through art. According to Kermode, like ideal poetry she was deemed able to conjure up a "radiant truth out of space and time" (*Image* 2), non-discursively transmitting a pure and unambiguous meaning, providing "a means to truth, a truth unrelated to, and more exalted than, that of positive science" (44), which participates in "a higher order of existence" where "free from Adam's curse, beauty is born of itself, without the labour of childbirth or the labour of art where art means wholly what it *is*" (85). In Kermode's view, the Symbolist dancer functioned as a self-sufficient symbol that could heal divisions and inspire the artist with visions of Truth and Beauty emanating from her; Kermode saw her as a unique utopian refuge for Mallarmé and Symons, their ideal bridge to the poetic Absolute.

My analysis of Symons' fascination with Decadence's and Symbolism's ambiguous poetic spirituality, however, suggests a rather different reading of Symons' dancer figures as symbols of his aesthetic endeavor than Kermode submits. In accordance with his Decadent approach to Mallarmé's Symbolism, I contend, Symons practiced a much more cautious and profoundly skeptical view of dance and dancers as emblems of the *fin de siècle* poetic quest. As Kerry Powell has argued, Symons stressed aesthetic escapism rather than idealist fulfillment in his approach to Symbolism, and his stance toward the literary symbol itself was a Decadent, not a Romantic one: "the symbol does not finally express an ineffable and benign spiritual reality (however much [Symons] would like it to), but rather provides an avenue of escape from a world darker and more foreboding than most Romantic authors ever conceived" (157).[5] In Symons the symbol becomes an artistic "performance whose goal is escape and forgetfulness of objective reality through illusion," "a charm for dreaming oneself into forgetfulness" that "clears a path of temporary escape from the vicissitudes of life and death alike" (166). Powell writes further that Symons' understanding of dance itself encapsulated his Decadent sensibility, by "serv[ing] Symons as the concretion of what he understood 'symbol' to mean; it was 'an escape into fairy-land,' a means by which the artist could bring forgetfulness of the oppressive shadow-life of reality and create, at best, an 'illusion' (perhaps no less real than so-called reality) in the theatre of his own mind" (163). While Symons' poetry of the 1890s celebrates dance and dancers, it also conveys a discernible aspect of melancholy and sadness, a note of isolation and insatiable longing, embodied in the poet's yearning for, and separation from, the self-contained, enigmatic figure of the dancer on stage, who can be watched but not mastered or preserved. Symons' dancers are solitary dream figures whose very ephemeral and evasive nature paral-

---

[5] The argument about Symbolism's placement "in between" Decadence and Romanticism is of course an old one, going back at least to Mario Praz's *The Romantic Agony*. Kerry Powell's view of Symons' dancers as tending toward a full-blown Decadent rather than lingering Romantic sensibility is an exception to the critical landscape, however. Most scholars who have studied the dancer as a central figure for Symbolist aesthetics and pointed out important cultural connections it provides between Mallarmé, Symons, and ultimately Yeats, have tended to follow or implicitly assume Frank Kermode's influential presentation as sketched above (e.g. Fletcher, Gordon, Ellis; cf. also Morris ["Form"], Beckson ["Tumbler"]). While I would of course acknowledge the unquestionable importance of Symbolism's Romantic heritage overall, on the question of Arthur Symons' *understanding* of Symbolism, I wholeheartedly agree with Powell that it is a skeptical Decadent rather than a Romantic-Idealist one.

lels the beckoning flight of the word in the Symbolist literary consciousness – an aspect that, as I have attempted to show above, also
preoccupied Symons in his commentaries on Mallarmé.

His essay "The World as Ballet" directly echoes many of Mallarmé's ideas on dance and dancers, but again gives them a decidedly Decadent bent. At first sight, Symons seems to develop the
dancer as an optimistic model of aesthetic evocation akin to Mallarmé's ideal of Symbolist poetry, but in fact she carries the same
fundamental spiritual ambiguities which Symons identifies in Mallarmé. In "Ballets," Mallarmé famously described the dancer as an
inhuman, desexed metaphor, whose bodily language produces a
freer and more perfect poem than the poet's: "*elle n'est pas une
femme,* mais une métaphore [. . .] avec une écriture corporelle ce
qu'il faudrait des paragraphes en prose dialoguée autant que descriptive, pur exprimer, dans la rédaction: poème dégagé de tout appareil
du scribe" (*Œuvres* 229-30).[6] Mallarmé's ballet dancer is pure figuration: not a "woman," but a mere figure of speech, a depersonalized rhetorical cipher – a body that writes, and writing that is body.
Her "corporal writing" is portrayed as more perfect and suggestive
an act of poetry than a writer's: she is language set free from the bal-
last of human intervention, or the ordering direction of a "script-
writer" (*scribe*). Her unparalleled direct embodiment of art makes
her a rival as well as an ideal for the poet, who can never achieve
perfect mimesis such as hers. Inhuman and impersonal, she can
momentarily become a physical-rhetorical vehicle for complete representation without words; seemingly emptied out of individual
traits, the dancer is able to transcend the limits of her humanity and

---

[6] "*[S]he is not a woman,* but a metaphor [. . .] with a corporal writing, what it
would take paragraphs of prose, in dialogue and description, to express: she is
a poem set free of any scribe's apparatus" (*Mallarmé in Prose* 109).

become, as Mallarmé writes in "Les Fonds dans le Ballet," profoundly moving "poésie par excellence" (*Œuvres* 234).

Symons' "The World as Ballet" at first similarly describes the ballet dancer as "pure symbol," able to create a powerful intuitive understanding in the onlooker. The dancer is an amazing mistress of worlds without words ("Nothing is stated, there is no intrusion of words used for the irrelevant purpose of describing"), whose body language speaks directly, momentarily to the senses: she has "the intellectual as well as sensuous appeal of a living symbol, which can but reach the brain through the eyes, in the visual, concrete, imaginative way" (250). For Symons as well as for Mallarmé, the dancer became a fitting emblem for the Symbolist ideal of seemingly effortless evocation and sensation because in the merging of her body with her work of art she was supposedly able to disappear into her creation and thus consummate the illusion of a radiant, seemingly self-begotten aesthetics. Symons had stressed just such an effort to "be a disembodied voice, and yet the voice of a human soul" as the ideal of Decadence ("The Decadent Movement" (867), and in his essay on Mallarmé he made it clear that the unattainable goal of the Symbolist poet was to fully merge with his creation: "[i]n the final result, there must be no sign of the making, there must be only the thing made" (*Symbolist Movement* 197).

But if "The World as Ballet" praises the superior ability of the dancer to evoke "with her gesture, all pure symbol" a whole "world" of "idea, sensation, all that one need ever know of event," the same essay also makes it clear that the illusion, perfect in the moment, will and cannot last. The world the dancer creates on stage is only a transitory one, itself mortal: "the picture lasts only long enough to have been there" (251). For Symons the dancer creates a potent aesthetic dream space with vaguely sacred qualities, like Mallarmé's ballerinas in "Crayonné au Théâtre," who "in the flotation of daydream" are able to effect the impression of a poetic *sacre*, a "conse-

cration" (*Mallarmé in Prose* 104), in the moment of their dance.
They are soothing figures of forgetfulness, "so human, so remote, so
desirable, so evasive," who "seem to sum up in themselves the appeal of everything in the world that is passing, and coloured, and to
be enjoyed; everything that bids us take no thought for the morrow,
and dissolve the will into slumber, and give way luxuriously to the
delightful present" (249-50). But when their performance ends, the
dream must inevitably rupture, and emptiness set in again. Even
though Symons never goes as far as Nietzsche did in openly declar-
ing the death of God, his portrayal of the precarious human condition between desire, dream, and disillusion often seems to assume
an already empty, god-forsaken world. "The World as Ballet" again
carries a strong sense of spiritual crisis, as it puts forward a rather
dark allegory of the dance stage as a last refuge, a besieged bastion
in a death-ridden world in which humanity which can only find
momentary relief in immersing itself in aesthetic illusion, and "pathetic[ally]" desire the forgetfulness the dancers' performance offers,
knowingly craving their deception:

> Realising all humanity to be but a masque of shadows, and
> this solid world an impromptu stage as temporary as they, it
> is with a pathetic desire of some last illusion, which shall
> deceive even ourselves, that we are consumed with this
> hunger to create, to make something for ourselves, of at
> least the same shadowy reality as that about us. The art of
> the ballet awaits us, with its shadowy and real life, its
> power of letting humanity drift into a rhythm so much of its
> own. (250)

It is clear from these passages that for Symons the ballet can only
function as a temporary answer to humanity's hunger for the solace
of illusion, not as a radiant promise of true metaphysical salvation.
The ecstatic experience the dancer creates is the result of potent arti-

fice and inherent "contradictions" which cause "boundless bewilderments"; it is decidedly not the work of a savior (248). Perhaps not surprisingly, "The World as Ballet" begins with a rumination on the expulsion of dance from traditional religious discourse. Here Symons' difference to Mallarmé's emphasis on the intuitively spiritual, elating effect of the dancer ("cet effet spirituel"), in this case Loïe Fuller's in "Les Fonds dans le Ballet," becomes apparent (*Œuvres* 234).

Symons' interpretations of Mallarmé and the Symbolist dance aesthetic ultimately promote a secular view of art marked by the metaphysical uncertainty of the late nineteenth century, the age of Nietzsche, who had rejected the notion of art as an entryway to the Divine, but recognized its importance as a temporary aesthetic refuge and escape from a harsh reality. In *The Will to Power*, for example, Nietzsche declares art an antidote to reality ("Truth is ugly. We possess art lest we perish of the truth" [435; fragment 822]; humans need to lie to themselves in art because they cannot live by the gleaming light of truth: "man must be a liar by nature, he must be above all an artist. And he is one: metaphysics, religion, morality, science – all of them only products of [man's] will to art, to lie, to flight from 'truth', to negation of 'truth'" [451-52; fragment 853]). In his conclusion to *The Symbolist Movement* (which carries overtones of Walter Pater's famous conclusion to *The Renaissance*, another of Symons' influences), Symons' interpretation of Symbolist art indirectly meets a Nietzschean sensibility, as Symons describes art as a means to deal with the sense of human mortality and lack of agency in the greater scheme of things, as a powerful "escape" into forgetfulness and dream, an aesthetic ecstasy akin to religion and passion (erotic love): "And so there is a great, silent conspiracy between us to forget death; all our lives are spent in busily forgetting death. [. . .] we find our escape from its sterile, annihilating reality in many dreams, in religion, passion, art; each a forgetfulness, each a symbol of creation" (*Symbolist Movement* 325).

"The Dance of the Daughters of Herodias" from *Images of Good and Evil* (1899), a poem that alludes to the Irish Sidhe myth, is a poignant example of Symons' Decadent and incipiently modern reading of art as intoxicating dream, passive forgetting instead of active perfecting of the true human condition.[7] Similar to Nietzsche, for Symons literature and art could intercept the inescapable, painful awareness of death, providing a soothing, if only momentary, refuge from reality; like a protective shield, they could postpone the cruel vision of the end to come. In the poem, Symons' dancing Daughters of Herodias openly offer themselves as beautiful and deceiving "mirrors," aesthetic reflections or deflectors of reality which shield men from seeing "Far-off, disastrous, unattainable things," and instead provide them with a pleasing aesthetic vision at hand. The poem reverses the physical order of reality and dream, insisting that the aesthetic choice of a beautiful dream, signified by the dancers, is the preferable mode of being: "We, we alone among all beautiful things, / We only are real: for the rest are dreams" (*Images* 46.91-92). The Daughters of Herodias offer a more intense artificial existential experience to the onlooker than life itself, since "all this tossing of our freighted lives / Is but the restless shadow of a dream" (lines 99-100), in which "the whole world, and we that walk in it" (101) as well as "all our loves, and birth, and death, are all / Shad-

---

[7] Symons' poem bears a strong thematic similarity to Yeats' "The Hosting of the Sidhe" from *The Wind Among the Reeds* (1899), a collection published almost simultaneously with Symons' *Images of Good and Evil* and *The Symbolist Movement in Literature* (see Ellmann 25-26), exemplifying the degree to which Yeats was involved in Symons' interest in Symbolist aesthetics. Yeats himself contributed several essays on Symbolist art to Symons' magazine *The Savoy*, and in 1900, he published his own essay, "The Symbolism of Poetry," partly as a reaction and expansion of Symons' points in *The Symbolist Movement in Literature*.

ows, and a rejoicing spectacle / Dreamed out of utter darkness and the void" (105-07). And so the rhetorical trajectory of the poem, similar to the close of "The World as Ballet," merges into a longing invocation begging the dancers to dance on, and intoxicate the mortal world of "perishable" human "shapes" into blissful forgetfulness, despite the inevitable fleetingness of the beautiful illusion:

> Shapes on a mirror, perishable shapes,
> Fleeting, and without substance, or abode
> In a fixed place, or knowledge of ourselves,
> Poor, fleeting, fretful, little arrogant shapes;
> Let us dream on, forgetting that we dream! (112-16)

For Symons as well as for Nietzsche, nineteenth-century literature and culture grappled with the impossibility of an organic, ecstatic unity with the Divine, finding refuge in figurations of aesthetic dream and erotic desire. As Symons recognized, Symbolism itself found a temporary secular substitute for religion in the aesthetic adoration of the dancer's body and the ecstatic (if impermanent) sensation she was able to incite in the poet. Ultimately, however, Symons had no illusions about either art´s final inadequacy as a means to lasting fulfillment, or the dancer´s independence as an aesthetic sign. In "The World as Ballet," the paradise of physical poetry the dancer creates on stage is but aesthetic artifice, and inevitably recognized as such by the viewer:

> Here are all those young bodies, made more alluring by an artificial heightening of whites and reds on the face, displaying, employing, all their natural beauty, themselves full of the sense of joy in motion, or affecting that enjoyment, offering to our eyes like a bouquet of flowers, a bouquet of living flowers, which have all the glitter of artificial ones.
>
> (249)

Many of Symons' dance poems in *London Nights*, Symons' most Decadent poetry collection (for which Symons had trouble finding a publisher), mark this awareness of artifice through deliberate irony towards the ways in which the dancers work their magic via make-up, wigs, costumes, and lighting. Rather than developing the dancer as a perfect, radiant, and complete symbol (as Mallarmé had done), Symons makes visible the rather mundane tools of her trade. In "On the Stage" (from the cycle of poems dedicated to "Lilian") he describes the "whirling mist of multi-coloured lights" (15.3), "And rouge, and always tights, and wigs, and tights" (line 7); "Behind the Scenes: Empire" (from the "Décor de Théâtre" section) paints a picture of a throng of dancers rushing on stage like "little painted angels" (21.1) with "pink legs" (3), "Blonde, and bewigged, and winged with gold" (4) with "cheeks and nose / Rouged to the colour of the rose. / All wigs and paint" (8-10); the post-performance dancers in "At the Stage-Door" (another "Lilian" cycle poem) have "Cheeks with the blush of paint still lingering, eyes / Still with their circle of black ..." (16.16-17). "Nini Patte-en-l'Air (Casino de Paris)," written in May 1892 but not included in Symons' poetry collections until the 1920 volume *Lesbia and Other Poems*, even presents the dancer Nini as a full-blown emblem of Decadent artifice and eroticism, expertly practicing her "science" of seduction and deception through physical illusion:

> What exquisite indecency
> Select, supreme, severe, an art!
> The art of knowing how to be
> Part lewd, aesthetical in part,
> And *fin de siècle* essentially.
> The Maenad of the Decadence
> Collectedly extravagant,
> Her learned fury wakes the sense

That, fainting, needs for excitant
This science of concupiscence. (*Lesbia* 27-28.6-25)

Here again Symons' Decadent interpretation of the dancer figure makes itself felt. In the remaining pages, I want to give a brief overview of a few other conjoined Decadent and Symbolist influences in Symons' dance poems, the interpretation of Mallarmé's principal dance writings as channeled through Symons' larger Decadent perspective.

In keeping with Mallarmé's emphasis on the dancers' alluring mystery but adding a Decadent twist (the sense of human loneliness and isolation in an indifferent universe), in several of the dance poems in *London Nights*, the dancer appears as a fascinating vision, whose femininity stands in for a greater enigma the poet wishes to explore, but whom he can only watch from a distance; she appears as an existential paradox, both elating and deeply troubling. "La Mélinite: Moulin Rouge" from "Décor de Théâtre," a poem about one of Symons' lovers, the dancer Jane Avril (nicknamed La Mélinite), invests both the dancer and the poet-spectator with a note of isolation and vague, unfulfilled longing, dramatizing both the dancer's ultimate unavailability and her aesthetic and erotic impenetrability. Symons places a dancing Jane Avril in front of a mirror, "Alone, apart," but looking at her own reflection as she dances at some distance from the other ballet dancers, and "watches / Her mirrored, morbid grace; / Before the mirror, face to face" (24.11-13), stressing the quality of mystery of this "dance of shadows" (16). The artificiality of the dancer's illusion on the stage again offers the experience of a beautiful dream; the dancer is a remote and elusive figure immersed in her own mysterious *rêverie*, which invites the isolated poet-onlooker to follow her into her own realm of mirrors, shadows, and aesthetic intoxication. Indifferent to anything but her own reflection, the strangely "morbid" (15) and "enigmatically smiling" dancer (26) appears self-contained within her own empty hall

of illusions, which throws her own manifold image back at her, as
well as at the spectator in the wings, the mirror's multiplicity calling
into question the authenticity of the human being as opposed to the
aesthetic image.

The main themes of "La Mélinite," which Yeats praised as "one of
the most perfect lyrics of [its] time (*Uncollected Prose* 40; qtd. in
Beckson, *Life* 85) again echo those of Mallarmé's *Hérodiade* , parts
of which Symons included in his own 1899 poetry collection *Images of Good and Evil*. The fragment Symons translates (from "La
Scène, Hérodiade – Nourrice") focuses on a powerful image of
Hérodiade (a stylized Salome) in front of her mirror, addressing her
own reflection and ruminating on her loneliness and isolation. Similar to La Mélinite, this Hérodiade seems to have lost her humanity,
her sense of self among others' mirroring gazes:

> I live in a monotonous land alone,
> And all about me lives but in mine own
> Image, the idolatrous mirror of my pride,
> Mirroring this Hérodiade diamond-eyed. (*Images* 77.30-34)

In "La Mélinite" as well as in *Hérodiade,* the theme of aesthetic
looking and looked-at-ness versus authentic being separates the
world into two halves, bodily reality and its aesthetic reflection or
imagination, physicality and image. La Mélinite's mirror produces
mysterious shadows and reflections, and the poem seems to ask
about the possibility of telling apart the shadow in front of the mirror from the one behind it, physical reality from aesthetic dream: the
self in front of the mirror is possibly as much an illusion as its own
reflection, a remote, elusive figure on the threshold between the
physical and the dream world:

> Before the mirror's dance of shadows
> She dances in a dream,
> And she and they together seem

A dance of shadows;
Alike the shadows of a dream. (*London Nights* 24.16-20)

Dream and reality seem to merge in the timeless space of the dance, a site that seems precarious and precious at the same time. In Symons' "White Heliotrope," itself a poem about a moment between dream and waking, a mirror "has sucked" a young girl's "face / Into its secret deep of deeps, / And there mysteriously keeps / Forgotten memories of grace" (50.5-8), again echoing Mallarmé's connection between mirrors and a sense of lost authenticity in *Hérodiade*.

The idea of aesthetic distance and isolation of the poet from the dancer also appears in "To a Dancer" and "Prologue," two of the opening poems of *London Nights*. "To a Dancer" stresses the separation of the dancer from the spectator "across the footlights" (5.2); the speaker's separation from the life on stage is also palpable here, as in "Prologue," where the music-hall itself becomes a metaphor and textual mirror for the life of the spectator, who remains "Chained by enchantment to [his] stall," separated from the action on stage by a cloud of cigarette smoke (3.3). Unable to join the dancers on the stage, he remains a longing recipient, drawn into the spectacle in his imagination, but also ultimately unable to lose himself in it. As in "The World as Ballet," the male spectator is irresistibly attracted to the stage, but remains too aware of its artifice and transience to be able to fully merge with it except in elusive moments, captured ecstatically "in mid-flight."

Despite the demonstrated awareness in Symons' poems that the world of the ballet is an illusionary one, Symons often portrays the dancer's art as a seductive physical rather than metaphysical language, a powerful discourse of female bodies fantastically geared at him across a great divide. In many of Symons' dance poems of *London Nights* there is a strong suggestion of intimate communication between the dancer on stage and the poet in the wings, who senses that the dancer may offer a special revelation of herself, and thus inspire powerful thrills in him. In "To a Dancer," the speaker imagines the girl on stage dancing just for him ("Her eyes, that gleam for me" [5.8], "Her feet that poise to me" [12],) and experiences her dancing body as a "melody" that "In silent waves of wandering sound, / Thrills to the sense of all around, / Yet thrills alone for me!" (13-16). "On the Stage" even formulates the speaker's sense that the dancer secretly communicates only with him, sending him "memories and messages":

> You see a dance of phantoms, but I see
> A girl, who smiles to me,
> Her cheeks, across the rouge, and in her eyes
> I know what memories,
> What memories and messages for me.
>
> (*London Nights* 15.10-14)

The aspect of elemental communication between poet and dancer is reminiscent of Mallarmé's closing passage in "Ballets," which portrays the relation between the spectator-stranger and the Dancer-as-Symbol as a process of singular erotic intimation and intimacy:

> Oui, celle-là (serais-tu perdu en une salle, spectateur très étranger, Ami) pour peu que tu déposes avec soumission à ses pieds [. . .] la Fleur d'abord *de ton poétique instinct*, n'attendant de rien autre la mise en évidence et sous le vrai jour des mille imaginations latentes: alors, par un commerce dont paraît son sourire verser le secret, sans tarder elle te livre à travers le voile dernier qui toujours reste, la nudité de tes concepts et silencieusement écrira ta vision à la façon d'un Signe, qu'elle est. (*Œuvres* 233)

Mallarmé portrays the transaction between the poet and the dancer in quasi-religious terms, like a sacrificial prayer – the process centers on the dancer's erotic body, which the poet worships, and it is a game of seduction as much as it is a quasi-religious service. At his own initiative, the poet places "the Flower [. . .] of [his] poetic instinct" at the dancer's feet. He wishes that the dancer would "provide the revelation in its true light of thousands of latent imaginations" and reflect back at him "unhesitating, through the last veil which will always remain," his own "vision in the form of a Sign, the sign that she herself is," hence functioning as a powerful inspiration to his own aesthetic vision (*Mallarmé in Prose* 113). In "Poem," Symons similarly praised the dancer Lilian as "the artificial flower of my ideal" (*London Nights* 9.16).

But while Mallarmé preserves the poet´s sense of agency (the dancer gives him back his own imaginings, functioning as a mere catalyst rather than an independent agent of her own poiesis), Symons' speakers in his poems often appear disempowered, if fascinated, victims of the dancer's enchantment, who must answer to her powerful "magic." In "Nora on the Pavement," for example, a young dancer spontaneously charts out a "magic circle" on a city pavement at midnight, and draws the spectator into "the laughing circle of her power" through her dance (*London Nights* 7.3-4). An inexplicable mistress of time and space, she appears elusive, irresistible, and strangely free as she is "Leaping and joyous, keeping time alone / With Life's capricious rhythm, and all her own" (17-18). Nora appears to have an independent, godlike power to let time (and hence, death) stand still for the duration of her dance, a theme that also appears in "To a Gitana Dancing," where the dancer, this "witch of desire" (*Images* 108.23), "beckon[s], repel[s], / Entreat[s], and entice[s], and bewilder[s], and build[s] up the spell" in her dance (107-108.10-11), so that "the world is as nought" ((line 8) and "Time [. . .] is as nought, and the moments seem / Swift as eternity" (25-26). In *London Nights*, too, the female dancer speaks a potent and irresistible language that impresses itself on the senses like no other and works its magic, leading the speaker of these poems to crave her ecstatic, if momentary, sensual enchantment as a means of forgetting death (through her aesthetic realignment of time), but at the cost of his ultimate loss of agency.

As this brief discussion indicates, in Symons' female figures in *London Nights* we often see Symons pairing the Symbolist conceptual desire to forge out of aesthetic creation a deeply moving or ecstatic self-experience, with the Decadent fascination with the erotic *femme fatale*. In many of the *London Nights* poems, Symons follows Mallarmé's initial figuration of the dancer's femininity as an instrument of inspiration and identification for the poet, but keeps her highly eroticized, so that her very eroticism becomes the basis for her power. Whereas Mallarmé often paradoxically desexes the female body of the dancer as he tries to identify with her, placing "female sexuality under erasure" as the female body "turns out to be both the source of poetic inspiration and the obstacle to its accomplishment" (Townsend 130), Symons' women remain strongly sexed, depersonalized tools for aesthetic and erotic ecstasy. Symons' investment in femininity as a tool for secular ecstatic experience also appears with striking intensity in related figurations of erotic encounters with seductive women in *London Nights* – female bodies in erotic performance that emulate and echo the effects of Symons' dancers. Among such related encounters are the invocation of a Nereid-like prostitute in the infamous poem "Stella Maris" (which provoked an outcry and garnered Symons his reputation as an immoral decadent), and the musical imagery of a woman's body as a heavenly "instrument" playing to the poet's desires in "Idealism." The prostitute in "Stella Maris" arises and smiles to the male speaker "Out of the night, out of the sea" (*London Nights* 40.25), and comes "to call [him], come[s] to claim / [His] share of [her] delicious shame" (41.30-31). In the speaker's memory, the sexual encounter with the enigmatic woman assumes an almost religious quality of ecstasy, as he regrets the loss of

> [. . .] that ineffable delight
> When souls turn bodies, and unite
> In the intolerable, the whole
> Rapture of the embodied soul

which her advances used to produce in him (46-49). Here as well as in the poignant "Idealism," the female body becomes a conduit for the poet's metaphysical desires and fantasies, which beckons to him and offers itself for his exploration and possession. In "Idealism," Symons' erotic yet inhuman figuration of femininity reaches a grotesque climax in the speaker's cynical praise of the woman he desires as a "masterpiece of flesh" (*London Nights* 44.4), a "splendid body" (10), which flat-out denies her human subjectivity:

> The woman has no possibilities
> Of soul or mind or heart, but merely is
> The masterpiece of flesh: well, be it so.
> It is her flesh that I adore [. . .] (2-5)

The poem's synecdochal presentation of the woman as mere "flesh" can itself be seen as an expression of Symons' occasionally surfacing misogyny, but it is the self-conscious egomania of the poem's speaker himself – his desire to use the woman's body as an "instrument" to experience sensations he has otherwise only been able to dream of – that remains the most interesting element of this poem, and most characterizes its overall tone and purpose:

> Tyrannously I crave, I crave alone,
> Her splendid body, Earth's most eloquent
> Music, divinest human harmony;
> Her body now a silent instrument,
> That 'neath my touch shall wake and make for me
> The strains I have but dreamed of, never known. (9-14)

For Symons the female body in physical performance (musical, erotic, dancing) hence effectively becomes the poet's means to actively transport and dream himself into a physical (rather than metaphysical) Beyond. Ultimately, however, this aesthetic movies an illusionary one: just like Huysmans' Decadent protagonist Des Esseintes in *À rebours*, who is addicted to artifice in the objects he collects, yet remains deeply unsatisfied with their sensual effects (so that he keeps searching endlessly for the perfect sensation, the ultimate aesthetic-erotic experience), the male speakers of Symons' poems crave the dancers on stage and the sexual encounters with alluring women, while already aware that they will only find imperfect satisfaction in passing moments of aesthetic dream, the short-lived forgetfulness afforded by artifice.

In Symons' poetic universe which admires Symbolism's aesthetic-spiritual project and yet cannot deny its own Decadent notion of metaphysical disillusion, figurations of the spiritual-physical threshold, the very Limit of aesthetic representation and erotic satisfaction itself, become highly attractive as paradoxical metaphors of desire and thwarted fulfillment, transgressive flights of the poetic imagination which must ultimately remain confined to the stage of the poem itself. As we have seen, Symons' dance poems often reflect this ambiguity, which celebrates the anticipation and the memory of blissful aesthetic and erotic dreams, but ultimately denies or suspends any possibility of lasting metaphysical fulfillment. For the poet, one path remains: to describe and explore, from all different angles, this very state of desire and non-fulfillment between Symbolism and Decadence, in which the constant disillusion of erotic and spiritual desires paradoxically merge to intensify sensation; the very oscillation on the threshold of satisfaction – never the crossing of it – hence becomes eroticized. In "Liber Amoris" (one of the closing poems of *London Nights* about Symons' lover Lydia who was also a dancer), it is paradoxically the very quality of elusiveness, the erotically teasing aspect of Bianca, Lydia's nemesis, that makes her highly desirable to the speaker:

Nay, but a subtlier intense
Unsatisfied appeal of sense,
Ever desiring, ever near
The goal of all its hope and fear,
Ever a hair's breadth from the goal.
So Bianca satisfies my soul. (105.102-07)

Commenting indirectly on the phenomenon of Symons' predilection for figurations of suspended and withheld (instead of fulfilled) desire in Symons' *London Nights* dance poems, Jan B. Gordon (440) writes, "The final irony is that [Symons] reaps a kind of satisfaction from the denial of satisfaction, part of the ontology of *fin-de-siècle* desire." The emphasis on this paradoxical invocation and denial of aesthetic-erotic satisfaction puts Arthur Symons in close proximity to the Modernism of W. B. Yeats and T. S. Eliot, who learned much from their encounters with the poetry of Stéphane Mallarmé, and the Symbolist and Decadent aesthetic, which Symons had facilitated. Like Moreau's iconic dancer "the eternal Salome," whom Symons describes as a perpetual figure of the Limit in *Studies in Seven Arts* (and who always "fumbl[es]" in vain about the outskirts of evil, of beauty, and of mystery" [50]),[8] as a writer and theorist Arthur Symons positioned himself on the threshold between Symbolism,

---

[8] Notably, Symons' description of Salome in the essay "Gustave Moreau" is again marked by the twin influences of Symbolism and Decadence, Mallarmé's Symbolist dancer and Huysmans' Decadent transposition of Moreau's Salome in *À rebours*. Symons (*Studies* 51) writes,

She is not a woman, but a gesture, a symbol of delirium; a fixed dream transforms itself into cruel and troubling hallucinations of colour; strange vaults arch over her, dim and glimmering, pierced by shafts of light, starting into blood-red splendours, through which she moves robed in flowers or jewels, with a hieratic lasciviousness.

Decadence, and Modernism; between eroticism and aesthetics; language and the Absolute; and ultimately between despair and hope for modern poetic agency.

As this essay has argued, Symons' 1890s major dance writings imitate many of Mallarmé's conceptual connections between the dancer, the poet, and the aesthetics of Symbolist evocation that foster dynamic suspension rather than stable reference of meaning, and acknowledge the absence of an immutable metaphysical referent. Reading the Symbolist trope of the dancer through an essentially Decadent lens, Symons creatively fused his admiration for Symbolist aesthetic ideas and techniques with an already disenchanted, Decadent sensibility that celebrated physical sensation rather than metaphysical inspiration. Via Mallarmé's formulations of Symbolist evocation on the one hand, and Decadent intellectual figurations of eroticism and death on the other, Symons found his own way to representing dancers as remote, erotically alluring yet ultimately mysteriously unavailable figures, of whose illusionary stage craft and artifice the poet is only too well aware: they serve as nagging reminders of an already lost connection to the metaphysical Absolute. For Symons, the dancer became inextricably linked with *fin de siècle* literature's struggle with language, a literature self-consciously skeptical of its own presupposed mimetic, spiritual, and even religious faculties. Reconfigured as a symbolic breaking point, an indication of poetic and religious crisis rather than a utopian model for a unification with the Sublime through art, the dancer was Symons' emblem of choice to express and negotiate the modern writer's own precarious, perhaps even doomed, dance with language after the aesthetic Fall. Arthur Symons' dancers thus stand out as powerful images for the poetic and spiritual crisis of the late nineteenth century, reflecting the *fin de siècle* poet's own desires, doubts, and fears as in the depths of a distant mirror.

Works Cited

Bargainnier, Earl F. "Arthur Symons' Music-Hall Poems." *Four Decades of Poetry (1890-1930)* 1 (1977): 189-200.

Beckson, Karl. *Arthur Symons: A Life.* Oxford: Clarendon, 1987.

---. "The Tumbler of Water and the Cup of Wine: Symons, Yeats, and the Symbolist Movement." *Victorian Poetry* 28 (1990): 125-33.

Block, Haskell M. "Yeats, Symons and *The Symbolist Movement in Literature.*" *Yeats: An Annual of Critical and Textual Studies* 8 (1990): 9-18.

Bristow, Joseph. "'Sterile Ecstasies': The Perversity of the Decadent Movement." *Essays and Studies* 48 (1995): 65-88.

Eliot, T. S. *The Sacred Wood: Essays on Poetry and Criticism.* London: Methuen, 1920.

Ellis, Sylvia. *The Plays of W. B. Yeats: Yeats and the Dancer.* New York: St. Martin's, 1995.

Ellmann, Richard. *Eminent Domain: Yeats among Wilde, Joyce, Pound, Eliot and Auden.* New York: Oxford UP, 1967.

Fletcher, Ian. "Explorations and Recoveries, II: Symons, Yeats, and the Demonic Dance." *London Magazine* 7 (June 1960): 46-60.

Gordon, Jan B. "The Danse Macabre of Arthur Symons' *London Nights.*" *Victorian Poetry* 9 (1971): 430-32.

Kermode, Frank. *Romantic Image.* New York: Vintage, 1964.

---. "Poet and Dancer Before Diaghilev." *Puzzles and Epiphanies: Essays and Reviews 1958-1961.* London: Routledge and Kegan Paul, 1962. 1-28.

Mallarmé, Stéphane. *Œuvres: Textes ablis avec chronologie, intro-ductions, notes, choix de variantes et bibliographie.* Ed. Yves-Palain Favre. Paris: Garnier, 1985.

64   *Petra Dierkes-Thrun*

---. *Mallarmé in Prose.* Ed. Mary Ann Caws, trans. Jill Anderson, Malcolm Bowie, Mary Ann Caws, Rosemary Lloyd, Richard Sieburth, and Patricia Terry. New York: New Directions, 2001.

Morris, Bruce. "Elaborate Form: Symons, Yeats, and Mallarmé." *Yeats: An Annual of Critical and Textual Studies* 4 (1986): 99-119.

---. "Mallarmé's Letters to Arthur Symons: Origins of the Symbolist Movement." *English Literature in Transition, 1880-1920* 28 (1985): 346-53.

Munro, John M. *Arthur Symons.* Twayne English Authors Series. New York: Twayne, 1969.

Nietzsche, Friedrich. *The Will to Power.* Ed. Walter Kaufmann, trans. Walter Kaufmann and J. R. Hollingdale. New York: Random House, 1967.

Powell, Kerry. "Arthur Symons, Symbolism, and the Aesthetics of Escape." *Renascence: Essays on Value in Literature* 29 (1977): 157-67.

Praz, Mario. *The Romantic Agony.* Trans. Angus Davidson. 2nd ed. Oxford UP, 1970.

Symons, Arthur. *Arthur Symons: Selected Letters, 1880-1935.* Ed. Karl Beckson and John M. Munro. London: Macmillan, 1989.

---. "The Decadent Movement in Literature." *Harper's New Monthly Magazine* 87 (November 1893): 858-67.

---. *Images of Good and Evil.* 1899. Poole, UK: Woodstock, 1996.

---. *Lesbia and Other Poems.* New York: E. P. Dutton, 1920.

---. *London Nights.* 2nd ed. London: Leonard Smithers, 1897.

---, trans. *Poésies.* [Translations of selected poems by Stéphane Mallarmé.] Ed. and bibliog. Bruce Morris. Edinburgh: Tragara, 1986.

---. *Studies in Seven Arts.* New York: E. P. Dutton, 1925.

--. *The Symbolist Movement in Literature.* Reprinted, revised and enlarged ed. New York: Haskell House, 1971.

Townsend, Julie. "Synaesthetics: Symbolism, Dance, and the Failure of Metaphor." *The Yale Journal of Criticism* 18.1 (2005): 126-48.

Yeats, William Butler. *Autobiographies*. Ed. William H. O'Donnell, Douglas N. Archibald. Vol. 3 of *The Collected Works of W. B. Yeats*. Ed. Richard J. Finneran and George Mills Harper. New York: Scribner, 1999.

---. "The Symbolism of Poetry." *W. B. Yeats, Essays and Introductions*. London: Macmillan, 1961. 153-64.

---. Rev. of *Amoris Victima*, by Arthur Symons. April 1897. *Uncollected Prose by W. B. Yeats*. Ed. John P. Frayne and Colton Johnson. Vol. 2. London: Macmillan, 1975.

Cultural Decline and Alienation
in Vernon Lee's
"Prince Alberic and the Snake Lady"

Peter G. Christensen
Cardinal Stritch University

Abstract: In this essay, after considering the critical response to Vernon Lee's supernatural story, "Prince Alberic and the Snake Lady" (1896), I claim that Lee uses decadence less as a literary strategy than as a set of tropes in order to call us to remember the loss of native Italian Renaissance culture under foreign cultural and political domination.

Recovering from the bout of fever precipitated by the old man's story of Alberic the Blond and the Fairy Oriana, young Prince Alberic, the protagonist of Vernon Lee's "Prince Alberic and the Snake Lady," tells the priest attending him, "My father [. . .] I have seen and heard strange things in my sickness, and I cannot tell for certain now what belongs to the reality of my previous life, and what is merely the remembrance of delirium" (1896: 321, 1954: 53).[1] These words have resonance beyond the personal psychology of the young, misunderstood hero. They capture in a nutshell the historical change taking place in the year of his death, 1700, as Italy moves into a period of cultural decline. Through Alberic's distress the story engages larger issues which have been raised before about Lee's work: whether the story should be labeled "decadent," whether decadence here is a group of tropes or rather a set of strategies, and whether decadence has a repressive or liberating force for the reader. For example, in "'Still Burning from This Strangling

---

[1] My quotations from the story will refer to the page numbers in the 1896 *Yellow Book* edition and the widely available 1954 edition edited by Horace Gregory. Where there is a slight punctuation variation, I have used the 1896 version. Other changes are noted.

Embrace,'" Kathy Alexis Psomiades, discussing the contrast between the more liberatory aestheticism described by Jonathan Dollimore and Richard Dellamora and the more repressive brand described by Elaine Showalter and Griselda Pollock, notes that Vernon Lee's work "complicates any easy opposition between literary and conservatory aestheticism and complicates too our ideas about Victorian dissidence" (21). Earlier this year, Dellamora discussed Lee's relationship to decadence with reference to Lee's review of the English translation of Max Nordau's *Degeneration* under the title of "Deterioration of Soul," which he reads as Lee's defense of "sexual dissidence as necessary to the very existence of reason" (Dellamora 2005: 531). After considering the many different interpretations that "Prince Alberic and the Snake Lady" has received, I will use the trope of cultural decline to discuss Lee's presentation of the loss of a vital Italian culture at a fin-de-siècle two hundred years anterior to her own writing in the 1890s.

"Prince Alberic and the Snake Lady" was the only contribution that Vernon Lee made to *The Yellow Book* (July 1896), and it was reprinted in her collection of stories, *Pope Jacynth and Other Fantastic Tales* (1904). Over the years most people have known it from the collection of Lee's stories edited by Horace Gregory, *The Snake Lady and Other Stories* (1954), from the one compiled by Irene Cooper Willis, *Supernatural Tales: Excursions into Fantasy* (1955), or from the reprinting of *The Yellow Book* in 1967. It now appears in the collected edition (600 copies only were printed) of Vernon Lee's fantastic stories, *Hauntings*, with an introduction by David G. Rowlands, published by Ash-Tree Press (2002). This volume contains her eighteen fantastic short stories and sketches plus the essay, "Faustus and Helen: The Supernatural in Art" from *Belcaro* (1887). In addition, the story is available online through both *Gaslight* and *HorrorMasters*.

Although "Prince Alberic and the Snake Lady" is only about forty-five pages long, it is not easy to summarize because in a fantastic tale explanations are not simple. The story begins in 1701 but then immediately tells what happened over the last decade, that is, the series of events which followed when the room of eleven-year-old Prince Alberic was redecorated. He had been much smitten by the figure of a Lady in a faded tapestry on his wall, but he had never seen her whole picture, since a chest and heavy iron crucifix concealed the bottom part. When the tapestry was accessed and replaced, he could tell that the Lady had a snake's tale. He slashed to pieces the replacement tapestry of *Susanna and the Elders*, and he was banished from the Red Palace by his grandfather, Balthasar Maria, Duke of Luna, to the dilapidated Castle of Sparkling Waters. In the garden he met a snake, whom he befriended, and when the snake was away, a woman like a fairy godmother took her place. Eventually the Duke and his ambassadors came and killed the snake, precipitating soon after the deaths of both Alberic and the Duke. At this point we are back to the situation given in the story's opening paragraph.[2]

---

[2] "Prince Alberic and the Snake Lady" was not one of the few works of fiction of Vernon Lee analyzed briefly in Peter Gunn's pioneering biography of Vernon Lee (1964). However, it has become more and more central to considerations of the author's achievements. Commentary by the following critics has appeared: Burdett Gardner, Horace Gregory, Mario Praz, Catherine Rancy, Gunnar Schmidt, Ruth Robbins, Martha Vicinus, Jane Hotchkiss, Carolyn Christensen Nelson, Sophie Geoffroy-Menoux (in "L'imaginaire" and in somewhat different form in "Le fantastique"), Brian Stableford, Vineta Colby, Christa Zorn, and Mary Patricia Kane. The last three authors have all written full-length books on Lee. Increased interest in Vernon Lee's writing was demonstrated by the dedication of a conference entirely to her work, Vernon Lee: Literary Revenant, at the Senate House at the University of London, hosted by Patricia Pulham and Catherine Maxwell on 10 June 2003, where Margaret Stetz delivered a paper on "Vernon Lee and the Bruised Bodley Head."

Christa Zorn suggested for origins of this story primarily the melusine legend (as did Mario Praz [294], writing in 1955) and secon-
darily *Amadis de Gaule* (191). Vineta Colby stresses the influence
of E. T. A. Hoffmann's "The Golden Pot" and points out that the ge-
ography of her story is imaginative. She notes that Lee wrote to
Maurice Baring, who wanted to set a story in Italy of the same period, suggesting to him on 20 February 1906, "In your place, I
should boldly invent a state to suit my purpose (as I did in *Alberic*,
if you remember, though I had Massa Carrara in my mind). It leaves
one free to be as detailed as one wishes" (Colby 354). In addition,
the extinction of the family of Luna will remind many readers of the
tragedy of the di Luna family in Verdi's *Il Trovatore*, where the
Duke kills Manrico, the dashing Troubadour, only to find out from
the gypsy Azucena, as the opera closes, that he has killed his own
brother, who was long ago presumed dead. As a person knowledge-
able about opera, Lee's choice of the family name must have been
deliberate.

"Prince Alberic and the Snake Lady" is a masterfully ambiguous
story, which has provoked many different readings.[3] There is no

---

[3] Horace Gregory finds much of the ambiguity in the Snake Lady herself, writing, "This snake descends from the benevolent dragon of the East and is the
heiress of Good now transformed in the Christian world to Evil. It is this mu-
tation of the snake lady and her magic qualities, compounded of both Good
and Evil which endows Vernon Lee's version of the legend with its undercur-
rents of inherited fears and ecstasies" (22). The Snake Lady's ambiguity not
surprisingly has provoked various psychoanalytical readings, as in Burdett
Gardner's *The Lesbian Imagination* and Gunnar Schmidt's *Die Literarisierung
des Unbewussten*. Gardner speculates on Lee's own identification with the
characters in the story and suggests that it may be a symbolic presentation of
her own personal struggle as a lesbian to attain psychic wholeness (28).
Schmidt, even more restrictively Freudian, concentrates on Alberic's Oedipus
complex, the incest taboo, and the Snake Lady as a symbol for the return of
the repressed (105), thus closing off any liberating possibility of the story
from the start.

agreement on the meaning of the story because there is no consensus on the ending. Jane Hotchkiss is the one critic who sees the story as optimistic. Christa Zorn, Mary Patricia Kane, Martha Vicinius, and Sophie Geoffroy-Menoux find some optimistic notes. Finally, Ruth Robbins reads the ending as a complete defeat.[4]

In an extended post-Freudian study, "(P)revising Freud, Vernon Lee's Castration Fantasy," Jane Hotchkiss praises Lee's strong feminist stance. She claims, "The tale's many warnings that patriarchy cannot survive its imposition of castration upon the feminine come to fruition" (35). For Hotchkiss, the story "connects patriarchal domination and cultural 'decadence' with rape and with colonization of feminine body/space" (32).

Christa Zorn, who sees the Snake Lady as a "symbiotic other," is somewhat less optimistic about the ending of the story. She writes that the relationship of the Prince and the Snake Lady undercuts the norms of heterosexuality and that the bond between Alberic and the Snake Lady "establishes a principle beyond patriarchal authority." Although the Snake Lady is murdered, the ending of the story "does

---

[4] Vineta Colby warns against simplified psychoanalytic explanations of the story. She writes that the "erotic implications" are "undeniable" yet at the same time "only matters of speculation" (229). She stresses the goodness of the Snake Lady (similarly see Rancy 162) and the optimistic nature of the story because Lee, here influenced by E. T. A. Hoffmann's "The Golden Pot," with its positive relationship between Serpentina and Anselmus, does not create, as she usually does, a "malign femme fatale" (230). More pessimistically than Colby, Brian Stableford writes in "Haunted by the Past," "Like Gautier and Keats, Lee takes the side of the tempting serpent against those who would banish her, and sees her removal from the world – representative of a reluctant acceptance of brute reality – as a tragedy best delayed for as long as humanly possible" (Stableford). Like Colby, Carolyn Christensen Nelson stresses the importance of the "perverse women characters" to Lee, and goes so far as to say that she does not see her as a feminist short story writer (70).

not reinstate patriarchal rule since the duke survives the prince by only a few months, and the 'House of Luna' becomes extinct" (157).

In a study which stresses the similarity in outlook between Lee and Hélène Cixous, Mary Patricia Kane (61) writes that the story exposes the fact that "repression and control over what is feminine is an untenable position destined to lead to the fall of the House of Luna, the metaphoric figuration of the House of Patriarchy." However, it is only the reader who gets the benefit of this exposition. In contrast, tourists in the story at the end only know that chairs and tables in the porter's lodge have been upholstered with pieces of a damaged tapestry from the Red Palace, which told the story of Alberic the Blond and the Snake Lady.

Martha Vicinus (100) responds to Burdett Gardner's Freudian study by asking whether Lee could not just as well have imagined herself as the "victimized Snake Lady," "the destructive, false Duke," or the "youthful, idealistic Prince Alberic." Vicinus states, "[t]he Oedipal implications of a boy fixated on an erotic mother are irrelevant, for Lee is constructing the ideal lesbian romance" in which the "godmother has created Alberic without reproduction" and engages with him in a relationship of "reciprocal need" (97). She considers the story double-edged, claiming that Decadent aesthetics was both "imaginatively freeing" and "isolating" for Lee (100-01). Vicinus writes, Lee's "tales of frustrated desire, impossible love – who could be more impossible as a recipient of physical love than a woman whose lower half is a snake's tale? – seem to confirm this pervasive feeling of defeat" (100).

Sophie Geoffroy-Menoux ("L'imaginaire" 192) considers the Snake Lady to be a Jungian figure, an archetype of the Dame-Serpent, an ambivalent chthonic mother. She assists the Prince in his rite of passage against the old Duke, whose architectural delights represent anti-nature and decadent perversion ("Le fantastique"

157). For Geoffroy-Menoux, the story represents the sad triumph of Artifice over Nature.

Ruth Robbins, who stresses the pessimism of the ending and its symbolic defeat of woman, is more interested in the problematics of labeling Lee's stories as Decadent, given that Decadence was a term applied to male writers. In the end, "the tapestry world is more valuable than the forces which defeat it" and "the perspective offered by history, that of the impartial overview, is cold" (156). History "survives because there is nothing outside it to consume it in its turn" (156). Robbins's attention to history in Lee's story in relationship to decadence opened up a new approach to the story.

Subsequently, Catherine Maxwell in "Vernon Lee and the Ghosts of Italy" (206) has pointed out the importance of the idea of the "culture-ghost" to Lee, who used this phrase in her preface to the reprint of her early story, "Winthrop's Ghost" in the collection, *For Maurice* (1927). In a related vein, Angela Leighton also mentions the culture ghosts ("Ghosts" 1) and writes that "Lee brings the past, figured as Italy, the Renaissance, the ghost, the portrait to the very doorstep of who we are" ("Resurrections" 234).

Lee both stresses the conflict between historical periods and gives us a sense that the weightiness of history is a characteristic of decadence. Thus I am not taking the approach of the editors of *Perennial Decay*, Liz Constable, Matthew Potolsky, and Dennis Dennisoff, who write, "On the other hand, we can look at decadence not as a literary period or a set of tropes such as perversions, artificialities, illnesses, and blasphemies, but as an array of destabilizing literary strategies" that disrupt older patterns of reading and interpretation" (11). This approach is also endorsed by Richard Dellamora in his article, "Productive Decadence" (529). However, given the fact that there is no consensus among critics as to whether the story is destabilizing in a progressive sense or not, I feel that an approach by tropes such as artificiality and decline is still significant.

In "Prince Alberic and the Snake Lady," I argue, Lee offers us a picture of decadence that she has developed as a cultural historian. Lee is lamenting the end of the native Renaissance culture in the seventeenth and eighteenth centuries, as northern Italy fell under French and Austrian cultural and political influence. We can see this theme by paying attention to three topics. First, in her own essays, such as "Carlo Gozzi and the Venetian Fairy Comedy" in *Studies in the Eighteenth Century in Italy* and "The Outdoor Poetry" and "The School of Boiardo" in *Euphorion*, Lee shows her regret for what was lost from the imaginative world of the Middle Ages, as reason becomes more important with the revival of classical learning. Second, the network of historical and cultural references in the story itself, which takes place shortly before the War of the Spanish Succession, shows Italy's historical decline. Third, Lee evokes the French classical fairy tale, through enchanted serpent and fairy godmother figures, even as she writes in the tradition of the German fairy tale of alienation.

First, since the historical element of "Prince Alberic and the Snake Lady" is sometimes overlooked, it is important to relate it to Lee's own *Studies of the Eighteenth Century in Italy*, published at the beginning of her career, Lee announces the historical theme that appears in this story about fifteen years later. For her, the eighteenth century is a period which has been lost to students of history. Here, as Hilary Fraser (230) points out, Lee is interested in popular culture as well as elite culture. In her essay "Carlo Gozzi and the Venetian Fairy Comedy" (415-36), Lee pays little specific attention to his play, *The Serpent Woman*, a theatre piece which constitutes one part of the literary historical legacy of the figure of the Serpent Woman across time (427); instead she discusses Gozzi's theatre in general.

Lee concludes that Gozzi is a chief victim of the disappearance of artists of eighteenth-century Italy from the annals of significant world cultural periods. She remarks that Gozzi's grotesque and fantastic world was brought to life on the stage of San Samuele. However without the Sacchi company to perform his work, he was forgotten "unlike the greater masters of the art, Shakespeare, Beckford, and Hoffmann" (427). In the conclusion she states resignedly:

> Moreover, we must repeat it, the art of the Italian eighteenth century is extremely forgotten; indeed, with the exception of a few plays by Goldoni, wholly forgotten. The music and the drama may, will, nay certainly must, sooner or later be exhumed; but the revival will have taken place too late, they will be things of culture and eclecticism, the tradition will be gone. [. . .] The Italian eighteenth century will, like Antiquity, like the Middle Ages, like the Renaissance, contribute its share to our eclectic culture; its men and women will be exhumed, restored, put into glass cases and exhibited mummy-fashion in our historical museum; we shall gape at them, pry into them, hit upon them, just as we do for all the other classified human fossils which we possess; but that time has not yet come. The men and women of the Italian eighteenth century are still mere ghosts whom we have scared in our search for art; for whom we feel we know not what vague friendship and pity.
>
> (439-40)

One would have to agree that Goldoni and Gozzi are not considered as important even today as Boiardo, Ariosto, and Tasso, who rank as some of the greatest Italian poets since Dante. Lee's story begins by asking us to think of Prince Alberic's ancestors in relationship to Boiardo and his legacy. Alberic the Blond, a hero of an earlier, happier period, appears as both cultural and physical ancestor.

Lee discusses the Italian Renaissance epic writers with enthusiasm in her essay, "The Outdoor Poetry" from *Euphorion* (109-66): "Huon of Bordeaux" is generally considered the poem on Carolingian themes which leads most directly through fantasy to the school of Boiardo. The fairies in this tradition are of particular interest to Lee. In "The Imaginative Art of the Renaissance" from *Renaissance Fancies and Studies* (65-133), Lee claims, "The actual fairy story becomes, little by little, more complete – the painters of the fifteenth century [. . .] little guessing it, are precursors of Walter Crane" (113). This interest led her to publish a collection of traditional *Tuscan Fairy Tales*.

In "The School of Boiardo," also from *Euphorion* (261-333), Lee remembers that when she first began to read Boiardo years earlier she could not put him down because he had some of the appealing quality of "some fairy books of Walter Crane's" (319). She says admiringly of Boiardo's world at the expense of Ariosto's and Tasso's:

> This is the real Fairyland, this of Boiardo: no mere outskirts of Ferrara, with real, playfully cynical Ferrarese men and women tricked out as paladins and Amazons, and making fun of their disguise, as in Ariosto; no wonderland of Tasso, with enchanted gardens copied out of Bolognese pictures and miraculous forests learned from theatre mechanicians [. . .]. (320)

Lee believes that the fairy epics represented by *Orlando Innamorato* and *Orlando Furioso* with their "peculiar combination of chivalric and classic elements" (326) continued to excite poet and public, but the Age of Exploration finished off this kind of interest, and Spanish picaresque moved in, reflecting a less hopeful world (332). In "Prince Alberic and the Snake Lady" the end of this earlier world is emblematized by the death of the Snake Lady herself. The narrator writes, "[. . .] the Dwarf had given it two cuts with his Turkish scimitar" and the Duke "kicked its mangled head with his ribboned shoe, and turned away laughing" (1896: 342, 1954: 71). With the map of the world being filled in, there was no longer a realm in which this Snake Lady could convincingly be placed.

Turning to our second category, we see that the set of references in the story suggests something additional to the murder of women by men, the havoc that the older generation wreaks on the younger generation, or the destruction of paganism by Christianity. Lee's story is told by a third-person narrator as a flashback about the end of a ducal family at the end of the 1600s. The story begins ominously. In 1701 the Duchy of Luna is united to the Holy Roman Empire because of the extinction of the royal family line with Prince Alberic III. The story then offers a net of possible connections both literary and historical. The passing away of a family may call to mind the end of the Este household in Ferrara. With the title to the city taken away by the Vatican, the last Este Duke left for Modena in 1598. Because of this event, the court that nourished Boiardo and then Ariosto and many other artists passed out of cultural visibility. Furthermore, the Red Palace of old Duke Balthasar may remind us of the Palazzo Rosso in Genoa, a sixteenth-century building now a museum of sixteenth-century artists such as Titian, Veronese, and the later Caravaggio.

Lee skillfully blends faked references with actual ones, and a reader may not be able to distinguish between representatives of the two categories without some background reading. Church figures are noticeable among the complete fabrications. There is first of all no St. Paschal Babylon. Pope Paschal I (817-24), Saint, and Pachal II (1099-1118) had nothing to do with Babylon. There does not seem to be any Saint Fredevaldus as far as I can tell. Saint Romwald is a very little known Saxon saint, probably not too popular in Italy, said to have preached the gospel shortly after his baptism as an infant. The bizarre luxuriousness of these confused historical references reminds us of the happily disordered world of the tapestry and of medieval quasi-historical epic poems.

On the other hand, the verifiable references give a concrete sense of setting for this fantasy. For example, once famous was the Military Order of the Knights of St. Stephen, which was founded in Pisa by Cosimo I de' Medici, Grand Duke of Tuscany. So too there really was a famous alchemist from Milan named Giuseppe Francesco Borri, patronized by Queen Christina of Sweden. In 1670 Christina died, and when Innocent XII ascended to the Holy See, he revoked the privileges granted to Borri. Then Borri was imprisoned in Castel S. Angelo, where he was to die of disease in 1695, age 68 (see Cosmacini's book passim).

The story ends at the time of the beginning of the War of the Spanish Succession, which is adumbrated by the semi-ridiculous rivalry between the Jesuit, the Jester, and the Dwarf, with the Dwarf representing the King of Spain; the Jester, the Holy Roman Emperor; and the Jesuit, the Papacy. Two possible eventualities of the War, as it began in 1701, were the union of Spain and France under the Bourbons, on the one hand; and the union of Spain and the Holy Roman Empire under the Hapsburgs, on the other. The war began when Pope Innocent XII advised King Charles II of Spain to make a Frenchman, the Duke of Anjou, his testamentary successor. Spain was the dominant power in Italy until Austria replaced it in the War of the Spanish Succession. Prince Alberic, as the heir to a petty duchy in northern Italy, is subject to the power politics of the neighboring political units. The end of the story is meant to remind us of the death of Italian Renaissance culture under Austrian domination.

The Renaissance world is displaced in stages. Balthasar Maria follows the classical example of the Sun King in the arts. France had first invaded Italy two centuries earlier under Charles VIII. Although he replaces the tapestry of *Prince Alberic and the Snake Lady* with Gobelins of *Susanna and the Elders*, the Duke allows the older work of art to remain in a back room like the cultural unconscious.

The old Duke is interested in French ballet, in which he dances the part of Phoebus Apollo in *Daphne Transformed*. Daphne is culturally the earliest of the metamorphosed females suggested by references in the story, appearing in book 1 of Ovid's *Metamorphoses*. Meanwhile, Ovidian metamorphosis is also recalled by Lee with reference to the Narcissus and Echo story. When Alberic as a boy looks into a well, he is in for a shock:

> Alberic, as he bent over, was startled by suddenly seeing what seemed a face filling up part of the shining circle; but he remembered it must be his own reflection, and felt ashamed. So, to give himself courage, he bent over again, and sang his own name to the image. But instead of his own boyish voice he was answered by wonderful tones, high and deep alternatively, running through the notes of a long, long cadence, as he had heard them on holidays at the Ducal Chapel at Luna. (1896: 303, 1954: 38)

After this incident a snake appears, and Alberic is surprised that it had such a little head since it did not match the head in the tapestry (where the snake's upper part was a woman). The motif of a boy looking at his own face and hearing a type of echo recalls Book 3 of the *Metamorphoses,* but Alberic is under no curse of Nemesis to love without winning his love, although ironically it turns out that this is indeed his fate.

Third, we should note that the time of the story is the period of the beginning of the classical fairy tale in Europe, a tradition about two hundred years old as Lee wrote, and one strongly influenced in the last hundred years by German Romanticism. In the time of Louis XIV the transformation story of the classical Cupid and Psyche from Apuleius showed itself in the classic fairy tale, "Beauty and the Beast," by Jeanne-Marie Leprince de Beaumont. The 1690s was the decade when marginalized members of the court of Louis XIV produced the first great outpouring of literary fairy tales, in the famous stories by Charles Perrault, as well as the lesser known ones by Mme. D'Aulnoy (author of "Le serpent vert") and a half-dozen other women. As Lewis Seifert writes, in the Quarrel of the Ancients and the Moderns the fairy tale writers at Louis XIV's court were on the side of the Moderns. Nearly half of the writers of the vogue between 1690 and 1715 were women, and they accounted for two thirds of all the fairy tales of this period (922). The happy fairy tale ending often showed hope for social mobility for the good, cultured young woman.

The insert story of Alberic I's entry into Oriana's castle deliberately works and re-genders "Beauty and the Beast" motifs. Lee's story asks us not only to examine one culture that arises organically out of another one but also to see how treacherous it is to try to understand the world when one culture is fossilized in another. Although Lee in her essayistic writings clearly showed that she was interested in the survival of the pagan gods, perhaps nowhere in these writings did she give the theme the complexity it has in this story.

We may at first feel that the killing of the snake is simply the killing of a woman by the three lackeys of Duke Balthasar Maria, but there are complications. It is true that after the killing of the snake, there is no body of the snake that remains but rather "the body of a woman, naked, and miserably disfigured with blows and saber cuts" (1896: 343, 1954: 72). As the story makes clear, the three men kill the snake because as a snake it represents the devil (1896: 342; 1954: 70). Their frame of reference is different from that of the reader who has been introduced to the story of the Snake Lady both in the tapestry and in the life of Prince Alberic III. The woman in the tapestry, when the table with the crucifix on it is removed in Alberic III's youth, is found to have a "big snake's tale" (1896: 294,

1954: 31). In the life of Alberic III, as he grows into maturity (approximately age twenty-two) in the course of the story, we never see the Snake Lady in this form. She is either snake or Lady (but not both at once) at different times. According to the priest:

"--- let me see, how does the story go? – ah yes – this demon, I mean this Snake Lady was a – what they call a fairy – or witch, malefica or strix is, I believe, the proper Latin expression – who has been turned into a snake lady for her sins – good woman. [. . .] The Snake Lady – let me see – was to cease altogether being a snake if a cavalier remained faithful to her for ten years; and at any rate turned into a woman every time a cavalier was found who had the courage to give her a kiss as if she were not a snake – a disagreeable thing besides being mortal sin. As I said just now, this enabled her to resume temporarily her human shape, which is said to have been fair enough; but how can one tell? I believe she was allowed to change into a woman for an hour at sunset, in any case and without anybody kissing her, but only for an hour. A very unlikely story, my Lord, and not a very moral one, to my thinking!"

(1896: 323, 1954: 55)

Thus it seems that the source of the story within the story is not even believed by its own teller, the priest. He may be wrong, and at some point the Snake Lady may have features of both serpent and woman as in the tapestry, thus causing us to think of the tapestry's representation as symbolic. However, this solution to the problem is not as simple as it seems because the narrator connects the Snake Lady with Boiardo, writing, "This tapestry was of old and Gothic taste, extremely worn, and represented Alberic and the Snake Lady Oriana, alluded to in the poems of Boiardo and the chronicles of the

Crusaders" (1896: 290).[5] However, there is no such story in Boiardo's *Orlando Innamorato*, unless it is to be found in one of the several continuations made when Boiardo died with the poem unfinished as the French under Charles VIII were invading Italy. Since the story is a fabrication of Lee, not Boiardo, it would seem as if she wants to point to his poem as another marker of Italian cultural disappearance, the French invasion.

It was a typical pattern for Boiardo to use monstrous creatures in his epic, and so a hypothetical Snake Lady is not far-fetched. As Julia M. Kisacky (41) writes, "[. . .] of the three most important fays in the *Innamorato*, Dragontina, Falerina, and Morgana, only one is explicitly a fay in the poem." It is "on Ariosto's authority that Dragontina and Falerina are known as fays." Dragontina is associated with the water of forgetfulness, Falerina with the seductive garden, and Morgana with the temptation of wealth. Thus they have allegorical trappings to them. Such associations are not carried into Lee's story where the temptation is the woman herself, the woman who may be what? Snake? Demon? Fairy? Enchantress? Godmother?

As the priest himself indicates, he does not have the right vocabulary for the Snake Lady, and he cannot have it because it is not available to him or to anyone. She can not correspond historically to a *malefica* or *strix*. The Roman world is gone. The passage of the classical gods is not a simple one to demons but rather a complicated one in which Celtic folklore blends with classical mythology.

Laurence Harf-Lancner's *Les fées au Moyen Âge* offers much insight into this melding. The fairies melusine and morgana developed in the XIIth century in the period Lee designates when she mentions

---

[5] Horace Gregory's edition reads, "This tapestry was of old and Gothic taste, extremely worn, and represented Alberic the Blond and the Snake Lady Oriana, as described in the *Chronicles of Archbishop Turpin* and the poems of Boiardo" (1954: 27).

the *Chronicles of Archbishop Turpin* (i. e. pseudo-chronicles). First of all the fairies are split into two groups. In the first group are the fairy godmother types who, as heirs of the Parcae, decide human destinies (9). Second we find the fairy who engages in a love affair with a mortal and who dominates "l'imaginaire érotique" of the Middle Ages (9). The melusine of this second group is a supernatural creature who falls in love with a human, follows it into the human world and marries its beloved while imposing on it an interdiction. The melusine goes back to the Other World after the transgression of the pact, leaving descendants behind. The morgana represents the flip side of this set of characteristics. The morgana is a supernatural figure who falls in love with a human and carries it off to the Other World. A return to this world comes only with obeying an interdiction. Disobeying it results in either death for the hero or else his final disappearance into the Other World. There are no offspring from this union (9-10).

Neither of these paradigms from the Middle Ages applies to the Snake Lady, since she appears to Prince Alberic as his Fairy Godmother and refers to herself by that name. Perhaps the *locus classicus* for the appearance of the Fairy Godmother in appropriated folklore is in Charles Perrault's "Cinderella" of 1697. Here the paradigm that kept the melusines and morganas together in their separation from the fairy godmother no longer holds. If indeed the woman is not lying, when she tells Alberic that she is his Fairy Godmother, then the paradigm that is being used to interpret her by the establishment culture has not yet moved ahead with the times. The priest is still looking backward to Alberic I and Alberic II.

Yet even here there is a problem as to what we actually know about the Snake Lady. According to the priest, Alberic I supposedly disenchanted his Snake Lady. The priest says, "I cannot exactly remember what princess [married Alberic I], but it was a very suitable marriage, no doubt, from which Your Highness is of course descended" (1896: 324, 1954: 55).[6] The possibility is left open that the Princess appeared after the disenchantment because this Princess was the disenchanted Snake Lady, a typical enough pattern in magical tales. Further argument for this view is offered by young Alberic III's response to his nurse when the crucifix is removed for the first time. She says, "it's only Duke Alberic the Blond, who was your ancestor, and the Snake Lady" (1896: 294, 1954: 31). Her view, informed by folklore, implies that Alberic the Blond did end up with his Snake Lady. Young Alberic thinks that the painting shows that "the knight was so very good to her" (1896: 295, 1954: 31). Later Alberic II gave up his Snake Lady in order to enter a monastery, where he died. Thus the two earlier stories of the Snake Lady never reached completion. The reader does not get to find out whether she was a melusine or a morgana, since in neither case did the prince love her for the ten years.

It may be argued that the truth of the Nurse's story that Alberic and the Snake Lady did indeed wed is vouched for by the appearance of the old man who mends crockery and tells fairy tales. However, in my view, Lee means this matter to be questionable. First of all, the old man is said to be able to recite "some of the many stanzas of *Orlando* or *Jerusalem Delivered*, which he knew by heart" (1896: 315, 1954: 48). If he knew them by heart, then he could use them for motifs in fantasy stories. Second, he is specifically presented as a reciter of "fairy tales" (1896: 315, 1954: 48). He does not make any truth claims. Third, when the usually subdued Prince Alberic asks the man for a story of his ancestor, he threatens the man with physical punishment if he does not overcome his reluctance to say anything. Thus the old man's story of Alberic kissing the Snake with the Golden Crown and watching her turn into a beautiful damsel may just be a lie to save his life. This story is so

---

[6] 1954 capitalizes the word "Princess."

disturbing to Prince Alberic that he falls into a fever. Does he react this way because he would then think of himself as descended from a snake for a mother? Until this point he has always dreaded asking for more details about his disturbing ancestry and issues of succession.

It is worth noting that the tapestry of the Snake Lady may have had been spun less to suggest magic than to suggest legitimate princely succession. As recent work by Stephen G. Nichols on the *Roman de Mélusine*, written in 1393 by Jean D'Arras under the patronage of Jean, Duke of Berri, indicates, the story served not only as a reworking of the melusine myth but also as a response to the justifications made by Froissart in his chronicles for English rule of France (Nichols 137-38). Thus the point of a melusine story may be less about an otherworldly love and the problems it entails than a statement that the origin of a certain ruling family is not indebted to another ruling family. The family holds its origin in an imaginary, independent moment. Of course, D'Arras' version of the story is built around the fact that descendants of Mélusine rule Lusignan to this day, whereas in Lee's story Alberic I may or may not have married the Snake Lady, depending on whom you believe. Indeed, it is only a "rumor" that the snake was ever part lady. The figure in the tapestry might better be called a lamia rather than a melusine since she is a female monster. There may be an allusion to the treacherous snake in the "Lamia" of John Keats in the motif of the serpent shedding tears (426; pt. 2.60-68).

Even short allusions such as the one to Keats indicate that Lee is guiding us on a trip about the metamorphosis of women throughout different literary-historical periods. After she takes us from Ovid's Daphne to the romances of Boiardo and his successor Ariosto, we are made to consider through the green snake the literary fairy tale of the court of Louis XIV. As Marina Warner notes in *From the Beast to the Blonde*, one of Mme. D'Aulnay's most famous fairy tales, was "Le serpent vert." It deals with the situation of being an unlovely woman in the marriage market of France c. 1700 (Warner 288-89). In this story the green serpent is a man. The heroine is a very ugly woman Hidessa, and her true match turns out to be the Green Serpent. The wicked fairy in this story is called Magotine. However, the story is quite different from Lee's because the Green Serpent takes Hidessa away to an enchanted world, an escape Prince Alberic cannot make.

Mme. D'Aulnoy's story is not at all the same story as Carlo Gozzi's more earthy play *The Serpent Woman* (1762), which features a magical female creature named Cherestani, married to Farruscad, who wants to renounce her powers and immortality and become a human wife. However, she has to act toward Farruscad in a way that looks malicious as part of the trials that she has to go through, and these culminate in Farruscad having to kiss Cherestani in the form of a serpent. In the end she does become a normal wife and offers her realm to Farruscad. Ted Emery, who translated this play, sees it in his Freudian study as a comedy enforcing the patriarchal order (16-17).

As Jane Hotchkiss pointed out, Lee is resisting the patriarchal order. In order to do so she grafts herself on to the tradition of the Romantic literary fairy tale of alienation, such as E. T. A. Hoffmann's "The Golden Pot" (1814), which I read in a different way than Vineta Colby does. Lee's story, unlike the Louis XIV-period fairy tales and the earlier Italian epics, ends in the pessimistic fashion of the literary fairy tales of the German Romantic movement, discussed by Jack Zipes in *Breaking the Magic Spell*. E. T. A. Hoffmann is called to mind when Lee mentions the "Cremona viols" (21), which figure prominently in one of his stories, "The Cremona Violin," about Councillor Cresperl. Zipes points out how alienation is a key to these Romantic tales such as Hoffmann's. "The Golden Pot" is a story in which the protagonist, a young German student of the period of the Napoleonic invasion, has doubts about becoming a privy councilor after he sees Serpentina, a snake with blue eyes, who is actually the daughter of an archivist named Lindhorst, who had earlier been banished from the otherworldly kingdom of Atlantis. The story is one in which Anselmus, who represents the forces of the imagination, is pitted against repression. In the end he jumps into water to go off with Serpentina, and he disappears, perhaps to Atlantis, but possibly to his death. Her reality status is questionable, a noteworthy fact that contrasts with the concrete reality status of the earlier melusines and morganas, since Anselmus may be crazy. He is a literary ancestor of the disturbed Prince Alberic. As Zipes points out, the Romantic German writers used the fairy tale to "question the limits of change in a conservative society" and their studies of alienation influenced scores of writers after them (39). In the end, Serpentina represents less the lover or the temptress than the absolute.

This new concern with alienation turns the fairy tale into a direction far away from the view of love we see in Ariosto and Tasso for example. The Christian humanist allegorical elements are gone, and love is now a way to overcome individual alienation from society. How far we are from what we read in the *Orlando Innamorato*:

> But he who knows the power of Love
> Will offer to excuse that knight,
> Since Love is stronger than the mind,
> Beyond all skill and intellect.
> Both young and old join in his dance
> The peasant and the mighty lord:
> There's no relief from Love, or death;
> All feel them, every kind and class.
>
> (Boiardo 204; canto 27.2)

In Lee's story the mighty lord, Duke Balthasar Maria, is incapable of love, unlike Alberic.

In *Jerusalem Delivered*, Armida, the chief temptress, makes heroes forget God, as Rinaldo the hero learns: "She, with sweet words and false enticing smiles, / Infused love among the dainties set, / And with empoison'd cups our souls beguiles, / And made each knight himself and God forget" (Tasso 217; canto 10.60). God no longer matters as he did for Tasso in this Hoffmannesque tradition of writing. If Lee replaces God at all, it is with the fairy godmother figure.

As we conclude and return to the questions that have been asked about Lee's relationship to decadence, it is worth keeping in mind that decadence is predicated on alienation. This alienation may itself be caused by the weight of history. In the recently published posthumous essay, "Flaubert's *Salammbô*: History in Decadence," Charles Bernheimer defends Flaubert against the claims first made by Saint-Beuve and then much later by Lukács that *Salammbô* was an ahistorical failure:

> However, what Lukács interprets as a failure of historical vision may rather be an assertion that history lacks vision. What he sees as the decadence of historical fiction may be a fiction generated by history's decadence. Flaubert feels himself to be at an end – which he variously describes as that of nineteenth-century France, of the Latin race, even of the world – but he associates this ending not with a poverty of history but with its excess. Flaubert's conception of what it means to be historical destroys history as a mode of insight and understanding. To be historical, he says, is to lose any elevated perspective, any spatial or temporal distance from events and persons, and to adopt an entirely contingent point of view, "le point de vue de la chose." History

for Flaubert is no more than its objects and exists nowhere else than in its objects. (42-43)

Lee did not look at the ruins of Carthage, but she did write a story in which there is no elevated perspective on history or on the Snake Lady. With the duchy passing from the House of Luna, all that re-mains behind are the chairs in the porter's lodge, the Red Palace, the Porphyry Rhinoceros, etc. The story contains too much literary his-tory to allow easy interpretation and too little material history be-sides these scattered artifacts as Italy settles down into its eight-eenth-century cultural slumber. Ultimately, the story asks us to re-flect on the idea of decadence as it is communicated to us through material culture (in part, archaeology) and literary culture (in part, intellectual history). Whereas material culture captures better the sense of loss, without literary culture we would largely be deprived of understanding alienation.

Works Cited

Bernheimer, Charles. *Decadent Subjects: The Idea of Decadence in Art, Literature, Philosophy, and Culture of the Fin de Siècle in Europe.* Ed. T. Jefferson Kline and Naomi Schor. Baltimore: Johns Hopkins UP, 2002. 33-55.

Boiardo, Matteo. *Orlando Innamorato.* Trans. Charles Stanley Ross. Berkeley: U of California P, 1989.

Chapman, Alison, and Jane Stabler, eds. *Unfolding the South: Nine-teenth-Century British Women Writers and Artists in Italy 1789-1900.* Manchester: Manchester UP, 2003.

Colby, Vineta. *Vernon Lee: A Literary Biography.* Charlottesville: U of Virginia P, 2003.

Constable, Liz, Matthew Potolsky, and Dennis Denisoff. Introduc-tion. *Perennial Decay: On the Aesthetics and Politics of Deca-dence.* Ed. Liz Constable, Dennis Denisoff, and Matthew Potol-sky. Philadelphia: U of Pennsylvania P, 1999. 1-32.

90   *Peter G. Christensen*

Cosmacini, Giorgio. *Il medico ciarlatano: Vita inimitabile di un europeo del Seicento.* Rome: Laterza, 1998.

Dellamora, Richard. "Productive Decadence: 'The Queer Comradeship of Outlawed Thought': Vernon Lee, Max Nordau, and Oscar Wilde." *New Literary History* 35 (2005): 529-46.

Emery, Ted. "Carlo Gozzi in Context." Introduction. *Five Tales for the Theatre.* By Carlo Gozzi. Trans. Albert Bermel and Ted Emery. Chicago: U of Chicago P, 1989. 1-19.

Fraser, Hillary. "Regarding the Eighteenth Century: Vernon Lee and Emilia Dilke Construct a Period." *The Victorians and the Eighteenth Century: Reassessing the Tradition.* Ed. Francis O'Gorman and Katherine Turner. Aldershot, Eng.: Ashgate, 2004. 223-49.

Gardner, Burdett. *The Lesbian Imagination (Victorian Style): A Psychological and Critical Study of "Vernon Lee."* Ph. D. Diss. Harvard U, 1954. New York: Garland, 1987.

Geoffroy-Menoux, Sophie. "L'imaginaire du souterrain/souterrain de l'imaginaire: Vernon Lee." *Le Souterrain.* Ed. Aurelia Gaillard. Paris: L'Harmattan, 1998. 185-95.

---. "Le fantastique de Vernon Lee au tournant du siècle: entre baroque et grotesque." *La littérature fantastique en Grande-Bretagne au tournant du siècle.* Ed. Max Duperray. Presses Universitaires de Provence, 1997. 147-70.

Gregory, Horace. "The Romantic Inventions of Vernon Lee." Introduction. *The Snake Lady and Other Stories.* By Vernon Lee. Ed. and introd. Horace Gregory. New York: Grove, 1954. 6-24.

Gunn, Peter. *Vernon Lee: Violet Paget, 1856-1934.* New York: Oxford UP, 1964.

Harf-Lancner, Laurence. *Les fées au Moyen Âge: Morgane et Mélusine. La naissance des fées.* Nouvelle bibliothèque du Moyen Âge. Geneva: Slatkine, 1984.

Hotchkiss, Jane. "(P)revising Freud: Vernon Lee's Castration Phantasy." Ed. Carola M. Kaplan and Anne B. Simpson. *Seeing*

Double: Revisioning Edwardian and Modernist Literature. London: Macmillan, 1996. 21-38.

Kane, Mary Patricia. "Threadbare and Faded History: Tapestry in 'Prince Alberic and the Snake Lady.'" *Spurious Ghosts: The Fantastic Tales of Vernon Lee.* Rome: Carocci, 2004. 45-67.

Keats, John. *The Complete Poems.* Ed John Barnard. 2nd ed. New York: Penguin, 1976.

Kisacky, Julia M. *Magic in Boiardo and Ariosto.* New York: Peter Lang, 2000.

Lee, Vernon. *Belcaro: Being Essays on Sundry Aesthetic Questions.* London: W. Satchell, 1887.

---. "Deterioration of Soul." *Fortnightly Review* 59 (June 1896): 938.

---. *Euphorion: Being Studies of the Antique and the Mediaeval in the Renaissance.* 2nd ed. London: Unwin, 1885.

---. *For Maurice.* London: John Lane, The Bodley Head, 1927.

---. *Hauntings: The Supernatural Stories.* Introd. David G. Rowlands. Ashcroft, BC: Ash-Tree, 2002.

---. "Prince Alberic and the Snake Lady." *The Yellow Book* 10 (July 1896): 289-344. Rpt. *The Yellow Book* 10. New York: AMSP and Arno, 1967. 289-344.

---. "Prince Alberic and the Snake Lady." *The Snake Lady and Other Stories.* By Lee. Ed. and introd. Horace Gregory. New York: Grove, 1954. 27-72.

---. "Prince Alberic and the Snake Lady." *Gaslight.* 20 Oct. 2005 <http://gaslight.mtroyal.ab.ca/princalb.htm>.

---. "Prince Alberic and the Snake Lady." *HorrorMasters.* 20 Oct. 2005 <http://www.horrormasters.com/Themes/horror_classics.htm>.

---. *Pope Jacynth and Other Fantastic Tales.* London: Grant Richards, 1904. 2nd ed. New York: J. Lane, 1907.

---. "Prince Alberic and the Snake Lady." *The Snake Lady and Other Stories* Introd. Horace Gregory. New York: Grove, 1954. 27-72.

---. *Supernatural Tales: Excursions into Fantasy.* Introd. Irene Cooper Willis. London: Peter Owen, 1955.

---. *Renaissance Fancies and Studies.* London: Smith, Elder, 1895. New York: Garland, 1977.

---. *Studies in the Eighteenth Century in Italy.* 2nd ed. London: Unwin, 1907.

Leighton, Angela. "Ghosts, Aestheticism, and 'Vernon Lee.'" *Victorian Literature and Culture* 28.1 (2000): 1-14.

---. "Resurrections of the Body: Women Writers and the Idea of the Renaissance." Chapman and Stabler 222-38.

Maxwell, Catherine. "Vernon Lee and the Ghosts of Italy." Chapman and Stabler 201-21.

Nelson, Carolyn Christensen. "Vernon Lee and the Short Story." *British Women Fiction Writers of the 1890s.* New York: Twayne, 1996. 70-79.

Nichols, Stephen G. "Melusine between Myth and History: Profile of a Female Demon." *Melusine of Lusignan: Founding Fiction in Late Medieval France.* Ed. Donald Maddox and Sara Sturm-Maddox. Athens: U of Georgia P, 1996. 137-64.

Praz, Mario. "Fantasmi culturali." *Il patto col serpente: Paralipomeni di "La carne, la morte e il diavolo nella letteratura romantica."* Milan: Mondadori, 1972. 292-97.

Psomiades, Kathy Alexis. "'Still Burning from This Strangling Embrace': Vernon Lee on Desire and Aesthetics." *Victorian Sexual Dissidence.* Ed. Richard Dellamora. Chicago: U of Chicago P, 1999. 21-41.

Rancy, Catherine. "Étude d'un cas: 'Vernon Lee.'" *Fantastique et décadence en Angleterre, 1890-1914.* Toulouse: CNRS, 1982. 157-80.

Robbins, Ruth. "Vernon Lee: Decadent Woman?" *Fin de Siècle/Fin du Globe: Fears and Fantasies of the Late Nineteenth Century.* Ed. John Stokes. London: Macmillan, 1992. 139-61.

Schmidt, Gunnar. *Die Literarisierung des Unbewussten: Studien zu den phantastischen Erzählungen von Oliver Onions und Vernon Lee*. Frankfurt: Peter Lang, 1984.

Seifert, Louis. "The Marvelous in Context: The Place of the Contes de Fées in Late Seventeenth-Century France." *Fairy Tales, Sexuality and Gender in France, 1690-1715: Nostalgic Utopias*. Cambridge: Cambridge UP, 1996. 59-97. Rpt. *The Great Fairy Tale Traditions: From Straparola and Basile to the Brothers Grimm*. Ed. Jack Zipes. Norton Critical Editions. New York: Norton, 2001. 902-33.

Stableford, Brian. "Haunted by the Past: An Introduction to Vernon Lee." *Infinity Plus*. Dec. 2001. 20 May 2005 <http://www.iplus.zetnet.co.uk/introduces/lee.htm>.

Stetz, Margaret. "The Snake Lady and the Bruised Bodley Head." Conference on Vernon Lee: Literary Revenant. Institute of English Studies, School of Advanced Study, University of London and the Queen Mary School of English and Drama, London. 10 June 2003.

Tasso, Torquato. *Jerusalem Delivered*. Trans. Edward Fairfax. Introd. John Charles Nelson. New York: Capricorn, 1963.

Vicinus, Martha. "The Adolescent Boy: Fin de Siècle Femme Fatale." *Journal of the History of Homosexuality* 5 (1994): 90-104. Rpt. *Victorian Sexual Dissidence*. Ed. Richard Dellamora. Chicago: U of Chicago P, 1999. 83-106.

Warner, Marina. *From the Beast to the Blonde: On Fairy Tales and Their Tellers*. New York: Farrar, Straus, and Giroux, 1994.

Zipes, Jack. *Breaking the Magic Spell: Radical Theories of Folk & Fairy Tales*. New York; Routledge, 1979.

Zorn, Christa. *Vernon Lee; Aesthetics, History and the Victorian Female Intellectual*. Athens: Ohio UP, 2003.

A Decadent Discord: George Egerton

Sarah E. Maier
University of New Brunswick

> Neither does it avail anything to say that the *nature* of the two sexes adapts them to their present functions and position [. . .] What is now called the nature of women is an eminently artificial thing [. . .]. John Stuart Mill, *The Subjection of Women* (1869)

> Femininity in this sense is on the same side as madness. It is because madness secretly prevails that it must be normalized [. . .] It is because femininity secretly prevails that it must be recycled and normalized (in sexual liberation in particular).
> Jean Baudrillard, *Seduction* (1979)

In the 1880s and 1890s, a new type of fiction emerged in the United Kingdom which male critics sought to normalize, then marginalize, as the mad fiction of suffragette minds. Far from being the trivial scribblings of unbalanced minds, the New Woman fiction, much of which appeared in the infamous periodical *The Yellow Book* and in John Lane's equally notorious *Keynotes* series[1] became persistently identified with the decadent male artist because "the ambitions of both [presented] a profound threat to established culture" (Dowling 434-35); indeed, Lane's infamous series was named for its first volume, *Keynotes* (1893) by George Egerton, which sold over 6000 copies in 1893, ran through eight printings by 1898 and was translated into seven languages. It was the second edition, issued in 1894, which was used to launch the series. The author of two wildly suc-

---

[1] Both *The Yellow Book* and the *Keynotes* series were published at the Bodley Head, a result of the 1887 partnership of John Lane and Elkin Matthews. *The Yellow Book* went to thirteen issues under the editorship of Henry Harland and Aubrey Beardsley, while the series produced thirty three volumes of *avant garde* work by both well-known and new writers.

cessful collections of short stories, the second being *Discords* (1894, sixth volume of the series), with less successful collections of stories (*Symphonies* [1897], *Fantasias* [1898] and *Flies in Amber* [1905]) and two novels (*The Wheel of God* [1898], *Rosa Amorosa* [1901]) as her *oeuvre*, George Egerton – pseudonym of Mary Chavelita Dunne Golding Bright – was a sensation of the 1890s. Her texts are influential precursors to modernism and are now recognized as paradigmatic texts of the *fin de siecle*. Variously labelled as a premodernist, a virago, a mannish writer and a New Woman, Egerton's narratives might best be read in the *milieu* of decadence.

Born in Australia in 1859, Mary Chavelita Dunne (later Golding Bright) was a child of travel; raised in Ireland, Chile, Germany and New York, Chav (as she was known) began her life as an adventurous woman with an elopement at the age of twenty eight with Henry Higginson, a much older friend of her father who was a bigamist. They ran away to Norway where her greatest influences in literature entered her life: Ibsen, Strindberg and Knut Hamsun whose novel *Hunger* she translated into English in 1899. Moving back to Ireland, she was forced to find work due to the recklessness of her then husband, Egerton Clairmonte, until her eventual marriage to Reginald Golding Bright, a theatre critic. Writing became her work; her first notebook of six stories, the eventual core of *Keynotes*, was rejected by T. P. Gill, a reviewer for *The Weekly Sun*, and by the publishers at Heinemann, before finding their way to the Bodley Head. Signed only 'Ardath,' reflecting where they had been written, the immediate mystery as to the gender of the author was only broken when she arrived at the offices to inquire as to the status of her submission.

With plenty of life-experience to draw upon, and as a strong advocate of what she believed to be the "eternal feminine" or wildness of Woman, Egerton's texts have most often been placed within the confining parameters of New Woman fiction. The New Women writers themselves are generally considered to fall into two main camps.[2] First, there is the "purity school" which includes such authors as Sarah Grand, Iota and Grant Allen, who desired to maintain the traditional, middle-class Victorian ideal of femininity while approaching equality, and to emphasize the belief that the most important principle for the woman was purity that cannot be enforced; rather, it has to be chosen by young women well-informed on the issues of sexuality such as venereal disease, adultery and seduction. In contrast, there is the "neurotic" school, a more radical feminism that considers the attainment of sexual freedom to be one element in the attainment of equality. Traditionally, the decadent male and the New Woman have been acknowledged as literary figures[3] who share few similarities in agenda such as their attempt to represent categories of gender as an unnatural manifestation that can be transcended, and their disdain for conventions of matrimony. According to Elaine Showalter in *Sexual Anarchy* (169), "the decadent or the aesthete was the masculine counterpart to the New Woman"; however, in an ironic twist, the Decadents distinguish themselves from the New Woman along biological lines; the "decadent aesthetic rejected all that was natural and biological in favour of the inner life of art, artifice, sensation, and imagination," which leads to a blatant anti-feminist, anti-Woman stance. Woman is seen as immanent and closer "to the body, and to a crude materialism, while men were aligned with 'Art,' to the intellect, and to spiritualism" (170).

---

[2] The complexity of the New Woman has been well explored by writers such as Gail Cunningham, Ann Heilmann, Sally Ledger, as well as challenged as a construct of the periodical press in more recent considerations such as Richardson and Willis's edited collection, *New Women in Fiction and in Fact*. I only offer this brief introduction to the "camps" as a way in to the main subject here.

[3] The most important discussion around which these dichotomies hinge is Linda Dowling's.

Although perceived as unified in the nefarious purpose of creating degenerate, apocalyptic visions of culture, due to the oft blurred boundary between the nihilism of the male decadent and the "neurotic" desire of some women writers for independence from social conventions, the 'New Woman Sphinx,' Oscar Wilde and Richard Le Gallienne's name for their female friends who were writers such as Egerton, "Vernon Lee" and Ada Leverson, represents a complex challenge to the decadent male with her condemnation of those male writers' destructive impulses towards women. Female authors have been forbidden inclusion within the elitism of decadence by contemporary and modern critics; even fictions with many similarities of style and content by women were categorized within an overly-homogeneous understanding of New Women writers, or were dismissed as "popular" fictions rather than as high art because "women's writing was coded as mass culture in relation to male expressions of artistic genius" (Pykett 23). Egerton's *Keynotes* attracted much attention with its publication and was variously referred to as hysteric, inappropriately erotic and as the shameful production of another "yellow lady novelist." The complexity lauded by the epithet 'Sphinx' soon came to be applied in a derogatory manner. The pathologization of women's writing as hysterical, which results in the exclusion of women from such a philosophic fraternity, was a further result of patriarchal, heterosexual ideals.

Decadence has been described as the disruptive act of annihilation and recreation in a work of art, conjoined with symptoms of cultural decay (including sexual dysfunction or perversion, nihilism, and degeneracy) as well as with certain character/human types (including effete men, destructive women and decaying aristocratic families). Criticism to this point seems to suggest that a "decadent is a *man* caught between two opposite and apparently incompatible pulls: on the one had, he is drawn by the world, its necessities, and the attractive impressions he derives from it, while on the other hand, he yearns toward the eternal, the ideal and the unworldly" (Thornton 26; my italics). The uncontested assumption here is that a decadent is by definition male and that male objectivity necessarily excludes female subjectivity. However, I would argue that Egerton, with her *avant garde* prose with decadent tropes and themes, does qualify.

Scholars have, for the most part, viewed both aestheticism and decadence, if and when separated, as the revenge of the Victorian male imagination on women. Bram Dijkstra has shown how this exploitation and appropriation of an exoticized feminine decadent aestheticism creates monstrous women as objects of desire;[4] Elaine Showalter has pointed to the widespread "misogyny, homophobia, and racism" (*Sexual Anarchy* 11) of many *fin de siècle* texts, and Rita Felski sees that *l'art pour l'art* "sought transcendence through a denial and repression of the (female) body" (104). Kathy Alexis Psomiades (33) argues that women "are both the content of the Aestheticism art and its necessary support"; while still denying them entrance to decadence. To a certain extent, I do agree with these critics and with Martha Vicinius (91) who believes decadence exhibits "Gynophobia"; however, there is another possibility: the possibility of a woman decadent or female decadents/ce in late-nineteenth century prose. Some of these women writers of the *fin de siècle*, often categorized with or as New Women, are, in a very strong sense, creators and participants of a decadent aesthetic while they attempt to disrupt the conventional dialectics of the late-Victorian age. Some writers, such as Marie Corelli, claimed to be "counter-decadence," yet authored fictions such as *Wormwood* (1895) which can be argued to exemplify the strongest aspects of decadence in spite of its polemical preface which argues to the contrary.[5] The ex-

---

[4] See Dijkstra for discussion of the many stereotypes of Woman as devouring, dangerous *femme fatale* but as object of desire.

[5] As part of a larger project on nineteenth-century female decadents/ce, I argue that four women usually categorized otherwise, "M. Barnard" (Louisa May

clusive domain of the male author/character must make space for female decadents/ce and texts which include female decadent characters who go beyond the politics of the New Woman. In particular, the short fictions of George Egerton[6] exemplify an important moment in women's construction of artistic narrative where fantasy is interrupted with interpretive dialogue, and where critical discussion is entwined with seductive description. The dialectics of Egerton's stories include a deliberative interaction between private brooding and public dialogue; this interaction, as well as this intervention into gender politics through the exercise of an hermeneutic of suspicion, creates a type of female decadent aesthetic when combined with linguistically stylized descriptions, non-realist moments or eruptions, themes of the beautiful and the psychological, when told from a woman's point of view.

In June 1895, Hugh Stutfield's article, "Tommyrotics," warns that society's "most dangerous and subtle foes are beyond question 'neurotics' and hysteri[cs] in their manifold forms" (833). He claims that texts such as George Egerton's *Keynotes* and *Discords* (and Ella D'Arcy's *Monochromes* [1895] and *Modern Instances* [1898])[7] are written by a degenerate group of women who are the "offspring of hysteria" who write repulsive fiction because to "be a woman is to be mad" but even worse, "the woman of the new Ibsenite [neurotic] school is not only mad herself, but she does her best to drive those

Alcott), Ella D'Arcy, "George Egerton" (Mary Chavelita Dunne Bright), and "Rachilde" (Marguerite Emery), as well as "Vernon Lee" and Marie Corelli – create a performativity of gender which embodies a discursive position disruptive to received notions of decadents/ce.

[6] I have speculated in "Trivialized Female Idealism or Valourized Male Realism" that the continuous use of the male pseudonym "George" may trace a lineage of female authors who pay homage to "George Sand's" writing, philosophy and reputation.

[7] Indeed, D'Arcy was immersed in the culture of aestheticism and decadence as the sub-editor of and writer for, *The Yellow Book.*

around her crazed" (835). Stutfield believes that these "neurotic" writers "are simply sick [. . .] degenerates to be shunned like any other manifestations of disease" (836) because they need sedatives rather than mental excitants to feed their psychoses. He dismisses their unconventional views and disruptive fictional techniques as forms of literary and social corruption; further, he argues against their presumed agenda because they "are wrong when they turn women away from the duties of their sex and when they turn their heads with illusory emancipatory ideas, which are unrealizable and absurd. Let woman remain what Nature has made her: an ideal woman, the companion and lover of a man, the mistress of the home" (117). In other words, let woman be content with the role assigned to her as man's designated Other.

Against Stutfield, I would argue that these women, upon whom I focus in my problematization of George Egerton's confinement within the category of New Woman writer, are neither psychologically classic hysterics nor neurotics; indeed, his own argument allies them with definitive ideas on male decadents who set out to violate what is 'natural' in human experience by resorting to drugs, depravity, or sexual deviation in order to achieve the systematic derangement of all the senses to transcend everyday realities. For such reasons, their fiction is not strictly limited to the realm of the New Woman because these women are acutely aware of the fact that "the sedimentation of gender norms produces the peculiar phenomenon of a 'natural sex' or a 'real woman' or any number of prevalent and compelling social fictions" (Butler 140) which may be antithetical to their aesthetic project. Such a violation of the 'natural' vision of Woman could only be interpreted as degenerate or as constructive of an 'artificial' other to man. In fact, in decadent literature, "women are left out of the celebration of perversity for their lack of imagination and artistry even as they are cannibalized for their coveted traits of 'artificiality' and social marginality" (Hamilton 77).

Seen as purveyors of social corruption combining the negative features of both screeching suffragettes and effeminate decadents, Egerton's texts were greeted by the 1890s media as symptomatic of "the Beerbohmic plague" of literature (*The Bookbuyer* XVIII: 184; qtd. in Mix 172). Her fictions are threatening to patriarchal culture because they do not replicate acceptable nineteenth-century stereotypes of a deviant woman, a madwoman in an attic, a fallen Magdalen or an Ophelian passive and victimized woman.[8] Instead, Egerton creates actively erotic female characters who challenge existing notions of idealized woman as an ahistorical, non-subjective Other who exists only to define the masculine in culture where the central recognition is that a subject is not determined by the rules through which it is generated because signification is not a founding act, but rather a regulated process of repetition that both conceals itself and enforces its rules (Butler 145).

To contextualize Egerton and other possibly decadent women writers, it is important to remember woman's categorization in the nineteenth century. Positioned outside of history proper, woman is identified instead with the immediacy and intimacy of social life. Man is a generic or universal category that is constituted through violently hierarchical differences; the main difference is that woman must be radically other to history and to men. The later nineteenth century is the time of the Woman Question. Men are constituted as historical subjects and find man in history by locating woman Other-wise. The spectacular inflation of women's ideal value, assumed to be endowed by nature, and the consequent repression of her subjective reality is inextricably a part of the nineteenth-century investment in history. The tremendous effort to understand women, to manage them, to find out what they want, the asking of the

---

[8] Margaret Stetz has an excellent discussion of how Egerton, as a Catholic, rejects the virgin/whore dichotomy.

Woman Question, occurs at the expense of the real woman as the price of discovering the truth of man in the far reaches of history. For a Victorian Englishman, historical consciousness is a mode of self-consciousness, an awareness of the self by means of woman as Other; this ostracization of woman as the otherness of Victorian history must be read as a problem, not an answer, a process in which differences are produced only to reflect the truths of certain men, a process which constructs an imaginary unity of English/ British men which is then projected as an image of universal white men and then mankind; this entire process entails the radical exclusion of women from the historical construction of subjectivity. To look at Victorian writing without asking how it produces or disrupts these images would be to necessarily reflect, beyond question, its truths, including woman's exclusion from decadence.

In *Writing a Woman's Life* (1988), Carolyn Heilbrun reminds us that

> Women have long searched, and continue to search, for an identity "other" than their own. Caught in the conventions of their sex, they have sought an escape from gender. A woman author who was not content to expound the titillations of romance, or to live out Freud's family romance, had two means of escape. One was to hide her identity as an author within the shelter of anonymity, the safety of secrecy, to write while protecting the quotidian self leading her appropriate life. The other was to create in her writings women characters, and sometimes male characters, who might openly enact the dangerous adventures of a woman's life, unconstrained by female propriety. (111-12)

As an exemplar of both of these facts in women's literary history, the pseudonymous George Egerton categorically refuses to allow her writing to reflect the limitation of conventional gender dialectics "which condition the problematics of identity that it seeks to solve" (Butler 144). Her writing is critical of the use of such dialectics by male decadent authors and theorists whose fantasies of aestheticism and femininity are, as Felski (113) points out, "defined and valorized in opposition to the naiveté of feminist struggles for social change; accused of either vulgar essentialism or phallic identification, real women are, it appears, incapable of 'becoming woman'". While "the aesthete's performance of femininity is depicted as authentically modern precisely because of its self-conscious transcendence of the constraints of corporeality and natural sexual identity within which woman remains imprisoned" (112) both in image and in society.

Egerton questions stereotypes of the "natural" and the implications of woman's corporeal being as she demystifies the ideology and/or epistemology of the representation of woman in male-authored decadence. Provocative stylistics are appropriate to her material because it was episodic, full of narrative gaps and it showed an almost complete lack of interest in causal relations relying instead upon psychological impressions and details, as well as philosophical meanderings. While not perhaps intentionally or programmatically doing so, Egerton lays the groundwork for the project of a decadent woman with a frank exploration of woman's role in society and her right to a self-defined sexuality; rather than assuming that art imitates reality and represents something both external and prior to the work of fiction, she prominently figures female desire in her fiction in a reclaiming of the female body from appropriation by male decadents' effeminacy or sterile feminization. Egerton states clearly that she writes "for the love of writing [. . .] not with a view to usher in a revolt, or preach a propaganda" but "merely to strike a few notes on the phases of female character I knew to exist" (*Discords* 58) as "the *terra incognita* of herself, as she knew herself to be, not as man liked to imagine her" ("Keynote"

58). To explore what is woman, for this reason, Egerton's narrators focalize through her female characters. This creates psychological immediacy and allows her to explore the decadent obsession with the distinctions between the ideal and the real, the artificial and the organic, as well as to explode the polarization of the male decadent and the New Woman by showing that either

> women are subsumed into supposedly general and objective norms derived from male experience, or they are represented as other, as the polar opposite of man. In both cases, they are judged by *male norms masquerading as universal values.* There thus appears to be no standpoint which would allow woman to be valued in and for herself. Almost all discussions about women represent only what they are in their real, ideal, or value relationship to men. No one asks what they are for themselves [. . .] the conclusion is drawn that for herself she is *nothing.* (Felski 44; my italics)

To debunk further this socially unquestioned myth, Egerton disrupts the male decadent projection, or fetishistic aestheticization, of women's sexuality as evil or hysteric, where a "male theorist's fantasy of 'becoming woman' is defined and valorized (sic) in opposition to the naiveté of feminist struggles for social change; accused of either vulgar essentialism or phallic identification" she posits instead an erotic, detailed female sexuality or "becoming woman" (Felski 113) by performing a new type of woman with decadent precision. Her fiction calls for a resistance to and subversion of the imposition of the ideal image upon real women because both the projection and the results are degrading and debilitating to a woman's individuality. She refuses to give credence to either the derision of her writing of woman as merely madness, or, as in the *Athenaeum* review which declares her collection of stories laudable if only for "the hysterical frankness of its amatory abandonment"

(18). The psychological immediacy Egerton creates in her texts is no less than seeing the woman as self-creator which assists her confrontation of Victorian conventions that deny women artistic and sexual means of self-expression. She dismantles the main mythologies, conventional and decadent, which construct woman: the definition of marriage as happy closure, the regulation of active sexuality as moral, or conversely immoral and/or decadent, only in men, and the aesthetic construction of woman by patriarchal society and, by extension, in decadent male fictions.

"An Empty Frame" in *Keynotes* deals with a short moment in a woman's life where she stands gazing intently at an empty picture frame while she contemplates her husband's ongoing and multiple infidelities which she is expected to forgive and forget. She thinks of an earlier time and of another man who desired her as an equal, wanted a life-long relationship based on mutual respect, but who refused to subsume her identity in a conventional marriage. Her thoughts range from anger to regret in a humorous but revealing reversal of a social cliché; this woman knows that "with a great man [she] might have made a great woman" (*Keynotes* 122) if she had only had the courage to refuse to conform to convention and had filled the blank canvas, *tabula rasa*, of the empty frame with the artwork of her own life. Under her aesthetic gaze, the "plain white space becomes alive to her" (117) with lost possibilities of a bohemian and artistic relationship but the woman has never been given a chance to express herself as an individual. Her current situation confines and defines her as a "little woman" (119)[9] who is controlled by her husband, whereas an artistic/sexual liaison or free union (as in another of her stories, "The Regeneration of Two") with a more

---

[9] There are several uses of the phrase "little woman" in the stories of Egerton where men demean their wives with its use which is reminiscent of the many diminutive names used for Nora in Ibsen's *fin de siècle* drama, *A Doll's House*.

progressive man would have possibly enabled her to fulfil her potential and define her own identity rather than feeling, as she daydreams, that "her head is wedged in a huge frame, the top of her head touches its top, the sides its sides, and it keeps growing larger and larger and her head with it, until she seems to be sitting inside her own head, and the inside is one vast hollow" (123).

Once Egerton has defined her perceptions of these restrictions endured in the institution of marriage by women, she reveals the degrading effects of institutionalized male sexual predation on women and the resulting power dynamics in "Virgin Soil," a story in the collection *Discords* which also challenges the arrogant morality of the ideal marriage. In this story, Flo is a malleable seventeen-year-old who has just married Philip, a man with grey hair whom she does not love. While Philip waits to embark on their honeymoon, Flo cries upstairs in her mother's arms and asks "What is it that I do not know, mother? What is it? [. . .] There is something more – I have felt it all these last weeks in your and the others' looks – in his, in the very atmosphere – but why have you not told me before" (146). Her mother denies her empathy and chastises her with the voice of society: "You are married now, darling, and you must obey [. . .] your husband in all things – there are things you should know – but marriage is a serious thing, a sacred thing – you must believe what your husband tells you is right – let him guide you" (146). Treated like the girl-child in "Little Red Riding Hood," Flo encounters Egerton's eroticized but dangerous revision of the wolf who "comes for her; his hot breath smells of champagne, and it strikes her that his eyes are fearfully big and bright, and he offers her his arm with such a curious amused proprietary air that the girl shivers as she lays her hand in it" (147-48). Flo's marriage is quickly filled with "bitter disillusion" (149) by a bestial husband who demonstrates the hypocrisy of any politically detached understanding of male sexuality:

[Men] finesse and flatter and wheedle and coax, but truth there is none. I couldn't do that you see, and so I went to the wall. I don't blame them; it must be so, as long as marriage is based on such unequal terms, as long as man demands from a wife as a right, what he must sue from a mistress as a favour; until marriage becomes for many women a legal prostitution, a nightly degradation, a hateful yoke under which they age, mere bearers of children conceived in a sense of duty, not love [. . .] they submit to [sex] with distaste instead of a favour granted to a husband who must become a new lover to obtain it. (155)

Further, with an exultant cry "like the fancied echo of the laughter of hell," she claims that a man "is responsible for his own sins, we [as women], are not bound to dry nurse his morality [. . .] No wife is bound to set aside the demands of her individual soul for the sake of imbecile obedience" (155). Flo leaves to claim her own life outside of the role dictated to her by society and her husband that has dehumanized and repressed her intellect as well as her sexuality; at the same time, Egerton has aligned herself with the decadent stance of mutual alienation between the sexes.

Egerton's narrative makes a strong case for woman's right to sexual experimentation and expression, rather than the enforcement, through women's complicity, of patriarchal conventions which subsume woman as a passive function of her body rather than as an active, intellectual, desiring sexual entity. Again, through an indictment of Flo's mother, society is condemned:

it is your fault, because you reared me a fool, an idiot, ignorant of everything I ought to have known, everything that concerned me and the life I was bound to lead as a wife; my physical needs, my coming passion, the very meaning of my sex, my wifehood and motherhood to follow. You gave me

not one weapon in my hand to defend myself against the possible attacks of man at his worst. You sent me out to fight the
biggest battle of a woman's life with only maiden purity as a
shield to wear in the battle of the sexes. (157)

Egerton's stories suggest that women must create an educated,
creative and compassionate community of women in order to combat the repression imposed on them by society. In another story with
similar implications, "A Psychological Moment," Egerton (*Discords*
13) declares that women have been alienated from each other by socially imposed conventions, such as religion, to the point where "the
subdued soul of [a] still young woman has disciplined [her]
thoughts and feelings and soul and body into a machine"; clearly,
society does not "encourage independence in women" because patriarchy believes that "when they lose this hold on [women] they'll
lose their hold on humanity" (57). Egerton exposes the extent to
which Victorian women have internalized the conventional ideal of
womanhood and demonstrates by example why woman's complicity
in this form of patriarchal oppression must end.

Convention creates the reality that women are "prey to every man
who thinks she has given him a right to her person" (61); for this
reason, woman must redefine herself without all "the systems of
philosophy or treatises of moral science, all the religious codes devised by the imagination of men [that] will not save" her (64). One
such step is to explore woman's sexuality without the limitations of
male-defined morality. It is crucial to understanding Egerton's fiction that each pivotal restraint that is placed upon woman by society
is exposed before she is able to advance and subvert the role of
woman's sexuality to recreate a decadent woman. Perhaps not as
blatant as the sexual characters of Rachilde,[10] Egerton's critics un-

---

[10] Rachilde's first novel, *Monsieur Vénus* (1884) was banned from publication in
Paris due to its sexual and decadent content.

derstood that her writing and her characters posed a threat to Victorian proper culture:

> The physiological excursions of our writers of neuropathic fiction are usually confined to one field – that of sex. Their chief delight seems to be in making their characters discuss matters which would not have been tolerated in the novels of a decade ago. Emancipated woman in particular loves to show her independence by dealing freely with the relations of the sexes. Hence all the prating of passion, animalism, "the natural workings of sex," and so forth, with which we are nauseated. Most of the characters in these books seem to be erotomaniacs.
>
> (Stutfield, "Tommyrotics" 836)

While not necessarily erotomaniacs or nymphomaniacs, the characters in Egerton's narratives do, in fact, use healthy sexuality to resist the construction of woman as passionless and to create a transitional picture of woman's potential strength. Egerton's fledgling female decadent may not obviously be sexually dominant or malicious, but her rejection of society's normalizing processes makes her female characters perverse in their desire to create themselves as significant moral agents.

"A Shadow's Slant" argues her belief in the need of internal resistance to a life of possession and objectification. Exposing socially accepted dialectics, the husband in this story considers his wife as his property, but he realizes there is something in her that he cannot possess: "You wait on me, no slave better, and yet, I can't get at you, near you; that little soul of yours is as free as if I hadn't bought you, as if I didn't own you, as if you were not my chattel, my thing to do what I please with; do you hear [. . .] to degrade, to treat as I please [. . .] your spirit is out of my grasp" (*Discords* 146). This woman's stoicism is her only resistance to her captivity; Egerton calls the bluff of a detached male and exposes him as "an animal with strong passions [who] avails himself of the latitude permitted him by the laws of society" (156). It is these social laws, both explicit and implicit, that Egerton's narratives confront to deconstruct the claim that only men are cerebral and have control of the artificial as represented in their wilful misunderstanding of woman's "nature"; then, she reconstructs the wildness of the sexuality of woman as not merely physical, but also including an understanding of woman's erotic nature.

To define women as desiring subjects, not merely as objects of man's pleasure leads George Egerton to construct many of her heroines as forthright, sensual women who freely express their sexual natures. It is her female characters' expression of their personal sexuality which causes them to be classified, by some of her male characters (and by literary critics) as neurotic rather than as true, pleasure-seeking decadents. Granted, Egerton's heroines have often internalized societal conventions to the point that they break into hysterical laughter or manifest hysterical/neurotic symptoms when they are forced to repress their desire in order to maintain their social masks/masquerades. For example, Mrs Grey in "A Psychological Moment" (a woman thrown aside from her husband via a fraudulent claim of adultery) is only able to discuss her sexual desire with shame:

> I was lonely and wretched, and I don't know what madness possessed me, you can't understand. One just gets insane, and lets oneself be carried away. I think the devil gets hold of one. I tried to attract him; there was a kind of excitement in it [. . .] there was a kind of fascination in the danger [. . .] I had no control over myself, something used to possess me; it is always like that, one stifles the memory of the first [encounter] with the excitement of the second.
>
> (*Discords* 102-04)

While Egerton does not make it immediately possible for Mrs. Grey to overcome her imposed guilt, she exposes the inadequacy of patriarchal language to discuss her physical desires and emotional needs as limited to the claim of temporary insanity.

Martha Vicinus argues that "[u]nlike other *fin de siècle* writers [. . .] Egerton was not influenced by French Decadence" (Vicinus xii); nevertheless, the precision of Egerton's detailed consideration of woman's sexual desire, her ornamentation and exotic detail, and her intense subjectivity create the possibility of a female decadent. Heavily influenced by Scandanavian Realists and Naturalists, Egerton's consideration of woman's potent(ial) sexuality exposes the fact that men are frightened by what a decadent woman represents because "when a Strindberg or a Nietzsche[11] arises and peers into the recesses of her nature and dissects her ruthlessly, the men shriek out louder than the women, because the truth is at all times unpalatable, and the gods they have set up are dear to them" (*Keynotes* 23); consequently, in a social "system that means war, and always war, [. . .] it is a struggle between instinctive truths and cultivated lies" (4This celebration of female eroticism allows for the potential power to disrupt this closed binary system by displaying openly and without male mediation – thereby proving – the existence of her own and her female characters' individual and subjective sexuality through the minute details of the moment juxtaposed with fantastic images. Egerton's "A Cross Line" is a rare re-visioning by a woman writer of the Salome story which so obsessed men of the *fin de siècle* like Moreau, Huysmans and Wilde (and later Strauß),[12] not to forget Mallarmé, Laforgue, Klimt and Beardsley. It is important to

---

[11] According to Terence De Vere White, editor of the correspondence of George Egerton in his *A Leaf from The Yellow Book*, this is the first reference to Nietzsche in English (18).

[12] Oscar Wilde was a friend of George Egerton; interestingly, this may hold suggestive possibilities for the above depiction of the Salome legend.

note that this story was part of Egerton's collection which was the lead monograph of John Lane's Keynote Series; in addition to being illustrated by Beardsley, the Bodley Head would also publish Beardsley's infamous illustrated version of Oscar Wilde's translated *Salome,* a fact which places Egerton in the nexus of decadent controversy. In her story, the most notorious (and most discussed) instance of woman exultant takes place in the unnamed female protagonist's ornamented and detailed fantasy where first she rides astride "in Arabia on the back of a swift steed," the eroticized female controlling the male animal:

Her thoughts shape themselves into a wild song [. . .] an uncouth rhythmical jingle with a feverish beat [. . .] to the untamed spirit which dwells in her. Then she fancies she is on the stage of an ancient theatre out in the open air, with hundreds of faces upturned towards her. Her arms are clasped by jewelled snakes and one with quivering diamond fangs coils round her hips [. . .] She bounds forward and dances, bends her lissom waist, and curves her slender arms, and gives to the soul of each man what he craves, be it good or evil. And she can feel now [. . .] the grand intoxicating power of swaying all these human souls to wonder and applause [. . .] She can see herself [. . .] sway voluptuously to the wild music that rises, now slow, now fast, now deliriously wild, seductive, intoxicating [. . .] She can feel the answering shiver of feeling that quivers up to her from the dense audience, spellbound by the motion of her glancing feet, and she flies swifter and swifter, and lighter and lighter [. . .] One quivering, gleaming, daring bound and she stands with outstretched arms and passion filled eyes, poised on one slender foot, asking a supreme note to finish her dream of motion. And the men rise to a man and answer her. (*Keynotes* 15)

This passage does not simply reinscribe an essentialistic definition of female sexual nature. Egerton endorses intense, if imagined or subjective, autoerotic female desire and ambition against the naturalistic imperative of the body. The men answer that she has usurped the position of speaking, active subject with the female language of the body. As Judith Butler points out in *Gender Trouble* (vii),

> for that masculine subject of desire, trouble became a scandal with the sudden intrusion, the unanticipated agency, of a female "Object" who inexplicably returns the glance, reverses the gaze, and contests the place and authority of the masculine position. The radical dependence of the masculine subject on the female "Other" suddenly exposes his autonomy as illusory.

In the culture that the protagonist dreams about, Woman returns the gaze and she is able to take pleasure in both her erotic fantasy and her fantasy of success as a female artist in a public forum. Significantly, Egerton's protagonist fantasises about her life in a different, perhaps Hellenic, orientalized and exotic cultural context, and ironically, her husband names her only 'Gypsy'; thus, the protagonist crosses several lines in her impressionistic dream-vision combining Apollonian intellectual culture with Dionysian nature and art. Egerton moves outside the inscribed circle that middle-class culture draws around correct female behaviour: eroticism and ambition are co-mingled in this dream in a way that the cultural ideology of female passivity would not allow. This untamed woman defies the Victorian ideology of sexual passionlessness by describing sexuality as the core or centre of human personality, and by rejecting the dichotomization of mind/body, reason/passion and St. John/Salome to establish the body and desire as a co-determinant of a decadent female mind and subjectivity.

Egerton's demythologization or revisioning of the possibilities of Salome's sisters as the Decadents' central, "obsessive icon of female sexuality" (Showalter, *Sexual Anarchy* 149) literarily unveils the male or patriarchal bias in previous decadent depictions, an assault upon male sensibility that did not go unnoticed by literary critics. In March 1894, "SHE-NOTES" by "Borgia Smudgiton" appeared in *Punch; or the London Charivari* which directly links Egerton to the contemporary decadent tradition, both in style and in content. The parody acknowledges her ornate and elliptical style and is illustrated, à la Wilde's *Salome*, by a Beardsley-esque "Mortarthurio Whiskersley" both of which pay bitextual[13] homage to her decadent affinities. In Egerton's text, her female body artist's hunger for the Baptist's head is thus proved to be a mere pretext for the need to find the source, in woman's insatiable and demonic sexuality, of all the wrongs and rejections men may perceive are visited upon them by the social milieu of the contextualizing culture. Any envisioning of Salome as *femme fatale* had become the *fin de siècle* male's favourite scapegoat, the creature whose death might permit them to drive woman from them in the final climax of their search to transcend the flesh and approach the pure mysticism of the male decadent project. The empowered woman of the vision in "A Cross Line" disrupts archaic truths about woman as the Natural against which the male subject defines himself in culture. Clearly, Egerton (*Keynotes* 22) builds the argument that Victorian man "has fashioned a model on imaginary lines" of self-preservatory devotion to the female ideal which shields him from a real woman's possibilities. The unnamed dancer notes that if men were observant, then they would see that the "[s]tray words, half confidences, glimpses through soul-chinks of suppressed fires, actual outbreaks, domestic

---

[13] For an excellent discussion of the bitextuality and inter-reliance of fiction and illustration at the Bodley Head, see Kooistra.

catastrophes" hint at the "untamed primitive savage temperament that lurks in the mildest, best woman" (*Keynotes* 22); such an understanding of Woman's "eternal wildness" may potentially lead to seditious, sadistic or perverse desire, or more subversively, to a conjoining of the sexes.

Egerton presents an alternative image of a self-creating, self-aware decadent woman in her stories with characters such as Mrs. Grey who not only challenge the Victorian ideals of feminine conduct, but who are also desired by men because "the pout of the wine-red lips, the soft receding chin, and the strange indefinable expression that lurks about [her] rather fits a priestess of passion [. . .] her forehead is a child-girl's; her mouth a courtesan's of forty" (*Discords* 91). Through this woman who is full of Pre-Raphaelite eroticism and conspicuous desire, Egerton implores men to "see the real woman" (*Discords* 101);[14] further, she calls for a complete disruption of Victorian dialectics and convention because

> men have manufactured an artificial [and gendered] morality; made sins of things that were clean in themselves as the pairing of birds on the wing; crushed nature, robbed it of its beauty and meaning, and established a system that means war, and always war, because it is a struggle between instinctive truths and cultivated lies [. . .] In one word, the untrue feminine is of man's making, a creation that must be undone by women in the arts. (*Keynotes* 49-50)

---

[14] Ella D'Arcy's "The Pleasure Pilgrim," a powerful story in her first, and best, collection *Monochromes* (1896), has a comparable scene of aestheticization of a Pre-Raphaelite beauty, Lulie, who is destined to a spectacular, performative suicide by a male writer/artist's inability to accept her desire as a real woman, who nevertheless can easily objectify her as his ideal vision of desirable womanhood. Notably, Lulie is derided as an American version of the New Woman.

Egerton's female protagónists are seen by many reviewers to possess a decadent and "morbid perversion of the natural feelings, affections, inclination, temper, habits, moral dispositions and natural impulses, without any remarkable disorder or defect of the intellect, or knowing faculties, and particularly without any insane illusion or hallucination" (Hogarth 590); however, at least one contemporary, continental reader, Laura Marholm Hansson, understood that *Keynotes* "is not addressed to men, and it will not please them. [. . .] There is nothing of the man in this book, and no attempt is made to imitate him [. . .] Neither is it a book which favors [sic] men; it is a book written against them, a book for our private use" because it is "a liberal book, indiscreet in respect of intimacies of married life, and entirely without respect for the husband; it is a book with claws and teeth ready to scratch and bite when the occasion offers" (62-63). I agree; I would argue that Egerton was initially categorized as perverse and neurotic, rather than decadent, in order to attempt to marginalize her and minimalize her potential societal impact because to label her as decadent would present even more of a disruptive threat to the definition of Victorian ideal womanhood. The problem is, it is a resistant and historically situated masculine Victorian world-view that decides what is rational or objective, and delusional or decadent. This labelling of 'neurotic' is not the same as what Stutfield sees as neurotic psychoses; in fact, Breuer and Freud (4) himself claimed that "Neurotic impulses were due to non-psychological causes and are evident when sexuality is repressed." Egerton's progressive ideas of a woman combine the explosive chaos of her potentially decadent sexuality with a thinking, active subject who constitutes herself historically and contextually. By virtue of the nature of the society that defined her, Egerton is a neurotic, a degenerate, a decadent *and* a New Woman because, as one of her characters says, she believed that "[d]eep through ages of convention, [woman's] primeval trait of [eternal wildness] burns, an untameable quantity that may be concealed but is never eradicated by culture [because it is] the keynote of woman's strength" (*Keynotes* 22) and the key to her redefinition. Perhaps best expressing the *ennui* and ambivalence of many women writers which caused the flame to burn bright but briefly at the *Keynotes* series and *The Yellow Book,* Ella D'Arcy claimed that the *fin de siècle* in Britain "is a weird world, and I'm inclined to give up Art and Literature", indeed, "Decadence, and go back to the comfortably prosaic circles" (qtd. in Mix 147) of a woman writer not aligned with such a complex study of human nature.

Works Cited

Baudrillard, Jean. *Seduction.* 1979. Trans. Brian Singer. New York: St. Martin's, 1990.

Breuer, Joseph and Sigmund Freud. *Studies on Hysteria.* 1895. Trans. J. Strachey. New York: Basic, 1992.

Butler, Judith. *Gender Trouble: Feminism and the Subversion of Identity.* New York: Routledge, 1990.

Cunningham, Gail. *The New Woman and the Victorian Novel.* New York: Macmillan, 1978.

Cunningham, A. R. "The New Woman Fiction of the 1890s." *Victorian Studies* 18.2 (1973): 177-86.

D'Arcy, Ella. *Monochromes.* London: John Lane, 1895.

D'Arcy, Ella. *Modern Instances.* London: John Lane, 1895.

D'Arcy, Ella. "The Pleasure-Pilgrim." *The Yellow Book* 5 (April 1895): 34-67.

Dijkstra, Bram. *Idols of Perversity: Fantasies of Feminine Evil in Fin-de-Siècle Culture.* New York: Oxford UP, 1986.

Dowling, Linda. "The Decadent and the New Woman." *Nineteenth-Century Fiction* 33 (1979): 434-53.

Egerton, George. "A Keynote to *Keynotes.*" *Ten Contemporaries.* Ed. John Gawsworth. London: Ernest Benn, 1932. 57-60.

Egerton, George. *Discords.* London: John Lane, 1894.

Egerton, George. "How to Court the Advanced Woman." *The Idler* (1905): 194-96.

Egerton, George. *Keynotes.* London: John Lane, 1893.

Felski, Rita. *The Gender of Modernity.* Cambridge: Harvard UP, 1995.

Hamilton, Lisa K. "New Women and 'Old' Men." *Women and British Aestheticism.* Ed. Talia Schaffer and Kathy Alexis Psomiades. Charlottesville: UP of Virginia, 1999. 62-80.

Hansson, Laura M. *Six Modern Women: Psychological Sketches.* Trans. Hermione Ramsden. Boston: Roberts, 1896.

Heilbrun, Carolyn. *Writing a Woman's Life.* New York: Ballantine, 1988.

Heilmann, Ann. *New Woman Fiction.* New York: St. Martin's, 2000.

Hogarth, J. "Literary Degenerates." *Fortnightly Review.* (April 1895): 586-92.

Janzen Kooistra, Lorraine. *The Artist as Critic: Bitextuality in Fin de Siècle Books* . Menston: Scolar, 1995.

Ledger, Sally. *The New Woman: Fiction and Feminism at the Fin de Siècle.* Manchester: Manchester UP 1997.

Maier, Sarah. "Trivialized Female Idealism or Valourized Male Realism: The Importance of Being 'George.'" *Canadian Review of Comparative Literature 31* (Summer 2005), forthcoming.

Mill, John Stuart. "The Subjection of Women." *Feminism: The Essential Historical Writings.* Ed. Miriam Schneir. New York: Vintage, 1972. 162-79.

Mix, Katherine. L. *A Study in Yellow: The Yellow Book and Its Contributors.* Lawrence: U of Kansas P, 1960.

Psomiades, Kathy Alexis. *Beauty's Body: Femininity and Representation in British Aestheticism.* Stanford: Stanford UP, 1997.

Pykett, Lyn. *Engendering Fictions: The English Novel in the Early Twentieth Century.* New York: St. Martin's, 1995.

Rachilde. *Monsieur Vénus.* Paris: Flammarion, 1888.

Rev. of *Keynotes. Athenaeum* (6 Jan. 1894): 18.

Richardson, Angelique, and Chris Willis, eds. *New Women in Fiction and in Fact*. Basingstoke: Palgrave, 2000.

Showalter, Elaine, ed. *Daughters of Decadence: Women Writers of the Fin de Siècle*. London: Virago, 1993.

Showalter, Elaine. *Sexual Anarchy: Gender and Culture at the Fin de Siècle*. New York: PBC, 1990.

Smudgiton, Borgia [pseudonym]. "'SHE-NOTES' with Japanese *Fin de Siècle* Illustrations by Mortarthurio Whiskersly." *Punch, or the London Charivari* 10 March 1894: 109, 17 March 1894: 129.

Stetz, Margaret D. "Turning Points: 'George Egerton' (Mary Chavelita Dunne Bright)." *Turn-of-the-Century Women* 1.1 (1984): 2-8.

Stutfield, Hugh. "The Psychology of Feminism." *Blackwood's Magazine* (January 1897): 104-17.

Stutfield, Hugh. "Tommyrotics." *Blackwood's Magazine* (June 1895): 833-45.

Thornton, R. K. R. *The Decadent Dilemma*. London: Edward Arnold, 1983.

Vicinus, Martha, ed. *George Egerton: Keynotes and Discords*. London: Virago, 1983.

White, Terence De Vere, ed. *A Leaf from the Yellow Book*. London: Richards, 1958.

"Lifeless, inane, dawdling": Decadence, Femininity and Olive Schreiner's *Woman and Labour*

Ewa Macura
The Warsaw School of Social Psychology

Abstract: This essay is about an encounter between women/femininity and the rhetoric of decadence (and/or degeneration), and the various ways in which metaphors of illness (or its literal renditions) congealed on the body of the Victorian "angel in the house" to yield a solid narrative of social and economic success. It is also about how writers such as Olive Schreiner (in her *Woman and Labour*) tampered with these metaphors in order to stake out particular claims and undo particular stories.

Images of emaciated, safely passive, permanently enervated women came to populate, as Bram Dijkstra (25-63) argues, the late nineteenth-century cultural scene, becoming a desired and desirable ideal of femininity. Tirelessly emulated by middle-class women, they shared in what was called the "cult of invalidism" whose popularity gave rise to a new breed of "the dwarfed, miserable, sickly specimens of feminine humanity" (Cooke; qtd. in Dijkstra 26). Dressed out in the garb of inanition, female weaklings were thought to epitomise the highest standards of womanhood as the physical weakness they displayed never ceased to announce, and affirm, their delicacy, fragility, passivity, and self-sacrificial nature. Abba Goold Woolson, an American writer, argued:

> With us, to be ladylike is to be lifeless, inane and dawdling. Since people who are ill must necessarily possess these qualities of manner, from lack of vital energy and spirits, it follows that they are the ones studiously copied as models of female attractiveness. (Qtd. in Dijkstra 27)

In Elaine Showalter's (140) words, the invalid woman was "a model of ladylike deportment and hyperfemininity, a paradigm of that wasting beauty that the Victorians found so compelling." Thus illness was a graphic visualisation of femininity, its evidence and repository; it kept the woman homebound and immobile, sapped her energies, and secured her idleness of which she was, paradoxically, frequently accused. It also manifested the necessary sacrifice she was to make as she exchanged her vitality and health for the moral well-being of her husband. Dijkstra writes, "This principle of 'spiritual' transference came more and more to be 'validated' by the wife's physical, and hence visible [. . .] degeneration" (30). The sicklier the wife was, the healthier the husband was assumed to be. Women in a state of, as Dijkstra (28) puts it, "abject physical degeneration," signalled the husband's not only moral and physical, but also economic strength. They demonstrated that the wealth he was able to amass was ample enough to "allow him to support such a helpless elegance" (Woolson; qtd. in Dijkstra 27).

Thus the invalid woman, a badge of her husband's pecuniary achievements, meets, as Dijkstra points out, the demands of what Thorstein Veblen (48) called "the law of conspicuous leisure,"[1] putting to test, and on display, "his ability to sustain large pecuniary damage without impairing his superior opulence." Just as he accumulates wealth, he must also accumulate tangible evidence thereof. In Veblen's theory, this opulence – constantly subject to scopic practices of verification – is the supreme marker of reputability, which the wife helps to sustain through her performance of vicarious leisure and consumption. "The ceremonial consumer of goods" (63), she consumes for the good name of the household(er) and not for herself (55), thus evidencing both the money, which enables, and

---

[1] Dijkstra (27) discusses the economic aspect of the cult of invalidism in relation to Thorstein Veblen's notion of "conspicuous leisure."

underlies, her consumptive appetite on the one hand, and the necessarily spectacular amount of waste, on the other. Ostensible consumption and leisure are useful in the production of reputability provided an "element of waste" (64) has been invested in them. Indeed, the "fundamental canon of conspicuous waste" (68) canonises consumption.

In Veblen's theory, the vicariously consuming and leisurely wife produces (also reproduces) evidence of wealth and, at the same time, is a product, herself evidence, of a high pecuniary standard. Given the double role she performs, she is both an "investment for a profit" (41) and a profitable object invested with waste and accumulated wealth that can be spent *ad infinitum*; in other words, she both expends wastefully and is a profligate expenditure. Thus she is a woman in abundance that must be constantly produced in order to be subjected to endless spending. Veblen emphasises that conspicuous consumption, if it should assure fame and repute, has to be "an expenditure of superfluities" (which "must be wasteful") because "No merit would accrue from the consumption of the bare necessaries of life [. . .]" (72). The consumptive woman in plenty must expend (herself) superfluously in order to produce conspicuous worth. This economic excess (or economy of excess) contains, however, a form of control for it keeps the feminine at the right size. Here, spending amounts to the trimming of what is superfluous, and therefore redundant, of what would distort certain symmetry. The profusely feminine that is subject to regular expenditure does not overgrow, and thus secures economic flow and balance.

Femininity emerges thus as a superfluity of sorts, whose disproportionate value within the economic system of the leisure class is, and can only be, regulated by a constant and wasteful expenditure, which, in turn, necessitates its endless production. The economic and aesthetic requirements that she wastes (away), foreground the abundance that the sickly woman incessantly turns into a most productive (and profitable) effect. Hence, the cult of what Dijkstra (29) calls the "consumptive sublime" resonates, in fact, with a double meaning. Combining illness with dissipation it encapsulates two potent images of the feminine: one implicated in an exemplary emulation of weakness, the other aligned with excessive consumption, both laced with enough waste to produce the householder's economic prestige and taste.

What the costly, lifeless wife makes evident is not only the husband's sufficient means but also the exemption from the necessity to labour, which Veblen identifies as the hallmark of the leisure class.[2] In her "conspicuous abstention from labour" (Veblen 30) the invalid woman validates the husband's claims to economic power. Also, embodying the ideal of a non-labouring womanhood (and in fact making evident that she is not predisposed to labour) she fits neatly into the ideology of the separate spheres corroborating the naturalness of the division of labour.[3] Social health clearly depended upon the unhealthy woman whose physical weakness and visible degeneration kept regenerating the natural order of things.

Healthiness in women, Dijkstra (26) argues, came to be associated with a serious violation against nature as it connoted "dangerous, masculinizing attitudes. A healthy woman, it was often thought, was likely to be an 'unnatural' woman." A veritable femininity, then, found its fullest realisation in an immobilising, mental or physical, deterioration. The feminisation of illness (or the "diseasing" of femininity), which no doubt occurs here, not only shares in repro-

---

[2] Veblen (44) states that this exemption was most desirable in relation to two groups in particular, servants and women. Their manifestation of unproductive labour served to enhance the master's wealth.

[3] As Dijkstra (31) points out, the invalid woman had an important ideological role to play: "just when, toward the final years of the century, feminists had become quite vociferous and daring, ideologically charged counterimages of women ill, dying, or already safely dead proliferated."

ducing illness as a natural condition of women,[4] but also turns them into constituent elements of nineteenth-century theories of social evolution. Always part of the natural order of things in her enactment of nature's laws of decay, the sickly woman thus fitt into, and corroborated, the scenario of progress where degeneration was acknowledged as advancement's inevitably enabling condition. Indeed, as Robert A. Nye (49) points out, in nineteenth-century theories of social evolution "the concept of decline was conceptually inseparable from that of progress." To make the idea of progress conceivable and to assure its credibility was to rely on the idea of degeneration. Barbara Spackman (5) makes a similar point: "The very epithet 'decadent,' uttered first by critics camped on the island of normalcy, is filtered through a positivistic progressive ideology that

---

[4] That physical strength was considered an evolutionary quality of men was "scientifically proved" by Darwin. In her discussion of the various representations of "decadence," Sandra Siegel (204) thus writes on Darwin's theory:

> In the course of fighting for the possession of their women, men rivalled other men. Through the law of battle he became greater in strength and in intelligence [. . .]. Thus civilisation evolved and progressed. Darwin [*The Descent of Man*, ch. 19] repeatedly reminds his readers that man's greater physical, mental, and moral strength is due to his inheritance from his half-human male ancestors. During the "long ages of man's savagery" these characters would have been preserved, or even augmented, "by the success of the strongest and boldest men, both in the general struggle for life and in their contests for wives; [. . .]" The characteristics of primeval male progenitors – physical strength, perseverance, courage, intellectual vigor, the power of invention, and determined energy – are precisely those qualities that continue to separate male from female.

Jean Lorrain offers a literary version of this separation in his story "The Man Who Loved Consumptives." Couched in a decadent aesthetics that turns decomposing flesh into a most lovely image, it rehearses the gendered healthy/unhealthy opposition eroticising the sickly woman as a lover *par excellence*.

can define itself only against a negative regressive pole." It was through recourse to the degenerate/decadent that progress, in its various forms, could be tangibly and convincingly demonstrated and sketched. Such indispensability of the notions of degeneration resulted from a largely biologised view of progress, spelled out most pronouncedly by Herbert Spencer (Gagnier 95).

Claiming that it is "an art of nature" Spencer was convinced that "the law of organic progress is the law of all progress" ("Progress") and consequently credited the social organism with truly metabolic functions that allowed it to keep its body healthy and clean: "under the natural order of things society is constantly excreting its unhealthy, imbecile, slow, vacillating, faithless members." This "purifying process" (*Social Statistics* 180) carried out in the name of natural self-regulation and in perfect accord with "biological truths" ("Study of Sociology" 278), testifies to a more general necessity to shed off (to a variety of margins) that which mars the appearance of health. Excretion becomes a sign of the organism's good health, fending off the threat of constipation that might make the body rot inside. "The natural workings of things" with which Spencer explains social phenomena (the division of labour among others ["Art" 84]) obviously include, and entail, decaying as a process of doing away with what is useless and excessive. Spencer builds his argument upon a dichotomy between the strong/progressive and the weak/regressive where the latter literally enables the former's advancement.[5]

---

[5] To prevent the purifying process "increases the vitiation" and encourages the multiplication of the reckless and incompetent by offering them an unfailing provision, and discourages the multiplication of the competent and provident by heightening the difficulty of maintaining a family. And thus, in their eagerness to prevent the salutary sufferings that surround us, these sigh-wise and groan-

Also, the concept of evolution, as elaborated by Spencer, was based upon an ineradicable fixity of different groups of people in their "proper" places (in spite of the organism's potential for adaptation which Spencer singled out as the motor of development). An undoing of such natural allocations would mean unnatural arrangements, degeneration and a regression or collapse of the evolutionary machine. Hence, any claim to emancipation was, from the point of view of evolution, unjustified and unjustifiable. Rita Felski points out that "any challenge to the established division of the sexes would lead not to further progress but to the inevitable decline of the race. For society 'as a whole' to develop, women had to stay as they were. In other words, male advancement required female stasis" (155). Since both the law and the cause of progress are manifestations of a "universal principle" (Spencer, "Progress") conflated with the natural and explained as inevitability beyond anybody's control,[6] attempts to steer its course are rendered futile from the very beginning. Progress produces itself and does so according to rules that cannot be contravened.

Thus, naturalisation of femininity as illness fits the Victorian vision of progress in a double way. It makes progress visible and possible, and keeps women returning to their traditional locations. Sickness was considered a naturally feminine property as it coincided, in medical discourses of the nineteenth century, with

---

foolish people bequeath to posterity a continually increasing curse. (Spencer, "Progress")

Such members of a population as do not take care of themselves, but are taken care of by the rest, inevitably bring on the rest extra exertion [. . .]. Fostering the good-for-nothing at the expense of the good, is an extreme cruelty. It is a deliberate storing-up of miseries for future generations. (Spencer, "Study" 283)

[6] Spencer writes, "Progress is not an accident, not a thing within human control, but a beneficent necessity" ("Progress").

women's physiology.[7] Thus congenitally diseased, women were expected to cultivate their permanent impairment in order to keep their femininity intact. This enacting of "herself" was often assisted by the medical profession as doctors themselves proscribed debilitation as the best remedy for women's afflictions. Ellen L. Bassuk's discussion of the late nineteenth-century "rest cure" (developed by a neurologist, Silas Weir Mitchell[8]) reveals how the Victorian medical discourse participated in literally producing the invalid woman,[9] for what Mitchell's therapy administered was "complete rest, seclusion, and excessive feeding" (Bassuk 141). Refused any activity whatsoever (except for cleaning the teeth), bathed and spoonfed, having her vagina douched and her rectum cleaned with enema by a nurse, the sick woman was invalidated into an almost lifeless creature. What was to restore vitality in a thoroughly immobilised woman, among other things,[10] was a special diet meant to rebuild the deposits of fat. Thus, in Mitchell's rationale, she might regain her well-

---

[7] Ellen L. Bassuk, discussing the ideological underpinnings of a popular treatment devised by an American doctor, Silas Weir Mitchell, writes:

> Like his contemporaries, Mitchell believed that women were fundamentally inferior to men and that their nervous systems were more irritable; both 'facts' contributed to a woman's greater susceptibility to disease. And female irritability was firmly rooted in women's reproductive physiology and sexuality. 'The great physiological revolutions of a woman's life' such as menstruation, menopause, lactation etc., were viewed as a frequent cause of nervous disorders. In fact, normal female functions or femininity were considered diseases. (145)

[8] Mitchell developed the cure in the early seventies in America. In the eighties, it was introduced in England by W. S. Playfair (Showalter 139).

[9] For the list of diseases that were cured with the rest treatment, see Bassuk (141).

[10] The special diet was accompanied by tonics and stimulants, sometimes sleeping pills, a number of "passive exercises" like "massage, electricity, and hydrotherapy," and a total seclusion from relatives (Bassuk 141-42).

being by excessive consumption of food,[11] where getting fatter was concomitant with, and indicative of, getting better, and the surplus flesh a clear evidence of health restored. In Mitchell's medical logic, then, the most feminine labour[12] was the (re)production of surplus body (indeed, he associated obesity with the best reproductive capacity). Conservation of health, which clearly amounts to the conservation of traditional gender roles, entails, Mitchell seems convinced,[13] excessive consumption (inextricable from excessive production) that is, ideally, carried out in confinement, appended by inactivity as the best exercise of femininity. Thus medical inventions such as the rest cure made woman return to her proper place that was carefully marked by practices, which defined her most desirable mode of being. A woman under the treatment not only heals into idleness *par excellence* but also responds to the demand that she both consume and produce. Caught in a hyperbolic act that inscribes consumption (food) and production (fat) into her body as a stipula-

---

[11] At the beginning of the treatment, the patient was on a milk diet exclusively, given "four-ounce doses every two hours" simply to get fat (Bassuk 142).

[12] Mitchell was convinced that physiology disqualified women from "continuous labour of the mind," and that their attempts to act against this natural disposition jeopardised their health (Mitchell 15; qtd. in Bassuk 146).

[13] According to Bassuk (143), Mitchell believed that in order to properly nurse their health women "should model their lives on the principles underlying the rest cure." Moreover, Mitchell's understanding of health is clearly Spencerian in that he claimed that "to remain healthy, persons must achieve a harmonious relationship with their environment [. . .]" (Bassuk 144). Spencer (*Social Statistics* 41) emphasised harmony between organisms and circumstances as essential for their well-being: "Every suffering incident to the human body, from a headache up to fatal illness – from a burn or a sprain, up to accidental loss of life, is similarly traceable to the having placed that body in a situation for which its powers did not fit it." He thus introduced a moral aspect to his theory claiming that evil "is invariably referable to the one generic cause – want of congruity between the faculties and their spheres of action."

tion for health, she epitomises an economy that conjures up illness to make itself visible on the one hand, and workable, on the other.

(Woman's) dawdling was thus inscribed, or stipulated, in the family's financial prosperity, her degeneration a prerequisite for the middle-class man's economic progress, her physical deterioration an emblem of his financial success and reputation, her abundance an unlimited source of spending. Whether she dawdled away time, or herself, in the bouts of consumptive feasts/fits, she served well the health of the (masculine) body economic. As Spackman succinctly puts it, "A touch of sickness makes health more visible" (14). Busy (re)producing evidence of health, the diseased middle-class woman becomes a locus of ideological labour where evolutionary concerns are amplified, supposedly common interests preserved and promoted, justifications of gendered divisions advertised as priceless. Couched in decadent images of withering flesh and stultifying weariness, she is defined antithetically to the "domain of productive and social labour" (Schreiner 50). Indeed, driven by aesthetic necessity to cultivate invalidism and dissipation she helped re-create work as a masculine domain.

In his essay, "The Part played by Labour in the Transition from Ape to Man," Friedrich Engels leaves no doubt that what is at stake in the history of evolutionary progression is labour. Furnished with almost god-like causative powers, labour is credited with a humanising force, which set progress in motion instituting the metamorphosis of apes into men. Locating this revolutionary change in a rather imaginary, and indeterminate, past of "the Tertiary period," Engels situates labour as, and at the beginning of, human history and body. Becoming thus a boundary which separates, and keeps distinctly apart, what is animal and what is human, labour acquires a generic value in the constitution of man. The time of no-labour is a time beyond history (however illogical this may sound) and beyond humanity. It is also a time in which the body ("of anthropoid apes") still gropes, out of adaptive necessity, in search for the perfectly laborious posture to finally culminate into the most human(e) and belaboured shape – erection.

It is not surprising, perhaps, that, erecting this Darwinesque theory of the labour movement,[14] Engels has history and men originate with an erectile body, whose humanness is measured by its ability to permanently adopt an up-right position, which will, in time, qualify the simian "ancestors of ours" (Engels) for the full membership in the human society, and thrust its future onto the path of progress. Bodies half-erect won't make a true man, Engels explains, too impotent to perform the erectable labour that begets mankind. Meanwhile, the "man in the making," busy labouring the "origin of man," cultivates labour's power of begetting, handing down "from generation to generation," through the law of inheritance, "the prime basic condition for all human existence" (Engels) plus the fully developed and grown organs to perform it.

Thus laboured into erection the human body also marks the moment of man's emancipation from nature. Instrumental in this liberating move is the hand, both "the organ of labour" and "*the product of labour*" (Engels; emphasis original), whose production and productive potential entail, for Engels, the conquest of and control over nature's provisions. The supreme hand, then, somehow abstracted from the material it will master, in a truly imperial fashion proceeds to execute man's will paving the way for knowledge and humanity. Engels writes: "Mastery over nature began with the development of the hand, with labour, and widened man's horizon at every new advance." The violent gesture of the free hand, inscribed into the scenario of evolution, happens obviously naturally, for paradoxically, it

---

[14] Engels' indebtedness to Darwin would be discernible even without his references to Darwin's theories. For a discussion of Engels' enchantment with Darwin's evolutionary theory, see Stuart C. Gilman.

is itself quite a natural product, an evolutionary outcome of nature's laws, sanctioned by biological necessity and hence neutralised under the guise of progress.

This naturalisation of subjugation becomes the foundation for the emergence of freedom – "the decisive step had been taken, *the hand had become free* (Engels; emphasis original) – its binding promise and a form of its pursuit. The freedom of the dexterous hand, which for Engels is genuine evidence of the transition accomplished and of labour's productive capacity, is inseparable from the subjection of what comes within its reach. Moreover, the employment of the upper-hand that works the miracle of evolution, extricates the natural from the realm of productive labour. Thus subjected to the mastering hand that requires its submission, it becomes a material whose use consists in servility. The indisputable value of labour, therefore, inheres in a devaluation of what is belaboured. Engels states it explicitly when he summarises the fundamental difference between animals and men:

> In short, the animal merely *uses* its environment, and brings about changes in it simply by its presence; man by his changes makes it serve his ends, *masters* it. This is the final, essential distinction between man and other animals, and once again it is labour that brings about this distinction.
>
> (Engels; emphasis original)

Interestingly, the origin of man laboured into existence is predicated on a quite economic transaction where the freedom of the hand as the supreme instrument of labour is obtained at the cost of nature's subjection, which amounts to a mutilation of her body. The task man was to carry out, in contrast to animals, was to consciously impress "the stamp of [his] will upon the earth" (Engels). Thus the scar, left as an authorial mark attains an economic value being turned into a trademark, which is to advertise more the producer than the produce and to secure his proprietary (copy)right. Consequently, branded human, the marked earth also brings out the difference between the owner and the owned as impressions are produced and left according to rules of belonging. The primal exchange, then, sets economy in motion introducing property as its indispensable condition and underlying principle.

Engels' theory of the ape made man opens up, however, gloomy vistas on this rather optimistic narrative of human progress as the regressive fall of men remains a possibility within the evolutionary mechanism. Failure to perform labour, Engels makes it clear, dehumanises man into "savages" whose "regression to a more animal-like condition" brings about "a simultaneous physical degeneration." The atavistic "savage," however suspended between the animal and the human, is undeniably excluded from the family of man as his degenerate condition places him outside the generically human. To regress into degeneration is to "fall from the genus or stock" (Gilman 169), as the etymological roots of the word suggest, thus into a region outside humanity. In Engels' narrative, this falling is equivalent to losing the humanising potential for labour. The loss of physical strength invalidates the body that, curiously enough, becomes both the cause and effect of degeneration. The body, which does not labour, is implicitly posited as a dis-abled body, in a double sense. In a way, it is a handless body, deprived of the instrumental organs of productive labour. Also, and consequently, it is a powerless body, unable to master nature as it cannot secure the mastering freedom of the hand, thus bound to be mastered by it. The story of the transition from ape to man is built upon a dichotomy of physical degeneration and health, where the latter, clearly privileged, becomes the badge of this transition and its condition. Labour, in its turn, calls for sturdy bodies while degeneration disqualifies them from its humanising realm.

The explicit equation of idleness with degeneration and the rele-
gation of the idle to the margins of humanity bring out the instances
when labour fails to create man. Or, differently put, it becomes a
gesture of exclusion without which the creative, begetting, power of
labour would not be conceivable and measurable. That this exclusion seems permanent is suggested, not only by the phallic origin of
labour, but also by a certain conceptual limit to Engels' evolutionary
thinking. That is, Engels' is a dead-end logic, for how might a
physically degenerate body, incapable of working, hope for regeneration and inclusion back into the genus, once it is locked in the in-
decipherable conflation of causes and effects? And yet, it is impossible not to see that this logic undermines, not to say invalidates,
Engels' myth of the labour-inflected origin of man, as it claims the
end of evolution as its fundamental premise and renders it a finite
project, quite against the logic of advance.

As has been rightly appreciated, Olive Schreiner's *Woman and
Labour* is a valiant attempt "to chronicle the epic unfolding of the
world historical condition of women" (McClintock 291) and "to locate women's oppression economically" (Ledger 41). Underlying
Schreiner's arguments is a conviction that "the lessons of gender are
not written immemorially in the blood," as well as a rejection of the
"notion of women's subjection as universal, natural and inevitable"
(McClintock 291).[15] Turning to nature to de-naturalise gender roles
Schreiner overturns some dogmas of science, remaining, however,
within that same science's argumentation. A project to trace back in

---

[15] Schreiner wrote in the introduction to the book:
  sex relationships may assume almost any form on earth as the conditions of life vary; [. . .] even in their sexual relations towards offspring, those differences which we, conventionally, are apt to sup-
  pose are inherent in the paternal or the maternal sex form, are not
  inherent. (12)

history, investigate at present, and delineate for the future, the condition of women in relation to labour, Schreiner's impassioned text resonates with forceful, and repeatedly voiced, demands: "Give us labour and the training which fits for labour!" (33). Familiar with the socio-scientific discourses on sex of her time,[16] Schreiner sets out to counter theories that relegate women to a home-bound idleness on the pretext of her "Divine Child-bearer" (200) role. Convinced that women's exclusion from "active productive exertion" (89) and fields of labour opened by the modern world constantly transformed by technological inventions will lead to the decay of the whole society, she pleads for women's access to education and workplace challenging the separate-spheres ideology. Framed by evolutionary discourse,[17] *Woman and Labour* puts forward an indo-

---

[16] For example with Geddes and Thomson's *The Evolution of Sex*. Burdett (47) and Felski (156) both mention this fact.

[17] Schreiner's reliance on evolutionary narrative continues to be a complex, and widely discussed issue. For example, Rita Felski argues that it needs to be related to the context of the nineteenth-century male discourses of evolution which invariably produced women as much less developed than men, and repeatedly located them in the home proving, on the basis of scientific data, that it was unquestionably natural. Moreover, as she notes, the "evolutionary paradigm" enjoyed a ubiquitous presence in Victorian thought regardless of ideological alliances: "Rather than an analytical tool to be adopted or cast off at will, this paradigm was so deeply embedded in common-sense attitudes of the period as to be almost invisible, shaping the discourse of critics as well as of supporters of the status quo" (156). Carolyn Burdett, in turn, points to the ways in which the language, and the idea, of progress provided a means of empowerment and struggle. She argues that for many women

> progress was a precious idea precisely because they had, as yet, been excluded from its benefits. By the final two decades of the nineteenth century, middle-class women were beginning to insist that they, too, wanted to join the fast track of social transformation. Many found in the languages of evolution new and powerful ways to articulate their aspirations. (2)

lent woman who, corrupted by lack of activity, may become a dead end of progress.

To envisage the demise of humanity, Olive Schreiner evokes the figure of the (bourgeois) woman as a degenerate invalid, shrouded in "metaphors of corruption, contagion, and disease" (Felski 157), in order to posit her as the herald of the end and its loathsome personification. A tell-tale symptom of decadence, she is compared to a parasitic organism with the infective potential to blight the social structure: "Everywhere, in the past as in the present, the parasitism of the female heralds the decay of a nation or a class, and as invariably indicates disease as the pustules of smallpox upon the skin indicate the existence of a purulent virus in the system" (Schreiner 98).

The female parasite, "the fine lady" (Schreiner 82) of the "dominant class or race" (83), is one of the main characters, so to speak, in Schreiner's text. Depicted as a completely inert figure, caught in the state of "supine inaction" (86), she is cast outside the realm of productive activity. The parasite's passivity is often vividly represented through images of prostration. Thus she "reposes among pillows" (89), or "recline[s] on her sofa" (89), virtually unable to move. Having become "stationary and inactive" (106), the female parasite is wedged securely in one location, the home, where "immured within the walls" (84) she wastes time, and others' labour, gratifying her appetites.

In Schreiner, this statically rendered parasitic woman figures as an obstruction, and a threat, to the movement of progress, as a retrograde tendency that makes the notion of futurity less and less tenable. Incapacitated for movement, she represents, in fact, the frightening impossibility of mobility, a more or less permanent arrest in the here and now which impedes the move towards there which takes place elsewhere. The image of the female parasite is an image of impotence and futility, both linked irrevocably to stasis, because it is set against the progressive which belongs to a different sphere, a sphere which is not where *she* is. Inimical to the advancement of the nations, she is also inimical to the Woman's Movement which Schreiner depicts explicitly as a literally active undertaking which involves exertion, an undertaking whose progression entails women's movement. As she writes, it "is a movement steady and persistent in one direction, the direction of increased activity and culture, and towards the negation of all possibility of parasitism in the human female" (139). It is, she adds, "in its ultimate essence, an endeavour on the part of a section of the race to save itself from inactivity and degeneration" (123).

To make progress and survival of the race possible, the parasite woman has to be "animated into action" (129), brought to life again where living equals doing and acting. In Schreiner's project, to be able to undergo this vitalisation, she will need to take what she clearly does not have. In order to move, and to move forward, she must be infused with virility, to use Schreiner's own expression, virility which becomes the most progressive disposition. Counterposed to virility are enervation, effeteness, emasculation, degeneration, epithets she uses to describe the condition of both parasitic women and parasitised men, which point up to the loss of vigour at stake in the process of feminine decay. Sterilising weakness, intimated in these epithets, can affect also men:

> only an effete and inactive male can ultimately be produced by an effete and inactive womanhood. The curled darling, scented and languid, with his drawl, his delicate apparel, his devotion to the rarity and variety of his viands, whose severest labour is the search after pleasure, and for whom even the chase, which was for his remote ancestor an invigorating and manly toil essential for the meat and life of his people, becomes a luxurious and farcical amusement; –

this male [. . .] is possible only because generations of parasitic women have preceded him. More repulsive than the parasite female herself, because a yet further product of decay, it is yet only the scent of his mother's boudoir that we smell in his hair. (107-08)[18]

Thus the female parasite feminises women and men alike. The effete man, dwelling in aesthetics and delicacy which are clearly not his own, redolent of feminine spaces, woman's private rooms, manifests the distortions brought upon the vigorous and laborious body of his ancestors. The parasite herself, on the other hand, embodies this space where feminisation takes place, the boudoir becoming the metaphor of her womb, where feminised males originate and are bound to return through an olfactory bond productive of decadence.

Schreiner's persistent use of the word "virile" may smack of what for contemporary readers might sound like an undesired eulogy of virility where what is masculine or manly is a norm to which women should necessarily aspire. However, in Schreiner's text "virile" is not, strictly speaking, a provenance of men. It transcends genders becoming a universal disposition of a human subjectivity. It is a condition of health – both physical and moral, of life, and of activity; indeed, the highest standard of humanity. In her parlance, it will refer to both the physical and mental, meaning vigorous, reso-

---

[18] Despite the eugenic overtones in this passage Schreiner in fact does not evoke ideas of hereditary transmission of certain traits but rather what could in today's parlance be called the process of socialisation:

> As we have said it is the power of the human female to impress herself on her descendants, male and female, not only through germinal inheritance, through influence during the period of gestation, but above all by producing the mental atmosphere in which the impressionable infant years of life are passed, which makes the condition of the child-bearing female one of paramount interest of the race. (108)

lute, mighty, fearless, able, and laborious. Schreiner will, therefore, juxtapose the idle and static female parasite with an "active, virile, laborious" (106) woman of the past[19] and the future to come, who will, leading the Woman's Movement, lead the race toward harmonious equality. Throughout the text, virility, activity and laboriousness are conflated into a token of socially useful productiveness and valorised in opposition to a feebleness which ultimately entails the abuse of others' work and regress. In the ideal of "virile womanhood" (82), a womanhood furnished with attributes necessary to perform "useful human toil" (68), virility is what will qualify women for labour. It is, in fact, its enabling condition to virtually produce itself. It also provides a space of regeneration where decadent parasites can be virilised and thus recreated as human.

It is appropriate, it seems, to note that given Schreiner's indebtedness to social Darwinism inflected with Spencerian thought and to Karl Pearson's ideas, she has inevitably taken over the language these discourses deploy.[20] The discourses of evolutionary science, saturated with the notion of progress, posited weakness and feebleness as a regressive tendency valorising, instead, strength. That progress required healthy bodies and healthy minds was a fact recognised and shared by many. For example, Herbert Spencer's hostility towards welfare-state socialism and the care of "enfeebled individu-

---

[19] For example, describing women of the past ages Schreiner frequently deploys this quality as something women used to have before they reached the condition of parasitism.

[20] Darwin's *The Variation of Animals and Plants under Domestication* was one of the books Olive Schreiner read early in her life (Burdett 10). Also, she read Herbert Spencer's *First Principles* at the age of sixteen (Ledger 73). Sally Ledger argues that Schreiner's fascination with Spencer and Darwin was "a result of an early crisis of religious faith." As she says, "Spencer's work provided Schreiner with an alternative credo – scientific naturalism" (73).

als" (Nye 58)[21] testifies to the importance of, and foregrounds, the idea of vigour both intellectual and physical. Despite Schreiner's problematic deployment of the idea of virility, the figure of the female parasite, sketched in a stark contrast to the virile body of usefulness, offers itself for a reading where the ways in which she is described nonetheless contest certain assumptions of the evolutionary discourse.[22] Here, virility, in its claims to social usefulness and productiveness, becomes a backdrop against which the notion of Victorian femininity enacts its own de-composition.

Middle-class women's parasitism is "an inevitable result of long-term patterns of social change, as industry and technology slowly take the place of traditional feminine skills" (Felski 157). The figure of the female parasite, a contemptuous metaphor Schreiner uses to describe the idle woman, combines images of decadent weariness, excessive consumption, and a surfeit of pleasure, amongst which emerge both aesthetic and economic concerns:

> The truth is that, if at the present day, woman, after her long upward march side by side with man, developing with him through the countless ages, by means of the endless

In "The Coming of Slavery," for instance, Spencer writes:

> There seems no getting people to accept the truth, which nevertheless is conspicuous enough, that the welfare of a society and the justice of its arrangements are at bottom dependent on the characters of its members; and that improvement in neither can take place without that improvement in character which results from carrying on peaceful industry under the restraints imposed by an orderly social life. The belief, not only of the socialists but also of those so-called Liberals who are diligently preparing the way for them, is that by due skill an ill-working humanity may be framed into well-working institutions. It is a delusion. The defective natures of citizens will show themselves in the bad acting of whatever social structure they are arranged into.

[22] I return to this contestation by the end of my essay.

exercise of the faculties of mind and body, has now, at last, reached her ultimate limit of growth, and can progress no farther; that, then, here also, to-day, the growth of the human spirit is to be stayed; that here, on the spot of woman's arrest, is the standard of the race to be finally planted, to move forward no more, for ever: – that, if the parasite woman on her couch, loaded with gewgaws, the plaything and amusement of man, be the permanent and final manifestation of female human life on the globe, then that couch is also the death-bed of human evolution. (132-33)

Then, in the place of the active labouring woman, upholding society by her toil, has come the effete wife, concubine, or prostitute, clad in fine raiment, the work of others' fingers; fed on luxurious viands, the result of others' toil, waited on and tended by the labour of others. [. . .] she bedecked and scented her person, or had it bedecked and scented for her. She lay upon her sofa, or drove or was carried out in her vehicle, and, loaded with jewels, she sought by dissipation and amusements to fill up the inordinate blank left by the lack of productive activity. (81)

Schreiner equates the decay of human evolution with the decaying of the female body – both suggested by the evocation of the death-bed where one who lapsed into illness awaits the end slowly withering away – a gesture which inscribes the feminine as a threshold that designates an outside of nothingness. Embodied in the figure of a woman coming to a developmental standstill, "the limit of growth" is the limit of history as the contours of her body sketch the borders of humanity, beyond which no "human spirit" is conceivable. In this strange mixture of stasis and dynamics, her almost death-like figure, solidified in passivity, comes to animate the process of decline. The prophesised dissolution of the social body infected with the ills of

parasite women is implicitly contrasted with the integrity of progress summoned up by the image of a concerted movement of the
body of human history.

Schreiner locates the end of humanity amidst accessories of economy: sofas, ornaments, clothes, perfumes, (the parasite herself) –
trivia at the periphery of serious business. "The presence of endless
purchasable objects" that threatens the smooth run of human evolution, and that confuses women with commodities (Psomiades 198),
in a sense turns humanity into yet another object(ive), traded, in the
worst scenario, for the all-accommodating sofa. Commodity culture,
then, is where human progress encounters (stumbles over) bourgeois
femininity. It is also where the end of this progress is forever turned
into a ghastly spectacle of a woman with extra (feminine) things (all
expendable and exchangeable). And yet this culture of petty commodities is what she can properly have. What she has (can only
have) is always some small possessions, accessories, indeed paraphernalia. Originally being, according to the *Oxford English Reference Dictionary*, "personal articles which a woman could keep after
marriage, as opposed to the dowry which went to her husband," and
as opposed to herself who went to the husband, paraphernalia is
what is rescued from giving, what resists taking. Over the blatant
deprivations that underlie the marriage transaction, and the consoling function of paraphernalia she is left with an illusion of keeping
the house ("within his house, as ruled by her," as John Ruskin [136]
puts it).

There is a limit to this decadent profligacy as the female parasite,
in her thoughtless, exploitative and unrestrained consumption will
ultimately devour the entire race. Curiously enough, her overly consumptive existence translates into an over-productive one, despite
the passivity she is drugged into by her love of comfort and fashion.
Lurking behind this scene of death-begetting femininity is the fear
of uncontrolled re-production for clearly what is intimated in the

image of the parasitic woman is a possibility of interminable contamination where parasites beget parasites and the contagious femininity turns into congenital disease that spreads to global proportions. The female parasite is a figuration of femininity unbound that
reproduces itself beyond limits to finally eat away the social organism on which it breeds. Held responsible for the disease of society,
"the human female parasite – the most deadly microbe which can
make its appearance on the surface of any social organism"
(Schreiner 82) keeps carrying out its monstrous work despite its
seeming slothfulness. Cast outside the realm of productive labour,
she is nonetheless locked in the deplorable production of the terminally diseased society. In a sense, the end of evolution is envisioned
as an excess of/ in the bourgeois feminine.

Laden with jewels she herself comes to be reduced to a rather
gruesome ornament of the social body, an excessive tumour, deca-
dently useless, which disfigures it and incapacitates for labour. A
superfluous decoration, she embodies decadence as a cult of the ornamental and reiterates the conflation of the feminine and the decorative.[23] In "neo-classical aesthetics," as Naomi Schor argues, the
ornament bears a feminine burden of "the decorative, the natural,
the impure, and the monstrous" (45). The female parasite, herself a
painted trinket of the house's interior scenery, is a lifeless monstrosity whose dubious decorativeness is an offence to the healthy usefulness of things and people. In Schreiner's aesthetics of labour the
most beautiful is the practical, that which never surpasses the limits
of utility, while "ugliness is pegged to waste" (Schor 54). Useless-
ness fosters, in Veblen's words, "an abiding sense of the odiousness
and aesthetic impossibility of what is obviously futile" (70). In
Schreiner, too, this aesthetic impossibility is persistently opposed to

---

[23] On the conflation of the feminine, the ornamental, and decadence, see Naomi
Schor.

the beauty of the useful and productive. Thus beauty and ugliness come to be defined by economic concerns. The waste at stake in ugliness, is a waste of labour which might have been performed by the parasite, who, cast in the state of "supine inaction" (Schreiner 86), participates in the myriad of useless objects. It is also a waste of usefulness, of the potential for "active productive exertion" (89) which decays amidst the "excessive wealth and luxury" (99).

The female parasite is, as Schreiner puts it, "tenderly housed" (82), provided with a pleasant and luxurious home but also carefully stored as a good, kept (she is, Schreiner (82) says, a "kept wife," "kept mistress"), and owned, maintained in return for sexual favours. The home is a storage, a place for storing things and women who are to help amass items of the familial felicity. According to Schreiner, woman's slide into parasitism brings about her objectification where even for herself she becomes an owned person, an "it" she owns, possesses, and *handl*es (after all, wealth is "*in the hands* of the dominant class or race*" [98; emphasis mine]): "she bedecked and scented *her person*, or had *it* bedecked and scented for her" (81; emphasis mine). The shift from "her" to "it," and the distance it introduces, turns the parasite into a lifeless object to be adorned. And yet Schreiner persistently implies that this beautification only yields an "appalling," "terrible" (91), and "repulsive" (108) picture of a static and decaying womanhood that grows limitlessly and hideously (the parasite accepts, Schreiner (91) tells us, "unlimited consumption") as if beyond the control of the wielding, manipulating hands.

There is a close affinity between monstrosity and commodities, as Thomas Keenan has shown in his reading of Marx's *Capital*. In Schreiner, the bourgeois home is a site for the storing of "unlaboured-for wealth" (101), a place where wealth is displayed (conspicuously consumed, as Veblen would put it) and accumulated, with the parasite as the most precious good and consumer. Here, she is depicted by Schreiner as part of the assortment of objects all of which bespeak "ease in the place of exertion, and an unlimited consumption in the place of production" (91). According to Marx, wealth "appears as a monstrous collection of commodities" (Marx 49; qtd. in Keenan 157), the monster becoming a figuration for wealth, its ghastly representation whose most palpable shape is, at best, that of appearance. "The monstrous," writes Keenan, "is the form of appearance of wealth, the way it signifies itself, as something(s) else" (157). "As" signals the moment of deception which forever withholds wealth from an immediate access (and, rhetorically, from possession). Because wealth never is but appears, in Keenan's reading of Marx, it requires someone (something) else's form, someone (something) else's body in/with which to appear (in order to hide). It needs a commodious body, first of all, for example of a monster, to disguise itself ("something (economic) shows itself by hiding itself, by announcing itself as something else or in another form" [Keenan 157]), to offer, or present, itself at all.

The female parasite, "a monster, carrier" (Keenan 157) for unlaboured-for wealth, lends her monstrous body to the bourgeois household commodities, a body in/with which they can appear. A collectivity of sorts, she becomes the form for, and herself part of, "something(s) assembled" (Keenan 157). If in Marx wealth appears as a monster, in Schreiner it appears as a parasite. Yet this parasite must still borrow its body from the body of someone else, assume its attributes all of which add to a form of appearance, semblance. Schreiner makes this assumption particularly noticeable when she turns those attributes into an image of dissimulation.[24] Gestures of theatricality and elements of disguise shape the parasitic woman,

---

[24] "The matter at issue is the appearance or self-announcement of something as something else, the rhetorical structure of simile or metaphor (*als, comme*): semblance, shine, simulation or dissimulation" (Keenan 157).

yet, at the same time, they constitute, and partake of, (traditional) femininity. Thus, writes Olive Schreiner, the female parasite of the Roman Empire, "like more modern counterparts, painted herself, wore patches, affected an artistic walk, and a handshake with the elbow raised and the fingers hanging down" (89). In the image Schreiner offers, it is femininity that becomes a body for the parasite, a body made up of disguise, posing and simulation. But then again, femininity emerges out of this composite as nothing less and nothing more than an assumption where what is assumed is a body of Victorian womanliness.

If, as Rita Felski rightly points out, Schreiner's *Woman and Labour* "in its plea for female liberation [. . .] reproduces a powerfully gendered cluster of metaphors which counterposes the labouring, healthy, and virile body to the insidious threat of passivity, femininity, and disease" (157), then it seems it does so strategically. Not only does it argue that the ideals of Victorian femininity, if cultivated, are bound to head for degeneration, of her and society, but it also intimates the unnaturalness of the dispositions that are taken to constitute this feminine ideal. Schreiner's depiction of the female parasite who embodies some of the standards cherished by Victorians suggests that the parasitic woman is a product of specific historical and social conditions and not a natural given. Thus the lifeless, inane, dawdling darling of the Victorian bourgeois home that Schreiner renders in a much less pleasing manner than her proponents, indeed, the angel of the sweet Victorian hearth, in *Woman and Labour* comes in for an open critique.

Schreiner's statically rendered female parasite addresses, if implicitly, the ubiquitous premise underlying evolutionary theories of progress that "male advancement required female stasis" (Felski 155). Nineteenth-century male discourses of evolution invariably produced women as much less developed than men, and repeatedly located them in the home proving, on the basis of scientific data, that it was unquestionably natural.[25] The progress of civilisation depended directly on "the retarded development of women" (Felski 155), which, in turn, was "necessitated by the reservation of vital power to meet the costs of reproduction," according to Herbert Spencer (*Study of Sociology* 373; qtd. in Felski 155). The very "alignment of the modern woman with a narrative of progress" (Felski 155) was in itself a daring and challenging act, an unsettling intervention into a man-created and man-dominated discourse. Undermining the tenets of evolutionary thought, Schreiner argues that the desired stasis would, in the worst scenario, also entail the stasis of the whole race. Thus if the different modes of science persistently excluded women from the narratives of advancement, Schreiner contends, instead, that having women barred at home and steeped in idleness is certainly anti-progressive.

If some of Olive Schreiner's ideas, elaborated in her *Woman and Labour*, may be nowadays seen as attenuating her feminist politics, it is worth remembering, perhaps, that what may be considered feminist or radical is always contingent. As Elizabeth Grosz reminds us, stressing the importance of historicity and alerting our sensitivity to the many aspects that contribute to a text's designations, "feminist" (and, it can as well be argued, "radical") is not a universal appellation:

> It is nonetheless necessary to understand that no text wears
> its political status as a nameplate or label, no text can be
> classified once and for all as wholly feminist or wholly pa-

---

[25] It is interesting and important to note that the "evolutionary paradigm," in Felski's words, enjoyed a ubiquitous presence in Victorian thought regardless of one's ideological alliances: "Rather than an analytical tool to be adopted or cast off at will, this paradigm was so deeply embedded in common-sense attitudes of the period as to be almost invisible, shaping the discourse of critics as well as of supporters of the status quo" (156).

triarchal: these appellations depend on its context, its place within that context, how it is used, by whom and to what effect. These various contingencies dictate that at best a text is feminist or patriarchal only provisionally, only momentarily, only in some but not in all its possible readings, and in some but not all of its possible effects. (23-24)

Works Cited

Bassuk, Ellen L. "The Rest Cure: Repetition or Resolution of Victorian Women's Conflicts?" *The Female Body in Western Culture.* Ed. Susan Rubin Suleiman. Cambridge: Harvard UP, 1986. 139-51.

Burdett, Carolyn. *Olive Schreiner and the Progress of Feminism: Evolution, Gender, Empire.* Basingstoke: Palgrave Macmillan, 2001.

Chamberlain, J. Edward, and Sander L. Gilman, eds. *Degeneration: The Dark Side of Progress.* New York: Columbia UP, 1985.

[Cooke, Nicholas Francis]. *Satan in Society.* 1870. By "A Physician". Cincinnati: C. F. Vent, 1876.

Dijkstra, Bram. *Idols of Perversity: Fantasies of Feminine Evil in Fin-de-Siècle Culture.* Oxford: Oxford UP, 1986.

Engels, Friedrich. "The Part Played by Labour in the Transition from Ape to Man." 1876. Trans. Clemens Dutt. *Marxists.org Internet Archive.* 12 Oct. 2005 <http://www.marxists.org/arch ive/marx/works/1876/part-played-labour>.

Felski, Rita. *The Gender of Modernity.* Cambridge and London: Harvard UP, 1995.

Gagnier, Regenia. *The Insatiability of Human Wants: Economics and Aesthetics in Market Society.* Chicago and London: The U of Chicago P, 2000.

Gilman, Stuart C. "Political Theory: Left to Right, Up to Down." *Degeneration: The Dark Side of Progress.* Chamberlain and Gilman 165-97.

Grosz, Elizabeth. *Space, Time, and Perversion.* New York and London: Routledge, 1995.

Guy, Josephine M., ed. *The Victorian Age: An Anthology of Sources and Documents.* New York and London: Routledge, 2002.

Keenan, Thomas. "The Point is to (Ex)Change it: Reading *Capital,* Rhetorically." *Fetishism as Cultural Discourse.* Ed. Emily Apter and William Pietz. Ithaca and London: Cornell UP, 1993. 152-85.

Ledger, Sally. *The New Woman: Fiction and Feminism at the* fin de siècle. Manchester and New York: Manchester UP, 1997.

Lorrain, Jean. "The Man Who Loved Consumptives." *The Decadent Reader: Fiction, Fantasy, and Perversion from Fin-De-Siecle France.* Ed. Asti Hustvedt. New York: Zone, 1998. 891-94.

Marx, Karl. *Capital: A Critique of Political Economy.* Trans. Ben Fowkes. New York: Vintage, 1977.

McClintock, Anne. *Imperial Leather: Race, Gender and Sexuality in the Colonial Context.* New York and London: Routledge, 1995.

Mitchell, Silas Weir. *Lectures on Diseases of the Nervous System Especially in Women.* Philadelphia: Lea Bros. and Co. 1885.

Nye, Robert A. "Sociology and Degeneration: The Irony of Progress." *Degeneration: The Dark Side of Progress.* Chamberlain and Gilman 49-71.

"Paraphernalia." *Oxford English Reference Dictionary.* 1995.

Psomiades, Kathy Alexis. *Beauty's Body: Femininity and Representation in British Aestheticism.* Stanford: Stanford UP, 1997.

Ruskin, John. "Of Queens' Gardens." 1865. *Sesame and Lilies.* London: George Allen and Sons, 1907. 110-80.

Schor, Naomi. "Decadence: Wey, Loos, Lukács." *Reading in Detail: Aesthetics and the Feminine*. New York and London: Methuen, 1987.

Schreiner, Olive. *Woman and Labour*. 1911. London: Virago, 1988.

Showalter, Elaine. *The Female Malady: Women, Madness, and English Culture, 1830-1980*. London: Virago, 1998.

Siegel, Sandra. "Literature: The Representation of 'Decadence.'" *Degeneration: The Dark Side of Progress*. Chamberlain and Gilman 199-219.

Spackman, Barbara. *Decadent Genealogies: The Rhetoric of Sickness from Baudelaire to D'Annunzio*. Ithaca and London: Cornell UP, 1989.

Spencer, Herbert. "Art IV. – The Social Organism." *Westminster Review* 27 (January 1860): 90-121. Rpt. in Guy 83-91.

---. "The Coming Slavery." *Illustrations of Universal Progress*. 1857. Columbia University. 12 Oct. 2005 <http://www.colum bia.edu/acis/ets/CCREAD/etscc/spencer.htm>.

---. "Progress: Its Law and Cause." *Illustrations of Universal Progress*. 1857. Columbia University. 12 Oct. 2005 <http://www.columbia.edu/acis/ets/CCREAD/etscc/spencer.htm>.

---. *Social Statics: Or, the Conditions Essential to Human Happiness Specified, and the First of Them Developed*. London: Chapman, 1851. *The Online Library of Liberty*. 7 Apr. 2004. 18 Dec. 2005 <http://oll.libertyfund.org/Texts/LFBooks/Spencer02 36/SocialStatics/0331_eBk.pdf>.

---. "The Study of Sociology. XIV. – Preparation in Biology." *Contemporary Review* 22 (August 1873): 325-46. Rpt. in Guy 278-88.

---. *The Study of Sociology. New York, 1893*.

Veblen, Thorstein. *The Theory of the Leisure Class*. 1899. New York: The Modern Library, 2001.

Woolson, Abba Goold. *Woman in American Society*. Boston, 1873.

The Perversion of Decadence:
The Cases of Oscar Wilde's Dorian Gray and Salome

Bonnie J. Robinson
North Georgia College & State University

Abstract: This essay establishes the affinities of Wilde's concept of the individual with Decadent qualities of self-absorption and aestheticism, by drawing upon Wilde's own work as well as influences upon it by Huysmans, Baudelaire, and Pater. It delineates successful Decadent individuals in Wilde's work, then considers the unsuccessful Decadent individuals, Dorian Gray and Salome. It explores how they pervert Decadence through failed self-realization. This argument emphasizes Wilde's positive attitude towards and use of the Decadent movement in literature.

Wilde's concept of the individual, the center of his philosophy of Individualism, relies on Decadent qualities of artificiality, aestheticism, contemplation, and relativity. While his works present successful Decadent individualists in such characters as Ernest Worthing and Lord Goring, the two Wildean figures that critics most often hail as epitomizing Decadence in British literature, that is, Dorian Gray and Salome, are actually failed individualists. Rather than realize themselves through Decadent qualities of self-absorption and Aestheticism, they turn instead to action and influence. In effect, they pervert Decadence and its positive values.

These positive values of Decadence support Individualism. As Koenraad W. Swart (77) writes, early Decadents began by

> Repudiating traditional morality, rejecting all social restraints, defying society, and taking a morbid delight in corruption [. . .] It was this consciously adopted ideology of [. . .] individualism, and estheticism that formed the most important legacy of French Romanticism to the so-called

Decadent movement in literature at the end of the nineteenth century.

Aestheticism and artificiality, for Decadents, go hand in hand.
Charles Baudelaire privileged art and artificiality in "In Praise of
Cosmetics," Max Beerbohm did the same in "A Defense of Cosmet-
ics," and Wilde famously reversed the values of mimesis in his "The
Decay of Lying" (33), when he declared that "Nature imitates Art."

Wilde's perfect personality indeed resembles a work of the Aesthetic Movement's art by being autonomous, non-doctrinal, complex, and non-discursive. Wilde, for example, has Dorian think of
the individual thus: "To him, man was a being with myriad lives and
myriad sensations, a complex multiform creature that bore within itself legacies of thought and passion" (171-72). And one of Wilde's
early prose works delineates the individual's autonomy: "Bodies or
organisms progress toward greater and greater multiformity or
structural differentiation when not subjected to undue external influence" ("The Rise of Historical Criticism" 210). Wilde's individual
develops himself out of himself, entirely rejecting external, natural –
or naturalized – standards. Thus, Wilde's self-developing individual,
like the Decadent, subverts Victorian concepts of "natural" manli-
ness and morality. It eschews such Victorian values as conformity,
consistency, and sincerity. As Jonathan Dollimore points out in
"Desire and Difference" (41), this rejection assists Wilde's aim to
escape the prescribed gender expectations of his day: "[Individual-
ism] is both desire for a radical personal freedom and a desire for
society itself to be radically different, the first being inseparable
from the second." Decadence becomes a means for "social change."
As Richard Dellamora writes in "Productive Decadence" (529),

> Revolutionary impulses and experience within liberalism
> depend upon a view of change in time as catastrophic and
> potentially liberating. I am principally interested in deca-

dent culture as an element of critique and utopian aspiration within the liberal tradition. In the aesthetic and decadent movements, one of the ways in which this possibility is imagined is in terms of the creation of a modern counter-culture.

The self-absorption and mental stimulation practiced by such Decadents as Des Esseintes in Joris-Karl Huysman's À *rebours* further exemplify the positive values of self-realization and autonomy for Wilde. For example, Des Esseintes secludes himself with his own fancies, nightmares, and visions – stimulated by art and literature. And in Wilde's concept of Individualism, self-realization involves bringing to the surface, through expression, what lies "hidden" within. As Wilde writes in *De Profundis*, "at every single moment of one's life one is what one is going to be no less than what one has been. Art is a symbol because man is a symbol" (476). These words echo Walter Pater's observation in his conclusion to *The Renaissance: Studies in Art and Poetry* (238) that art "comes to you proposing frankly to give nothing but the highest quality to your moments as they pass, and simply for those moments' sake." Like Pater, Baudelaire, and Huysmans, then, Wilde insists on art's autonomy, adding the idea that man can be a work of art, even a masterpiece. As Wilde writes in "The Soul of Man Under Socialism" (285), "What a man really has is what is in him. What is outside of him should be a matter of no importance."

Aestheticism, as opposed to actual experience, allows the individual self-perfecting development. As Wilde writes in "The Critic as Artist" (221), "Aesthetics, like sexual selection, make life lovely and wonderful, fill it with new forms, and give it progress, and variety, and change." Wilde applies this value to the individual: "What Individualism seeks to disturb is monotony of type, slavery of custom, tyranny of habit, and the reduction of man to the level of a machine"

("Soul" 293). Like the title character of Pater's *Marius the Epicurean*, Wilde's individual refuses to adhere to any single interest in order to maintain this variety and change. Further, the individual refines him/herself not through actual experience or action but through contemplation, aesthetic experience, and expression. Action maims and mars the individual by subjecting him to pain and peril; art, on the other hand, shields the individual from hurt while providing access to joy and sorrow. Because of its inherent humanity, Wilde privileges expression over action: "It is very much more difficult to talk about a thing than to do it [. . .] There is no mode of action, no form of emotion, that we do not share with the lower animals. It is only by language that we rise above them, or above each other" ("Critic" 132). Verbal expression allows the individual self-objectification because "expression is the only mode under which [the individual] can conceive life at all. To him, what is dumb is dead" (*De Profundis* 481). The individual best achieves perfection through forms of art because such forms possess self-consciousness, completeness, coherence, and correspondence of form and spirit:

> As a physiologist and psychologist, [Aristotle] knows that the health of a function resides in energy. To have a capacity for a passion and not to realise it, is to make oneself incomplete and limited. The mimic spectacle of life that Tragedy affords cleanses the bosom of much 'perilous stuff,' and by presenting high and worthy objects for the exercise of the emotions purifies and spiritualises the man.
>
> ("Critic" 40)

Wilde thus supports the aesthetic experience Pater propounds in his conclusion because "[i]n the spectacle of the lives of those who have never existed one [finds] the true secret of joy and [weeps] away one's tears over their deaths who, like Cordelia and Brabantio, can never die" ("Critic" 74).

Wilde presents examples of successful Decadent individuals throughout his work. Lord Goring of *An Ideal Husband* derives "everything" from himself, asking almost nothing from the world around him. He thus enjoys a security that the title character Lord Chiltern entirely lacks. Goring represents the self-originating and self-absorbed Decadent individual most aptly in his exchange with his valet in act 2 when he observes that "fashion is what one wears oneself. What is unfashionable is what other people wear [. . .] Just as vulgarity is simply the conduct of other people [. . .] And falsehoods the truths of other people [. . .] The only possible society is oneself" (137-39).

Lord Goring's self-contemplation admirably contrasts with Robert Chiltern's conformative probity and sensible marriage with a good woman (145). The latter's probity's coming into question almost destroys his marriage with a too good woman. Lord Chiltern has himself succumbed to Baron Arnheim's influence, taking from him the "shallow" creed that power over the world was the one thing worth having (81). In order to obtain wealth and power, he sells to Arnheim private information, thus becoming vulnerable to Mrs. Cheveley's blackmail. Lord Goring, in contrast, remains inviolable, himself defeating Mrs. Cheveley's attempt at blackmailing him into marrying her. He later receives his "reward" by marrying Mabel Chiltern who, unlike Lady Chiltern, only wants her husband to "be what he chooses" (239).

Similarly, Ernest Worthing of *The Importance of Being Earnest* proves his self-"worth" not by discovering his parents' identity but by having himself arranged the vital statistics of his life with remarkable prescience: his name is indeed Ernest; he has indeed a brother, Algernon Moncrieff. Further, the women of this play prove suitable counterparts to the men. Gwendolen Fairfax, despite having fallen in love with a man named Jack, achieves her self-generated ambition of marrying an Ernest. And Cecily Cardew not only derives an entire courtship out of herself, from its wooing and marriage proposal to its quarrels and reconciliations, but also easily incorporates the object of her affection, when he actually appears, into her creation.

Wilde presents successful Decadent individuals in not only his comedies but also his prose works, most notably the Man in "The House of Judgment," who denies God's power to condemn him to either heaven or hell because he has "never in no place [. . .] been able to imagine [hell or heaven]" (*Poems in Prose* 211). And Wilde emblemizes the successful Decadent individual in *The Portrait of W. H.* through the actor Willie Hughes, the homoerotic W. H. of Shakespeare's sonnets. This Willie Hughes is so self-originating that he is, like a fine lie, his own evidence ("Decay" 14). His existence makes no reference at all to external facts; rather, he derives solely from "himself," as Shakespeare expresses him in the Sonnets. Indeed, his physical portrait, itself a forgery, far from offering concrete proof of his existence only leaves the narrator Gilbert a prey to perpetual doubt and uncertainty concerning the actual existence of Willie Hughes.

These individuals comprehend the positive creative and original qualities of Decadence. Nevertheless, when discussing Wilde's Decadence, critics focus not on these characters but on the unsuccessful Decadent individuals Dorian Gray and Salome. In his chapter "The Damnation of Decadence," from *London in the 1890s*, Karl Beckson, for instance, includes only these two characters' respective works. About *Dorian Gray,* he writes, this "most famous Decadent novel of the British 1890s [. . .] sums up – and radicalizes – much that Wilde had read in Pater and in French literature" (47). And he describes how *Salome* fuses "erotic Decadence and Christian myth" (51).

In particular, critics assign Dorian's hedonism, immorality, and androgyny to decadence; likewise, they point to his portrait's corruption and decay as illustrating this decadence. For example, Barbara Belford writes,

> One is never sure of the extent of Dorian's sins, but it is his disregard for humanity and lack of generosity rather than any sexual act that determine his destruction [. . .] when Lord Henry wants to seduce Dorian into the hedonistic life, he supplies him with a "poisonous" book, assumed to be *À rebours*, Wilde's bible of the Decadence. (173)

Thomas Wright (218) examines what he calls "the decadent sections of the novel" to point to its precursors in Pater, Théophile Gautier, and Huysmans:

> The decadent sections of the novel, such as chapter 11, in which Dorian delights in such artistic pleasures as music, perfumes, embroidery, jewels, and stones [has] Théophile Gautier [as] an important influence [. . .] Wilde's most significant precursor was [. . .] J.-K. Huysmans, whose novel *À Rebours* influenced the subject and the style of *Dorian Gray*, especially its jeweled and purple passages.

If these qualities of guilt and connoisseurship along with his interaction with his portrait helped Dorian realize himself, then they would be Decadent and "golden." But he "delights" in the artistic pleasures of chapter 11, for example, not for their own sake but to escape himself. Indeed, almost from the beginning of his story, Dorian deflects self-development through absorption with not himself but his portrait.

This novel presents three characters in all who betray and lose themselves by succumbing to externals and external influence. Basil Hallward, the artist, suffers his true death, the death of his soul, when he becomes "absorbed" by Dorian Gray: "He is all my art to me now" (11). This absorption stifles Basil's variety and freedom of expression and self-realization.

After Dorian behaves thoughtlessly and cruelly to both Basil Hallward and Sibyl Vane, Basil feels that he has "given away [his] whole soul to someone who treats it as if it were a flower to put in his coat, a bit of decoration to charm his vanity, an ornament for a summer's day" (14). In an interesting parallel, then, Basil becomes a trivialized version of Dorian's portrait, a piece of decorative art. Basil's version, though, emphasizes life's transitoriness while Dorian's portrait's stasis – transferred to Dorian – has the bleakness of an ever-increasing winter's blight.

When he loses Dorian to Lord Henry's influence, Basil loses his art's inspiration; he never paints as well again. Although he later disclaims any consequences from his thralldom to Dorian, Basil yet acknowledges responsibility to him as his voice of conscience, a responsibility for which Dorian exacts a fitting punishment. Dorian murders Basil and has his body chemically disintegrated – as thoroughly as if he had indeed been nothing more than a flower, a summer's decoration.

Basil Hallward's dependence on Dorian Gray for his art's inspiration finds its echo in Lord Henry Wotton who condemns influence as immoral: "All influence is immoral [. . .] because to influence a person is to give him one's own soul. He does not think his natural thoughts, or burn with his natural passions [. . .] He becomes an echo of someone else's music" (21). Lord Henry who, purportedly, never says a moral or does an immoral thing, nevertheless commits the "immoral" act of trying to influence Dorian. "Yes," he thinks to himself, "he would try to be to Dorian Gray what, without knowing it, the lad was to the painter [. . .] He would seek to dominate him [. . .] make that wonderful spirit his own" (44).

Through this resolve, however, Lord Henry loses his own spirit. Like Basil Hallward, Lord Henry fades away and, by the end of the novel, loses whatever Individualism he possessed. For example, the man who had acclaimed marriage's ability to organize a complex personality through lies and masks laments his wife's desertion: "The house is rather lonely without her. Of course, married life is merely a habit – a bad habit. But then one regrets the loss even of one's worst habits" (257). Failure for Decadents is to form habits, not lose them. Also, when Dorian tries to confess to Lord Henry his having murdered Basil, Lord Henry fails to absorb this difference, this complex event into his personality; instead, he contradicts Dorian, laughs at him, and refuses to understand him.

Lord Henry becomes, in effect, an echo of himself, a type of mirror image of Dorian who puts into action what Lord Henry's soul concocts: "There was something terribly enthralling in the exercise of influence" (43), Lord Henry learns to his own detriment. He becomes untrue to himself, as he enjoys the sensation of influencing Dorian: "No other activity was like it. To project one's soul into some gracious form [. . .] to convey one's temperament into another, as though it were a subtle fluid or a strange perfume: there was real joy in that" (43). He succeeds so well in projecting his soul into Dorian that Lord Henry becomes but half a man; he becomes heartless. He lacks the complexity he advocates, as appears when he considers telling Dorian that "art had a soul but [. . .] man had not" (261).

Although Dorian acknowledges his having absorbed Lord Henry Wotton's temperament when he says that "I am putting [one of Lord Henry's aphorisms] into practice, as I do everything you say" (56), he does not lose himself to Lord Henry. Rather, he loses himself to his own portrait when he influences this external object, this finished work of art, by imposing upon it his heart's desire: "If thought could exercise its influence upon a living organism, might not thought exercise an influence upon dead and inorganic things?" (128). Dorian realizes his desire to influence something external to himself when he declares that he would give everything, even his own soul, to retain youth and beauty.

In a strange echo of Lord Henry's desire to influence Dorian, Dorian Gray succeeds in conveying into another object his temperament, as though it were a subtle fluid or a strange perfume. At first, the "horrible sympathy" (127) and "strange affinity" (128) between the picture and himself seems to intensify Dorian's self-consciousness. For instance, it makes him "conscious of how unjust, how cruel, he had been to Sibyl Vane" when he rejects her (115). He does not, however, express this self-realization, at first, because it comes after Sibyl Vane has already committed suicide, and later, because he does not want to do so. When observing the picture's transformation, Dorian momentarily considers praying in order to break "the horrible sympathy that existed between him and the picture [. . .] It had changed in answer to a prayer; perhaps in answer to a prayer it might remain unchanged" (127). But he resists such a prayer, fatalistically accepting his relationship with the picture as a *fait accompli*. Then he consoles himself with the pleasure he will derive from watching it carry the burden of his actions:

> For there would be a real pleasure in watching it. He would be able to follow his mind into its secret places. This portrait would be to him the most magical of mirrors. As it had revealed to him his own body, so it would reveal to him his own soul [. . .] Not one blossom of his loveliness would ever fade. Not one pulse of his life would ever weaken. Like the gods of the Greeks, he would be strong, and fleet, and joyous. What did it matter what happened to the coloured image on the canvas? He would be safe. That was everything. (128)

As Charles Bernheimer (60) writes, "Dorian equates his soul, that is,
his moral center, his essential being, with a perfectly static image of
his unchanging physical beauty." Not he but the "misshapen
shadow" bears the burden of his soul's realization (169), the passions that "find terrible outlet" (144), and the evil dreams that become real.

Consequently, his personality simplifies as he loses his creative,
imaginative will: "Men and women at such moments lose the freedom of their will. They move to their terrible ends as automatons
move. Choice is taken from them." Dorian Gray becomes "callous,
concentrated on evil" (230). Even this concentration on evil could
have been a form of Decadent self-realization had Dorian maintained a stance of inaction, detachment, and observation.

For example, Dorian discovers his own "world spirit and its various moods" when he contemplates the yellow-backed novel Lord
Henry gives him; this living in his imagination allows Dorian momentarily to manifest extraordinary complexity:

> One had ancestors in literature [. . .] There were times when
> it appeared to Dorian Gray that the whole of history was
> merely the record of his own life, not as he had lived it in
> circumstances, but as his imagination had created it for
> him, as it had been in his brain and in his passions. (173)

And when contemplating his ancestor's portraits, Dorian realizes
himself through Lady Elizabeth Devereaux as well as George Wil-
loughby of the eighteenth century and Lord Beckenham of the Regency days. But the multi-valent identity that these portraits suggest
remains external to Dorian, embodied by his picture and its "evil"
changes. Rather than internalize this identity through self-
expression, Dorian resorts to action.

Consequently, even the philosophy he considers promulgating, the New Hedonism, fails to develop Dorian, for ultimately it serves him as a means of escape – not into pleasure, but from himself:

> For these treasures [gems, ecclesiastical vestments, etc.], and everything that he collected in his lovely house, were to be to him means of forgetfulness, modes by which he could escape, for a season, from the fear that seemed to him at times to be almost too great to be borne. Upon the walls of the lonely locked room where he had spent so much of his boyhood, he had hung with his own hands the terrible portrait whose changing features showed him the real degradation of his life. (218)

Dorian's error is not that he believes his picture releases him from moral judgment, as critics such as Philip Cohen, Christopher Nassaar, and Epifanio San Juan suggest; or releases him from causality, as Richard Ellmann, for instance, argues. Rather, he thinks it releases him from the expression. As Ed Cohen and Alan Sinfield, among others, note, Wilde vaguely suggests most of Dorian's physical crimes. However, Wilde explicitly depicts Dorian's crimes against Decadent Individualism.

Rather than realize the effects of his rejecting Sibyl Vane, the rejection that leads to her suicide, for example, Dorian allows Lord Henry to rationalize them away. He deliberately avoids expression when he says, "But we will not talk again of what has happened. It has all been a marvelous experience" (125). And he cultivates forgetfulness, saying, "I must sow poppies in my garden" (127).

Absorbing the horror of the picture's change, on the other hand, Basil Hallward insists that Dorian confess himself in prayer. Rather than do that, Dorian stabs Basil, then deliberately resists absorbing this act: "the secret of the whole thing [the murder] was not to realize the situation" (192). As he waits for Alan Campbell, who will destroy Basil's corpse, Dorian draws and reads, trying to keep at bay thoughts of Basil Hallward, the murdered man, the dead thing. For Basil's corpse allies with the picture as a visible emblem of Dorian's deeds.

Far from being able to detach himself from externals, Dorian is haunted by them, haunted by his desire to escape himself. He does not maintain aesthetic detachment and vicarious pleasure. Instead, he resorts again and again to action – as a means of escape.

> Ugliness that had once been hateful to him because it made things real, became dear to him now for that very reason. Ugliness was the one reality. The coarse brawl, the loathsome den, the crude violence of this disordered life, the very vileness of thief and outcast, were more vivid, in their intense actuality of impression, than all the gracious shapes of art, the dreamy shadows of song. They were what he needed for forgetfulness. (228)

As he later laments to Lord Henry, "My own personality has become a burden to me. I want to escape, to go away, to forget" (248).

This desire to forget himself culminates in his attack on his picture when it, like Basil, urges upon him expression rather than action: "Confess? Did it mean that he was to confess?" (269). Instead of detaching himself from the picture, contemplating and absorbing himself through it, Dorian sees it as evidence he must destroy. So he stabs it and, thereby, himself; he thus unwittingly identifies himself through his picture, an identification he has resisted. Wilde leaves the knife not in the picture but in Dorian Gray to illustrate the failure to absorb the picture, the art, that constitutes Dorian Gray's fatal error, his perversion of Decadence.

The female type of this perversion occurs with Salome, a character and play that also epitomizes decadence for many critics. However, Salome, like Dorian, fails in self-realization and self-absorption when she rejects imagination and thought for action. Like Dorian when he relies on contemplation and imagination, Salome potentially transforms a succession of identities into intense self-realization. Each of her identities – virgin/whore, princess/dead woman – overlap, like the layers of veils she dons then doffs for her dance. Yet her thwarted will, her thwarted love, unravels this intensification, strips her multiplied selves down to a concentration, a single focus on her physical desire for Iokanaan.

This loss of Decadent identity fans out to other characters, to perspectives other than Salome's. For example, the Page of Herodias and the young Syrian confuse God's identity. He is unseen like Iokanaan; He is fond of blood like Salome (264). They also confuse Iokanaan's identity: he is the prophet Abraham; he is Jesus Christ. Iokanaan confuses Herodias with Salome: she has drunk the wine of iniquities and succumbed to the concupiscence of her eyes; she has become drunk with Iokanaan's voice (270). Herod confuses himself with the King of Cappadocia: "He [Iokanaan] is not speaking about me. Nothing that he says is ever against me" (284-85). Each character seems both identifiable and unidentifiable, seems like Jesus Christ, who is "everywhere [. . .] but [. . .] hard to find" (281).

In effect, the characters in this play, but most particularly Salome, lack Decadent subjectivity. And Salome's fate illustrates the danger of this failed subjectivity. Gilbert (147) calls Salome "Wilde's daring exploration of the possibilities and limits of a self-reflexive life." Also, Shewan (135) describes Salome as "the supreme egotist of a cast imprisoned by indifference or introspection." Indeed, the characters reflect only partial aspects of Salome without absorbing or accepting her differences to either themselves or their conceptions of her. Although they systematically confuse their identity with hers, they do not see like God; they do not see everything.

The page sees the moon as a "dead woman. She might be seeking for the dead" (263). The Young Syrian, on the other hand, sees it as "a princess with little white doves for feet [who] might be dancing" (263). As Salome later prepares to dance, Herod declares that "Your little white feet will be like white doves. They will resemble white flowers" (263). Thus Salome's partial identities accumulate. Soon to die, she seeks for the dead; she "kills" the Young Syrian by looking at him: "If I [the Page of Herodias] had hidden him [the Young Syrian] in a cave she would not have seen him" and he would not have committed suicide (274). With her dance, Salome seeks to kill Iokanaan who hides in a cave and will not look at her.

Salome sees her own virginal aspect in the moon: "She [the Moon] is cold and chaste [. . .] I am positive that she is a virgin" (264). But Herod sees the moon as "a madwoman [. . .] seeking everywhere for lovers [. . .] She reels through the clouds like a drunken woman" (274). After hearing Iokanaan's voice, Salome becomes drunk – like the drunken woman/Moon – "with the wine of Iokanaan's voice, drunk with the wine of iniquities" (273), as she seeks "everywhere" for lovers.

This virginal Salome imagines Iokanaan to be like herself: "I am sure that he is chaste, chaste as the moon [. . .] His flesh must be very cold, like ivory" (271). She is sensual; he, ascetic. She lives on the surface; he, in the depths of the cistern. And he describes her as her own opposite: "The Wanton! the Prostitute [. . .] Let them crush her beneath their shields" (282).

Even though presenting Salome's potential Decadent individuality through these simplistic dichotomies of virgin/whore, princess/dead woman, Wilde does suggest that Salome could extend her experience through self-cultivation in these aesthetic exchanges with other characters, most especially with Iokanaan. Wilde reduces morality, principles, and integrity to sensations that allow self-cultivation through absorption of "difference," thus presenting Decadence as a powerful mode of self-realization.

But Iokanaan denies Salome their potential exchange of consciousness. This man of the depths, the dark, the shadow, ignores what Wolfgang Iser calls the disturbing quality of "luminous beauty as pure appearances," the "generative matrix of [. . .] opaque appearances" that Salome manifests (63-65). He prefers instead the invisible mystery of God: "I do not wish to listen to you. I hear none but the words of the Lord God" (272).

These simplistic dichotomies – that could be extended through self-cultivation – appear also in the play's opposing descriptions of Iokanaan: his body is white like lilies; it is like "a plastered wall where vipers have crawled" (273); his hair is like clusters of grapes; his hair is "like a knot of serpents coiled round thy neck" (274).

He resists Salome, refusing to look at her. His adamantine rejection hardens her nature until Salome's will, her desire, focuses only on his mouth – not on his whole physical and spiritual being but on the too feminine hole of his mouth: "It is thy mouth that I desire, Iokanaan" (274). Rather than becoming masculine, absorbing masculine characteristics – and thus surpassing the female stereotypes of virgin/whore – Salome fails to realize her extended self when her desire for Iokanaan centers on his mouth. Other critics have noticed this gender appropriation on Salome's part. As Helen Tookey writes,

> Salome ascribes to Jokanaan *female* signifiers [. . .] we may
> perhaps read in the lines [Salome's to Iokanaan's head] both
> a further hint of the homoerotic nature of Salome's desire
> and a final image of menstrual sexuality: the taste of love,
> for Salome, is the taste of blood. (35)

As he seeks the cover the cistern affords, Iokanaan seems as "the hand of a dead woman pulling at her shroud to cover herself" (270). Salome's perverted, thwarted self-realization begins as she pulls off her veils to uncover herself. And her dance of the seven veils perverts Decadence because she paradoxically dances not in a self-realizing form of expression but as a simple, straightforward action. With it, her perverted, rather than creative, will desires to win Iokanaan's head. Heidi Hartwig (25) argues that this dance is not action but a form of aesthetic expression because it "is performed in exchange for an oath" and so is a "speech act." However, Salome does not realize herself with this expression; rather, she gains Iokanaan's decapitated head.

Because of this dance, Peter Raby (116) compares *Salome* with Yeats's plays, especially with *The Death of Cuchulain*: "Yeats's use of the dancer suggests a process of refining through successive experiments until he reaches the purity of his last dance. It does not seem far from the kind of theatre Wilde was intuitively making." Gilbert also believes that Salome's dance strips her down to her essence. But Salome's refinement seems only simplification, only loss of potential complexity. As Jane Marcus points out, Salome's possessing John's head on a platter shows the resisting John "only half a man" (102). By resorting to dangerous action to effect her exchange with Iokanaan, Salome shows herself as only half a woman – as not "virgin" and "Prostitute" (and thus complicating gendered stereotypes) but as "Prostitute" alone. She does not depict, as Regenia Gagnier believes, "the triumph of sexual love over the repressive forces of society" (169). Rather, Salome's "triumph" only sterilizes her creative imagination.

Her hardened nature deafens Salome to Herod's pleas that she ask for another reward than Iokanaan's head. She even resists his prediction that Iokanaan's head will offer only a sexual intensification: "A man's decapitated head is an ugly thing, do you not realize? Not a thing for a virgin to look at" (289).

When looking at Iokanaan's severed head, Salome states the great truth that "Love is greater than the mystery of death" (295). This statement paradoxically revitalizes the figure of Jesus Christ as a self-realized individual who expresses the mystery of love being greater than the mystery of death. But Salome, a failed Decadent individual, relates neither love and art, nor love and imagination, but love and death. Consequently, she speaks of her deathly physical desire for Iokanaan as love: "I have kissed your mouth. Your lips had a bitter taste. Was it the taste of blood? [. . .] Perhaps it was the taste of love" (295). In her sterile, fruitless and yet active (rather than contemplative) exchange, Salome possesses only her simplified self; with Iokanaan's decapitated head, she consummates her self-marriage with what critics like Nassaar and Frank Kermode see as only the archetypal, cruel and destructive woman.

Herod perceives Salome's monstrous identity illuminated in a shaft of moonlight. And his reaction, his order to the soldiers to "Kill that woman" emphasizes Salome's simplified identification as a "wanton" or "prostitute" (295). The soldiers crush her to death beneath their shields as Wilde resoundingly identifies her: "Salome, daughter of Herodias, Princess of Judea" (295).

Wilde relished the positive opportunities that Decadence afforded the individual. While his works can hardly be called "prescriptive," they do offer readers successful as well as unsuccessful Decadent individuals. That in perverting Decadence both Dorian Gray and Salome fail to realize themselves and so end tragically casts into relief this positive view of Decadence that Wilde holds and supports.

Works Cited

Beckson, Karl. *London in the 1890s: A Cultural History*. New York: W. W. Norton, 1992.

Belford, Barbara. *Oscar Wilde: A Certain Genius*. New York: Random House, 2000.

Bernheimer, Charles. "Unknowing Decadence." *Perennial Decay: On the Aesthetics and Politics of Decadence*. Ed. Liz Constable, Dennis Denisoff and Matthew Potolsky. Philadelphia: U of Pennsylvania P, 1999. 50-64.

Cohen, Ed. *Talk on the Wilde Side: Toward a Genealogy of a Discourse on Male Sexualities.* New York: Routledge, 1993.

Cohen, Philip. *The Moral Vision of Oscar Wilde.* Cranbury: Associated UP, 1978.

Dellamora, Richard. "Productive Decadence: 'The Queer Comradeship of Outlawed Thought: Vernon Lee, Max Nordau, and Oscar Wilde." *New Literary History: A Journal of Theory and Interpretation* 35.4 (2004): 529-46.

Dollimore, Jonathan. "Desire and Difference: Homosexuality, Race and Masculinity." *Race and Subject Masculinities.* Ed. Harry Stecopoulos. Durham: Duke UP, 1997. 17-44.

Dowling, Linda. *Language and Decadence in the Victorian Fin de Siècle.* Oxford: Princeton UP, 1989.

---. "The Decadent and the New Woman in the 1890's," *Nineteenth-Century Fiction.* 33.4 (1979): 434-53.

Ellmann, Richard. *Oscar Wilde.* New York: Alfred A. Knopf, 1988.

Gagnier, Regenia. *Idylls of the Marketplace: Oscar Wilde and the Victorian Public.* Stanford: Stanford UP, 1986.

Gilbert, Elliot L. "Tumult of Images: Wilde, Beardsley, and *Salome.*" *Victorian Studies* 26.2 (1983): 133-59.

Hartwig, Heidi. "Dancing for an Oath: Salome's Revaluation of Word and Gesture." *Modern Drama* 45.1 (2002): 23-34.

Iser, Wolfgang. *Walter Pater: The Aesthetic Moment.* Trans. David Henry Wilson. European Studies in English Literature. Cambridge: Cambridge UP, 1987.

Kermode, Frank. *The Romantic Image.* New York: Routledge, 2001.

Marcus, Jane. "*Salome*: The Jewish Princess was a New Woman." *Bulletin of the New York Public Library* 78 (1976-77): 95-112.

Nassaar, Christopher S. *Into the Demon Universe: A Literary Exploration of Oscar Wilde.* New Haven: Yale UP, 1974.

Pater, Walter. *The Renaissance: Studies in Art and Poetry.* Ed. Adam Phillips. Oxford: Oxford UP, 1986.

Raby, Peter. *Oscar Wilde.* Cambridge: Cambridge UP, 1988.

San Juan, Epifanio. *The Art of Oscar Wilde.* Princeton: Princeton UP, 1967.

Sinfield, Alan. *The Wilde Century: Effeminacy, Oscar Wilde and the Queer Moment.* New York: Columbia UP, 1994.

Swart, Konraad W. *The Sense of Decadence in Nineteenth-Century France.* The Hague: Marginus Niijhoff, 1964.

Tookey, Helen. "'The Fiend That Smites with a Look': The Monstrous/Menstruous Woman and the Danger of the Gaze in Oscar Wilde's *Salome.*" *Literature and Theology: An International Journal of Religion, Theory, and Culture* 18.1 (2004): 23-37.

Wilde, Oscar. "The Critic as Artist." *Intentions.* Ed. Robert Ross. London: Methuen, 1904. 99-224. Vol. 7 of *The Complete Writings of Oscar Wilde.* 10 vols.

---. "The Decay of Lying." *Intentions.* Ed. Robert Ross. London: Methuen, 1904. 3-57. Vol. 7 of *The Collected Writings of Oscar Wilde.* 10 vols.

---. *De Profundis. The House of Pomegranates.* Ed. Robert Ross. London: Methuen, 1904. 29-165. Vol. 3 of *The Collected Writings of Oscar Wilde.* 10 vols.

---. *An Ideal Husband. The Duchess of Padua.* Ed. Robert Ross. London: Methuen, 1904. 1-239. Vol. 1 of *The Complete Writings of Oscar Wilde.* 10 vols.

---. *The Importance of Being Earnest. Salome, The Importance of Being Earnest.* Ed. Robert Ross. London: Methuen, 1904. 1-187. Vol. 2 of *The Complete Writings of Oscar Wilde.* 10 vols.

---. *The Picture of Dorian Gray. Dorian Gray.* Ed. Robert Ross. London: Methuen, 1904. 1-272. Vol. 10 of *The Complete Writings of Oscar Wilde.* 10 vols.

---. *Poems in Prose. Lord Arthur Saville's Crime.* Ed. Robert Ross. London: Methuen, 1904. 203-19. Vol. 8 of *The Complete Writings of Oscar Wilde.* 10 vols.

---. "The Rise of Historical Criticism." *Miscellanies.* Ed. Robert Ross. London: Methuen, 1904. 181-228. Vol. 6 of *The Collected Writings of Oscar Wilde.* 10 vols.

---. *Salome. Salome, The Importance of Being Earnest.* Ed. Robert Ross. London: Methuen, 1904. 1-82. Vol. 2 of *The Complete Writings of Oscar Wilde.* 10 vols.

---. "The Soul of Man Under Socialism." *Intentions.* Ed. Robert Ross. London: Methuen, 1904. 273-335. Vol. 7 of *The Collected Writings of Oscar Wilde.* 10 vols.

Shewan, Robert. *Oscar Wilde: Art and Egotism.* London: Macmillan, 1977.

Wright, Thomas. "Oscar Wilde's *The Picture of Dorian Gray.*" *British Writers: Classics, Volume II.* New York: Scribner's, 2004: 211-28.

A Moment's Fixation:
Aesthetic Time and Dialectical Progress

Paul Fox
Zayed University

Abstract: The late nineteenth-century polity encouraged a faith in progress and a nostalgia for past glories that was necessarily based on a linear model of time. I analyze the manner in which the Decadent Movement broke from this model and introduced a synthetic concept of time, one that privileged the aesthetic moment.

In his funeral oration for Victoria, Lord Salisbury, her last Prime Minister, remarked that future historians would look back upon the changes undergone by Britain during the old Queen's reign as exemplifying a "constant increase of public prosperity, without any friction to endanger the peace or stability of our civil life and at the same time with a constant expansion of an Empire which every year grows more and more powerful" (qtd. in Beckson 376). This presentation of time as limitless progress into the future was the common line drawn out by the late nineteenth-century polity. But along with such an optimistic view came dire warnings of potential disaster. In 1897, for Victoria's jubilee, Kipling (262) wrote perhaps his most famous verse "Recessional" in which he claimed that "all our pomp of yesterday / Is one with Ninevah and Tyre," that the Empire, like those ancient cities, was in danger of terminal decline. The poem was originally entitled "After," before being sent to press in the *Times* newspaper, and this former title suggests Salisbury's politically representative eulogy with its emphasis on living up to past glories and the present's relationship to that past. As Gilmour (123) states in *The Long Recessional*, his biography of Kipling, "the response to the poem was astounding, surprising even the author, [. . .] now widely acclaimed the 'Laureate of the Empire.'" The poem clearly proclaimed that which the general public was used to hearing, and wanted to hear: of past splendors and the need for constant vigilance to defend a rightful inheritance.

Both Salisbury's speech at Victoria's funeral and "Recessional" maintain this same conception of time as linear, moving from past to future; if the poet's tone is pessimistic and the politician's buoyant, that is secondary to the presentiment that the present is simply a moment on a longer pathway, whether toward greater glories or disaster being as yet unknown. Past and future are thusly privileged at the expense of the present, the present employed simply as a means toward politic ends. The dialectic of progress and potential degeneration removes the nineteenth century's focus from contemporary time in its emphasis on history and the future.

Kipling's poem does not diagnose an irreversible trend. The political paradigm of progress/ regress requires hope that the future will not be one of cataclysmic failure. The refrain of "Recessional" explains that the poem is written "Lest we forget" and encourages a remembrance of things past as both bolster for the present and spur toward a hopefully gilded future, one simultaneously deserved and requiring effort to claim it. If Kipling holds out little hope for such splendid outcomes, he is only representative of his society's obsessive regard for warning signs of cultural and national decline. And the poet was by no means the lone spokesman of his historical moment.

One of the best-selling books of the 1890s was the Austro-Hungarian Max Nordau's *Degeneration* (1893), translated into English in 1895 and an immediate bestseller, going through several reprints in a few years.[1] It is a vitriolic jeremiad upon the then con-

---

[1] Nordau is the critic to whom most 1890s critics and artists responded. He was only one of many authors publishing texts expressing concern with, and charting the downward path of, society's cultural and moral degeneration. R. K. R. Thornton discusses some of these texts, most notably Havelock Ellis' "A Note on Paul Bourget" (1889), and Cesare Lombroso's "Atavism and Evolution"

temporary trends in European art and literature, and reads like a *Who's Who* of the most famous literary names of the period: Nietzsche, Shaw, Ibsen, Tolstoy and Wilde, amongst others, come in for vituperative condemnation as unhealthy degenerates. The fact that the most prominent artistic movement of the 1890s in England had been named 'Decadent' and that the decade's moniker of *fin de siècle* emphasized the unhappy conclusion of something generally considered, in Salisbury's typical view, glorious, underlines this compulsion to scrutinise the nation's health, to examine the body politic for symptoms of corruption. That this corruption was generally referred to in temporal terms as 'degenerative,' 'decadent,' and 'regressive' would suggest that the artistic milieu was one which opposed the potential for progress along the line of time; instead, at best partaking in, and at worst encouraging, this perceived decline from past splendor. Alison Hennegan discusses Nordau's portrayal of

a lurid picture of a century engulfed in a tidal wave of neurasthenia, indecency, female erotomania, diabolism and some ill-defined but much feared 'unnaturalness' [. . .] Degenerate, once solely an adjective, had become a noun: people could be 'degenerates'. This change (in which a grammatical shift accurately reflects a considerable movement in thought) is important for the period [. . .] First iden-

---

(1895; 10, 38). Thornton makes clear the reliance of many of the texts of the period on the then dominant scientific discourse of Darwin, and the importance of Classical studies at Oxbridge in the cultural belief of the British nation (1-10). Charles Bernheimer has made a detailed analysis of the work of Nordau and Lombroso in terms of their Darwinian context in his book *Decadent Subjects* (139-62). A broader nineteenth-century history of the development of concepts of degeneration is discussed in Daniel Pick's *Faces of Degeneration*. My concern in this essay is primarily that of the aesthetic response to this discursive paradigm.

tify accurately the enemy, then isolate, eject, eradicate it, and all will be well. The body politic is purged of its canker. (189)

Hennegan employs the same metaphors of illness and health, of change, "movement" and periods in time to articulate Nordau's own position, one that ironically is based upon the very system of linear temporality, of the dialectic of progress and regress, for which Nordau claims disdain. As Bernheimer (*Decadent Subjects* 161) has written of the Austro-Hungarian author, "many more of the traits he applies to degenerates could be used to describe qualities of his own writing – hysterical, egotistic, unbalanced, emotional, pessimistic, imitative." And yet the text was one of the most popular of its decade. Clearly the vitriol of *Degeneration* catered to the tastes of its popular audience.

However, it is not that the Decadent artists of the Nineties were unconcerned with this prevailing sense of decline. Indeed, the cultural disagreement concerning Decadence and the movement's role in undercutting moral and spiritual values is apparent in Holbrook Jackson's near contemporary account of the period:

The Eighteen Nineties, however, were not entirely decadent and hopeless; and even their decadence was often decadence only in name, for much of the genius denounced by Max Nordau as degeneration was a sane and healthy expression of a vitality which, as it is not difficult to show, would have been better named regeneration. (23)

It is interesting to note that even a critic sympathetic to the aesthetic of the period discusses Decadence in dialectical terms, of regeneration and degeneration, health and sickness inflected by a linear model of time. The impact of the cultural discussion on the artists themselves would seem to be similarly rendered: one need only think of Ernest Dowson's poignant lament that the days of wine and roses are not long, of Dorian Gray's desire to remain young and beautiful, of Yeats' glamorization of the "Tragic Generation" of his dead contemporaries of youth. But rather than accepting the linear conception of time, with its seemingly oppositional progressive/ regressive binary, I would suggest that the so-called, and often self-styled, "Decadent" artists were consciously seeking a temporal model that opposed the weight of history along with its expectations for the future, that deliberately rejected Kipling's warnings concerning forgetting, Nordau's of degeneration, and proposed art as contrary to, and a redemption from, time.

The temporal model forwarded by Decadence was one of the "moment," but a peculiar form of presentism unburdened by history.[2] Its chief proponent in England had been Walter Pater, and the basis for the aesthetic of the Nineties was the conclusion to his study of the Renaissance, a text published in 1873, but still being referred to by Wilde almost two decades later as his own "Golden Book." Pater's radical departure from the contemporary liberal progressivism is remarked upon by Peter Allan Dale when he writes,

> Where the inspiration for Pater's aesthetic philosophy is coming from ultimately is, in fact, not the nineteenth-century empiricist tradition at all but the more ancient em-

---

[2] The manner in which artists of the late nineteenth century represented history is a telling trait of an aesthetic that rejected the 'truth' of the past. Pater, Wilde and Beardsley, to name just those artists I deal with in this essay, all made use of the redrawing of past time in favor of a more appealing, because aesthetically rendered, fiction of the moment. The title of *Studies in the History of the Renaissance* was changed in the second edition of 1877 to *The Renaissance; Studies in Art and Poetry*, to emphasize the impressionistic and aesthetic, rather than the factual and historical aspects of Pater's text. Jan B. Gordon suggests further, when she writes of Pater's alteration of the title, that "he recognized that history is redeemed by its transposition to art. It is surely evidence of the extent to which nineteenth-century historicism is challenged" (40).

piricist [. . .] tradition which had not yet learned the modern faith in endless intellectual and material progress. (182)

The illiberal life described by Pater in the conclusion had been infamous from its publication, being almost single-handedly responsible for the artistic perspective of a generation of aesthetes and Decadents.[3] Of this life he wrote:

> Fix upon it in one of its more exquisite intervals, the moment, for instance, of delicious recoil from the flood of water in the summer heat. What is the whole physical life in that moment but a combination of natural elements to which science gives their names? [. . .] Our physical life is a perpetual motion of them [. . .] This at least of flame-like our life has, that it is but the concurrence, renewed from moment to moment, of forces parting sooner or later on their ways. (150)

Pater clearly recognizes the flux of existence caused by the movement of linear time, but sees in the moment a chance to "fix upon" what is not simply important in life, but its only, and saving, grace. This art of the moment is employed "proposing frankly to give nothing but the highest quality to your moments as they pass, and simply for those moments' sake" (153). To discriminate the moment of concurrence is, for Pater, the chief aim of the individual, to be able to fix upon the process of experience as it flows by and through us.[4] And the moment is of sole, and solitary, importance.

---

[3] So controversial was the initial publication of the "Conclusion" that it was subsequently removed by Pater from the 1877 edition, to appear again only in later editions after *Marius the Epicurean* had been published in 1885.

[4] Pater wrote that "what is secure in our existence is but the sharp apex of the present moment [. . .] and all that is real in our experience a series of fleeting impressions" (*Marius* 84). In contrast to the moment, 'process' suggests movement along a static line of time toward an inevitable and conclusive end.

Such temporal discrimination is clearly antithetical to a view of linearity (whilst recognizing the actuality of the flow of time), of the present bound up inextricably with the past and the future. It exists as a moment onto itself, exterior to the flux of history. The aesthetic character, along with his impressionistic experience, is described as impermanent, as "that continual vanishing away, that strange, perpetual, weaving and unweaving of ourselves" (152). Pater concludes that the lived experience of the aesthetic man is the impetus for the creation of "poetic passion," the fruit of which is a "quickened, multiplied consciousness" (153).

The artist, then, becomes the site of experience, and in his capacity as an artist orders those experiences by "fixing" upon them, construing them in a way meaningful to his own personality. It is unsurprising, therefore, to see in the texts of the late nineteenth century a great emphasis placed upon making oneself a work of art, upon the importance of developing one's receptive personality and aesthetic consciousness. "Fine art, as Pater understood it, is an expression of self" (Bullen 157). This aesthetic, developed by Pater, and continued by the 1890's generation of Decadent artists, would be to discriminate the moment, inflected by the artist's personality, in, and out of, time. And the re-presentation of history was central to this aesthetic sensibility.[5]

Pater's two major texts, *The Renaissance* and the 1885 novel *Marius the Epicurean*, renegotiate history, forgetting what is inconvenient and unexceptional and reinterpreting from an always present perspective the so-called 'facts' of the past. In a study of his life and work published in 1906, A. C. Benson (92) wrote that *Marius the*

Thus to "fix upon" a moment in time's process is to discriminate a singularity from out of the "fleeting" movement of time.

[5] I use the hyphenated term "re-presentation" to avoid the suggestion of mimetic "representation" and to underline the fictionalization of history, the reproduction of the past in different, and new, guises in the Decadent aesthetic.

Epicurean benefited from its author's only superficial knowledge of Italy, of Pater that this "helped him to make his picture so clear and vivid; he was always at his best when he was amplifying slender hints and recollected glimpses." Benson was a member of the critical camp that recognized the deliberation of the artist in the depiction of history not as fact, but as impressed upon the mind of an individual and one true to his solitary aesthetic temperament. Laurel Brake (31), in a short modern study, suggests this same idea of *The Renaissance* when she writes that "Pater has created a book whose 'subjects' are primarily his theories, language, and style, rather than the Renaissance, the lives of the artists, or their work *per se.*"

The rendition of second-century Rome in decline in *Marius the Epicurean*, as a world seen momentarily through the eyes of its eponymous hero, was of particular resonance with the contemporary Victorian audience. Drawing parallels between the Roman and British Empires was a commonplace (an examination of late nineteenth-century sales figures for Gibbon's *Decline and Fall* make that immediately apparent). But Pater's second- and sixteenth-century Italies were often barely recognizable to his audience, and the author came in for equal amounts of praise and criticism for the license he displayed in his texts. He combined his imaginative and highly individualized rendering of history with a dense allusion to, quotation and translation of, Classical learning, and thereby warped traditional historicity into a novel form. Benson (116) remarks upon Pater having offered to the reading public a "new possibility in the composition of English prose" and praises the imagination required to unify these varied elements. For the artist, remembering is a rememberment, a personal and creative constitution of history where past details are accepted or disregarded as impressed upon the spectator as experientially valuable.[6] Pater's historical method was, and

---

[6] Josephine M. Guy and Ian Small remark upon the re-presentation by Pater of

still is, the basis for the vastly different assessments of his texts. Megan Becker-Leckrone writes,

> The idea that Pater's prose would lead readers to regard its author retrospectively is in keeping with the broader dynamics of his historicism [. . .] critical determinations of historical reference are especially difficult [. . .] because he so studiously invokes the historical past as his immediate context (288).

Pater acknowledges that his own texts will be read as historical documents one day, and he expects the same critical treatment that he employs in his own criticism, one of fluid interpretation meaningful only from each contemporary moment to the next. To enforce an absolute interpretation is to quench the aesthetic life of the artist's perpetual reconfiguration of his past.

Speaking about Nietzsche and his theory of time, one which mirrors Pater's theory closely, Max Nordau (418) froths, "Blow away the lather from these phrases. What do they really say? The fleeting instant of the present is the point of contact of the past and future.

---

a speech by a character from *Marius the Epicurean*. They write:
> Pater describes the Roman Stoic and orator Cornelius Fronto delivering a discourse on 'The Nature of Morals'. From the textual signals in the novel, there is no way in which even the most careful reader may detect that Fronto's discourse is authoritative or less 'real' than any of the other classical source material quoted in the novel [. . .] 'The Nature of Morals' does not exist; nor is there any record of the discourse ever having existed [. . . T]o complicate matters further, in reality, it is not fictional at all, in the sense that it is composed of material derived from the *Meditations* of Marcus Aurelius. Pater, however, edits and reorders Aurelius's work so substantially that in effect it comprises another work. (153-54)

This re-memberment and deliberate misattribution of textual material, apparently historically real, for the artist's own purposes is precisely the method of Decadent aesthetics.

Can one call this self-evident thought a fact?" Nordau's sarcastic query unintentionally touches upon the crux of both the ontological and epistemological concerns of Decadence: what constitutes the self if it is constantly dissolved by the passing of time, and how can it know anything in this maelstrom of dissolution? Nordau presumes on his artistic targets' perception of time, and takes as a given the definition of the present, one that had been reformulated by Pater and his aesthetic heirs. The present for them had become not a 'fact' but a creative expedient, contingent upon a moment's perception and beyond a linear time that must needs bring dissolution in its wake. It is only in living in the moment, beyond the reality of what has come before and what will come thereafter, that the self *can* be evidenced to Pater's mind. This constitution of the present is a fabrication, a pretence, a beautiful lie "of which it may be more truly said that it has ceased to be than that it is" (*Renaissance* 151). And for Pater, this 'truth' of time's passing is precisely what he wishes to escape through his aesthetic revision of time. The moment might be a fiction, but it affords the individual the capacity to *live*, unburdened by a sense of the past that bears down upon every aspect of existence.

This artistic redrawing of linear time was taken up with zest by the authors of the Nineties. In Oscar Wilde's sole novel, Dorian Gray synopsizes within himself "the whole of history" and treats it "merely as the record of his own life, not as he had lived it [. . .] but as his imagination had created it for him" (*Dorian* 113). Such a stylish re-presentation of history in reference solely to oneself at each given moment finds its aesthetic correspondence in the stylistic playfulness of decadent authors. Wilde's constant use of puns in his texts effects a reversal of expectation that plays with contemporary critical views of meaningful linear progress. The necessity to reconstrue verbal moments in Wilde's works matches the Paterian aesthetic and its perpetual reconstitution of comprehension in the texts.

The structuring of Nineties' witticism was also descended from Pater's style, one of the most remarked upon aspects of his works. In the reconfiguration of the prosaic sentence through the use of euphuism Pater disrupts the linearity of sentence structure with an emphasis upon the transient, the contingent and, once more, the momentary. Linda Dowling (130) expresses this in *Language and Decadence in the Victorian Fin de Siècle* writing that Pater "puts off the moment of cognitive closure [. . .] And he does this not simply by writing long sentences, but by so structuring his sentences as to thwart – at times even to the point of disruption – our usual expectations of English syntax." The style that Pater employed denied a teleological function to art and knowledge, relying rather on fragmentary moments of meaning and reconstituted cognition, rejecting the traditional sense of narrative closure. His style, therefore, operates in a fashion antipathetic to expectations of linear progress toward some presumed end. It reflects in its fragmented form the aesthetic philosophy of the moment that Pater had presented in his texts. This formal quality of Pater's (de)composition becomes evident in an anecdote related by Matthew Sturgis (51):

> It is said that he composed his sentences by first writing out the bald argument upon alternate lines of his page and then filling the interstices with qualifying sub-clauses; and then repeating the process. It is believable. As is the tale that, on his death, hundreds of slips of paper were found in his study drawers, each with a disembodied phrase awaiting its place in some still unwritten sentence.

The method of Pater's writing here described highlights the interstitial spaces between literary moments, which become moments themselves as they are filled by Pater. And the overarching philosophy is the ever-*present* refusal to write in a linear manner.

Combining his aesthetic view of history, and the subjectively impressionistic, with his personal style, Pater's language is used to *create* histories, meaningful only for the moment, because constantly dissolved in the passing of time. Meaning alters with each new utterance as with each new impression, as language reconstrues existence and experience. Like Wilde's, Pater's style requires a constant reconstitution of meaning by the reader in his texts. There is no mimetic correspondence between the word and a 'real' second-century or Renaissance world; in fact (or, rather, in fictions) words create Pater's world. The reversal and repetition of construal makes a nonsense of meaning progressing through a text to a given conclusion. There are no conclusions, no ultimate meanings, and this "can be illustrated by citing virtually any passage of *Marius*, where every paragraph is studded with qualifiers, such as 'somewhat,' 'sort of,' 'rather,' 'perhaps,' and so on, and the verbs are more often than not conditional" (Weir 76).

Such a contingency suggests that dissolution and reconstitution are the conditions of existence, conditions which the aesthete embraces as an opportunity for experiencing life constantly, anew and in all its variety. And in his own prose style Pater reflects this view. His use of euphuism as a method of writing reclaims archaism and simultaneously employs neologisms to express meaning. Refurbishing what has gone before anew, whilst simultaneously creating the novel expresses linguistically and stylistically the Decadent theory of the temporal moment. As Wilde reinterprets the historical Salome's story as a symbolist drama, so Aubrey Beardsley, illustrating the published version of the play, reinterprets Wilde's contemporary stature in the literary world, inserting caricatures of him into scenes from the Judaean night.[7] Beardsley's reinterpretation of Wagner's

---

[7] Beardsley famously reworked Wilde's play from his own perspective, rather to the latter's annoyance. As Charles Bernheimer writes of Beardsley: "[T]he

Siegfried as a fey, aesthetic type subordinates pagan Germanic myth to his modern cosmopolitan dandyism.

Max Beerbohm had called the 1890s "the Beardsley decade," a timely attribution to the consumptive artist echoed by Holbrook Jackson (95) when he wrote: "Temporally he was so appropriate that an earlier appearance would have been as premature as a later would have been tardy. It was inevitable that he should have come with *The Yellow Book* and gone with *The Savoy*. The times demanded his presence." So Beardsley, perhaps more than any other artist of the period, was of the moment. And from his letters it is clear, and not surprisingly so, that he was more aware than most of the fleeting nature of time and existence, for he was fully conscious that his consumption was slowly killing him.[8] Jane Haville Desmarais (68) reads attacks on Beardsley's work couched, as is critically usual, in terms of sickness and degeneration, as "reflections of Britain's anxiety about the past and the future." This emphasis on linearity, and the progressive paradigm, Beardsley responded to in his art. A comparison of his early and later work will show that the

---

art of the illustrator, he claims implicitly, need not be subservient to the art of the writer; if the writer veils instead of mirroring nature, so the illustrator veils any resemblance his pictures may have to the external verbal world" (*Decadent Subjects* 135). This reference to art's veiling of nature describes Wilde's, and the Decadent aesthetic, stance against a slavish imitation of 'the real' in both the natural world, but also in the historical.

Lorraine Janzen Kooistra makes a similar point when she writes that Beardsley's approach "is actually authorized by Wilde's own theory for the (un)referential relations between critical and creative enterprises" (132). Wilde's text takes the place of the historical fact for Beardsley, his illustrations becoming the textual re-presentation of this given.

[8] A cursory survey of Beardsley's published letters makes quite apparent the constant return in the artist's mind to his condition (*The Letters of Aubrey Beardsley*).

artist made full use of his pen to reconstrue the movement of linear time in a manner similar to his literary fellows.

The early Arthurian drawings for Malory's *Morte D'Arthur* (1893-94) show Beardsley employing the style of Burne-Jones, representing an historical medievalism, if one somewhat reconfigured by the Pre-Raphaelites. From the artistic line imitating this medieval design of history, Beardsley would end his career contorting the line of his drawings into heavily baroque ornamentation, where linearity is folded back upon itself, highlighting a visual moment captured and stylized into art. The corinthian manner of his drawings is also literarily evident in Beardsley's one major prose work, *Venus and Tannhäuser*. With very little plot, Wagner's version of the story is rewritten to become less a dramatic narrative than a documentation of detail where the language employed pays clear homage to Paterian euphuism, capturing each visual moment in piling linguistic detail upon detail. One must distinguish between this captured momentariness and the action of the moment depicted, such as that of the illustration where the hero struggles through hedges, torn by the twisted lines of the thorns. In its momentariness the drawing warps and weaves the line into what the artist wills. In its depicted linearity, the picture's line is destructive and dangerous, the depiction of temporality's power rather than a controlled, momentary, rendition of it. Such danger is represented in the drawn lines of Beardsley's *The Return of Tannhäuser to the Venusberg* (1896) where the

> contrast between the spiny foliage and Tannhäuser's bare flesh, his scratched or flagellated shoulders and back, suggests his entanglement or entrapment in the vegetation, an oppressive mood augmented by the borders which close, top and bottom, on the central design. (Sutton 30-31)

Tannhäuser is depicted as a desperate pilgrim in the drawing, one who travels toward an end, in his case toward a hoped-for spiritual redemption. The twisted lines of the foliage and fauna tear the hero, the space of the action is claustrophobic and inescapable. I would suggest that here Beardsley specifically draws the Decadent's conception of the trials that must be undergone when time is lived as linear progress from the past to a longed-for end. Both visually, and symbolically, the line of the picture is wound at the heart of the 1890's aesthetic.

In his late drawings of Jonson's *Volpone* and Gautier's *Mademoiselle de Maupin* (1898), Beardsley recomposes literary history in his own image, just as Dorian Gray had done, fully controlling the representation of an impressionistic past to the contemporary moment. Peter Raby has remarked that

> paradoxically, as Beardsley grew weaker, his style was modified in the direction of greater elaboration: he tended to fill in more and more of his chosen frame, embroidering and decorating, in an impulse that required even more effort and concentration from himself, and that seems almost to be a self-imposed reaction to his early fluent mastery of line. (115)

As the artist's health slowly ebbed through the last years of his life, and in his awareness that he would die in the near future, the extraordinary effort made in the illustrations for Gautier's and Jonson's texts, the execution of as many details as possible, presents a striking parallel to Pater's call to experience as many "forces parting sooner or later on their ways" in each moment (*Renaissance* 150).[9]

---

[9] Desmarais writes that "Both the English and the French saw Beardsley's artistic imagination as growing out of his diminishing physical energy." The British saw the physical degeneration of the artist's health as corresponding to the moral decadence of his art. The French read Beardsley's work in psychological terms, his disease allowing him special access to a fevered subconscious (68). My reading of Beardsley is that his consumption rather emphasized the

Each frame suggests the plenitude of life in that momentary depiction of the past summoned into the present moment and re-presented through a startlingly original employment of the aesthetic line. Beardsley then, in his latter work, has subsumed historical texts and the energies of life into as pure a form of the moment as is possible. The extraordinary detail of each drawing contains the full awareness of the necessity laid upon the aesthete to live, and to live in, and for, only the moment.

A reinterpretation of the past is, of course, not uncommon to a linear view of time, but the 'ends' toward which Salisbury and Kipling, for example, might aim, as opposed to the purposiveness of Pater and Beardsley, are entirely different. The former propose eulogistic remembrances of historic glories as a goad to present efforts toward future achievement. The Decadent's perspective, in contrast, is impressed by the past as an artistic end in itself, relevant solely to the moment as it comes. It makes the present the sole arbiter of value and the past and future contingent upon the contemporary. The conception of time as flowing ever onward had been summarized by Beardsley's illustration of the ragged Tannhäuser, scrambling through a thorny landscape, yearning for some future possibility beyond his outstretched arms; or perhaps by Beerbohm's Enoch Soames who destroys himself by selling his soul to the devil, eager to know that his future success as an author is assured.

What might then be said to be 'decadent' about the aesthetic conception of time? There is certainly in the work of the period a general poignancy caused by its passing: I have already referred to Dowson's poem "Vitae Summa Brevis" and Dorian Gray's desire to remain young; one might add Beardsley's illustration of the twilight of the Wagnerian gods and the overwhelming pathos for lost tradi-

---

more important weight of time and its remaining allotment to the artist, and thus created an urgency, the need to aesthetically reconfigure that burden.

tions in Pater's *Marius the Epicurean*. The flux of time is clearly present to the Decadent consciousness. But it is precisely the fact that time is 'present' to the aesthete that allows his art to flourish: his work is this redemption of and from time in the creation of aesthetic moments from the debris of the past. Pater (*Renaissance* 150) may advise us to "fix upon the moment" but there is a clear understanding that the novelty of life and experience dwells in the repetition of difference as each moment passes away. The danger of static conceptions of art is obvious from Wilde's Dorian, where his refusal to allow change is the beginning, and basis, of his corruption and death.

Bernheimer ("Unknowing Decadence" 60) reads Dorian's failure in the latter's perception of the painting as a moral touchstone, saying "Dorian equates his soul, that is, his moral center, his essential being, with a perfectly static image of his unchanging physical beauty." I would suggest that it is precisely in the essentializing function, the stasis, of Dorian's desired beauty, that we see a symptom of the rejection of a Decadent aesthetic. Wilde's protagonist perceives his beauty within the context of linear time, of unchanging, and therefore uncreative, stasis. The painting shows Dorian not so much the state of his soul, but rather the effect of time, of becoming, on his longed-for essentialized being. There is no place in the character of Dorian for a renewal of creative energies. He has denied to himself the Paterian confluence of forces that constitute life itself. Life is thus corrupted, stultified and this is what is shown in the decaying picture. Wilde, in his story, writes a warning to would-be aesthetes: it is only in the fiction of the moment, and it *is* fiction despite Dorian's desire for it to be always true, that the degenerative energy of time can be escaped. But it is only through time that the moment can be creatively renewed. Decadent art is the ascription of value to the moment because the aesthete lives *as if* each moment is an eternity unto itself. The subsumption of the past into the present denies the burden of history, but it is the movement of time that allows ever refreshed configurations of its meaning.

In Wilde's poem in prose, "The Artist," a sculptor, unable to find enough bronze to form his conception of "The Pleasure that Abideth for a Moment," melts down one of his earlier sculptures entitled "The Sorrow that Endureth for Ever." This text might succinctly embody the relationship between the linear movement of time and the aesthetic moment in Decadent aesthetics: time's flow is eternal, and weighs down the individual beneath the twin burdens of history and the future. But from this existential pain might be forged an artfully rendered redemption – that of a moment. This moment is created necessarily out of linear time, from its reconstitution, affording to the artist a pleasure that might be repeated in different guises and indefinitely.

The Decadent aesthetic is revealed in Wilde's story as an escape not only from linear time and its destructive power, but also from the dialectic of progress and regress that constituted the Victorian polity. By synthesizing the privileged moment with passing time's affording of that moment's constant renewal, the artists of the late nineteenth century forged a means to live unburdened by nostalgia and by fear for the future. Time becomes an ontological tool rather than the basis of an existential imperative.

Pater's self-confessed symbol of the aesthetic moment was published as his infamous re-presentation of *La Gioconda*. In the passage describing his impressions of Leonardo's painting, Pater describes the Renaissance Madonna as having

> all the thoughts and experience of the world [. . .] etched and moulded there [. . .] the animalism of Greece, the lust of Rome, the mysticism of the middle age with its spiritual ambition and imaginative loves, the return of the Pagan world, the sins of the Borgias [. . .] a perpetual life, sweeping together ten thousand experiences [. . .] the idea of hu-

manity as wrought upon by, and summing up in itself, all modes of thought and life. Certainly Lady Lisa might stand as an embodiment of the old fancy, the symbol of the modern idea. (*Renaissance* 80)

Wilde, in a re-presentation of Pater's famous description of Leonardo's painting, would describe Dorian Gray pondering upon the

shallow psychology of those who conceive the Ego of man as a thing simple, reliable and of one essence. To him, man was a being of myriad lives and myriad sensations, a complex multiform creature that bore within itself strange legacies of thought and passion, and whose very flesh was tainted with the maladies of the dead. (107)[10]

This passage from *The Picture of Dorian Gray* shares an aesthetically rendered view of history with Pater's *La Gioconda* and an ontological view descended from that expressed in the conclusion to *The Renaissance*. Like Wilde's Dorian, *La Gioconda* contains the history of the world in her aesthetic form, subsuming innumerable momentary experiences from history into one interpretative rendition. She is eternal, and is immune to the vicissitudes of time, controlling them in her person and in her depiction. It is the impressionistic moment that allows her rebirthing, her return from the dead over and over again, that will allow the experience in her of the embodied facets of re-presented pasts rather than a chronicle of past

---

[10] Wilde also here echoes Pater's Marius when the latter reflects that "the individual is to himself the measure of all things" (*Marius* 76). This is another example of the Decadent reconstitution of history as a simply textual source that the artist draws upon in order to satisfy his own discretion and pleasure. The primary distinction between the art of a Kipling and that of the Decadents is that the former invests his text with what he considers to be given truths. The latter has an aesthetic version of history that is provisional, contingent upon the constitution of the artist from moment to moment.

times. And it is important to note that Pater highlights the peculiarly modern visage of Leonardo's sitter, for it is to the present that the aesthete would continually speak and through which his perceptions are inflected. The past is meaningful only in its conjured reconstitution in the moment, what Pater's Marius would call the "Ideal Now" (*Marius* 153). Kenneth Daley (98) writes: "Mysterious, expressive, eternal, archaic – Leonardo's *Mona Lisa* is Pater's quintessential artistic expression of the Renaissance spirit of unity." This unity is the coalescence not just of the Renaissance, but of that period into the contemporary moment, where a multitude of historical periods are subsumed into Pater's then present sensibility through the creative imagination, what Carolyn Williams (36) refers to as "the federating power of memory." It is a memory that re-members, that selectively orders only those parts of the past that are of aesthetic meaning to the artist in the creation of his moment. Memory is freed from a reliance on recollection, nostalgia and an essentialized, 'real' past.

And so Leonardo's painting re-presents for Pater not only the aesthetic power of the eternally present now, the subsumption of the past into that moment, but the means by which the moment can be renewed (the means that Dorian failed to appreciate): that time's passing should not *constitute* identity and life, but that it *affords* a perpetual, and perceptual, reconstitution of the same. This synthetic rendition of an aestheticized time redeems life from time's power, employing that power against itself. Decadence, passing away, is necessary to create anew, to allow the novel, but it is employed by the artist as a means to the end of the fiction of the eternal moment, not as the ground of existence itself. The moment synthesizes the present with the linear passing away that constitutes time, simultaneously living *as if* there is nothing but the eternity of that moment. Without art and the aesthetic temperament the past will weigh more and more heavily upon the present as it consumes the line of time into the future. It is this condition from which the Decadent aesthetic creates an escape.

Kipling's "Recessional" is written from under the burden of history. For the late Victorian polity, the fear was constant that the modern age was handing away the gains and glories fought for and earned by past generations. The Decadent artists were seen as a symptom of this decline into degeneracy, and betokening an end to Britain's seemingly unstoppable imperial march into the future. To the politicians and social critics espousing a faith in liberal progress, what once appeared on charts as empty spaces and oceans for the great British navy to explore and conquer had now been filled, and usually with Imperial red. In what direction did imperial progression lie on the globe of the late nineteenth century? Existence had become an enduring round of desire for the retention of old and dead achievement and of declining hopes for progress into the future.

But Wilde had written in "The Decay of Lying" (991) that through Art one might rather experience once more the novelty of the hatching of the Phoenix, of Behemoth and Leviathan rising from the sea. For the aesthete there should always be present time to write 'here be Dragons' upon the map. The Phoenix would be reborn, like *La Gioconda*, and each and every moment would return a new experience, redeeming the present from the condemnation and damnation of history.

It is in Wilde's story of "The Artist" that the true opposition between conceptions of time is told: not that of progress and regress, for both of these operate within the same linear model; but rather between the synthetic formulation of Pater and the linear model. Decadent time renovates every moment as it passes *as if* each is an eternity unto itself. Linear time brings the pain of change, and it is only in its redemption from moment to moment that it can be survived, let alone lived. Rather than dwelling upon the lost glories of the past, or hankering after the possibilities of the future, one should

live and value the present moment as its own end, a remarkably
higher system of valuation than a linear model allows.

Works Cited

Beardsley, Aubrey. *The Letters of Aubrey Beardsley*. Ed. Henry
    Maas, J. L. Duncan and W. G. Good. Deddington, Oxford:
    Plantin, 1990.

---. *Venus and Tannhäuser*. New York: Blue Moon, 1959.

Becker-Leckrone, Megan. "Pater's Critical Spirit." *Walter Pater:
    Transparencies of Desire*. Ed. Laurel Brake, Lesley Higgins
    and Carolyn Williams. 1880-1920 British Authors Series 16.
    Greensboro, North Carolina: ELT, 2002. 286-97.

Beckson, Karl. *London in the 1890s: A Cultural History*. New York:
    W. W. Norton, 1992.

Beerbohm, Max. "Enoch Soames." *Seven Men and Two Others*.
    London: Prion, 2001. 1-42.

Benson, A. C. *Walter Pater*. Honolulu, Hawaii: U P of the Pacific,
    2002.

Bernheimer, Charles. *Decadent Subjects: The Idea of Decadence in
    Art, Literature, Philosophy, and Culture of the Fin de Siècle in
    Europe*. Ed. T. Jefferson Kline and Naomi Schor. Baltimore,
    Maryland: Johns Hopkins UP, 2002.

---. "Unknowing Decadence." *Perennial Decay: On the Aesthetics
    and Politics of Decadence*. Ed. Liz Constable, Dennis Denisoff
    and Matthew Potolsky. Philadelphia: U of Pennsylvania P,
    1999. 50-64.

Brake, Laurel. *Walter Pater*. Plymouth, UK: Northcote House,
    1994.

Bullen, J. B. "The Historiography of *Studies in the History of the
    Renaissance*." *Pater in the 1990s*. Ed. Laurel Brake and Ian
    Small. 1880-1920 British Authors Series 6. Greensboro, North
    Carolina: ELT, 1991. 155-67.

Dale, Peter Allan. *The Victorian Critic and the Idea of History.* 1977. Cambridge, Massachusetts: Harvard UP, 1979.

Daley, Kenneth. *The Rescue of Romanticism: Walter Pater and John Ruskin.* Athens, Ohio: Ohio UP, 2001.

Desmarais, Jane Haville. *The Beardsley Industry: The Critical Reception in England and France 1893-1914.* Aldershot, England: Ashgate, 1998.

Dowling, Linda. *Language and Decadence in the Victorian Fin de Siècle.* Oxford: Princeton UP, 1989.

Dowson, Ernest. "Vitae Summa Brevis." *Collected Poems.* Ed. R. K. R. Thornton and Caroline Davies. Birmingham: Birmingham UP, 2003. 63.

Gilmour, David. *The Long Recessional: The Imperial Life of Rudyard Kipling.* London: Pimlico, 2003.

Gordon, Jan B. "'Decadent Spaces': Notes for a Phenomenology of the *Fin de Siècle.*" *Decadence and the 1890s.* Stratford-upon-Avon Studies 17. Ed. Malcolm Bradbury and David Palmer. London: Edward Arnold, 1979. 31-60.

Guy, Josephine M., and Ian Small. *Politics and Value in English Studies.* Cambridge: Cambridge UP, 1993.

Hennegan, Alison. "Personalities and Principles: Aspects of Literature and Life in *Fin de Siècle* England." *Fin de Siècle and its Legacy.* Ed. Mikuláš Teich and Roy Porter. Cambridge: Cambridge UP, 1990. 170-215.

Jackson, Holbrook. *The Eighteen Nineties.* Franklin, Tennessee: Tantallon, 2002.

Kipling, Rudyard. "Recessional." *Rudyard Kipling: The Complete Verse.* London: Kyle Cathie, 2002. 261-62.

Kooistra, Lorraine Janzen. *The Artist as Critic: Bitextuality in Fin-de-Siècle Illustrated Books.* 1995. Aldershot, England: Scolar, 1997.

Nordau, Max. *Degeneration.* 1895. Lincoln, Nebraska: Nebraska UP, 1993.

Pater, Walter. *Marius the Epicurean*. Ed. Ian Small. Oxford: Oxford UP, 1986.

---. *The Renaissance: Studies in Art and Poetry*. Ed. Adam Phillips. Oxford: Oxford UP, 1986.

Pick, Daniel. *Faces of Degeneration: A European Disorder, c.1848-c.1918*. Cambridge, Cambridge UP, 1989.

Raby, Peter. *Aubrey Beardsley and the Nineties*. London: Collins and Brown, 1998.

Sutton, Emma. *Aubrey Beardsley and British Wagnerism in the 1890s*. Oxford: Oxford UP, 2002.

Sturgis, Matthew. *Passionate Attitudes: The English Decadence of the 1890s*. London: Macmillan, 1995.

Thornton, R. K. R. *The Decadent Dilemma*. London: Edward Arnold, 1983.

Weir, David. *Decadence and the Making of Modernism*. Amherst, Massachusetts: U of Massachusetts P, 1995.

Wilde, Oscar. "The Artist." *Collin's Complete Works of Oscar Wilde*. Centenary ed. Glasgow: HarperCollins, 1999. 900.

---. "The Decay of Lying." *Collin's Complete Works of Oscar Wilde*. Centenary ed. Glasgow: HarperCollins, 1999. 1071-92.

---. *The Picture of Dorian Gray*. *Collin's Complete Works of Oscar Wilde*. Centenary ed. Glasgow: HarperCollins, 1999. 17-159.

Williams, Carolyn. *Transfigured World: Walter Pater's Aesthetic Historicism*. Ithaca, New York: Cornell UP, 1989.

Decadence in Post-Colonial British Dystopias

James Whitlark
Texas Tech University

Abstract: Amid the self-congratulation that concluded the nineteenth century, there was also worry that the Decadence indicated a failure of resolve that might eventually destroy the empire. Imperial implosion in the twentieth century seemed to fulfill that prophecy and thus inclined authors of dystopias (narratives about Hellish places) to associate these with the Decadence, as the model of an unhealthy society.

As an extensive exploration of the word 'degeneration' (in its many senses), the literature of 1870-1910 provided later British authors of imaginary societies with themes of decline they tended to make even darker and more extreme. For instance, at the climax of *She* (a typical fantasy of the 1880s), when Ayesha regresses into an ape amid the cannibalistic remnants of "mighty and imperial Kôr" (Haggard 315), that devolution of a once-great realm and its queen may foreshadow a similar fate for British imperialism – but only distantly. On his way back to a still-secure England, its hero, Leo, is even mistaken by natives for a god: evidence they are ripe for colonization. As the British empire shrank, however, many authors of dystopias were influenced by the Decadence and the controversies it stirred in their extrapolation of the universal stagnation they expected in a post-colonial globe.

That influence was a complex mixture of reaction against certain aspects of the Decadence and seduction by others – a process that had begun during it. Discussions of the Decadence contemporary to it were almost always denunciations, but in titillating ways that also promoted it. In another article in this volume, "A Moment's Fixation: Aesthetic Time and Dialectical Progress," Paul Fox has well argued that *The Portrait of Dorian Gray* criticizes its title character for failing to grasp the ideal of healthy Aestheticism: living for the constantly changing moment. To the extent that Wilde's novel is autobiographical, however, it confesses his own fascination with the unhealthy side of Aestheticism: clinging to commodified youth and beauty. By way of many sources including Schopenhauer, Nietzsche, and a Buddhist vogue stirred by Sir Edwin Arnold's *The Light of Asia* (1879), the Decadence drew on non-Victorian metaphysics such as the Buddhist concepts *anicca* (everything changes) and *anatta* (there is no self). Plunging beyond Western tradition, however, was sufficiently deracinating so that even if it were undertaken for the most intellectual reasons, it might easily open Aesthetes to feelings of guilt, especially if coupled with unconventional lifestyles. The self-doubts of the period provided models for dystopias; thus the *fin de siècle* writers most influential on these are the ones with the greatest ambivalence about the Decadence.

Among this group was H. G. Wells, who played a significant part in shaping the dystopian genre, both through his earliest works (which fall largely in this category) and through his later utopias (which others parodied with their own dystopias). Wells began writing on the periphery of the Decadence. He published in its infamous anthology *The Yellow Book* (Cevasco 35). Before that, his first publication in a national venue (an essay in the *Fortnightly Review*) occurred only with the help of Oscar Wilde (Foot 27). As a Cockney who resented the British class system but wished to rise within it, Wells reacted with distaste yet envy to the world of Decadent luxury. The most direct way of examining this ambivalence and its influence on later writers is to alternate between analyzing his attitudes and those of other authors reacting to them.

His first major novel, *The Time Machine* (1895) begins by parodying Wilde's philosophical dialogues of men discussing paradoxes while they smoke together in a sensuous (almost sensual) setting. "Our chairs, being his patents, embraced and caressed us rather than submitted to be sat upon, and there was that luxurious after-dinner atmosphere [. . .]" (3). The time-traveler tells of encountering in the far future the descendents of this privileged class, the small, degenerate Eloi: "[The Eloi young man] struck me as being a very beautiful and graceful creature, but indescribably frail. His flushed face reminded me of the more beautiful kind of consumptive [. . .]" (19). As Decadent literature generally sets sensuous enjoyment in the context of the class struggle, so the Elois indulge themselves until the Morlocks (subterranean-dwelling descendents of the worker class) devour them. Despite being an extrapolation of the Decadence, the Elois are preferable to the cannibalistic and bestial workers.

Michael Moorcock has built on Wells' allegory the trilogy "Dancers at the End of Time": *An Alien Heat* (1972), *The Hollow Lands* (1974), and *The End of All Songs* (1976). In these, a time-traveler from the far future visits H. G. Wells after the latter has published *The Time Machine*. The character H. G. Wells recognizes that the traveler, Jherek Carnelian, resembles an Eloi in his ignorance and innocence. Jherek's personality draws widely on the Decadence. Bisexual, he dresses like Oscar Wilde, and, when he falls in love with a married, Victorian woman, he time-travels to see her in 1896, his love journey likened to the way "Oscar sped to Bosie" (*Alien Heat* 100). To Jherek's frustration, she represents the Victorian side of the period, and thus rebuffs him repeatedly; taken to the future, she is incredulous that the British Empire has ended (87).

For Jherek's people (situated in the ruins of New York), British decline (along with the fall of many subsequent empires) is a fact so obvious that Victorian imperialism has been forgotten, whereas the Decadence is recalled as a treasured precursor of themselves. Indeed, this enshrining of the late nineteenth century as their origin seems to have continued for millions of years, including the era of a five-hundred-year-long nation modeled on the Celtic Twilight (45).

To set the mood for this obsession with the Decadence, the title of the first volume, *An Alien Heat*, comes from Theodore Wratislaw's 1896 poem "Hothouse," which praises artificially grown flowers as superior to natural ones. In "Dancers at the End of Time," advanced technology has converted the future to a manufactured paradise, so that it has perhaps some claim to be a utopia, but certainly not for abducted humans from the past and other sentient beings from outer space, reduced to the status of animals in menageries. Li Pao, one of the abductees, remarks that if he returned to his own people and period he would be cruel to reveal "[t]hat all their work, their self sacrifice, their idealism their establishment of justice, finally led to the creation of your putrid world [. . .] Would I describe your overripe and rotting technologies, your foul sexual practices, your degenerate bourgeois pastimes at which you idle away the centuries?" (*Alien Heat* 53). Although Li Pao sounds too narrow minded, Jherek's society constitutes a subtly evil dystopia, where the inhabitants are so open to all experience that they barely care if they are alive or dead and, quite literally, most of them have no understanding of the words 'virtue' or 'purpose.' This openness has not made them responsive to their moment's needs, but enamored of recreating their own and humanity's past – despite a cosmic entropy about to destroy the universe. Jherek's first act in the trilogy is to make love to his mother (one of his many metaphoric returns to origin). Despite a number of amusing turns in its plot, the trilogy expounds the same sense of pointlessness that has been a career-long sensibility for Moorcock. For instance, "[h]is magazine of 'speculative fiction,' *New Worlds*, from 1964 to 1971 proclaimed that no corner of society was henceforth free of the *fin de siècle* vision of Man the Life-Artist in a meaningless universe" (Griffin and Wingrove 4). "Dancers at the End of Time" concludes, as that title portends, with an 1896-themed party, interrupted by the news that the universe may soon no longer be habitable. After taking his beloved away from her husband, Jherek and she leave for another timeline where they can be an adulterous Adam and Eve.

Spiced with allusions to twentieth-century horrors, "Dancers at the End of Time" is a more extreme depiction of social decay than Wells ever wrote. Wells' view of his own period's degeneracy, however, grew more acerbic throughout the mid-1890s, as can be seen in *The Island of Dr. Moreau* (1896). The title character's French name associates him with what to Victorians was the evil flow of Aestheticism from the continent into England. Moreau vivisects animals to reshape them into anthropomorphic form because of his "artistic turn of mind." He sympathizes with inquisitors whose "chief aim was artistic torture." Furthermore, he denies having any practical application for his sadistic research (131-32). In other words, Moreau constitutes Wells' travesty of the art-for-art's sake movement, which had slipped from disrepute to scandal with the arrest of Wilde in 1895. Despite the book's metaphoric attack on the Decadence, *The Island of Dr. Moreau* "was soundly thrashed by the critics for its sensationalism" (Costa 39). Sensationalistic presentation of torture was, of course, itself associated with the Decadence as in Octave Mirbeau's *Garden of Tortures* (*Le Jardin des Supplices*), or Huysmans' agonized martyrs in Des Esseintes' murals.

Costa argues that *The Island of Dr. Moreau* is the model for the deterioration to bestial violence in William Golding's *Lord of the Flies* (Costa 37-39). A more obvious descendent of Wells' book is Brian Aldiss' *Moreau's Other Island*. It begins with a devastating world war: "A philosophical observer might see here an analogy with the human brain, between parts labeled, for convenience if not accuracy, conscious and unconscious [. . .] Until humanity comes to an armistice between these yin-yang factors, there is no armistice possible on Earth" (61). Because the existence of the unconscious implies severe limitations on conscious control, recognition of it underlay the Decadent assumption that temptations can never be re-

sisted completely and decisions are largely rationalizations for repressed instincts. Although the Romantics had portrayed this issue
metaphorically, the Decadence made it the subject of popular science and literature. During the Decadence, however, the surfacing
of the unconscious continued to seem a relatively limited problem:
merely the plight of such unusual beings as Dorian Gray or the
denizens of Moreau's island.

For Aldiss' version of the latter, though, there is no longer a Pax
Britannica, trying to spread throughout the empire such Victorian
bulwarks of conscious control as the "stiff upper lip" and the "cold
shower." World wars have swept that empire away and made even
more terrible conflagrations likely. His protagonist is an American
politician, who has crashed from a moon shuttle (a metaphor for the
falling American empire). His alter ego is Dart, Aldiss' Thalido-
mide-deformed version of Moreau: "There is the covert suggestion
(similar to that made by Wells of his Moreau) that Dart is in the image of God, [but, in Aldiss' novel,] a crippled and malicious deity"
rather than the merely insensitive and arrogant one of Wells (Griffin
and Wingrove 171).

Like Haggard's Decadent torture chambers of Kôr and her immortal white queen, Moreau's vivisections are linked by him to euro-
centric racism and colonialism, in that he repeatedly compares his
anthropomorphized animals favorably to colonized natives. His fall
suggests that Decadents cannot maintain the British empire – an
empire that Wells would not entirely miss.

Very casually, he tends to slip metaphors for Victorian imperialism into his early narratives as in his best-known short story "The
Country of the Blind" (1904). It begins with reference to refugees of
Spanish imperial tyranny and then presents an Ecuadorian dystopia,
caricaturing Victorian society as blinded by superstition and tradition. Whereas the proverb from which Wells took his title assumes
that even the one-eyed would be king among the blind, Wells has

the sighted seem insane to the sightless. Following this, Edmund Cooper's dystopia of the far future *The Overman Culture* has its protagonist think: "In the country of the mad, the sane man is crazy" (80). This thought comes to him several times, once while he is in the midst of reading Tennyson's *Idylls of the King* and H. G. Wells' *A Short History of the World*. These, however, are not his only ties to the past. A robot posing as Queen Victoria is nominally in charge of what appears to be London. Actually, he and the few remaining humans come from a sperm bank established by a British Mormon fleeing that "corrupt and decadent" country (174). Everyone else is a robot, who treats the humans as if they were insane, and the globe is run with more-than-imperial uniformity by computer banks.

As has often been noted, Wells' own best-known version of mankind brought to near extinction, *The War of the Worlds* (1898), begins with humanity complacently expecting its "empire" to last for ever. By the end, however, the Martian invasion "has robbed us forever of that serene confidence in the future which is the most fruitful source of decadence [. . .]"; therefore, the invasion is an "ultimate benefit" (452).

In *The Space Machine: A Scientific Romance*, Christopher Priest has rewritten *The War of the Worlds*, adding to it imagery from *The Time Machine* and other science-fiction classics. The protagonist is Edward Turnbull (i.e., the British John Bull turning, amid the massive technological changes that ushered in Edwardianism). H. G. Wells also figures in the narrative along with a machine that can travel through both time and space. Escaping from a future that seems fatal for his friend Amelia, Turnbull and she find themselves on the planet Mars. There the anthropomorphic inhabitants are enslaved by their own creations – the monsters that attack the earth in Wells' story. Underlying Wells' book is the notion popular at his time that Mars was a degenerate planet, its massive canals dug to compensate for a collapsing natural order. Hoping to stop this collapse (but actually dooming their own dominion) the original Martians (with too great faith in artifice) fashion the monsters. In this conception, Priest obviously owes much to *Frankenstein*, but the deliberate choice of Wells' 1890s as setting, underlines the importance of that period as one when the Occident was deliberately choosing artificiality over nature and spreading (Martian-like) to consume foreign resources. Turnbull works for "Josiah Westerman & Sons, Purveyors of Leather Fancy Goods" (Priest 11). In a punning manner, Priest, thus, situates Turnbull in the enterprise of Western man, turning the skin (of bulls and others) from nature to aesthetic commodities. Near the end of the novel, Priest's character H. G. Wells comments: "The Martian effort is at an end, because intelligence is no match for nature" (358). In stark contrast, the narrator of the real H. G. Wells' *War of the Worlds* concludes with a vision of a future with man traveling from planet to planet as the Martians do (Wells 453) – i.e., the science-based imperialism, which Wells wished to substitute for Victorian imperialism.

In contrast to Priest, most science-fiction versions of Wells recognize his being on the side of artifice, as In C. S. Lewis' *That Hideous Strength*, where Wells appears as the character Jules (presumably named for Wells' only peer, Jules Verne). Lewis' Jules is a has-been: "any science he knew was that taught him at the University of London over fifty years ago [. . .]" (338). Consequently, he is a relic of *fin de siècle* agnosticism and anti-traditionalism. The personal description of him is even more derogatory:

> Jules was a cockney. He was a very little man, whose legs were so short that he had unkindly been compared with a duck. He had a turned up nose and a face in which some original *bonhomie* had been much interfered with by years of good living and conceit. (338)

Stereotyped as decadent in their language and their adjustment to unhealthy city living, the cockneys figured as types of degeneracy in the late nineteenth century. As with the Eloi, being short was then deemed another degenerate characteristic. The comparison of him to an animal (duck) coins a stock metaphor for devolution. That he had declined through "good living and conceit" finishes the portrait of him as Decadent.

Lewis' irony is not just that Jules is a little man trying to seem important as the figurehead for an evil organization, bent on world domination. The irony is also that Jules' model Wells had established himself as a denouncer of degeneracy, against the Decadents, in his dystopias, so that Jules' alliance with villainous degenerates marks a fall from his early promise. More damningly, through the essentially Fascist global plans of Jules' organization, Lewis alludes to the embarrassing fact that Wells' battle against devolution took a racist turn in *Anticipations of the Reaction of Mechanical and Scientific Progress Upon Human Life and Thought* (1901). This latter envisions a new empire of English-speaking people, who will weed out the degenerates by imposing birth control and eugenics (i.e. sexual artifice at a time when such artifice brought the Decadence to mind). In *That Hideous Strength*, Lewis indulges in long diatribes against non-procreative sexuality, especially one where Merlin is resuscitated to condemn contraception as unholy, unnatural and perverse. An advocate of socialism, free love, science, and prophylactics, Wells came to embody a radical change of mores of which the Decadence might be considered the beginning.

Consider, for instance, Wells' impact on two of the most famous British dystopias – *Brave New World* (1932) and *1984* (1949). As Aldous Huxley revealed in a 1960 *Paris Review* interview, his *Brave New World* was at one stage a parody of Wells' 1923 utopia *Men Like Gods* ("Art of Fiction" 5), Wells' work purporting to embody all of humanity's highest ideals, including Aestheticism. Even before reacting to *Men Like Gods*, Huxley placed basic ideas of *Brave New World* into the mouth of the character Scogan in *Crome Yellow* (1922): "An impersonal generation will take the place of Nature's hideous system. In vast state incubators, row upon row of gravid bottles will supply the world with the population it requires" (22; qtd. In Meckier 176). Scogan was a caricature of Wells (Aldridge 51). This fact helps to explain why mass incubation (along with a caste system also advocated by Scogan) recurs when Huxley again tried to satirize Wells. Scogan's phrase "Nature's hideous system" expresses a preference for artifice over nature that makes him into an Aesthete (part of the novel's underlying metaphor that the 1920s is still a "yellow" period comparable to the 1890s). Not surprisingly (given its origin in two parodies of Wells and the Decadence), *Brave New World* portrays degeneracy institutionalized: required polymorphous sexuality, pervasive use of drugs, the extreme sensationalism of the "feelies," and a halt to evolution, particularly in the breeding of epsilons, whose genetic material is first chosen to be inferior, then further stunted with alcohol. The situation is as if the diabolic aesthete Dr. Moreau foreshadowed the future, including hypnotic conditioning, which he apparently employed on his subjects: "In our growing science of hypnotism we find the promise of a possibility of replacing old inherent instincts by new suggestions [. . .]" (*Moreau* 132). Ironically, *Brave New World* enjoys the loss of what the Aesthetes used to justify their existence: Art. *Fin de siècle* critics, nonetheless, had already charged Aestheticism with being deleterious to creativity. Even more ironically, in his 1946 preface, Huxley admitted that when he wrote the novel, he was himself "a Pyrrhonic aesthete" (xiv). In other words, he still had much in common with the *fin de siècle* ambience – an explanation for its prominent role in his early novels.

Being in many ways the opposite of *Brave New World*, *1984* has a less transparent connection with the Decadence, but its chief source is Wells' 1899 novel *When the Sleeper Wakes* (Hammond 171). By way of it, Orwell's "Newspeak" can be traced back to *fin de siècle* awareness of widespread misrepresentation in politics and the media (as in the comic allusions in Wilde's essay "The Decay of Lying"). As George Ridge has already noted of *Brave New World*, it prophesies humanity made robots by mass propaganda – a future predicted by Remy de Gourmont's *Les Chevaux de Diomède* as the ultimate result of the Decadence (Ridge 91). That prophecy applies equally to *1984*. Furthermore, Orwell's Ministry of Love is described with the graphic attention to morbid detail employed by Decadent sensationalism, a byproduct of media hype, which accelerated as the nineteenth century drew to its close.

One of the masters of that sensationalism, Rudyard Kipling (according to Oscar Wilde) created the intense feeling among his readers "[a]s if one were seated under a palm-tree reading life by superb flashes of vulgarity. The bright colours of the bazaars dazzle one's eyes" (Wilde 180). Wilde's oxymoronic impression of Kipling (e.g., "superb flashes of vulgarity") might be termed the Decadence reflecting back the ambivalence Kipling felt toward it. His happiest memories from childhood were his visits to the Aesthete Sir Edward Burne-Jones and his times with his art-historian father, but from his long, painful stay with a cruel evangelical, he seems to have acquired a fascination with work and the working class that made him what Linda Dowling calls a "Counter-Decadent" (214). Kipling's *The Light that Failed* (1890) is his casting his early traumas into the form of a Decadent novel, obsessed with the issue of what constitutes Art, but amid its occasionally poeticized sentences, it is far too full of the breezy colloquialisms of the young and adventuresome to sound like *Marius the Epicurean*.

Whereas Wells almost inevitably comes to mind when science-fiction authors think about the history of their genre, Kipling – particularly the Kipling of "Recessional" with its worries about imperial decay – stands as an important interpreter of a *fin de siècle* empire poised between complacency and dissolution. In this light, he continues to exert an influence on some politically minded science-fiction authors as evidenced by *A Separate Star: A Tribute to Rudyard Kipling* and the comparable volume *Heads to the Storm*. Typical of the contributors to these in his devotion to Kipling, John Brunner, whose short story "Mowgli" appeared in the latter volume, is editor of *Kipling's Fantasy*, a repackaging of Kipling's best known ghost and dream tales for late twentieth-century consumption. In "Brunner's Novels: A Posterity for Kipling," John R. Pfeiffer examines Brunner's *The Sheep Look Upward*, where Brunner borrows Kipling's practice of beginning chapters with verse epigraph's of his own invention (De Bolt 64). One of these, Brunner's "Lays of the Long Haul" (fictitiously attributed to 1905), is an unmistakable caricature of Kipling's style. It portrays its narrator as a brutal imperial, beating a "black" woman and leaving her pregnant. Pfeiffer (64) comments:

> The parody can highlight an earlier chapter's account of pathetic Philip Mason, insurance executive, whose travels also involved "lays" of ill-considered promiscuity. Mason caught gonorrhea [. . .] The "lay" further provides a sexual metaphor for imperialistic "rape" in the form of the hallucinogen-bearing "Nutripon," an unappetizing food manufactured in America specifically for the starving populations of "colonized" countries.

Although, in a sense, all of the verse epigraphs derive from Kipling's typically late nineteenth-century practice of setting the action in a fictionalized historical context, several of Brunner's poems are set in the Decadence, a period he associates with crazed environmental and social damage, metaphorically presented in terms of corruption and illness (i.e. recognizing that Victorian expansion and

Decadence were two sides of the same process). The novel is a dystopia of a future dominated by pollution and desolation. In that regard, it is like such of his other novels as *Stand on Zanzibar* or many of the short stories collected in *Foreign Constellations*, where one late nineteenth-century tendency or another has crystallized into a horrific future.

Whereas Brunner is representative of the majority attitude of British authors of dystopias (that the future is practically hopeless), a still fairly large number depict disaster averted. A significant influence on this stream is G. K. Chesterton. During the Decadence, he was one of the louder voices against it and continued to see it as a turning point into an industrialized, anti-traditional, capitalist society that he abhorred. His subsequent dystopias usually followed the formula: a group of conservatives revolt against the worsening of Decadence into Modernism, e.g., *The Flying Inn* (1914), where Modernist prohibitionists join forces with the Moslems and are thwarted by British traditionalists. In the case of *The Flying Inn*, the obvious joke is that Modernism is presented as being really more reactionary in its league with Islam than are the British conservatives. Comparably, in his very Chestertonian novel *That Hideous Strength*, Lewis has a university town (modeled on Oxford) fall under the power of Jules' organization, N.I.C.E. (The National Institute of Co-ordinated Experiments), which purports to be science but is a cover for devil worship, traceable back to the Templars. A small group of Christians (plus one agnostic) bring down fire from Heaven to destroy the new dystopia, to prevent it from spreading throughout the globe. It plans the elimination of nature, with the earth made as barren as the moon, and an elite maintained through entirely artificial means: "They do not need to be born and breed and die; only their common people, the *canaglia* do that" (176). This line echoes (delivered, of course, by a decadent European) one of the most famous expressions of the Decadence, the remark by

Villiers de l'Isle Adam's character Axel that he no longer needs to live, since his servants can do it for him. The demons inspire desire for an *À rebours* perversity: "Never before had he known the fruitful strength of the movement opposite to Nature which now had him in his grip, the impulse to reverse all reluctances and to draw every circle anti-clockwise." In 1943, the reversed circle alludes to the Nazi swastika, and (as aforementioned), by way of Jules, Lewis implies that this turning away from divinely fashioned nature to a satanic and fascist artificiality had roots in the Decadence.

Chesterton's tradition is the one most hostile to the Decadence, yet Chesterton spent most of his life writing narratives and literary criticism – an activity hardly antithetical to Aestheticism; and attachment to Art comes even closer to Aestheticism in some of his followers, such as Anthony Burgess. His most obviously Chestertonian work is *1985*, containing a novella where the premise of *The Flying Inn* (Moslem subjugation of England) is updated to the conditions of the 1970s. The volume (also a critique of Orwell's *1984* for not being Christian enough) concludes with an "Epilogue" acknowledging Burgess' debt to Chesterton (234). Running throughout *1985*, however, is an elitist condemnation of the working class for mishandling the English language and scorning literature, so that Burgess manages to sound both like an evangelical (albeit a Catholic one) and an Aesthete. Recognizing his Chestertonian orientation helps clarify his best-known dystopia, *A Clockwork Orange*. As in *That Hideous Strength*, evil psychologists use their skills to torture "criminals" and support a government opposed by the protagonist's group. What makes *A Clockwork Orange* so odd, of course, is that Alex and his friends really are criminals, whose brutal abuse of an author's wife was modeled on the gang rape of Burgess' own wife. Given, however, the extensive coverage Burgess gives in his autobiography to her flagrant promiscuity and how much agony it caused him, one can understand why he presents Alex with considerable sympathy.

In literary craftsmanship and obsession with music (both of which Burgess shared), Alex is portrayed as embodying those Aesthetic aspects of the Decadence Burgess esteemed, whereas the government represents what Burgess most hated: the turn that psychology took in the *fin de siècle*.

The influence of Wells, Kipling, and Chesterton has stimulated writers to think about the political and other intellectual ramifications of the Decadence, but perhaps the most popular continuing echo of the Decadence is sensual rather than cerebral. It comes largely from Bram Stoker's *Dracula*, where the title character is modeled on *fin de siècle* theories of criminality and degeneracy, while being hypnotic, charismatic, and erotic. Brian Aldiss' *Dracula Unbound*, takes its protagonist back to meet Bram Stoker, whose obsession about his sexual disease allegedly kept him from understanding the evidence he had come across that vampires from a future dystopia run by them had begun to invade the nineteenth century and were about to subvert all of time. Being so large a part of world culture, Dracula's literary progeny also appear in British comedy, as in Terry Pratchett's *Carpe Jugulum*, where they threaten to spread a "diskworld" dystopia from kingdom to kingdom.

As distant invader welcomed by his civilized victims, *Dracula* exemplifies the Decadent metaphor of masochistic imperials awaiting the Barbarians expectantly (for that trope, see Ridge 22-23). This metaphor is most pervasive throughout the dystopias of J. G. Ballard, virtually all of which are recastings of a trauma, when as a child he was a prisoner of the Japanese (Fletcher and Whitlark 3-13). Sometimes he identifies with Decadent versions of it, as with the title of his novel *Rushing to Paradise* (an allusion to Yeats' early poem, "Running to Paradise," about seduction by the fairies). Perhaps the most elaborate version of the metaphor runs throughout Moorcock's multivolume Elric series (e.g., *The Revenge of the Rose*), about an Aesthete warrior emperor – in a sense, an heir of both Oscar Wilde and Conan the Barbarian. Moorcock intertwines the Elric tales with a multiverse, where characters of many dimensions and times occasionally visit the late nineteenth century and where Jherek is a repeated character.

As the Decadence did not end abruptly with its concerns completely forgotten, so it arose gradually from many precursors, including Lewis Carroll's best-known works, *Alice in Wonderland* (1865) and *Through the Looking Glass* (1871); these are also seminal dystopias (Hadomi and Elbaz 139; Sisk 1-2). As to their origins, Jeffrey Stern has demonstrated that, despite being initially inspired by the child Alice Liddel, Carroll's own drawings of the character Alice derive from Dante Gabriel Rosetti's portraits of the model Annie Miller, particularly one of her as the sensuous Helen of Troy (Stern 166-71). These drawings are clues to the attitude of Carroll (i.e., of Dodgson), as also are his photographing nude little girls. He probably conflated innocent child and sexual woman – the kind of transgressive affect that permeates literature of the Decadence, and with the same result: a retreat from the external world of Victorian taboos into a purportedly autonomous fantasy. For proto-Decadent Carroll the genre is "nonsense"; for the full-blown Decadence, it is "art for art's sake" (associated with artifice and lying). David Sisk well begins his *Transformations of Language in Modern Dystopias* with the quotation from *Through the Looking Glass*: "'When *I* use a word,' Humpty Dumpty said in rather a scornful tone, 'it means just what I choose it to mean – neither more nor less'" (qtd. in Sisk 1). Selecting this quotation (which epitomizes the deliberately nonsensical strain in both Alice books), Sisk employs it to head his argument that many twentieth-century utopias have a common theme: linguistic distortion (e.g., Newspeak or Burgess' Nadsat), which promotes moral dissociation.

The Alice books have had so pervasive an influence on science fiction and fantasy, that any single example of it is taken almost at random, but Neil Gaiman's children's book *Coraline* is, at least, a good introduction to his interpretation of his dark fantasies. The title character finds herself trapped in a world behind the mirror, where an evil version of her mother plans to drain her real life away in a false life fabricated of lies. In such other works as *American Gods*, Gaiman gives histories (including the *fin de siècle* period) for looking-glass worlds that reflect the dystopian elements in the former British and present American empires.

Gaiman is but one of many British scribes of imperial decline (e.g., Kipling, Ballard, and Aldiss), who have been drawn to write about, visit and, in some cases, live in America. A complement to them is the American expatriate T. S. Eliot. Being poetry, his *The Waste Land* (1922) seems a very different genre from pessimistic science-fiction narratives about the future, but it so beautifully and influentially synthesizes the major currents in them that it may be viewed as quintessentially dystopian. Like them, it is a dark prophesy, extrapolating from past and present. Inspired partly by Oswald Spengler's *The Decline of the West* (1917), it describes the fall of empires before the barbarian 'hordes,' ending with a vision of the collapsing towers of London in some apocalyptic tomorrow (lines 367-76). Spengler's book itself is a culmination of the *fin de siècle* paranoia about degeneracy in Occidental civilization. From it and a disorienting array of other sources, *The Waste Land* builds a hell vision, depicting the world as decadent and damned.

Since its publication, much has been discovered about its development. Eliot first drafted its lines 25-29 in his poem "The Death of St. Narcissus," composed circa 1912, and accepted by the very prestigious magazine *Poetry*, but suppressed by Eliot before its publication (Southam 74), probably because of its blatantly homoerotic imagery. This has prompted much speculation about Eliot himself: how he may have related to the *fin de siècle* Uranian movement, a precursor of gay liberation; and what his sexual orientation may have had to do with the disintegration of his first marriage – the crisis period when he composed *The Waste Land* (Macdiarmid 11-12, 46-57). In his notes to *The Waste Land,* Eliot deemed the bi-sexual Tiresias, as "the most important personage in the poem, uniting all the rest" (Eliot 70). Tiresias' section (lines 215-48) appears directly after the narration of what Eliot eventually identified as a homosexual proposition made to him (lines 207-14). The poem, thus, has what for Eliot may have been a disturbing, sexual undercurrent – perhaps a reason for an all-covering obscurity, that brings it close to nonsense verse.

Given its beginnings in "The Death of St. Narcissus" (written only slightly after the Decadence, and its Uranian subject, *The Waste Land* is closer than is usually presumed to a *fin de siècle* sensibility (albeit cast in Modernist form). By its context, his "Lady of the Rocks" (line 49) alludes to the most famous passage in Decadent literature, Walter Pater's prose poem about the Mona Lisa in *The Renaissance* (Southam 75). Such an allusion is appropriate both because Pater's euphuistic obscurity has some affinities with Eliot's and because the Mona Lisa (now generally presumed to be a self-portrait by Leonardo da Vinci) elicits extreme sexual ambiguity from Pater.

Throughout *The Waste Land,* the unifying metaphors come primarily from James Frazer's *The Golden Bough* (12 volumes, 1890-1915). Contemporary with the early Freud, Frazer similarly reduces world religion to sexuality – theories very much in keeping with the Decadent sensibility. For *The Waste Land,* it is a sexuality titillating and sterile (again, as with the Decadence). Although Eliot refers directly to Frazer, he also mentions the second-generation Frazerian, Jessie Weston, whose *From Ritual to Romance* (1920) focuses on the grail legends. Because of her Arthurian sources, Eliot's Frazerian metaphors acquire a particularly British ambience, forming a contrast to a declining English empire, subsequent to the First World War. Any hopes Allied victory may have brought initially have dwindled into the sordid pub scene about Lil's abortion and her husband being "demobbed" from the Allied forces (139-72). Throughout the poem, London keeps reappearing as eerie and "Unreal," its splendors relics of the past.

If the West is falling, can hope be found in the East? *The Waste Land* reflects Eliot's ambivalence on this point, written as it was between the period when he was telling people he was studying Buddhism, and the time of his conversion to Anglican Christianity. In "What is Minor Poetry?" he divulges one of the origins of his Orientalism:

> I came across, as a boy, a poem for which I have preserved a warm affection: *The Light of Asia*, by Sir Edwin Arnold. It is a long epic poem on the life of Gautama Buddaha: I must have had a latent sympathy for the subject-matter, for I read it through with gusto, and more than once. (38)

As I have already mentioned, the 1879 publication of *The Light of Asia* occasioned a Buddhist fad among Aesthetes. They found (in the Buddhist recognition of universal suffering) a justification for Decadent world-weariness. Eliot interspersed Asian religious imagery throughout *The Waste Land,* culminating with the repeated word "Shantih" (peace) at its conclusion. In Eliot's context, that "Shantih" may be salvation or a sardonic acceptance of personal and imperial collapse.

Comparably, before Ezra Pound's revision of it, *The Waste Land* started with a quotation from Joseph Conrad's *The Heart of Darkness* (1902). Conrad's protagonist, Kurtz (whose last words Eliot quoted in his epigraph), is an epitome of Western civilization, yet degenerates not merely to savagery but to evil. As Conrad suggests, the Occident may as well, while the story is told from the perspective of its narrator, who is repeatedly compared to a Buddha.

To brand London as dystopia, fit for destruction, Eliot draws on what Victorians considered the roots of the Decadence: continental, particularly French, literature. His notes identify the source of his terming London the "Unreal City" as being Charles Baudelaire's *Fleurs du Mal*: "Fourmillante cité, cité pleine de rêves, / Où le spectre en plein jour raccroche le passant" (Eliot, *Selected Poems* 69). That dreams (i.e., the unconscious) should break forth in daylight is for Baudelaire and his nineteenth-century readers an ominous event, suggestive of evil, because imperialism took for granted that Western consciousness should dominate the globe, imposing Occidental mores and technology, presented as the light of reason, saving humanity from unconsciousness and savagery. Thus, for Baudelaire, the dreamlike flowers of the unconscious come at the price of accepting their evil. Sometimes in his poetry but more so in his life, particularly his affair with Rimbaud, Verlaine acquired similar associations, coloring Eliot's citation of him. Comparably, Wagner's reputation as pampered, sexually liberated artist, at least as much as his works, endeared him to the Aesthetes and probably has something to do with repeated references to him in *The Waste Land*. Of course, not all Eliot's sources are this controversial, but many of them, notably the seventeenth-century metaphysical poets, had regained their vogue near the end of the nineteenth century. If there is a common thread to Eliot's palimpsest of quotations and allusions, it is a taste for more difficult and/or adult literature than the Victorians approved. Adult, of course, meant more cognizant of evil and thus more willing to see the world as a chillingly bad place, a dystopia. Griffin's and Wingrove's *A Study of the Writings of Brian W. Aldiss* fifteen times likens Aldiss to Eliot, because Aldiss is almost equally erudite, allusive, and pessimistic. In its battle against Victorian propriety, the Decadence began to blur the distinction between a hyperconscious, high culture (once associated with health) and an ignorant, low culture (once associated with disease). Such twentieth-century dystopians as Eliot and Aldiss, jumble the two together in even more striking manners, as if the Occident has developed consciousness so far that a compensatory flood of material from the psychological and social depths – a Decadence – is an inevitable but very dangerous corrective.

Works Cited

Aldiss, Brian. *Dracula Unbound*. New York: HarperCollins, 1991.

---. *Moreau's Other Island*. London: Cape, 1980.

Aldridge, Alexandra. *The Scientific World View in Dystopia*. Ann Arbor, Michigan: UMI, 1984.

Ballard, J. G. *Rushing to Paradise*. New York: Picador, 1996.

Brunner, John. *Foreign Constellations: The Fantastic Worlds of John Brunner.*New York: Everest House, 1980.

---. *The Sheep Look Up*. New York: Ballantine, 1972.

---. *Stand on Zanzibar*. New York: Doubleday, 1968.

Burgess, Anthony. *A Clockwork Orange*. New York: Norton, 1962.

---. *1985*. London: Hutchinson, 1978.

Cevasco, G. A. *The Breviary of the Decadence: J.-K. Huysmans'* À rebours *and English Literature*. New York: AMS, 2001.

Chesterton, G. K. *The Flying Inn*. 1914. New York: Sheed and Ward, 1956.

Cooper, Edmund. *The Overman Culture*. New York: Berkley, 1972.

Costa, Richard Hauer. *H. G. Wells*. New York: Twayne, 1967.

De Bolt, Joe, ed. *The Happening Worlds of John Brunner: Critical Explorations in Science Fiction*. London: Kennikat, 1975.

Dowling, Linda. *Language and Decadence in the Victorian Fin de Siècle*. Princeton: Princeton UP, 1986.

Drake, David. *Heads to the Storm*. New York: Baen, 1989.

Drake, David, and Sandra Miesel, ed. *A Separate Star: A Tribute to Rudyard Kipling*. New York: Simon and Schuster, 1989.

Eliot, T. S. *On Poetry and Poets*. London: Farrar, Straus and Giroux, 1956.

---. *The Waste Land: A Facsimile and Transcript of the Original Drafts Including the Annotations of Ezra Pound.* Ed. Valerie Eliot. New York: Harvest, 1971.

---. *Selected Poems.* New York: Harcourt Brace Jovanovich, 1934.

Fletcher, John, and James Whitlark. "J. G Ballard." *British Novelists since 1960.* Ed. Merritt Moseley. London: Bruccoli Clark Layman, 1999. 3-13. Vol. 207 of *Dictionary of Literary Biography.*

Frazer, James George. *The Golden Bough: A Study in Magic and Religion.* 12 vols. 1911-1915. Rpt. London: Macmillan, 1955.

Foot, Michael. *The History of Mr. Wells.* Washington: Counterpoint, 1995.

Gaiman, Neil. *Coraline.* New York: HarperCollins, 2002.

Griffin, Brian, and David Wingrove. *Apertures: A Study of the Writings of Brian W. Aldiss.* Contributions to the Study of Science Fiction and Fantasy 8. Westport, Connecticut: Greenwood, 1984.

Hadomi, Leah, and Robert Elbaz. "*Alice in Wonderland* and Utopia," *Orbis Litterarum* 45.2 (1990): 136-53.

Hammond, J. R. *A George Orwell Companion.* New York: St. Martin's, 1982.

Huysmans, Joris-Karl. *À rebours.* 1884. Paris: Fasquelle [1974].

Huxley, Aldous. "The Art of Fiction," *Paris Review* 24 (1960): 1-5.

---. *Brave New World & Brave New World Revisited.* Introd. Martin Green. Harper and Row, 1965.

---. *Crome Yellow.* 1922. New York: Bantam, 1955.

Kipling, Rudyard. *Kipling's Fantasy.* Ed. John Brunner. New York: Tom Doherty, 1992.

---. The Light that Failed. 1890. New York: Wildside, 2002.

Lewis, C. S. *That Hideous Strength.* 1946. New York: Macmillan, 1965.

Macdiarmid, Laurie J. *T. S. Eliot's Civilized Savage: Religious Eroticism and Poetics.* London: Routledge, 2003.

Meckier, Jerome. *Aldous Huxley: Satire and Structure.* London: Chatto, 1969.

Moorcock, Michael. *An Alien Heat.* New York: Harper and Row, 1972.

---. *The End of All Songs.* New York: Harper and Row, 1976.

---. *The Hollow Land.* New York: Harper and Row,1974.

---. *The Revenge of the Rose.* New York: Ace, 1991.

Pfeiffer, John R. "Brunner's Novels: A Posterity for Kipling." *The Happening Worlds of John Brunner: Critical Explorations in Science Fiction.* Ed. Joe De Bolt. London: Kennikat, 1975: 63-77.

Pratchett, Terry. *Carpe Jugulum.* New York: HarperCollins, 1998.

Priest, Christopher. *The Space Machine: A Scientific Romance.* New York: Harper and Row, 1976.

Sisk, David W. *Transformations of Language in Modern Dystopias.* Contributions to the Study of Science Fiction and Fantasy 75. Westport, Connecticut: Greenwood, 1987.

Southam, B. C. *A Guide to the Selected Poems of T. S. Eliot.* New York: Harcourt, Brace and World, 1968.

Sterns, Jeffrey, "Lewis Carroll the Pre-Raphaelite: Fainting in Coils." *Lewis Carroll: A Celebration.* Ed. Edward Guiliano. New York: Clarkson N. Potter, 1982. 166-71.

Wells, H. G. *Anticipations of the Reaction of Mechanical and Scientific Progress Upon Human Life and Thought.* London: Chapman & Hall, 1901.

---. *The Island of Dr. Moreau.* New York: Stone & Kimball, 1896.

---. *The Time Machine.* New York: Holt, 1895.

---. *The War of the Worlds.* London: Heinemann, 1898.

Weston, Jessie L. *From Ritual to Romance.* London: Macmillan, 1920.

Wilde, Oscar. "The Decay of Lying." *Essays.* London: Methuen, 1950. 33-72.

"Lascivious Dialect": Decadent Rhetoric and the Early-Modern Pornographer

Eric Langley
University of St Andrews

Abstract:

NANNA: Rising to my feet, I put my eye to a crack in the wall
           [. . .] I stood on tiptoe, shut my left eye, and looking
           with my right through the slit between the bricks, I
           saw …
ANTONIA: What did you see? Tell me, please!

(Aretino's Dialogues 27)

This article considers the difficulty of representation in Renaissance erotica, analysing the rhetorical strategies of erotic display, the construction of a recognisable rhetoric of decadence, and exploring how the poet or prose writer responds to the pornographic consumer's plea, "what did you see? Tell me, please!"

Since the 1980s publication of Francis Baker's seminal and controversial study, *The Tremulous Private Body*, literary criticism has come to correlate the early-modern fascination with anatomy and dissection with the increasing popular demand for pornographic and erotic material.[1] The invasive eye of the anatomist, uncovering and exploring the subjected cadaver, is easily conflated with the gazing eyes and intrusive pens of the prevalent "Smutty Poets" (Brown prep. matter) of the seventeenth century. This study follows on from the work of Barker, as well as that of Patricia Parker, "body" critics such as Jonathan Sawday, and "hard-core" critics such as Ian Moulton, Bette Talvacchia, and James Turner; in it I shall accept a rhetorical similarity be-

---

[1] This correlation is appropriated by the infamous early-modern pornographer, Pietro Aretino when he explains that "I hope that my book will be like the scalpel, at once cruel and merciful, with which the good doctor cuts off the sick limb so that others will remain healthy" (*Dialogues* 13).

tween medical and erotic texts, revealing how the anatomic characteristic of list-making becomes integral to early-modern erotic poetry
and prose. The erotic list or sexualised anatomy, where its incremental structure builds towards what is typically a denied or unsatis-
factory climax, exemplifies the itemising tendency of the *ars erotica*
or "discourses of pleasure and desire" (Zimmerman 8), and demonstrates the verbal overabundance – which Puttenham would condemn
as "superfluous speech" (215) – of a decadent aesthetic. This article
considers the rhetoric of early-modern pornography and erotica, demonstrating how these frequently censored and morally censured decadent texts are constructed with a corresponding *verbal* decadence and
extravagance.[2] From privately circulated coterie manuscripts to vogue
erotic-narrative epyllia, moving between the "hard-core writing"
(Turner x) typically inspired by Pietro Aretino to the less graphic
Ovidian poetry of John Marston and others, I shall demonstrate how
libertine writing adopts the anatomising tendency to catalogue, putting lists into the mouths of its poetic and dramatic "Jilts, Cracks,
Prostitutes, Night-walkers, Whores, She-friends, Kind Women, and
others of the Linnen-lifting Tribe" (*Catalogue* 1).

I. "Here's your Ware boys": Erotic display

You have without the help of an Author, made yourselves
famous in the World: your Vertues are conspicuous to all
Eyes, and palpable by all hands too: your perfections are

---

[2] Applying the term 'pornography' (*porno* and *graphoi*) to early-modern texts is
contentious; "if we take pornography to be the explicit depiction of sexual organs and sexual practices with the aim of arousing sexual feelings," argues
Lynn Hunt (10), "then pornography was almost always an adjunct to something else until the middle or end of the eighteenth century." I use the term
principally in relation to early-modern texts that do at least attempt both
graphic depiction and to cause arousal in the reader. See also, Mudge.

the common Theme of the people, and your graces are daily exposed to publick view. (Pallavicino A3^v-A4^r)

Before arriving at a more specific rhetorical discussion, it is important to identify a kind of hard-core artistic proviso, an ambivalence towards aesthetic or poetic display central to, and always undercutting, the representational practices of these erotic texts. For example, in the sexually explicit hard-core texts that appear after the publication of Aretino's infamous *Ragionamenti* (in *Aretino's Dialogues*), which eagerly participate in, while satirically pseudo-censuring the consumption of pornographic material, the conspicuous and extrovert display of their prostitute protagonists is both celebrated and condemned. The reader is welcomed into these texts by women "stood upon their heads [. . .] with their cloathes and smock about their ears, bare breeches to the cold wall (like Monsters) leggs spread at large with the door of the Chuck office open," and invited to follow the example of the gulls and "Cully-Rumpers" and "chuck [their] half crowns in" (Aretine, *Strange & True Newes* A2^v).

The governing aesthetic principles of these texts rely on a fascination with the minutiae of erotic display; indeed the artistry of the texts is inextricable from the artistry of its whores, as poet and prostitute equally indulge in the packaging of their textual and sexual merchandise; there is, as in the Pallavicino quotation above, a sense that the book trade and "oldest trade" are mutually compatible; after all, men "are guided by the same principles of Fancy and Opinion, in their choice of Books, as in that of Women" (Pallavicino A7^r). We shall see, as I continue, how it is the list, or catalogue, that encapsulates this congruence of the text's construction and the mechanics of the sexual marketplace; the whore is anatomised and catalogued via the incremental layering of "looking-glasses, pinning, unpinning, setting, unsetting, formings and conformings, [. . .] Combs, scanets, Dressings, Purles, Falles, Squares, Bushes [. . .]"

(Tomkis G^r). These lists act as both marketing strategy and as the text's principal mode of construction; in short, the progressive, incremental dynamic of listing is central to the art of poet and whore alike.

> To entice young punys, I lye as open as Noon-day, sit down at the dore, set one foot to the right, the other to the left, as far distant as I can spread my imperfect Limbs, and cry Lads: here's a can of the best liquor in the fair, claping my hand on my market-place, and saying, here's your Ware boys, which invitation with a wink, a smile and a chuck under the Chin, brings in the bonny Lads.
>
> (Aretine, *Strange Newes* A3^r)

So, the erotic text appears not simply to revel in, but also to be constructed via, a kind of litany of display, offering unparalleled visual satisfaction, either provided in the addition of layer upon layer, or paradoxically – in the inversion of that excessive decoration – in the action of undressing and stripping which equally pretends to provide privileged visual access; "I spread my shrouds, unvail my Cabinet, disclose my secrets, and open the pure Linnen Curtains that hang before my chief Fortress" (A3^v).

However, it is during comparable sequences of striptease that these texts disclose the disgust only ever temporarily disguised in any celebration of display; ultimately, the erotic text is characterised by moments of grotesque revelation, disclosing the "rotten carkasse," "visage pale, / Over whose wrinckles, paint could not availe" (Markham D3^v). Implicated in the construction of the ideal prostitute's form, is the destruction of what threatens to reveal itself as corrupt corporeal deformity; in a catalogue of advice to the would-be pimp, an erotic author (in this instance in a crude translation of Aretino) cannot extricate increasing arousal from an underlying disgust:

Beware the [. . .] wenches smell not rammish (as all whores
do) under their Armpits, or have any Crabbie breeding there
for fear of discovering the loss of their Maiden-heads, but
give them instructions to paint, Powder, and perfume their
clothes and Carcasses, have five clean Holland-smocks,
kiss with their mouths open, put their tongues, as all wan-
tons do, in his mouth, and suck it, their left hand in his
Cod-piece, the right hand in his Pocket, commend his Trap
stick, pluck their coats above their thighes, their smocks
above their knees, bidding him thrust his hand to the best
C___ in christendom. (*Wandring Whore* B2^r-B2^v)

Artifice or "borrowed beautie" (Markham C4^v) is both that which
redeems corrupted nature and that which is corrupt: if Sidney cham-
pioned art's potential to improve on nature, the pornographer sees its
consequent potential to degrade it. The whore's "deformity" (D^r) is
only half hidden beneath the "Sheets rich perfumed [. . .] night attire
[. . .] cushion cloth [. . .] damask bags [. . .] casting pots" (C4^v) and
so on; the catalogue of disguise ("to hide corruption and to paint
their skinne, / The haire to curle, to help the loathsome breath"
[D2^r]) will finally be betrayed by a new anatomy of decay ("To
groane, to cough, to spaule, to spit, to raile" [E3^v]). Increasingly,
these hard-core texts, indebted to Aretino's dialogue between an
aged whore and her pupil, are conducted with a veneer of decadent
didacticism (hence *L'École des filles*), supposedly providing instruction to the apprentice prostitute while simultaneously providing a
cautionary explication of their deceitful craft; as Markham's noble
courtesan concedes, "lovely could I wantonize in bed [. . .] Not as I
was, but onely as I seeme" (D^r). Consequently, the pornographic
text both instructs and deconstructs the prostitute's careful façade,
creating a situation where, as Turner (vii) has argued, "sex as a 'discipline' [is] ambiguously situated between Nature and Art." Hence

the commonplace delusion of the gullible punter that confuses artifice with reality:

> Phyllis has a gentle heart,
> Willing to the Lovers courting,
> Wanton nature, all the Art,
> To direct her in her sporting.
> In th'embrace, the look, the kiss,
> All is real inclination;
> No false raptures in the bliss,
> No feign'd sighings in the passion.
> [. . .]
> Oh the freaks! When mad she grows,
> Raves all wild with the possessing,
> Oh the silent Trance! Which shows
> The delight above expressing. (Brown 83-84)

For every moment of assumed naivety, there is another of deliberate self-deception; in Brown's version of an epigram from Martial the poet complains that while his mature mistress is incomparable in her theatrics – "No Nymph alive with so much art / Receives her Shepherd's firing" – the relative novice, Chloe,

> to Love's great disgrace,
> In Bed nor falls, nor rises,
> And too much trusting to her face,
> All other Arts despises.

The knowing dupe, lying "Disabled after storming," actually demands the consoling pretence of "half form'd words" and "murmuring sighs" which might "Engage [him] to fresh performing" (Brown 6-8); "Move, riggle, heave, pant, clip me round like a Ring, / In short, be as lewd as a Strumpet" (75), he demands. The more graphic texts all participate in the construction of a self-denying yet exaggerated aesthetic, a decadent aesthetic caught in a limbic state of parody between delight and disgust in its own artistic practices.

"Is not the most erotic portion of a body where the garment gapes?" (Barthes 9).

In less explicit texts, there remains a titillating interaction of art and nature, such as in Herrick's "Delight in Disorder"; "A sweet disorder in the dress / Kindles in clothes a wantonness" (1-2). In Herrick's poem, we are asked to feel an understated tension in the dichotomy of careful artistry and the unadorned, disarranged natural. In praising the "fine distraction" of an "erring lace" (4-5), or a "cuff neglectful" (7), Herrick constructs a studied aesthetic of disorder and "wild civility" (12) charged with this interaction of the wild and the civilised. Enjoying its dynamic of titillation, of nearly showing or almost displaying, Herrick's poem accords with Barthes' (58) definition of "so-called 'erotic books'" which, he suggests, "represent not so much the erotic scene as the expectation of it, the preparation for it, its scent; that is what makes them 'exciting.'" Wanton excitement is fired by the friction of the artful and the artless, a teasing interaction of the mannered and the guileless. This knowingly unresolved tension of the natural and artistic implicates further tensions between the real and the representational, the discrete elements of signifying practice, body and word; all erotica participates in the aesthetic display and marketing of "the deed of nature" (Aretine, *Strange & True* A3^r).

This study is concerned with the aesthetic strategies of erotic literature, the decadent aesthetic that both attempts to encapsulate and exacerbate the natural sexual urges of both protagonist and reader, but meanwhile, grudgingly at times, accepts its essential status as an artful reconstruction or substitute for the actual activity of sexual intercourse; as Susanne Kappeler (2) argues, "pornography is not a special case of sexuality; it is a form of representation," so the writer engages in "representational practices, rather than sexual practices." The relationship between reader and text attempts to replicate the interaction and immediacy of sexual interaction, while ultimately acknowledging itself as a solitary pleasure, a Pyrrhic triumph of textual over sexual interaction. Consequently, these erotic texts are unusually explicit not just in their representation of the natural act – "view my rare agility of Body on the ground, bending backward and forward, heaving, thrusting and other Recreation" (Aretine, *Strange Newes* A2^r) – but in their representation of representation; "pardon if I doe trip, / Or if some loose lines from my pen doe slip" (Marston 19).

II. "Where we must not name":
The limitations of erotic representation

"If one were tempted to apply the term 'pornography' to any text of the English Renaissance," argues Ian Moulton (22), "it would be to John Marston's "Metamorphosis of Pigmalion's Image" – not because it is the most explicit in its sexual description but because it combines explicitly sexual language with a blatant objectification of the female and a deep concern with the power of the male gaze." Pigmalion, "striv[ing] to discry" (Marston 4) the "faire Image" and "wonderous rareness / Of his owne workmanships perfection" (2), subjects his naked statue to the itemising and cataloguing gaze of the blazoning poet, viewing "her lips [. . .] / Then her dimpled chin [. . .] / Her breasts [. . .]," until "each beauteous part" (4) has suffered his anatomising scrutiny. If all erotic texts demand iogophilic attention – arousal by narrative – Pigmalion's in particular discloses "how discourse and figuration themselves become the object of desire" (Turner xi), as the sculptor/pornographer scrutinises his erotic artwork:

> Untill his eye discended so farre downe
> That it discried Loves pavillion:
> [. . .]
> There would he winke, & winking looke againe,

Both eies & thoughts would gladly there remaine.
[. . .]
So would he view, and winke, and view againe,
A chaster thought could not his eyes retaine. (Marston 6)

What Marston indulges in during these seemingly graphic sections is an intricate game of poetic titillation, displaying not the subject of the gaze – those "parts of secrecie" (6) – but rather the gazing subject; it is the winking eye of Pigmalion that concerns Marston, his furtive look that is repeatedly described. The viewer, kept at one remove from the privileged position of actual participant, is no more than voyeur to an already voyeuristic scene until the erotic charge is ascribed not to the female body-part but to the act of male observation and hence representation itself; this model of sequential observation enacts an extreme version of what Francis Barker described when he suggested how "the carnality of the body, has been dissolved and dissipated until it can be reconstructed in writing at a distance from itself" (62-63).

Love's pavilion is open to observation, but not quite to us. Consequently the poet's excited outburst – "O that my Mistres were an Image too, / That I might blameles her perfections view" (Marston 6) – articulates the final recourse of this model of deferred gratification, where the reader/viewer is left to fantasise beyond the confines of the text, and the erotic charge is found not in the object of the gaze but in the act of gazing itself; "so would he view, and winke, and view againe." By focussing on how the body is seen, rather than how the body appears, Marston's text demonstrates what Turner (13) has described as the paradox of libertine literature: "the libertine remains profoundly uncertain whether language is a mediating force or an obstacle between physical desire and rational self-consciousness, an accessory to seduction or a substitute for it." As Steven Marcus (279) explains: "Language for pornography is a prison from which it is continually trying to escape [. . .] for its function [. . .] is to set going a series of non-verbal images, of fantasies, and if it could achieve this without the mediation of words it would."

Accordingly, the female body, and in particular its genitalia, is deanimated in its metamorphosis into a textual site, compared to a "two leaved book." But rather than making these intimate regions visible or readable, the seemingly inexhaustible desire to classify only refocuses attention on the textual surface. "It is a gash a slash a wound" enacts not a controlled encapsulation or graphic achievement but, as the catalogue continues with "a bogg a cliff sans ground / a watery fire a scalding well," has become caught up in the erotics of representation itself and somehow obscured the "torturing pleasure," the "pleasing hell"; "well what it is I cannot guess," these poets conclude, "but well I wott some thinge it is / Ile therefore conclude in English blunt / a Dutch cut is an English [ ]" (qtd. in Moulton 50).

Consequently, Marston's poem articulates a complicated attitude to its pornographic task. Having celebrated the erotic potential of voyeurism, the poem proceeds to offer a critique of his hero's potentially idolatrous preoccupation with the viewed image, and by proxy rebukes the furtive reader guiltily implicated in the exchange of these wanton glances:

> Looke how the Papists crouch, and kneele
> To some dum Idoll with their offering,
> As if senseless carved stone could feele
> The ardor of his bootles chattering. (7)

Marston, turning not just on the idolatry of Pigmalion's ardour but also upon the implicated reader, is now ready to expose the integral dilemma of the pornographer, beginning to disclose the inherent inability of the artist to go beyond "senceles" involvement with "senceles" display. Exemplifying a keynote of pornographic texts, the celebration of the artificial, the beautiful, the displayed, is shown to be inextricable from the condemnation of the "remorseles Image, dum and mute" (7). The erotic text, frustrated by the limitations inherent in its textuality, admonishes itself, its readership, and emphasises the inevitable disappointment awaiting the pleasure-seeking consumer of erotica – "Yet viewing, touching, kissing, (common favour,) / Could never satiat his loves ardencie" (10) – while acknowledging its own inability to provide anything beyond the merely graphic: "Yet all's conceit. But shadow of that blisse / Which now my Muse strives sweetly to display / In this my wonderous metamorphosis" (14).

For example, the poet of "The Lost Opportunity Recovered" guides his hero and surrogate reader, Lysander, on a "wandering [. . .] search" for the "chiefest Object of his Love; / Hid with her Robes" (Phillips 3). Cloris' gradual disrobing earns its sexual frisson via the friction of a discrepancy between abandoning and stripping away the aesthetic, metaphoric veils, and actually indulging in the incremental tumble of "that happy place [. . .] that shady Paradise [. . .] Living Throne" (3). We follow with Lysander through "a secret Avenue" until he the "Best Partment found where Cloris slept / Extended on her Bed":

> [. . .] drawing near, Oh most delicious sight,
> As Love had laid her for his own delight.
> Yet far more strange Surprisal of his Heart
> When he discern'd how her bare Thigh displai'd
> That which to Man Pleasure doth impart:
> 'Twas then he saw Loves Empire open layd. (10-11)

Cloris is "Publick made," her shift "now no Vail to Humane Eyes," but as Lysander "surveys all the Delights that Gods adore," it becomes increasingly clear that, far from enacting his increasingly graphic scrutiny, the text cannot offer its audience the same perspective, pulling back from the physical, retreating into a catalogue of "Tomb and Cradle joyn'd in one," of "Little pretty Treasure of Nature," layering up conceit in an inventory of only sporadically comic aggression:

Although a narrow, yet a Charming Jail,
Thou sweetest Tyrant over the Sex Male,
Thou fix'd and yet a moving Sepulcher,
Thou Alter which is best serv'd upon the Knees. (11)

Susan Zimmerman (2) suggests that "any theory of sexuality must recognize the interdependence of the material and the representational," and I simply add the coda, that it is the striving to display and the consequent frustration with conceit and image that is characteristic of early-modern erotic texts, caught up in the paradox at the heart of representation, celebrating the whore's display and apologising for it: "leave off these similes" (Brown 11) is the final instruction. While "libertine literature aspires to write the scriptures of a new religion: in the beginning was the flesh, and the flesh was made word" (Turner vii), in practice the poetic conceit can never satiate the reader's desire to possess, or the author's desire to realise, to embody the flesh in words; pornography's celebration of the word is a case of making-do, while aspiring to the lost paradise of the material flesh. These are, as Judith Butler (ix) has suggested, "troubled translations" that try to bridge the "linguistic distance between the writing and the written." The problem for the gender theorist, as Butler describes it, is remarkably similar to what I would describe as the preoccupation of the pornographer, namely, "What about the materiality of the body?" (ix):

Perhaps I really thought that words alone had the power to craft bodies from their own linguistic substance?

Couldn't someone simply take me aside? (x)

Perhaps, the pornographer too, needs taking aside. In representing the corporeal body, language, to quote Butler at length, can only be "a substitute satisfaction" (69):

The linguistic categories that are understood to "denote" the materiality of the body are themselves troubled by a referent that is never fully or permanently resolved or contained by any given signified. Indeed, that referent persists only as a kind of absence or loss, that which language does not capture, but, instead, that which impels language repeatedly to attempt that capture, that circumscription – and to fail. (67)

So the tenor of erotic description is notably violent in its attempt to, in Barthes' words, "exceed [. . .] demand, transcend [. . .] prattle [. . .] to overflow, to break through the constraint of adjectives" (13) – "Her Secret Fence he brake with Secret Force [. . .] He conquers now secure without remorse [. . .]" (Phillips 13) – but only succeeds in imposing Barthes' "state of loss" (14), Butler's "kind of absence," or Cloris' "where we must not name" (Phillips 13):

That lovely Labyrinth he now observ'd,
With sparkling fierce eyes, caus'd in his sense
An Ardour Burning with such vehemence
As you may guess the Object well deserv'd. (12)

It is this frustration with the limits of artistic representation, perfectly articulated in Pigmalion's Ovidian tale, that is inevitable in almost all of these erotic works, and why therefore Marston's version can be productively read not just as a influential text in the early modern pornographic canon but as a key, an articulation of its central tropes, methods, characteristic preoccupations, and as archetype of the governing pornographic mythology. In his attempts to copulate with the cold marble of his statue, Pigmalion becomes representative of the erotic consumer, subjecting the "Image" to a catalogue of sexual embraces, rehearsing the blazoning method of his Petrarchan contemporaries:

His eyes, her eyes, kindly encountered,
His breast, breast oft joined close unto,
His armes embracements oft she suffered,
Hards, armes, eyes, tongue, lips, and all parts did wo[o].
His thigh, with hers, his knee played with her knee,
A happy consort when all parts agree. (9)

But, in the urge to satiate his bodily desire with more than merely artistic pleasure, Pigmalion can stand as the figurehead of Renaissance
pornographers, acknowledging the inevitable ("Yet all's conceit")
while craving unattainable satiation, attempting to transcend the limitation of semiotics:

O gracious Gods, take compassion.
Instill into her some celestiall fire,
That she may equalize affection,
And have a mutual love, and loves desire. (12)

Via the metamorphosis of Pigmalion's image, her conversion from
"stonie substance [. . .] into a living creature" (14), from pornographic
subject and image to wanton participant, Galatea embodies an erotic
ideal, transformed from unwitting subject to equal partner, "yeelding
soft touch for touch, sweet kisse, for kisse, / He's well assur'd no faire
imagery / Could yeeld such pleasing, loves felicity" (16). The metamorphosis described is not only of stone to flesh but also a moment of
linguistic reconstruction, where word and image are allowed to transcend their semiotic status and take on material physicality – the word
made flesh – and the process of signification is transcended; Pigmalion has achieved the goal of Renaissance rhetoricians where "apt
word[s] [. . .] properly agree to that thing, which they signifie" (Wilson 84[v]). As art becomes nature for Pigmalion, now the most delighted of pornographic consumers, the poem allows him a glimpse of
the pornographic fantastic, where the viewed woman becomes a re-

ceptive, reciprocating body; "Then arms, eyes, hands, tong, lips, & wanton thigh, / Were willing agents in Loves Luxurie" (Marston 37).

Momentarily it seems that Marston allows the pornographic text, fixated upon the mechanics of an intrusive male vision, to become something more reciprocal, where the female has active "will," becoming an "agent" in an erotic exchange; this new topography of entwined limbs – arms, eyes, tongues, lips, and thighs – is less an anatomising dissection of an observed body than a material confusion of joining bodies. If Renaissance erotica has a sustaining fantasy – a delusional but inspirational myth that provides its ideal, its hope, and its founding fiction – it can be found here in the embrace of the pornographer and his creation.

But Marston is more self-aware than this suggests. In depicting the fantastic potential of erotic art, he also acknowledges its realistic limitations. Just as the reader's "wanton itching eare," pricks up with "lustfull thoughts," straining to hear the "amorous discription of that action" (17), Marston's poem, unlike Pigmalion's sculpture, concedes the inadequacy of its metamorphic ability:

Let him conceit but what himselfe would doe
When that he had obtained such a favour,
Of her to whom his thoughts were bound unto,
If she, in recompence of his loves labour,
   Would daine to let one payre if sheets containe
   The loving bodies of those loving twaine.

Could he, oh could he, when that each to either
Did yeeld kind kissing, and more kind embracing,
Could he when that they felt, and clipt together
And might enjoy the life of dallying,
   Could he abstaine midst such a wanton sporting
   From doing that, which is not fit reporting? (17-18)

In a manoeuvre typical of the erotic canon, the moment of consummation – "which is not fit reporting" – is deferred; ultimately, the pleasures of Pigmalion surpass the pleasures of the pornographic reader.
"Lost in the sweet tumultuous joy, / And pleas'd beyond expressing"
(Brown B^r), the pornographic hero experiences while the reader
merely imagines. Ultimately, there is something elusive about even
the most graphic descriptions, which pertain to detail while leaving
obfuscation, lacuna, lapses, or metaphoric allusions with their in-built
elisions:

> Two friends affecting one each other
> Did putt there bellies the one against the other
> and did when they were so disposed
> the thinge they would not have disclosed
> the work was sure they did so grinne
> The one sate up the other did put in. (Qtd. in Moulton 68)

Obscenity, perhaps etymologically connoting "not to be staged"
(Moulton 26), becomes inexpressible:

> Who knowes not what ensues? O pardon me
> Yee gaping eares that swallow up my lines
> Expect no more. Peace idle Poesie,
> Be not obsceane though wanton in thy rimes. (Marston 19)

It should be no surprise therefore, that the final moment of a pornographic text, already acknowledging its inability to represent or present the female genitalia, should turn its attention to the penis, and
predictably, that the male member, along with the pen of the poet,
proves inadequate:

> The great Dictator, Nature's Propagator,
> The Principle of Life, Father of Motion,
> From Victory retreats: This *Jupiter Stator*
> Both shape and vigor losing prov'd meer notion. (Phillips 4)

Again, by overloading the metaphoric surface of the text, the hard-core writer simultaneously suggests an aesthetic and sexual shortcoming; "'*tis in vain*," Cloris explains to the mortified Lysander, "*Since no Sollicitations can retrieve / This Sottish Lump: In vain dos't thou excite / This Coward Caytiff*" (4). As his penis "*weeps upon* [his] *hand*" (5), Lysander can be seen to represent not just the "sad and much Afflicted Lover" (4), but author too, who, unmanned by his own artistic inadequacies, "in this cruel and most sad disaster / Remain[s] confused, astonish'd to despair" (5); as "Life's engendering Root" grows "Limber and cold," it is both poet and Lysander who realise that they "could not do the Feat" (4). "Yet in that Active Moment out it flies, / With such speed, as had no fellow to't" (4); premature ejaculation is a comic yet apt conclusion to these merely textual erotic endings.

The final consummations of the pornographic text will, of course, occur outside the confines of the text, in the bedrooms and studies of the readership as "some other hand" takes over (note how in the following the masturbating hand takes over from the writing hand, how the penis is physically, not cerebrally, "inspire[d]" by "warm[ing of the] Veins" to "make a stand" as textual connotations are replaced by a purely extra-textual autoerotic pursuit):

> But now my Muse forbear to warm my Veins;
> And here allow me leave to make a stand.
> Or else inspire me from some other hand
> [. . .]
> For when I *Cloris* do remember, straight
> With strange *Chimaera's* is my Fancy fill'd;
> I am *Lysander*, and enjoy his Fate. (16)

Samuel Pepys, sat masturbating by his fire with a copy of Nicolas Chorier's 1659 work, the "mighty lewd" *L'École des filles* – an image so often evoked in discussions of early-modern erotica – provides a literal demonstration of the only fulfilment available to the erotic text whose textual strategies gesture beyond the page.[3]

III. "Thighs, tits, flutes, and bags": Decadent rhetoric

It is during the1520s that Pietro Aretino publishes his infamous *Postures*, a sequence of *sonnetti lussuriosi* written to accompany sixteen erotic plates, drawn by Giulio Romano and engraved by Marcantonio Raimondi, pictures that had already accrued infamy, attracted the attentions of Pope Clement VII, and which would, when allied with Aretino's graphic sonnets, become one of the most influential, imitated, and alluded to hard-core publications of the period.

> In our private rooms we have the picture of the Italian padlock, Peter Aretines postures curiously painted, with several beautiful pictures stary-naked [. . .] one beholding a Chamber-pot betwixt her Legs, another striving might and main to enlarge the Orifice of her Mystretium magnum that unfathomed bottom, a third laughing at the large pair of cheeks and haunches she hath got, a fourth pointing at one that hath lost the hair off her Whibb-bob.
>
> (*Wandring Whore* B3^r-B3^v)

The sixteen images coupled with Aretino's text effectively comprise a sexual instruction manual, a catalogue of positions that quickly find their place on the walls and in the libraries of a generation of literary whores. Markham's noble courtesan has learnt Aretino by rote and "had him read and in acquaintance got, / So that his booke-rules I could well discover / To every ignorant, yet wanton lover" (C4^v). Here we see how a list becomes so integral to the mock didactic dynamic that texts such as Aretino's *Ragionamenti*, Chorier's *L'École*

---

[3] See Laqueur for discussion of masturbation in the period.

des filles, and Pallavicino's *Whores Rhetorick* adopt.[4] If we have previously seen how a descriptive catalogue, so familiar from the poetic
work of the *blasonneur*, effectively acknowledges its own representational inadequacy, it is in these Aretino-inspired and supposedly didactic texts that the list comes into its own.[5] As it does so, the
Ragionamenti mocks the poetic postures of its less explicit Petrar-
chian peers and predecessors, satirising their blazon device whose
anatomising method the hard-core texts have appropriated aggressively; Nanna, the experienced madam, recalls receiving "a long, long
rodomontade" from a suitor which "began with my hair," and by way
of brow, eyebrows, cheeks, teeth, lips, "a grand preamble to my
hands," fingernails, and bosom, finally reaches "the fountain, proclaiming that all unworthily he had drunk at it, that it distilled a
health-giving syrup and manna," although keeping "silent about the
other side of the model, offering as his excuse that it would take the
poet Burchiello [. . .] to sing of even the smallest particle of its wonders" (51). While still suggesting a failed attempt at exhaustive representation, the list now celebrates that textual failure, safe in the pre-
supposition that the eventual pleasure of the text will occur beyond its
confines. The didactic list by its nature gestures beyond the text.

Typical passages from the *Ragionamenti* ("[. . .] I saw four sisters,
the General, and three milky white and ruby-red young friars [. . .] the
sisters removed their habits and the friars took off their tunics [. . .]"
[*Aretino's Dialogues* 27]) exemplify what Steven Marcus describes as
the literary ideals of "Pornotopia"; "the relations between persons set
forth in such passages are in fact combinations," explains Marcus;
"they are outlines or blueprints, diagrams of directions or vectors, and
they must be read diagrammatically" (277). Lost in its circuitous rendition of sexual positions and repositions, the text delights in its self-

---

[4] See Turner for extended discussion of the didactic nature of these texts.
[5] See Kritzman for extended discussion of the blazon tradition.

destructive anatomising, its cataloguing methodology, frequently drawing attention to its own excessive participation in a verbal surfeit designed to imitate the erotic excesses it presents; "all that one heard was 'Oh my God, oh my God!' 'Hug me!' 'Ream me!' 'Push out that sweet tongue!' 'Give it to me!' 'Holy God!' 'Hold me!' and 'Help!'" (29). Bombarding the reader with scenes of "eyes popping," "gasps and groans," "twitching and turnings," Aretino offers sustained sexual assault on textual propriety, offering a critique of aesthetic norms as he refashions a model of erotic expression that simultaneously celebrates cliché while championing a grosser, more corporeal alternative:

> Oh, I meant to tell you and then I forgot: Speak plainly and say 'fuck,' 'prick,' 'cunt,' and 'ass' if you want anyone except the scholars of the university in Rome to understand you. You with your 'rope in the ring,' your 'obelisk in the Colosseum,' your 'leek in the garden,' your 'key in the lock,' your 'nightingale in the nest,' your 'tree in the ditch,' your 'syringe in the flap-valve,' your 'sword in the scabbard,' not to mention your 'stake,' your 'crozier,' your 'parsnip,' your 'little monkey,' your 'this,' your 'that,' your 'him' and your 'her,' your 'apples,' 'leaves of the missal,' 'fact,' '*verbigratia*,' 'job,' 'affair,' 'big news,' 'handle,' 'arrow,' 'carrot,' 'root,' and all shit there is – why don't you say it straight out and stop going about on tiptoes? (*Aretino's Dialogues* 43-44)

Just as I earlier described how an erotic text simultaneously censures and condones the excesses of aesthetic ornamentation, how the whore's over- abundant display is both integral to and condemned by the pornographic author, Aretino's catalogue discards whilst enjoying these filthy epithets. Like descriptions of the whore unveiling, the text accumulates while it casts off, leaving the corporeal fetish words "'fuck,' 'prick,' 'cunt,' and 'ass,'" to stand as only partially ironic pretenders to a radically material ideal of signification.

"Poesie," as Puttenham instructs, "ought not to be abased and im-
ployed upon any unworthy subject matter" (18), but in the moral and
verbal liberality of erotic poetry and prose we see how the dictates of
Renaissance rhetoricians can be flouted and abused; "Will you," ask
the whores, "have a black, brown, flaxen, tall, short, slender, thick,
fat, or lean wench to try your valor on?" (*Wandring Whore* B1^r). One
rhetorician's description of the figure of "rekening" ("when many
things are numbred together"), makes this implicit association of verbal proliferation with moral profligacy: "this may be an example [of
the figure:] whatsoever he hadde [. . .] he hath wasted it [. . .] among
the beastly company of filthie queans, among abhominable harlots
with banqueting from day to daie, with sumptuous rare suppers, with
drinking in the night [. . .] with Dicing, Carding [. . .]" (Wilson 105^v).
It seems that inextricable from a sense of verbal impropriety is a preoccupation with moral impropriety; indeed Seneca (114) warned
"Wantonness in speech is proof of public luxury," and Jonson that
"wheresoever, manners, and fashions are corrupted; Language is. It
imitates the publicke riot [. . .] the wantonnesse of language [indi-
cates] a sick mind" (Jonson 39). "Thus these wordes [. . .] are dilated
and set forth at large," concludes Thomas Wilson's (105^v) description
of "rekening," "by rehearsing severally every thing one after an other"
in a catalogue of moral and specifically sexual decadence.

Patricia Parker's discussion of the word "dilation" – connoting both
unpacking the sense of a word and "the opening up of virginity"
(*Shakespeare from the Margins* 203) – cites numerous examples
where the rhetorical imperative of dilation, both via verbal ornamentation and clarification, has almost explicit sexual implications; for
example, to dilate is, according to Erasmus, "like displaying some object for sale first of all through a grill or inside a wrapping, and then
unwrapping it and opening it out and displaying it fully to the gaze"
(Erasmus 572). Parker associates the dynamic of dilation with the gy-
naecological practices of early-modern anatomists (Helkiah Crooke in

particular), and to focus specifically on the strategy of list-making (anatomisation) is to explore one aspect of the dilatory method of erotica. The erotic anatomy indeed works via dilation ("deliberately prying open with his fingers the leaves of her asshole [. . .] he contemplated her crotch [. . .]"), and adopts an anatomist's eye for detail ("[. . .] rounded, quivering, glistening like a piece of ivory that seems instinct with life" [*Aretino's Dialogues* 28]), and it is precisely this dilatory method that is articulated in this "multiplicity of strict imbraces [. . .] sometimes inclining to violent, sometimes slow and remiss; but still such as may seem natural" (Pallavicino 43).

It is in these lists and the text's habit "of infinite enumeration (of positions, of partners)" (Moulton 9) that the decadent author offers his challenge both to poetical and rhetorical propriety. For every rhetorician who demands that "wee must expresse readily, and fully, not profusely" (Jonson 75), is a prostitute, confessing her culpability – "Pardon my lavish speech, it is wrong" (Markham E4ᵛ) – while indulging her rapacious verbal appetite; "You must be furnished with a great variety of word," explains Pallavicino's Madam Creswel, explaining that "Rhetorick is necessary to fit you on all occasions [. . .] for ornament sometimes, [. . .] to equivocate, vary and double" (42-43). Puttenham (215) warns:

> The Poet or makers speech becomes vicious and unpleasant
> by nothing more than by using too much surplusage: and
> this lieth not only in a word or two more than ordinary, but
> in whole clauses, and peradventure large sentences imperti-
> nently spoken, or with more labour and curiositie than is
> requisite.

But the "lascivious dialect" of the "altogether insatiable" whore corresponds to her voracious sexuality, which "swalloweth & glutteth up al things, and is never content nor filled," and is figured to perfection in the accumulative impetus of the text; "the insatiable belly of an harlot neither the aire, the earth, the sea, nor the rivers suffice, but it swalloweth and devoureth fields, castels, and houses" (Beroaldo B^v).

To conclude, these pseudo-didactic texts, indulging in the "bombast of words [and] sleazy stuff" that James Howell (2) bemoans, construct their own decadent rhetoric, a "bawdy Science [. . .] regular and methodical" (Pallavicino B2^v), satirising via appropriation the rhetorician's moral structures of "Oration, Elocution, and the Doctrine of the Tropes and Figures" (39):

> I have given this small contexture the name of a Rhetorick; it being that which makes an absolute Orator, whom I have said, the Whore must imitate in many particulars.
>
> [. . .]
>
> The Whores Rhetorick is nothing else, but the art to multiply insinuating words, and feigned pretence; to persuade, and move the minds of men, who falling into their nets, do become the trophies of their victories. (Pallavicino B^v & 36)

Yet perhaps, as they delight in the tumble of "dainty words, sweet Kisses, pretty smiles, and charming Looks" (38), and the anatomies of "thighs, tits, flutes, and bags" (*Aretino's Dialogues* 21), the cataloguing exuberance of these hard-core authors is revealed not as exhaustive but as exhausting, compendious but incomplete. "Now [. . .] the pleasure," as Aretino (*Aretino's Dialogues* 21) finally acknowledges, "ha[s] turned into that peculiar sadness that overtakes some men right after performing a certain act." The sustained assault on the propriety of aesthetic display, articulated in extreme "rekening" and aggressive anatomies, ultimately turns away the once inquisitive eye.

> "ANTONIA: Oh, how disgusting! [. . .] I didn't want to see any more" (*Aretino's Dialogues* 47).

244   *Eric Langley*

Works Cited

Aretine, Peter [pseudonym]. *Strange and True Newes from Jack-a-Newberries Six Windmills; or, The Crafty, Impudent, Common-Whore (turnd Bawd) Anatomised.* London: for Rodricus & Casto, 1660.

Aretine, Peter [pseudonym]. *Strange Newes from Batholomew-Fair; or, The Wandring-Whore Discovered, Her Cabinet unlock't, her Secrets laid open, unveiled, and spread abroad.* London: for Theodorus Microcosmos, 1661.

Aretino, Pietro [pseudonym]. *The Wandring Whore Continued: A Dialogue.* London: n.k., 1660.

Aretino, Pietro. *Aretino's Dialogues.* Trans. Raymond Rosenthal. London: George Allen and Unwin, 1972.

Barker, Francis. *The Tremulous Private Body: Essays on Subjection.* London: Methuen, 1984.

Barthes, Roland. *The Pleasure of the Text.* Trans. Richard Miller. New York: Hill and Wang, 1975.

Beroaldo, Filippo. *The Contention Betweene three Brethren. The Whore-Monger, The Drunkard, and The Dice-Player. To Approve Which of them three is the Worst.* London: for Henry Gosson, 1608.

Brown, [Thomas]. *A Collection of Miscellany Poems, Letters, &c.* London: for John Sparks, 1699.

Butler, Judith. *Bodies That Matter: On the Discursive Limits of "Sex."* London: Routledge, 1993.

A Catalogue of Jilts, Cracks & Prostitutes, Night-walkers, Whores, She-friends, Kind Women, and others of the Linnen-lifting Tribe, who are to be seen every Night in the Cloysters in Smithfield, from the hours of Eight to Eleven, during the time of the FAIR, viz 28. Aug. 1691. London: for R. W., n.d. Wing 2308.

Erasmus, Desiderius. "Abundance of Subject-Matter." *De copia. Literary and Educational Writings 2: De copia. De ratione studii.* 1512. Ed. Craig R. Thompson. Trans. Betty I. Knott.

Vol. 24 of *The Collected Works of Erasmus*. Toronto: Toronto UP, 1978.

Foxon, David F. "Libertine Literature in England, 1660-1745." *The Book Collector* 12 (1963): 21-36. Pt. 1 of a series.

Herrick, Robert. "Delight in Disorder." *Seventeenth-Century Poetry: An Annotated Anthology*. Ed. Robert Cummings. Oxford: Blackwell, 2000. 147.

Howell, James. *Epistolæ Ho-Elianæ: Familiar Letters Domestic and Forren*. Vol. 1. London: for Humphrey Moseley, 1650.

Hunt, Lynn. *The Invention of Pornography: Obscenity and the Origins of Modernity, 1500-1800*. Ed. Lynn Hunt. New York: Zone, 1996.

Jonson, Ben. *Discoveries*. 1641. London: John Lane, 1923.

Kappeler, Susanne. *The Pornography of Representation*. Cambridge: Polity, 1986.

Keaney, Patrick J. *A History of Erotic Literature*. London: Macmillan, 1982.

Kritzman, Lawrence D. *The Rhetoric of Sexuality and the Literature of the French Renaissance*. Cambridge: Cambridge UP, 1991.

Laqueur, Thomas W. *Solitary Sex: A Cultural History of Masturbation*. New York: Zone, 2003.

Marcus, Steven. *The Other Victorians: A Study of Sexuality and Pornography in Mid-Nineteenth-Century England*. London: Weidenfeld and Nicholson, 1966.

Markham, Garvis. *The Famous Whore; or, Noble Curtizan*. London: for John Budge, 1609.

Marston, John. *The Metamorphosis of Pigmalions Image and Certaine Satyres*. London: for Edmond Matts, 1598.

Moulton, Ian Frederick. *Before Pornography: Erotic Writing in Early Modern England*. Oxford: Oxford UP, 2000.

Mudge, Bradford Keyes. *The Whore's Story: Pornography, and the British Novel, 1684-1830*. Oxford: Oxford UP, 2000.

Pallavicino, Ferrante. *The Whores Rhetorick*. Trans. John Wickens [attrib.]. London: for George Snell, 1683.

Parker, Patricia. *Shakespeare from the Margins: Language, Culture, Context.* Chicago: U of Chicago P, 1996.

---. "Virile Style." *Premodern Sexualities.* Ed. Louise Frandenburg and Carla Freccero. London: Routledge, 1996. 201-22.

Phillips, John, ed. *Wit and Drollery.* London: for Obadiah Blagrove, 1682.

Puttenham, George. *The Arte of English Poesie.*1598. Menston: Scolar, 1968.

Sawday, Jonathan. *The Body Emblazoned: Dissection and the Human Body in Renaissance Culture.* London: Routledge, 1995.

Seneca. *Ad Lucilium epistulae morales.* Trans. Richard M. Gummere. London: Heinemann, 1917-1925.

Talvacchia, Bette. *Taking Positions: On the Erotic in Renaissance Culture.* Princeton: Princeton UP, 1999.

Tomkis, Thomas. *Lingua: or, the Combat of the Tongue, and the Five Senses for Superiority.* London: for Simon Miller, 1657.

Turner, James Grantham. *Schooling Sex: Libertine Literature and Erotic Education in Italy, France, and England. 1534-1685.* Oxford: Oxford UP, 2003.

Wilson, Thomas. *The Art of Rhetorique.* London: John Kingston, 1567.

Zimmerman, Susan, ed. *Erotic Politics: Desire on the Renaissance Stage.* New York: Routledge, 1992.

Dandies, Libertines, and Byronic Lovers: Pornography and Erotic Decadence in Nineteenth-Century England

Deborah Lutz
Hunter College

Abstract: The construction of an erotic male subjectivity in nineteenth-century England centered initially on the Byronic hero and his sublime depths of passion. A closely related character that became common in a particular class of literature mid-century was the pornographic libertine and his meaningless repetition of sexual acts. The aesthetic dandy figure emerged late-century from a complicated weaving together of both these subjectivities, with his melancholy love for death, for the morbidly erotic, for sexuality steeped in luxurious debauchery.

In 1890's England the aesthetic dandy shines forth, a creature of extravagance, sensual beauty, lavish prodigality. Something of the erotic always lurks about the Aesthete: he faints with love; he luxuriates in exotic decadence; he tends even towards the perverse. He quivers, he throbs with the pure ecstasy of life, with the exquisiteness of his own experience. The "new hedonist," the dandy worships the senses, he cultivates a "strange and dangerous charm" for all those around him (Wilde 139). The cloth from which such a fully erotic male subjectivity was finally cut was woven from a number of threads throughout the nineteenth century. Two central figures that can be traced in the richly complicated tapestry of the Aesthete stretch back to free-thinking radicals of eighteenth-century France.

Many a highly sophisticated, worldly, erudite, and radical nineteenth-century English gentleman, with artistic or literary pretensions, rounded out his character with a racy sexual life, often in conscious imitation of Byron and his created heroes. Particularly with the Regency dandy during the late Romantic period (1810-1830)

and the Aesthetes and other Decadents during the late Victorian period (1880-1900) we see a type of male subjectivity developed
through consciously rakish poses of impious revelry in sensual
pleasures of the most exotic kind – sometimes with heady and idealistic passion, more often with cynical and jaded lassitude. Throughout the nineteenth century, cultivating an erotic 'secret life' developed a subjectivity that represented a combination of dark mystery,
rebellious individualism, and a sense of a privileged world philosophy. Looking more closely at the constitutive features of male eroticism – of sexualized masculine subjectivity – one can see how they
shifted throughout the century. Mapping these subjects leads to
three defining moments of the nineteenth-century erotic hero: the
Byronic hero, the pornographic libertine, and the Aesthete.

Early in the century, Romanticism fostered the ideal of the radical
genius, too passionate in his god-like profundity to stay within the
bounds of a narrow-minded social world. The transcendent mind,
soaring to infinity and eternal in its reaches, must ultimately be
doomed to the inquietude of lone wandering, to the spurning of
communion with the petty cares of the human sphere. The Romantics everywhere depicted the melancholy brooder, the tormented
outcast, the otherworldly passionate idealist: Shelley's Alastor,
Keats's Endymion, Coleridge's ancient mariner. Like his fellow
Romantics, Byron appropriated the Gothic novel villain, but he
eroticized him by placing him in a narrative of redemptive love: the
tortured, blighted hero might be redeemed by the love of a female
angelic double. Starting with the wildly successful Childe Harold
and then developing the darker figures of the Corsair, the Giaour,
Lara, etc., Byron successfully molded the dangerous lover – a
deeply sexualized hero/villain still highly visible and potent today in
popular romances.[1] With some nudging by Byron himself, readers

---

[1] See my literary-historical account of this figure from the late eighteenth cen-

of Byron's poetry conflated the actual Lord Byron with his created characters and further solidified the heady constellation of ideas – solitary idealism; deep interior blightedness; aristocratic genius; fashionable dandy; passionate, masterful lover; cynical promiscuity in need of salvation by a "pure" woman.

Romantic eroticism centers on infinite subjectivity, on the abyss inside as representative of endless desire, of tumultuous passions never to be sated. The romantic lover's need for sexual plenitude is so endless, he must either find the one beloved who can represent all the good in the world or he must work his way through many women in his search for limitless fulfillment. The corsair's desire for Medora has this boundless, sublime quality:

> Yes – it was Love – if thoughts of tenderness,
> Tried by temptation, strengthened by distress,
> Unmoved by absence, firm in every clime,
> And yet – Oh more than all! – untired by Time;
> Which nor defeated hope, nor baffled wile,
> Could render sullen were She near to smile [. . .] (1.293-98)

Such desire can not be affected by time, by "defeated hope," by temptation, by absence, yet such love is, in Byron's poetry, always defeated. The corsair's true love dies before the end of the poem. So too do the beloveds of the Giaour, of Lara, of Manfred, leaving them bereft wanderers of a world empty of meaning. Love stands as the Byronic hero's only access to divinity, as the Giaour exclaims:

> But Heaven itself descends in Love;
> A feeling from the Godhead caught,
> To wean from self each sordid thought;

---

tury to today in *The Dangerous Lover: Gothic Villains, Byronism, and the Nineteenth-Century Seduction Narrative.*

A ray of Him who formed the whole;
A Glory circling round the soul! (1136-40)

The "Glory," as the height of perfection, of salvation and final blessedness, becomes impossible to attain for a figure characterized by always just missing the full grasp of his ideals. The erotic sublime is structured such that it can be reached only for one ecstatic moment and then is instantly swept away by the inexorable movement of time. Desire works only in extremes – consummation and loss must strike at once.

Certain romantic heroes, such as Childe Harold, will search for erotic absolution by overindulging, by racing too quickly "through Sin's long labyrinth" (I.v.1), thus early tasting the jaded palate of the cynical roué.

His house, his home, his heritage, his lands,
The laughing dames in whom he did delight,
Whose large blue eyes, fair locks, and snowy hands,
Might shake the Saintship of an Anchorite,
And long had fed his youthful appetite;
His goblets brimmed with every costly wine,
And all that mote to luxury invite,
Without a sigh he left, to cross the brine [. . .] (1.11.1-8)

The erotic needs of the likes of Childe Harold, the corsair, or Manfred, depend on slaking an impossible spiritual thirst, therefore final fulfillment is impossible, leaving at the core of the subject a yearning wound. The eroticism of the Byronic lover is based on too much desire – on an endless need for plenitude. Romantic eroticism turns on failure; in fact, failure itself becomes erotic in Byronism. Startling in its strangeness, an erotic text (dependent so fully on eroticism for its meaning, we could call it a kind of pornography) centered on failure foregrounds the way that fully erotic texts such as pornography are generally cut from a utopian cloth – penises stand at ready, orgasms succeed in a timely manner, the whole narrative fabric of pleasures flows on in a sunny world of happy perfection.[2] A uniquely Romantic theme, eroticized failure originally developed out of radical sympathies with the French revolution. In their different ways, Byron, Shelley, and Wordsworth developed egalitarian poetic philosophies which glorified the commonplace and the imperfect. This interest in the imperfect led to the belief in the importance of infinite striving, of recognizing the possible failure that might come from looking infinity in the face. Such striving was represented in the poetry of Byron, Shelley, and Wordsworth as ecstatic, terrifiying, devastatingly erotic. Sublime moments such as

> that blessed mood,
> In which the burthen of the mystery,
> In which the heavy and weary weight
> Of all this unintelligible world
> Is lightened: [. . .]
> [. . .]
> [. . .] we are laid asleep
> In body and become a living soul [. . .].

in "Tintern Abbey" (37-41, 45-46) and the pleading to be taken and ravaged by the west wind in "Ode to the West Wind" are calls for the revolutionary regeneration of humanity at the same time they are orgasmic swoons. In Byron in particular, Romantic heroes fail grandly in their reaching for the sublime, and it is this failure that makes them inwardly tormented; that gives them the dark interior that mesmerizes and attracts others.

Byronism exploded well outside the bounds of Byron's poetry, permeating the larger culture and seeping pervasively into basic figurings of narrative style, gesture, and meaning. Many early to mid-

---

[2] Steven Marcus describes this as "pornotopia."

century men *lived* as romantic lovers, or attempted to. Falling under his magnetic eroticism, many fashionable men (and women) either wanted Byron or wanted to *be* Byron, spawning so many Byron imitators that Annabella Millbanke, later Lady Byron, coined the word "Byromania," and she observed that "the Byronic 'look' was mimicked everywhere by people who 'practised at the glass, in the hope of catching the curl of the upper lip, and the scowl of the brow'" (qtd. in *Byromania* 5). What Matthew Arnold described later as the "theatrical Byron" was also copied by various young dandies by means of "deranging their hair or of knotting their neck handkerchief or of leaving their shirt collar unbuttoned" (*Byromania* 5).[3] Among many who dandified themselves *à la* Byron, Edward Bulwer-Lytton, Benjamin Disraeli, Charles Dickens, and Oscar Wilde (who will be discussed at greater length later) not only imitated him in their lives, they brought the Byronic hero under various guises into their fiction. For instance, Allan Conrad Christensen details Bulwer's devastation upon Byron's death, his affair with Byron's ex-mistress Lady Caroline Lamb, and the repetition of this character in his writing. Linking him to certain aspects of Byronism, Richard Burton spent much of his life exploring exotic sexuality through his extensive travels and had his hand in the translation and publication of erotic classics such as the *Kama Sutra* and the *Ananga-Ranga*, as Lisa Sigel describes in her study of Victorian pornography. Richly weaving a sexual secret life, Burton joined the activities of the Cannibal Club – an elite group of the Victorian male intelligentsia who mixed their mutual interest in sexual anthropology with a dabbling in the writing, publication and collecting of pornographic books. Many clubmen developed proclivities for sadomasochistic sexual

---

[3] See especially the classic study of the appropriation of Byronism in the nineteenth century: Andrew Elfenbein's *Byron and the Victorians*.

practices of either the hetero- or homo-variety. The group included the famous sexual radicals Algernon Charles Swinburne and Richard Monkton Milnes whose interest in sexual flagellation and progressive politics led them to such writers as de Sade and Voltaire.[4] Kinship lines can be traced from the cockmanship of club members to the Byronic hero of *Don Juan*. And, indeed, it is in the character of Don Juan that we see most clearly the proto-Aesthete, or an early manifestation of the Decadent dandy who will appear again, with a difference, around sixty years later. Parodying his own character of the deeply-tormented lover, Byron uses a cynical, urbane, and jaded narrator to recount the romantic adventures of his seductive and dashing rakehell who women greedily consume. Meant to shock the 'chaste reader,' *Don Juan* makes light of a vast array of sexual adventures which include cross-dressing, orgies, and adultery. Casting his satirical eye on the institution of marriage, Byron prefigures the deconstruction of the values of domesticity in Wilde's *The Importance of Being Earnest*.

> 'Tis melancholy and a fearful sign
> Of human frailty, folly, also crime,
> That love and marriage rarely can combine,
> Although they both are born in the same clime.
> Marriage from love, like vinegar from wine –
> A sad, sour, sober beverage – by time
>
> Is sharpen'd from its high celestial flavour
> Down to a very homely household savour.
>
> (*Don Juan* 3..5.1-8)

---

[4] Sigel details the sexual interests and the imperialistic attitudes of the Cannibal Club in chapter 2 of her *Governing Pleasures: Pornography and Social Change in England, 1815-1914*.

Wilde's "divorces are made in heaven" and other such witticisms link Byron's Romantic poem and Wilde's Decadent play in their erotic levity, in their softly melancholy pessimism lost to a sense of redemption, of erotic teleology. Jack and Algernon wile away their idle lives in an epicurean ennui and an intermittent flirtation with secret selves that open spaces in their lives for illicit passions.

1890's Decadence, as many scholars have argued, can be understood as a kind of "late Romanticism"; and its "lateness" is never more present than in its morbidly erotic tone, in its close attention to overripe sexuality, and at its furthest extreme, in its interest in the attraction of "evil perversity."[5] Just as the Aesthetes appropriated aspects of the eroticized villain from the Romantics, the Romantics were themselves shaping an earlier set of theories and characteristics. In the constellation of ideas that come together in Byron's epic we can trace the outlines of another source of the Romantic hero – the libertine. And then again a trace of libertinism appears in the Aesthetes and their dandified circle.

Similar to the term 'Decadence,' the concept of libertinism has a complex history, but, as Iain McCalman explains, its general features include its height of influence in eighteenth-century European – especially French – literary and philosophical works; its representation in both ideas and actions of rebelliousness against orthodox morals and traditions; and its interconnectedness with skeptical rationalism. Libertines were particularly antagonistic to religious laws or dictates and actively sought to overthrow them through championing such causes as sexual licentiousness.[6] Byron's *Don Juan* reimagined the hedonistic morality and anti-clericalism of the earlier libertine movement and wedded it to a depoliticized, cynical dandy-

---

[5] David Weir chronicles theories of Aestheticism as late Romanticism in his *Decadence and the Making of Modernism*.
[6] See McCalman's *Radical Underworld* 208-11.

ism and a rampant individualism that separated itself from ties of responsibility to others. Byron's epicure aestheticized sexual freedom
and prowess; he made the frolicking boy whose main skill lay in his
penis and in his secret entrances and exits an artist, an aristocrat, a
philosophically-free subject. And this project was, of course, continued and elaborated by the later Aesthetes – the aestheticization of
eroticism, of sexualized masculinity.

Not surprisingly, libertinism found one of its few nineteenth-
century English voices in pornography. Particularly early in the century, the protagonist of 'obscene' works proclaimed that enlightenment beckoned via seduction, the trampling of virtue, the eradicat-
ing of false ideas of modesty and virtuousness. In these texts, to liberate one's sexuality was to become a freethinker. McCalman describes the way that, early in the century, strong ties existed between
working-class egalitarian politics and pornography: radical publishers such as George Cannon and John and William Dugdale printed
libertine tracts, ribald and bawdy satires on the King and his cronies,
and obscene publications such as Cleland's *Fanny Hill*. These ties
were quickly loosened. While 'obscenity' published early in the century maintained a kinship with social criticism and radical politics,
in later pornography the libertine voice still spoke, but his subjectivity found its essence in the purely erotic.[7] His political statement became muddied and his radicalism was simplified into only one
statement: a philosophy that sexuality must be freed from its stifling
repression by current rules of respectability.

We see such depoliticized libertines represented in numerous pornographic works of the time, and a close consideration of them il-
luminates the way that the profound eroticism of the romantic lover

---

[7] Lisa Sigel's chapter on "revolutionary pornography" is relevant here, in her
*Governing Pleasures: Pornography and Social Change in England, 1815-
1914*.

was flattened into the empty leer of the libertine. To take as an example, the narrator of *My Secret Life* – a voluminous and explicit sexual memoir published anonymously around 1880 – stands as an extreme version of such a character. This English gentleman, who calls himself Walter, devotes an extraordinary amount of time to pursuing sexual encounters with prostitutes and servants, ceaselessly discovering and trying out a large variety of sexual positions, combinations, locations, and toys – what Walter calls "letches" – and relentlessly recording, organizing, classifying, and theorizing these acts. Walter impressively brags: "I have probably fucked now [. . .] something like twelve hundred women" (2074). He is a veritable world traveler of sex, going on more than one erotic Grand Tour. "In my travels in various parts of the globe, I have never failed to have the women of the various countries passed through [. . .] I find that I have had women of twenty-seven different empires, kingdoms or countries, and eighty more different nationalities, including every one in Europe except a Laplander. I have stroked Negress, Mulatto, Creole, Indian half-breeds, Greek, Armenian, Turk, Egyptian, Hindu [. . .] and squaws of the wild and American and Canadian races" (2074). *My Secret Life* stands as one of the first accounts of sexual tourism. If we are to take his rather astounding account as true, we can indeed agree that Walter's life is consumed by erotic activities and thoughts and that his subjectivity itself develops and is sustained by the almost ceaseless repetition of sexual penetration.[8] Walter eroticizes existence itself and everything in it; suburbs

---

[8] A lively debate among scholars has sprung up about the veracity of *My Secret Life* –whether it is an extended fantasy and fiction or a recording of actual experience. I agree with Steven Marcus's convincing argument that the events recorded are for the most part true, given their understanding and explicit descriptions of the lives of prostitutes and working class girls and the sheer richness of detail. And the failures and humiliations Walter records also have

become dark open spaces for a quick encounter up against a fence, a park is good only for cruising low-class prostitutes at night; Europe's main attraction for the English tourist is its exotic brothels and the unusual prostitutes and sexual practices one meets with there. The author of *My Secret Life* develops and expounds an erotic philosophy which is ontological but also libertine. Not only does Walter assert his will and his rights as an individual through sexual intercourse, he also *lives* his theory of sexuality, which was radical for its time. Walter attempts to undermine his society's censorious-ness of sexualities that couldn't be reclaimed for the institutions of marriage and domestic duty. Sexuality in the 1860s and 70's Eng-land was 'natural' and 'divine' only within certain narrowly defined domestic strictures. Walter's sheer excessiveness overruns these boundaries and asserts sexuality of any type as 'natural,' 'sacred,' and even as the true meaning of life. Unlike much of the medical writing of the period, Walter exclaims again and again that promiscuity does not constitute a loss of energy, of the life-giving force of se-men, but rather it constantly reasserts life as a magical gift to be given and used freely. Walter proclaims his erotic ontology on nu-merous occasions; the following is typical and deserves to be quoted at length:[9]

Yet this divine function, this coupling of the man and woman in the supremest ecstacy of mind and body. This sexual conjunction, this fucking, which is the foundation and the stay of love between the sexes. This act which may form and give life to a sentient being, to a being with a soul, to one partaking of the ethereal life – of the Divine es-

---

the ring of truth. However, whether or not Walter's account is true is immate-rial to my argument.

[9] In quoting from *My Secret Life* throughout this essay, I have retained the original oddities and errors in grammar, typography and orthography.

sence. This act which by the law of nature may create in God's own image a being with a soul to be hereafter by him either blessed or damned in all eternity. This act of mighty power and eternal endowments is called foul, bestial, abominable! It may not be mentioned or talked about. – Yea, even when the law has sanctioned it, and the Priest has blest it, it may not be even hinted at in public! Nor may the sexual organs, those blessed implements of coition with which the pleasure is got, and the act is done, be named or alluded to. – Age after age has wasted its thoughts [. . .] under the false notion that the penis and pudenda are indecent, filthy things. Yet [. . .] The hopes of earthly happiness are mainly derived from them, and without their function life is worthless [. . .] We who know so little of the beginning or the end of all things instead of calling the sexual organs [. . .] foul and obscene should rather sing loud paeans in praise of them, for they are emblems of the Creator, and fucking is obedience to his laws, and is worship of him. (1621-22)

"Fucking" is not only life itself, we also "fuck" in God's image – "fucking is prayer" becomes a strange twist on Carlyle's famous "work is prayer." Here sexuality becomes a means of societal rebellion and perhaps even spiritual grace. The narrator seems always on the point of transcendence, of a final blessedness and immanence. But unlike the Byronic lover for whom such a sublime moment really is a possibility, the pornographic libertine never truly finds absolution.

Neo-libertine pornographic subjectivity revolves around loss – a paradoxically fulfilling loss. Being rests on an interaction with the other which has no use value and passes with no remainder just as the moment itself is always slipping away. For the pornographic subject, sexuality is an expression of a sublime. But while the Romantic sublime joyously and terrifically dissolves the self into the natural world, causing an inspiration and a vision of oneness with the infinite and eternal, the pornographic sublime becomes quickly an almost meaningless repetition. Because the orgasmic moment with an unknown other (prostitute, servant, temporary mistress) can only be fulfilling when it is repeated, repetition becomes its only meaning. As Steven Marcus describes in his exploration of Victorian pornography, the pornographer has no interest in generalizing, summary, or even, finally, in concluding. Each little narrative has its temporary and natural teleology in the orgasm. Once this climax comes, the narrative possibilities are limited to retelling the same story, with only slight variation. "But it is precisely in repetition, in repetition sustained to infinity and beyond, that pornography and its allied phenomena live and move and have their being" (51). The ontology of pornographic subjectivity contains at its heart an abysmal emptiness, a sense of reaching after something that can never be finally grasped.

Such moments of orgasmic politics, of libertine ecstasy, can be found sprinkled throughout the better-written pornography and they echo hollowly, their meaning lying only on the surface. Particularly after the 1830s such statements point more and more weakly to a political libertine tradition and become a formulaic and transparent means of titillation. The 1896 pornographic *Parisian Frolics* is one example of many:

> [. . .] there was nothing about her to betray the lascivious desires that had brought her here, or the lecherous fashion in which she was ready to conduct herself – unless it was that peculiar glance that allowed one to detect, beneath the woman dressed, the naked woman, and behind perfect So-

ciety manners the intimate familiarity with the most daring libertinage. (37-38)

Freedom to engage in anonymous sex encompasses the whole meaning of "libertinage" in this text. Additionally, a subtle sense of melancholy can be picked out from the background of these Victorian pornographic narratives. Melancholy comes when one finds oneself asking of the narrator of *My Secret Life*, what is he looking for? Why can't he find it? The desperate sexual energy of these neo-libertines borders on hysteria and one feels that, at times, sex becomes a staving off of death. Or, in another way, it points always to death, as Marcus describes:

> Nevertheless, we must also observe that in this one sense at least pornography is closer to certain existential realities than art or literature can usually be. For life itself does not end in the way that a work of literature does. It ends in the meaninglessness of non-existence, of nothing [. . .] And if one takes a work such as *My Secret Life* and strips away the superstructure of sexual fantasies, one discovers directly beneath them the meaningless void, the sense that life is founded on nothing and that there is nothing to hold on to.
>
> (196)

Pornography, when viewed in a certain way, mourns the meaninglessness of death.

The Decadent movement of the 1880s and 90s set up a male subjectivity that drew on both traditions – Byronism and the pornographic libertine. Aestheticism brought together the threads of Romantic subjectivity and the cynical eroticism of the flat character of the de- or pseudo-politicized libertine. Aestheticism turns the erotic into art, into an artistic way of life. Byron the dandy also lived his art, aestheticized an erotic subjectivity. The mesmerizing magnetism of the corsair or of Manfred came from their powerfully rebellious, passionate selves – their transcendental homelessness. Because the *Übermensch* quality of these characters turned on love and desire for a woman, Byron turned that erotic into an aesthetic philosophy. Yet we also see the libertine in the careless and cruel seduction Dorian Gray practices, ruining others' lives merely to live for intense pleasure, Sade-like. In *The Picture of Dorian Gray*, sexual debauchery equals freedom from stifling and boring convention.

Wilde and his artistic circle fed on the religion of Walter Pater. Pater's philosophy developed from theorizing the beauty of the flashing moment and from gazing steadily at the glimmer as the moment disappears. From Pater comes the construction of a subjectivity so pervaded by languid excess, by the pleasures of the senses, that life is *too* sweet, and the subject floats on a dream of ever-unfolding sensual scenes that titillate all the senses. The world becomes "like a painted toy," and brief existence is flamed away in moments of intensity. Pater's famous line speaks to us readily in this context: "To burn always with this hard, gem-like flame, to maintain this ecstasy, is success in life" (154). Wistfully yearning for all that is perfect and strange, the Decadent unwittingly rung into existence by Pater is everywhere full of the "last refinements." Always with a backward glance, he feels there is no future, "all is before, nothing after" (Weir 5). "We are all under sentence of death but with a sort of indefinite reprieve" (Pater 155). The Decadent subjectivity doesn't stave off death, as the energetic movements of the libertine attempt to do, but rather he makes death manifest always – he sees the overripe, the just about to swoon to death as present and immanent. The Byronic lover appears on the scene as already dead: the Giaour, Lara and Manfred have already lost their one reason for living when the poem starts, Childe Harold and the corsair find life hateful despite their one true love. Yet the Byronic hero's inner fire comes from a still-burning idealism – eternal life, redemption, still *might*

exalt his barren life. As the barren spirit of Manfred calls out to his
dead beloved:

> I know not what I ask, nor what I seek:
> I feel but what thou art, and what I am;
> And I would hear yet once before I perish
> The voice which was my music – Speak to me!
>
> (2.4.131-34)

Always there is this tiny flame of hope.

The libertine holds death at bay through repeating what represents
life to him, again and again. The Decadent has already given up; he
lives in the afterglow of an apocalypse already in the past. Thus
death – the pale, wan, dying self – is eroticized. Dorian Gray falls in
love with seducing men and women to their deaths: "He grew more
and more enamoured of his own beauty, more and more interested
in the corruption of his own soul" (Wilde 125). In *Teleny*, an
anonymous, homosexual, pornographic novel of the 1890s, once
thought to have been written by Wilde and clearly a product of aestheticism, enamored eroticism intensifies to such a high pitch, death
is the only experience fraught enough to express it.

> Nature, hushed and silent, seemed to hold her breath to look
> upon us, for such ecstasy of bliss had seldom, if ever, been
> felt here below. I was subdued, prostrated, shattered. The
> earth was spinning round me, sinking under my feet. I had
> no longer strength enough to stand. I felt sick and faint.
> Was I dying? If so, death must be the happiest moment of
> our life, for such rapturous joy could never be felt again.
>
> (84)

Such fainting *Liebestod* lives Pater's "burning with a hard, gem-like
flame" philosophy. One must grasp the moment just as the inexorable movement of time always sinks it into the lost past. Each mo-

ment moves us closer to inescapable death. Decadent eroticism dwells in this melancholy relationship to temporality. Once again, the orgasm is everywhere the *petit mort*. Such a sex/death linkage is almost indistinguishable from the eroticism of the Byronic hero. The subtle difference lies in Romanticism's idealism: even if buried deep within the secret heart of the blighted life of the Gothic villain, there burns still a real belief in the redemptive qualities of the sublime. But with the Decadents that flame can only burn for a moment and always encroaching is the darkness of a final lack of meaning behind the façade of the rich parade of life. It is precisely here that we see that the Decadents are early modernists – in their proto-existential despair. Such despair shifts decadent porn away from the utopia of everyday pornography. In *Teleny*, Beardsley's work, and *The Picture of Dorian Gray*, a central character longs for death and, in the case of Dorian and Teleny, actually dies. Thus again failure becomes erotic, as we saw in Byronism where blightedness makes the Byronic hero erotically attractive. Similarly, in *Teleny*, sharp pain and eager pleasures are barely distinguishable:

> Yes, but perfect happiness cannot last long. Hell gapes on the threshold of heaven, and one step plunges us from ethereal light into Cerberean darkness. So it has ever been with me in this chequered like of mine. A fortnight after that memorable night of unbearable anguish and of thrilling delight, I awoke in the midst of felicity to find myself in thorough wretchedness. (102-03)

Here we do not find ourselves in pornotopia, although *Teleny* is certainly a work of pornography, albeit with pretensions to high art. Rather we enter into the world of Keatsian dystopia, where pleasure and pain seep into each other. The mournful brooding of the sexual subject in decadence creates a general pessimism, a melancholy erotic.

The sexuality of the Byronic hero bores inward always; it swirls around the chaos of his infinite interior. The libertine pushes his eroticism relentlessly outward; its meaning lies on the surface in body moving against body. With the Decadent, eroticism also floats outward, permeating his subjectivity, yes, but also seeping into everything exterior. The aesthete eroticizes his exterior life as well as his interior one. This is why Dorian Gray is not only a masterful seducer of both men and women, he also "worships the senses" (127) in a wholesale way: he becomes an expert in perfumes, jewels, tapestries, and, first and foremost, fashion.

> And, certainly, to him Life itself was the first, the greatest, of the arts, and for it all the other arts seemed to be but a preparation. Fashion, by which what is really fantastic becomes for a moment universal, and Dandyism, which, in its own way, is an attempt to assert the absolute modernity of beauty, had, of course, their fascination for him. His mode of dressing, and the particular styles that from time to time he affected, had their marked influence on the young exquisites of the Mayfair balls and Pall Mall club windows, who copied him in everything that he did, and tried to reproduce the accidental charm of his graceful, though to him only half-serious, fopperies. (126-27)

As we found with Byron and his imitators, the dandy's skill and cunning goes into the dashing cut of his clothing, the studied carelessness of tying his cravat, his stylish gestures and his charmingly sharp wit. But unlike Byronism, the 90s dandy's eroticism adheres to the material rather than the spiritual. The dandy's attraction comes from his inimitable superficiality rather than his interior depths. His secrets are readable signs that he wears on his body, rather than mysterious inner wounds.

In the pornography of the Decadents, as one would suspect, the truly erotic moments come in the lush descriptions of material objects, just as *The Picture of Dorian Gray* is at its most excessively erotic in its pages-long descriptions of jewels, interiors, perfumes. Aubrey Beardsley emerges as an obvious choice to turn to in this regard. His morbidly erotic illustrations are famous for their sinuous, sensual lines, their sometimes ghastly orgasms – as in *The Climax*, a picture of Salomé floating with the severed head of John the Baptist – and their grotesque sexuality. His images dance with goblin-like figures stumbling under their erect penises, too large for their bodies; overweight women on poles being flagellated; starvation-thin men being blown down by women's flatulence. Beardsley's sense of the erotic moves often just on the other side of the line between perversely mesmerizing and repulsively obscene. And this is just the line the Decadents often placed before them as a boundary to cross and re-cross. In their project to shock society out of its complacent view of respectable sexuality, we are reminded of that radical libertine – the Marquis de Sade.

Beardsley's *The Story of Venus and Tannhäuser* illustrates the externalized eroticism of the Decadent movement. The graphic sexual scenes are over in a moment, are unsuccessful, or only mildly successful because either Venus or Tannhäuser is weary with the overcharged pleasures of the meal or the theater. Thus the pornography can be found not in the meeting of bodies in penetration, but in the sheer debauchery of materialism. The majority of the novel is taken up by long descriptions of lavish goods:

> The tray was freighted with the most exquisite and shapely pantoufles, sufficient to make Cluny a place of naught. There were shoes of grey and black and brown suède, of white silk and rose satin, and velvet sarcenet; there were some of sea-green sewn with cherry blossoms, some of red with willow branches, and some of grey with bright-winged

birds. There were heels of silver, of ivory, and of gilt; there
were buckles of very precious stones set in most strange
and esoteric devices; there were ribbons tied and twisted
into cunning forms; there were buttons so beautiful that the
buttonholes might have no pleasure till they closed upon
them; there were soles of delicate leathers scented with
maréchale, and linings of soft stuffs scented with the juice
of July flowers. But Venus, finding none of them to her
mind, called for a discarded pair of blood-red maroquin,
diapered with pearls. They looked very distinguished over
her white silk stockings. As the tray was being carried
away, the capricious Florizel snatched as usual a slipper
from it, and fitted the foot over his penis, and made the
necessary movements. (30-31)

Fetishistically, the shoes are the proper receptacles for the penis
rather than the vagina or another bodily orifice. The locating of the
orgasm is no longer the straight-forward manner that it is in previous pornography – it has now moved out into a jeweled materialism.
Ecstasy explodes out from the body to the folds of drapery, the
shine of a Sèvres china teacup, the whiff of Indian spice perfume. It
is here that we must locate the erotic sublime in Decadent works.
The overwrought senses inundated by beautiful objects bring the
aesthete to a transcendental place where his soul might dissolve out
into universality. But like the pornographic libertine, empty repetition rather than plenitude and profundity become the results. This
decadent luxuriousness plays on the surface of the void similarly to
the libertine repetition. The meaninglessness underneath the superficial glamour of this world points again and again to the nothingness of death. The endless lists of beautiful objects, scents and music in Decadent works mirror the inexhaustible stream of slightly
different stories of penetration, cunnilingus, fellatio, and other sex-

ual maneuvers in earlier porn and thus points to existential emptiness.

Yet the Decadents recognized the nothingness underneath it all; they recognized the rot and decay behind the glitter and celebrated it along with the beauty. Making immanent such complexities of life, in fact, aestheticizing them, made aestheticism an artistic movement, which pornographic libertinism never was. The Aesthetes not only made of their art an erotic statement, they eroticized their own lives, their own bodies. As Wilde famously explained, he put his genius into his life and only his talent into his writings. Thus Wilde and his ilk took a page from Byron's book; the Byron who put himself into his art and his art into himself, confusing his readers into thinking *he* was Childe Harold, *he* was the corsair.

Thus a constellation of similar ideas swirl around the three constructions of male erotic subjectivities, some in influence, others in counterpoint: the secret life; an erotic sublime; a staving-off, or giving-in to, death; a highly sophisticated dandyism; debauched promiscuity; melancholy emptiness and lack of meaning. We can trace a solid literary-historical itinerary from the Romantic hero, through the pornographic libertine, to the dandified Aesthete. And in tracing such an itinerary, it becomes everywhere apparent that artists, writers, and musicians today continue to recycle the combinations of attributes that came together in these three types of erotic subjectivities: the influence of these important historical and literary figures still reigns.

Works Cited

Beardsley, Aubrey. *The Climax.* 1893. *The Artchive.* Comp. Mark Harden. 1996. 23 Aug. 2005 <http://www.artchive.com/artch ive/B/beardsley/beardsley_climax.jpg.html>.

---. *The Story of Venus and Tannhäuser.* London: Wordsworth, 1995.

Belot, Adolphe. *Parisian Frolics*. New York: Grove, 1984.

Byron, George Gordon. *Byron's Poetry*. New York: Norton, 1978.

Christensen, Allan Conrad. *Edward Bulwer-Lytton: The Fiction of New Regions*. Athens: U of Georgia P, 1976.

Elfenbein, Andrew. *Byron and the Victorians*. Cambridge: Cambridge UP, 1996.

Lutz, Deborah. *The Dangerous Lover: Gothic Villains, Byronism, and the Nineteenth-Century Seduction Narrative*. Columbus: Ohio State UP, 2006.

Marcus, Steven. *The Other Victorians: A Study of Sexuality and Pornography in Mid-Nineteenth-Century England*. New York: Basic, 1966.

McCalman, Iain. *Radical Underworld: Prophets, Revolutionaries and Pornographers in London, 1795-1840*. New York: Cambridge UP, 1988.

My Secret Life. New York: Grove, 1966.

Pater, Walter. *The Renaissance: Studies in Art and Poetry*. New York: Dover, 2005.

Sigel, Lisa. *Governing Pleasures: Pornography and Social Change in England, 1815-1914*. New Brunswick, NJ: Rutgers UP, 2002.

Teleny. London: Wordsworth, 1995.

Weir, David. *Decadence and the Making of Modernism*. Amherst: U of Massachusetts P, 1995.

Wilde, Oscar. *The Picture of Dorian Gray*. New York: Books, Inc., 1944.

Wilson, Francis, ed. *Byromania: Portraits of the Artist in Nineteenth- and Twentieth-Century Culture*. New York: St. Martin's, 1999.

Sexual Literary Freedom vs. Societal Hypocrisy and Ignorance: Aleister Crowley and the Artistic Challenge

Michael R. Catanzaro
University of Toledo

Abstract: Edward Aleister Crowley's book of poetry, *White Stains*, is a response to the hypocrisy of late nineteenth-century attitudes that enabled censors to punish individuals who imitate life in their art, but applaud and reward individuals who present the same material as a work of science. The destruction of his work by H. M. Customs and the newspaper proclamation that the work was "the filthiest book of verse ever written" and that Crowley was "the wickedest man in the world" serve as a prophecy of the futile attempt of institutions to control the natural inclination of humanity to explore its developing sexuality.[1]

In his book of poetry, *White Stains*, Edward Aleister Crowley provides clear images and expressions of sexual intimacies that caused his poems to be censored for their decadent subject matter. In his work *The Confessions of Aleister Crowley*, Crowley defends his poems as a study in psychology. He states:

> The facts are as follows: In the course of my reading I had come across von Krafft-Ebing's *Psychopathia Sexualis*. The professor tries to prove that sexual aberrations are the result of disease. I did not agree. [. . .] I said to myself that I must confute the professor. I could only do this by employing the one form at my disposal: the artistic form. I therefore invented a poet who went wrong, who began with normal and

---

[1] This essay was originally presented in a shorter version as a conference paper at the Poetry and Sexuality Conference, Department of English Studies, at the University of Stirling, Scotland, July 2004.

innocent enthusiasms, and gradually developed various vices. He ends by being stricken with disease and madness, culminating in murder. In his poems he describes his downfall, always explaining the psychology of each act. [. . .] I wrote the book in absolute seriousness and in all innocence. It never occurred to me that a demonstration of the terrible results of misguided passion might be mistaken for pornography. Indeed now that I do understand that vile minds think it a vile book, I recognize with grim satisfaction that *Psychopathia Sexualis* itself has attained its enormous popularity because people love to gloat over such things. Its scientific form has not protected it from abuse, any more than the artistic form of my own reply to it. But von Krafft-Ebing has not been blackguarded as I have. The average man cannot believe that an artist may be as serious and high-minded an observer of life as the professed man of science. I was to find very shortly that the most innocent personal relations could be taken by filthy minds as the basis for their malicious imagination. (127)

Whether Crowley was motivated by a "noble" desire to argue a philosophical viewpoint or simply a desire to write poems about sexual material deemed taboo is not the issue; rather, the creation of his poems elucidates his perspective that society's members are ignorant and hypocritical because they censor and punish individuals who imitate life in their art, but applaud and reward individuals who present the identical material as a work of social science.

Since Crowley claims his poems "represent a gradual development of vices" (127), it is logical to begin an analysis of the poetry with the first piece and progressively but selectively work to the last in order to establish the psychological sequence of sensualism that is both explicitly and implicitly stated. Even the title of the work, *White Stains*, suggests that the contents will be stimulating, perhaps

enough to allow Crowley's reader to rise up with him and vicariously experience first hand that which has been damned. For many
readers, however, his sexual images reflect extreme morbid and
perverse tastes. Even those who accept homosexuality as a natural
practice are repulsed, appalled, and shocked by the coarse explicit
material that glorifies the degradation of the human experience more
than it does to prove its validity. Even though Crowley adheres to
sensational imagery by exulting the pleasures of sexual experiences,
the poems present the identical material found in Krafft-Ebing's
study; nevertheless, these poetically phrased experiences are rejected because the censors have deemed them as the artistic manifestation of a "sick" and "perverted" mind created by the "wickedest
man in the world" (d'Arch Smith 95) with the intent of providing
sexual stimuli and pleasure for ordinary people which, according to
them, lacks comparison to the intellectual caliber of a scientific
study intended for the exploration and development of the study of
psychology by educated individuals.

Crowley may have had the grim satisfaction of knowing that society's intolerance of perceived sexual topics was hypocrisy at its best,
but he still felt the power of this intolerance when his books were
confiscated and burned. The point of his poems was not the asser-
tion of his sexual preference, but his sexual literary freedom. The
denunciation and destruction of his work demonstrates that the same
sexual material presented in the guise of scientific pursuits is toler-
ated and enjoyed by a society where artistic endeavors are denounced as perverted. Even today this mind set is not difficult to
comprehend since the government of a powerful nation such as the
United States finds it difficult to exactly define the term pornography. In her article, "The Perils of Pornophobia," Nadine Strossen
states that "this dilemma was best summed up in former Justice Potter Stewart's now famous statement: 'I shall not today attempt further to define [obscenity]; and perhaps I could never succeed in in-

telligibly doing so. But I know it when I see it'" (551). If we believe this statement to be true, then everything ever written about "the most innocent personal relations could be taken by filthy minds as the basis for their malicious imagination" (Crowley, *Confessions* 127) and intentionally censored.

Perhaps reflecting the ideas of the adage "that which is always seen is seldom noticed and that which is seldom seen is always noticed," Crowley presents to his reading audience that which they know exists but have not noticed and then presents what they seldom see (an attempt to relate a realistic sketch of life) which causes them to take notice and, subsequently, reject his work. In his article, "Aleister Crowley's *White Stains*," Rictor Norton claims "the book attempts to trace the progress of diabolism in an unhinged mind." This implication suggests that either Crowley was completely deranged to believe that society was prepared to learn of the sordid depravities that he believes exist in life or that he was completely degenerate and has lost the ability to engage in "normal" sexual relationships without seeking progressive perversities as a stimulus. Beginning with the dedicatory poem that reveals a new experience, "each poem is successively more vile than the preceding, until we reach the penultimate 'Necrophilia' [. . .] that leaves us more numbed than repulsed" (Norton, Aleister Crowley's *White Stains*). For many others, however, it represents the ultimate sexual experience.

Although many Victorian writers presented material that later was classified as decadent because it embraced deviant, immoral, and counterproductive ideologies that reflected homoerotism, they were usually able to pass the scrutinizing eyes of the censors by encrypting their works with a coded language that was subject to interpretation by a select group of individuals. Interestingly enough, many teachers of the classics, like the censors, are either unaware of the encoding or choose to ignore the encryption, if evident. According to Philip Clark, this occurs because

> The term 'homoerotic' is frequently problematic in scholarly articles, especially those discussing works of art. While most scholars use it carefully, to represent works of art that depict themes related to love, sex, and sensuality between people of the same gender, the use of the term is tricky. The word can be, and has been, used in a misguided attempt to make an artist 'straight' – as an excuse for not discussing homosexuality.

As a consequence of this, some educators continue to offer instruction based on traditional interpretations of the works or on the merits and laurels of the authors.

When educators do not feel comfortable discussing decadent themes, which may include the topic of homosexuality, it is usually because it is outside of their experience or because it would necessitate an explanation of the author's lifestyle or interest in the subject. Many still do not understand that one need not be gay to write about or discuss gay themes in the same manner that one need not be a women to discuss women's issues or Hispanic to discuss Hispanic issues or even a "dead, white, male" to discuss "classic literature." However, those individuals who are able to overcome the aversion of salacious material that deals with themes of homoerotica have realized many teaching opportunities to discuss the tenacity, creativity, and genius of the writers who dared to challenge the censors and society by expressing themes of homosexuality during a climate of intolerance.

These writers when "objectionable" material was presented required an indirect approach. They did not explicitly state their subject matter, but they did manage to camouflage their implicit messages throughout the topic that became apparent to select readers/listeners who sought understanding in the duality of the words, phrases, and thoughts. Many writers who wished to present themes of homosexuality had to encrypt their works because of their fear of censorship, social reprisal, and punishment. Even though we may view their endeavors as a passive/aggressive approach, their voices enabled the torch of literary freedom to be lit and then carried forward by those who followed in their footsteps.[2]

An examination of a few of Crowley's poems from *White Stains* will reveal, through his descriptively explicit avowals of decadent subject matters, that he was not intimidated by the dictates of Victorian society. Instead, he asserted his sexual literary freedom, which reflects an aspect of his occultist belief that "a man can do what he likes" or "Do What Thou Wilt" (*White Stains* vii), by his intentional disregard for society's intolerance of graphically, specific sexual imagery. Although readers may interpret some of the poems as an overdose of eroticism or classify them as literary pornography, an explication of some of the poems may shed some light on the question of why Crowley's poems were censored.

---

[2] Among those censored is Crowley, whose books of poems, including those found in his edition of *White Stains*, were not available to his contemporaries or modern readers because of censorship. According to John Symonds, Crowley's book of poems "was privately and anonymously printed in 1898 in an edition of 100 copies, most of which were destroyed in 1924 by H. M. Customs" (x). Published shortly after the infamous Wilde trials when society was still in an uproar over the moral climate of the nation, this work was denounced by the press as "the filthiest book of verse ever written." In a sense, Crowley was the first direct recipient of Oscar Wilde's personal trials and tribulations because he dared to pick up the literary torch to present sexually blatant verse that leaves little to the imagination. Yet, there is still the presence of encoding that serves to heighten the topical themes and allows readers to bring their own experiences to the work. However, the mildly encoded passages still allow the erection of a flimsy barrier between the author, intolerant press/censors, and society in general.

One of the main reasons Crowley's poems are omitted from standard anthologies is that they reflect a sentiment that many scholars preferred to ignore as a vital aspect of Victorian literature – explicit homoerotism. To better understand his poems, one must try to understand Crowley as a man and as a professed "Uranian" or "urning," to use a less common term. According to Karl Beckson, this term carried great significance during the Victorian period because a "Uranian" was a male homosexual. Although homosexuality existed, many Victorians chose to ignore what they considered to be the "unnatural" nature of homosexuals since it conflicted with their religious and moral values. Beckson states that to ensure that homosexuals remained out of sight, "The crime of buggery [sodomy] had carried the death penalty from the time of Henry VIII. During Victoria's reign," the law was changed to reflect that "any homosexual act between males [. . .] could lead to imprisonment" (191). For fear of their lives or imprisonment, many homosexual poets hid their sexual preferences behind a religious veil or by addressing their poems to women.

Ian Young states that "other poets," such as Crowley, "with no deep interest in religion, still found" the attitudes "of Victorian society deeply frustrating and hurtful, and took refuge in the self-consciously sinister" (264). Concurring with this belief is Brian Reade who reveals that provocation delighted Crowley: "It is in *White Stains* that we notice for the first time since the eighteenth century the promise – not so long after the Wilde scandal – of a brutal, burlesque approach to sexual intimacies and emotions which was to become common in our century" (49). Other scholars of the Victorian period who agree with Young and Reade consider Crowley a decadent writer because of his bizarre intent. Crowley, however, did not believe his explicitly sexual poems were bizarre at all.

The opening poem, "Dédicace," reveals the first sexual experience of a man with another man. The appropriateness of this poem, from a psychological approach, is apparent in that it represents a new beginning, a change from that which may have been familiar to that which is, technically speaking, virgin ground. The speaker expresses himself in the language of heterosexual discourse where he assumes the role of woman. According to Caroll Smith-Rosenberg, many Victorians knew of C. H. Ulrichs' belief that "homosexuality was not an example of willful moral depravity but a congenital degenerative defect. A woman's soul was trapped in a man's body" (266-67).

Crowley's poetry, however, emphasizes that the speaker's preference is not caused by defect but by choice. The very first line, "You crown me king and queen," reveals the duality of his nature. He is both man and woman. That is, he is a man who wants to be dominated, to be used, and to be taken as a woman for the sake of experience. His desire to feel the "rhythmical Caress" and the "kiss" of his lover will enslave his will to a force stronger than that within his power to control. He begs his lover to come to his bed and rob him "of his maidenhead." He anticipates the pain but urges his lover to be "like a strong man who would constrain a maid." At the moment of penetration, the speaker is overwhelmed by pain and feelings of mixed emotions including the knowledge of his "shame," but his physical and emotional pain is outweighed by the pleasure of the experience. He cries:

> God! I shall faint with pain, I hide my face
> For shame. I am disturbed, I cannot rise,
> I breathe hard with thy breath; thy quick embrace
> Crushes; thy teeth are agony – pain dies
> In deadly passion. Ah! You come – you kill me!
> Christ! God! Bite! Bite! Ah Bite! Love's fountains fill me.
>
> ("Dédicace" 12)

The experience is over quickly but not before the speaker urges his lover to bite him as he is filled with the results of the union.

The pain of penetration is quickly replaced by a sense of pleasure as his body reacts to the new sensations, yet the speaker compels his lover to bite him to cause him more pain. Many readers may wish to interpret this request as a prelude to future anticipated experiences of sado-masochism. It is equally plausible that the speaker wants to be brought back to reality in order to heighten his own sensations of the moment in much the same manner that a hypnotist will snap his fingers to make his subject conscious of an experience. Because the "thick dear darkness" of the room provides a cover of secrecy for the speaker, he is protected from the visual evidence of his encounter. Mentally, he does not have to acknowledge that he is physically present because he cannot see himself, his lover, or the bed in which they pursue their sexual activity. His emotional awareness of his "sweet infamy," relies only on his sense of touch of where he is present. He is able to speak, but we only know what the speaker expresses, which reflects the emotional silent musings of his mind. We hear no response from the lover whose only apparent function in the poem is to facilitate the physical action. Although the inflicted bites may be a physical attempt to draw the speaker back to reality, "the meter genuinely parallels the delightful 'rushing-forward' sense of orgasm" (Norton, Aleister Crowley's *White Stains*) that may be found in several of the poems used in this study. Whether actual bites or staccato-like actions of ejaculation, the climactic pleasure of the rhythmical penetration conjoins his mind and body.

Today, in the twenty-first century, most people would hardly consider this poem decadent or pornographic, because we are more open-minded to life's experiences. Yet the moral majority of Victorian people represented by the censors and press deemed this book of poems decadent to the point of proclaiming it "the filthiest book of verse ever written" (d'Arch Smith 95). Is it sufficient to declare a work filthy without defining what makes it filthy or obscene? Is the work so perverted that it deserves to be destroyed and promote the concept of a book burning as a means to control the stimuli of the masses? Apparently, the censors and press were the self-imposed authorities. They did not feel compelled to justify their actions since they believed they were protecting people from being exposed to pornographic and erotic material. They formed their opinions solely on the perceived idea that two men were engaged in sexual intercourse. In his article, "High Moral Climates," Rictor Norton reveals:

> This is because a gay subject is automatically reviled as obscene in the same way that gay people are automatically despised as those who 'indulge in homosexual practices.' That is, most people fail to distinguish between homosexual acts on the one hand and homosexual persons/ feelings/ lifestyles on the other; this focus solely upon sex is perpetrated by the term 'homosexual,' though most people are content with the terms 'cocksucker,' 'bugger,' etc.

Today this concept is realized in the attitudes of people who accept media endorsed stereotypes as the determining analysis of the character of an individual within a subculture or group. Inevitably, these stereotypes foster ideas that promote prejudice and hatred that lead to discrimination and, in extreme cases, death.

The psychological progression of the poems develops quickly from an innocent first experience to an experimentation of first experiences with many different partners. The speaker does not restrict himself to male-male desire but arbitrarily continues to engage in male-female relations. The gender of his partner is of no consequence, as the sexual encounters serve to broaden his experience, knowledge, and abilities. As the speaker gains a fuller sense of his sexuality, the novelty of these encounters with multiple partners becomes mundane because they fail to produce the same self-excitement as when the act was perceived as sinful, dangerous, or erotic. Consequently, it becomes necessary to seek out broader experiences, oftentimes inspired by a self-willful active imagination and the power of fantasy, to stimulate and enable the speaker to achieve and maintain an erection. Once the stimulus becomes a mechanization of routine, an ordinary experience with anticipated results, the speaker loses interest (literally speaking since he is usually unable to achieve or maintain an erection) and seeks out a more unique experience. This progression leads to even more desirable, bizarre activities because of the element of danger.

In his poem, "Ballade De La Jolie Marion," Crowley explicitly expresses a carefree attitude towards his sexual activities indicating that he is content to remain in a relationship as long as the excitement of sexual intimacy is present; however, once the excitement is gone, the relationship need not be continued. Even though this poem reflects what society calls "normal" sexual activity, that is male and female conventional intercourse, it is an affirmation of "free love" which Wendell Stacy Johnson states is a sensitive subject "unmentionable in any but the lowest society" (127). Crowley, however, flaunts his conviction that love is transitory by repeating at the end of every verse that when the excitement ends "we must part, and love must die." This attitude reflects his belief that the existence of love is directly proportional to sexual involvement. Effectually, many of these encounters are superficially transient leading us to question the possibility of many "one night stands." After sex ceases to be pleasurable, whether this be after one night, one week, or any period of time, love dies. For the Victorians, this is a sensitive subject because it negates the belief that sex is only for the purpose of procreation and is separate from feelings of love.

This poem relates the speaker's knowledge that for most people sexual passion is replaced by memories of past pleasures. The recollection of initial passion (of first experiences) is the source of the excitement that enables men to achieve and maintain an erection. The emphasis is on the pleasure performance of the man because of the common misconception that women do not enjoy sex and only engage in sexual activity because of their subservient obligation to men. Crowley stimulates the unconscious power of sexual response by utilizing a rhythmical language that heightens his readers' sexual awareness, while, at the same time, psychologically advancing their experience by suggesting an alternative source of inspiration and pleasure. In "Ballade De La Jolie Marion," Crowley uses a double alliteration in the line: "My lover's limbs of lissome white" (16) employing the consonants "l" and "s" to create a sense of breathlessness, a whispering; a staccato-like rhythm that evokes a sexually seductive presence. As the poem continues, the language becomes more explicit. "Fond limbs with mine were intertwined, / A hand lascivious fondled me" (38). The memories become a fantasy, a fantasy in which the speaker is free to explore other sexual possibilities. Negating the assumption of women's sexual passivity, the speaker states that he is inspired by "her desire" and that it is she who "work[s] our pleasure till I tire" (39). Crowley continues to flaunt provocative subject matters by suggesting the possibility that sadism and masochism can be a source of extreme pleasures, a mixture of sensations that create an atmosphere of excitement. The pleasure of contentment is expressed as the speaker "suck[s] the sweetness from the night" and is heightened as he "steal[s] passion from reluctant pain" (39). The words used to convey the sexual imagery produce an effect that censors deem pornographic because they serve to excite the reader. Isolated, the words suggest innocent actions that can be applied to almost any situation, but when presented in conjunction with the idea of a sexual encounter, the words are perceived as perverse. In his essay, "Problems of Pornography," Rictor Norton states:

Good porn – often like good sex – is gradual, slow and methodic. The very word 'slowly' renders more exciting any description of rubbing, thrusting, stoking, whipping or whatever. The one exception is ejaculation, which is best described as 'spasmodic jerks.' But if the sexual narrative itself is spasmodic and jerky, it generally fails to produce the physical tension necessary for a good erotic read.

Although Wendell Stacey Johnson states that if "these sensitive subjects [. . .] were referred to at all [by society] it was in oblique language, and cautiously" (127), we find that Crowley does not try to hide his meaning. His words clearly state his sexual activity, his knowledge that women have sexual desires, and his willingness to explore sexual alternatives. Throughout the poem, the iambic rhythm emphasizes the words as if they are meant to imitate the rhythmic thrust of sexual intercourse, while the concluding lines of each verse announce the inevitable end of their passion. This iambic expression of desire is indistinguishable from the explicitness of the verbal desire because it arouses explicit meaning.

In the poem, "Ballade de la Jolie Marion," Crowley presents to his readers the possibility of "normal" sexual fulfillment through "free love," "fantasy," and "sexual exploration" that stretches the psychological limitations imposed by society. Once a new limit is established, it becomes the floor from which all new experiences are judged. In his poem, "All Night," Crowley moves the peg of sexual exploration up a notch by introducing the idea that it is possible to achieve greater sexual satisfaction and to entertain sexual fantasies through multiple sex partners. Initially, the focus of the poem is on the ménage of three individuals (two men and a woman) and the excitement to be found in the sensation of touch within a heterosexual exchange; however, the primary force of the poem quickly changes to a homoerotic desire. The psychological development by including a given factor often yields an unexpected reaction. When a man and a woman are placed in a sexual setting, it is expected that they will engage in sexual activity. When we include another man in this scenario, it is expected that both men will use the woman as a source of pleasure. They may take turns or they may engage in the activity at the same time but from different approaches. This in itself is a very erotic image. However, what is not expected or anticipated is that the two men will derive pleasure from each other. Yet this is exactly the image that Crowley conveys. In this poem, once the circle of touch is completed, the woman is excluded from the sexual pleasures, and the remaining emotional focus of the poem is on male flesh touching male flesh. The speaker states:

> [. . .] only through the lips
> Electric ardour kindles, flashes, slips
> Through all the circle to her lips again,
> And thence, unwavering, flies to mine, to drain
> All pleasure in one draught. No whispered sigh,
> No change of breast, love's posture perfectly
> Once gained, we change no more. ("All Night" 45)

Unable to control the homoerotic awakening, the woman is consumed by sexual desire, but she is forced into the position of a spectator as the male bond is established. The presence of her body is relegated to the role of one who facilitates the homoerotic desire and validates the activities of the men. The speaker, aware of the woman's frustration, acknowledges: "Yet, did I raise my head, throughout the gloom / I might behold thine eyes as red as fire, / A tigress maddened with supreme desire" (46). The speaker, however, does not raise his head because he does not want to admit that he desires only the touch of the other man or that he has made a conscious choice to exclude the woman from the circle of touch.

The male energy takes on an erotic tone, an unleashing of male flesh touching male flesh that creates a sexual intensity that is present in the steady rhythm of the poem. The two men experience a sexual affinity as they join their bodies together, and the intensity of their passion erupts as the intended climax of the poem. Crowley reveals the vitality of their union as one sustained sentence that culminates with the exclamation of the single, monosyllabic word "Ah!" The speaker is enthralled in a graphically sexual frenzy that is expressed in a "meter [that] genuinely parallels the delightful "rushing-forward" sense of orgasm" (Norton, Aleister Crowley's *White Stains*). Although Norton claims that a spasmodic and jerky narrative "generally fails to produce the physical tension necessary for a good erotic read" ("Problems of Pornography"), the poetic presentations of words imitate the "rubbing, thrusting, stroking, whipping" expression of sexual intercourse:

> So, blood and body furious with breath
> That pants through foaming kisses, let us stay
> Gripped hard together to kiss life away,
> Mouths drowned in murder, never satiate,
> Kissing away the hard decrees of Fate,
> Kissing insatiable in mad desire
> Kisses whose agony may never tire,
> Kissing the gates of hell, the sword of God,
> Each unto each a serpent or a rod,
> A well of wine and fire, each unto each,
> Whose lips are fain convulsively to reach
> A higher heaven, a deeper hell. Ah! ("All Night" 46)

The climax is obtained, and D. J. Enright states what he believes should be obvious about Crowley's poem: "It cannot be said to lack virility if for Crowley's [formation of the word kiss] we substitute, as the context of the quotations invites us to do, the four-letter word and its formations" (213). In many of Crowley's poems, the word "kiss" and its formations are abundantly found, yet there is an implicitly homoerotic sense of seduction once the word "kiss" is decoded and replaced perhaps with the "correct" formations of the contemporary four-letter word.

In this poem, the homosexual desire emerges through a triangular setting within a conventional heterosexual situation; nevertheless, once the Victorian gender code is broken, the awakening of the male-bonding sexual experience brings with it the dawning of desire, as the two men confront the realization of their passion and the knowledge that they have found their suppressed sexual destiny. When the intense moment passes, however, the speaker expresses his dismay that his desire to be with another man is less than conventional:

> So soon to dawn, delight to snatch away!
> Damned day, whose sunlight finds us as with wine
> Drunken, with lust made manifest divine
> Devils of darkness, servants unto hell. ("All Night" 47)

Although Crowley's poem begins as an exchange of male homosexual desire channeled through a heterosexual mask, the conclusion reveals that the sexual attraction of the two men is not only based on same-sex eroticism but also on same-sex desire, bringing with it the reality that they cannot openly express their love for each other:

> And we, one mouth to kiss, one soul to lure,
> For ever, wedded, one, divine, endure
> Far from sun, sea, and spring, from love or light,
> Imbedded in impenetrable night [. . .] ("All Night" 48)

The speaker then indicates that they must bear the knowledge of their love as a secret until they can obtain social and legal sanctions: "So in our lust, the monstrous burden borne / Heavy writhing the womb, we wait the morn / Of its fulfillment." Until that time arrives, however, they can only dream of "One writhing glory, an immortal kiss" (49).

Once again, a new breakthrough occurs in the progressively psychological exploration of sexual pleasures. The conclusion of "All Night" reveals that sexual pleasures derived by the two men outside the constraints of a perceived "normal" relationship (i.e. male-female interaction) are viewed as even more obscene by society because it suggests that, given an option, men could choose other men as a source of pleasure over women. This negates the fundamental heterosexual social, religious, and biological principles that advocate the sexual union of two people for the purposes of procreation only. Although the idea of a woman engaging in sexual activities with two men at the same time is viewed by society as an act of debauchery, this situation is preferential to the alternative that the woman is totally spurned. To this effect, there is an underlying message that intolerant people can become tolerant of suggested immoral behavior when an alternative choice is purveyed as more immoral than the original situation. Further conveyed is another underlying message that people who fall outside the delineated norms of society must fight for their rights to love as they please.

Sensitive subjects of so-called deviant sexual activities during the Victorian period included pederasty, which was a common theme in Uranian verse. The attraction often involved a man of high social position with a boy of a much lower social rank. Although many Victorians may have perceived this as an exploitation of the plight of the poor, Timothy d'Arch Smith reveals that "the Uranians' need to form alliances with working-class boys may well have arisen from an inferiority complex forbidding them to stand up to the rigours and responsibilities of a love affair with an intellectual equal" (191). Crowley, however, does not suffer from an inferiority complex. According to Smith, Crowley's poems are a reflection of his desire to obtain pleasure by "celebrating every form of sexual perversion" (98).

In his poem "Rondels," Crowley advances the sexual challenge of finding new sources of excitement and extends his quest to include children. He "sings luridly (but perhaps sincerely) of the joys of paederasty" (Smith 98). The speaker in this poem does not restrict his enthusiasm for children to a specific gender. He is content to find his pleasure with the "Maid of dark eyes" upon "the shadowy secret of [her] amorous thighs" or with the "boy of red lips" as he watches "how the fond ruby rapier glides and slips / 'Twixt the white hills thou spreadest for me there" (57). The ambiguity of this line is that we do not know for certain who is performing the act. For Victorians, as well as modern readers, the title of giver and receiver is unimportant as the idea of engaging in sexual activities with children is found to be immoral on the grounds that they are too immature to make sexual decisions. Crowley considered himself outside the governance of social dictates. Naive children, believing they had the ability of moral, social decision making, were, in fact, deluded into usury by an adult population that put forth their best interests. Although not included in this study, the poem, "With Dog and Dame," reflects this same line of thinking since animals are unable to communicate their willingness or lack of willingness to engage in sexual activities with humans.

The topic of sexual activity with children and animals aside, this poem promotes the theme of bisexuality, which does much to undermine the supposition of most Uranians seeking homosocial situations preferring the male-to-male experience of sex found in the pleasures of the "hot mouth passionate more than man may bear" ("Rondels" 58) offered by the "boy of red lips." For many Uranians, homosocial settings were the only opportunity to engage in male-to-male desire since, outside this sort of environment, they were expected to present male-to-female interests. Clark reveals that "Like 'homoerotic,' 'homosocial' is another problematic term occasionally used to deny the existence of homosexual sex acts. [. . .] [H]omosociality is the condition of being involved in a closely- knit environment consisting entirely of one gender."³ However, Crowley, a professed bisexual, finds great pleasure in anal intercourse and does not feel compelled to restrict his activities to boys unless it is his desire to be the recipient of the act. He does not desire a homosocial setting because it would restrict his sexual experiences to one gender and preclude the possibility of entertaining a new direction for his bisexual conquests.

Readers of Crowley's poems must remember that laws existed to discourage homosexuals from succumbing to what was considered by many to be their unnatural inclinations. Demonstrating his lack of regard for these laws, Crowley's poem "A Ballad of Passive Paederasty" flaunts his preference for anal intercourse; even when he is with women, Crowley reveals such a preference as he finds little excitement in conventional sex. Again, his explicitness graphically illustrates his sexual literary freedom as well as his pleasure in provocation:

Free women cast a lustful eye
On my gigantic charms, and seek
By word and touch with me to lie,
And vainly proffer cunt and cheek;
Then, angry, they miscall me weak,
Till one, divining me aright,

---

³ Clark further reveals that "Classic examples of homosocial environments include the male boarding school, [. . .] the military, the gentlemen's club, and the fraternity. [. . .] These institutions often give rise to intense and loving male-male relationships. They are also known as frequent breeding grounds for homosexual sex acts."

> Points to her buttocks, whispers 'Greek!' –
> A strong man's love is my delight! (67)

Through the frankness of his language, Crowley continues to flaunt his disregard for the law and deliberately sets out to shock the sensibilities of the Victorian people by indicating how he desires to be with a man:

> To feel him clamber on me, laid
> Prone on the couch of lust and shame,
> To feel him force me like a maid
> And his great sword within me flame
> His breath as hot and quick as fame
> To kiss him and to clasp him tight;
> This is my joy without a name,
> A strong man's love is my delight. (68)

Crowley incorporates into this poem the code word "shame" which Beckson states is often associated with "the most widely quoted line in Uranian literature – 'I am the love that dare not speak its name'" (Douglas 25; qtd in Beckson 189) – in other words, the love for the same sex. Unlike his first homosexual experience described in "Dédicace," this poem reveals the speaker as a much more aggressive individual who is not content to assume a passive role "like a maid." He engages in an aggressive/passive role in which he aggressively seeks the passive. He asserts his manhood by directing and instigating an action that reflects a new first experience.

Indicating the last of first experiences, the very title of the penultimate poem "Necrophilia" prepares us for an unusual sexual experience that is ultimately most appreciated by those individuals who have "progress[ed] through various initiations from a relatively unenlightened state to a state of pure selfhood, which is also paradoxically selfless" (Maroney). The uninitiated individual, which in many cases is the reader of Crowley's poetry, may have a difficult time disassociating the ideal concept of enlightenment from the actual reality of an act that reflects, according to *Webster's Dictionary*, an "obsession with and usually erotic interest in or stimulation by corpses" (790). The thought of having sexual relations with a corpse is repulsive to people with even the most unusual proclivities. Yet it is this sort of act that delighted Crowley because it allowed him to challenge Christian sexual taboos that restricted people from indulging in experiences profaning the mysteries of life and death. This type of interaction is the omega to the process of initiation that provides the impetus to grow and expand the knowledge of quested maximum sensuality. Arrival of the final experience reflects a progression through the "levels of initiatory truth" that effectively frees individuals from the constraints of society. In his essay, "First: 'Do What Thou Wilt,'" Tim Maroney reveals that Crowley's motto "'do what you will' was an ethical code bearing on how one should deal with others" that rejected any influence from Christian doctrines that restricted self-experience. His creed reflected a one-on-one interaction with individuals, animals, and the universe as a process of achieving perfect unity. Maroney claims that

> Since this new law replaces outdated moral codes based around sins and forbidden acts, a person knowing and doing the will might appear to be sinful from a traditional viewpoint. In Crowley's view the Thelemite is following a demanding code requiring great personal integrity even while, for instance, making love in ways that would be illegal in oppressive societies.

For Crowley, the legality of the speaker's actions in the poem is not a major consideration since he believed himself and his subjects to be outside the domain of socio-religious influence. It is only through this act that "the realization of one's true nature comes at the same time that one realizes one's unity with all beings" (Maroney).

In his desire to achieve this perfect unity, the speaker indulges all his senses in one last experience with his dead lover, perhaps as a final tribute to "the ecstasies of Art" that he learned since his first homoerotic experience with him. In "Necrophilia" the speaker reflects that each act, progressively more vile, fails to fulfill him. The thrill of each new experience leaves him craving a new and more erotic experience. He is like a drug addict who cannot achieve the same glorious sensation previously achieved without increasing his dosage of the drug that produced the desired effect. The progression of acts that propagate taboos with offensive speech and action are meant to strengthen the character and resolution of the individual engaged in the activities. Nevertheless, in this poem, reflecting the final earthly experience, the speaker is still unable to express his male-to-male encounters without thinking of "the things shameful that I hold." He is still a member of an intolerant society though his actions reflect his desire to be independent of societal attitudes and concerns that restrict knowledge through experience.

When we consider "the major variations of buggery, pederasty, heterosexual sodomy, fellatio, cunnilingus, rimming, rape, sapphism, impotence, bestiality, coprophilia and necrophila" (Norton, "Aleister Crowley's *White Stains*") presented in the poems, it is interesting that what the speaker finds "shameful" are the things he held (physically and mentally). Nevertheless, the necrophagous imagery advances the speaker into a new realm of sexual adventurism that surpasses all previous experiences. The sight of his dead lover inspires sad recollections of what is now lost to him. No longer will he know the "kisses" or the "heartbeat" or the "sweat" that provided the ecstasies that society deemed obscene and appalling; these thoughts enthralled him. He recollects the experiences he has shared with this man that have culminated in this final moment. His contemplative musings are interrupted when his "nostrils sniff the luxury / of flesh decaying" ("Necrophilia" 109). He envisions his dead lover not as he was, but as he is now, one who has been reunited with nature. As his lover's body decays, he becomes food for the "festive worms" that enables him to live again as part of the cycle of life, one creature feeding on the misfortunes of another as a means of survival.

This process reflects the endless cycle of life that will allow his lover to live forever. No longer does he envision a corpse but an object of nature that lies before him to give him substance. As he looks at his dead lover, he sees an invitation to life in the "buttocks [that] now are swan-soft" (109) that causes him to transcend the feeling of death and to arrive at a state of euphoria. Like the worms feeding on the entails of the decaying flesh, his body wants to live and seeks nourishment. As he speaks to his dead lover, he reveals a vision of horror that even the most stout-hearted of individuals would find repugnant:

> Yea, thou art dead. [. . .]
> And hast a strange desire begot
> In me, to lick thy bloody brow;
> To gnaw thy hollow cheeks, and pull
> Thy lustful tongue from out its sheath;
> To wallow in the bowels of death,
> And rip thy belly, and fill full
> My hands with all putridities;
> To chew thy dainty testicles. (109-10)

Explicitly, the image reveals what the speaker sees before him and what he wants to do to the decaying body, yet it is the implicit image that reveals the perversities and obscenities of his thoughts and actions. He gnaws the "hollow cheeks" of the buttocks and pulls the uncircumcised penis from "out its sheath." He then presents a scatological image as he "wallows" in the excrement found in the bowels. He "rips" the belly to enter deeper into the vessel of his affection and the source of his pleasure, to fill his "hands with all putridities" and then his mouth as he "chews" the testicles. Yet these acts do not satiate his appetite. He wants more; he needs more; he craves more. His infected penis drips the seed of gonorrhea's "poisonous discharge" as he engages in his act of coprophilia. He partakes in a blasphemous ritual of sacramental union by eating the stool and drinking the fluids of the "hanged corpse," his god. Each act announces the onset of the painful climactic orgasm that concludes with his death.

Although these represent only a few of Crowley's poems, readers receive a clear message that he will not be intimidated by the dictates of Victorian society. His poems include descriptively explicit avowals of decadent (bizarre) subject matters that include: bestiality, cunnilingus, necrophilia, orgies (with men, women, and animals), pederasty, diseases (gonorrhea, clap, and syphilis), sex and menstruation, and death as a pinnacle of sexual desire. It is certain that Crowley wanted to draw attention to himself as one of the most outrageously shocking poets of his time, expressing his contempt for the narrow-minded attitudes of his society. And, he was successful in his endeavors.

Edward Aleister Crowley may have been "The Wickedest Man in the World" (d'Arch Smith 95), but, according to Enright, he is a poet whose "favourite literary device" is alliteration, "and crude though it is, it works quite effectively when he is being indignant or contemptuous" (214). Clearly many of his poems can be viewed as pornographic and erotic; nevertheless, they do reflect many of the sentiments, beliefs, and tastes that collectively represent a segment of his era. For this reason, Crowley stands as an equal with other decadent figures and deserves the serious consideration of scholars who want to genuinely represent the Victorian period in an unbiased and un-suppressed manner.

Works Cited

Beckson, Karl, ed. *Aesthetes and Decadents of the 1890s: An Anthology of British Poetry and Prose*. New York: Random House, 1966.

---. *London in the 1890s: A Cultural History*. New York: W. W. Norton, 1992.

Clark, Philip. "Erotics in Arcadia: Symbolic Myth and Homosexuality in F. Holland Day's Photography." *Understudy: Undergraduate Scholarship Journal of the College of William and Mary* 2.2 (2001). May 2004 <http://www.wm.edu/SO/under study/volume2issue2/Clark/Clar k.html>

Crowley, Edward Aleister. *White Stains*. Ed. and introd. John Symonds. Re/set ed. London: Gerald Duckworth, 1973.

---. *The Confessions of Aleister Crowley: an Autohagiography*. Ed. John Symonds and Kenneth Grant. New York: Bantam, 1971.

Douglas, Alfred Bruce. "Two Loves." *"Two Loves" and Other Poems: A Selection*. Michigan: Bennett and Kitchel, 1990. 23-25.

Enright, D. J. *Man Is an Onion: Reviews and Essays*. London: Chatto & Windus, 1972.

Johnson, Wendell Stacy. *Living in Sin: The Victorian Sexual Revolution*. Chicago: Nelson-Hall, 1979.

Krafft-Ebing, R. von. *Psychopathia Sexualis*. New York: Physicians and Surgeons Book Company, 1927.

Maroney, Tim. "'Do What Thou Wilt.'" *Introduction to Crowley Studies (in Five Voices). The Tim Maroney Web Collection* 1980-2002. May 2004 <http://tim.maroney.org/CrowleyIntro/ Do_What_Thou_Wilt.ht ml>.

Norton, Rictor. Home Page. 18 Feb. 2005. "Aleister Crowley's *White Stains*." *Gay History and Literature. A History of Homo-*

erotica. May 2004 <http://www.infopt.demon.co.uk/homoeros.
htm>.

---. "High Moral Climates." *Gay History and Literature. A History
of Homoerotica*. May 2004 <http://www.infopt.demon.co.uk/
homoeros.htm>.

---. "Problems of Pornography." *Gay History and Literature. A History
of Homoerotica*. May 2004 <http://www.infopt.demon.
co.uk/homoeros.htm>.

Reade, Brian, ed. *Sexual Heretics: Male Homosexuality in English
Literature from 1850 to 1900: An Anthology*. London:
Routledge, 1970.

Smith-Rosenberg, Carroll. *Disorderly Conduct: Visions of Gender
in Victorian America*. New York: Alfred A. Knopf, 1985.

Smith, Timothy d'Arch. *Love in Earnest: Some Notes on the Lives
and Writings of English "Uranian" Poets from 1889 to 1930*.
London: Routledge, 1970.

Strossen, Nadine. "The Perils of Pornophobia." *Risking Contact*. Ed.
W. Royce Adams. New York: Houghton Mifflin, 1997. 550-56.

Young, Ian. *The Male Homosexual in Literature: A Bibliography*.
Metuchen, N.J. and London: Scarecrow, 1982.

Discourse of Pathology and the Vitalistic Desire for Unity in Lawrence Durrell's *The Black Book*

Ann-Catherine Nabholz
University of Basel and University of Orléans

Abstract: My chief concern lies in tracing literary Modernism's traumatic response to modernity. From the agonistic perspective characterising Modernist literature, modernity initiated the collapse of a premodern cultural framework. The resulting sense of disintegration was perceived as the primary sign of decadence. Throughout my analysis, the human body will appear as the principal witness of this modernist spectacle of decay. To elaborate on this suggestion, I shall analyse Lawrence Durrell's late Modernist attempt to recover the lost sense of unity through a vitalistic reevaluation of embodied experience.

The various Modernist movements of the beginning of the twentieth century have generally been understood as distressful attempts to come to terms with the destabilising experience of modern life. As a reaction to the period which provided it with a name, literary Modernism denotes an acute awareness of modernity with its changes that arose from the emergence of industrial development, technological progress and urbanisation. Even if the terminological debate around the term 'Modernism' has made clear that as a literary historical designation it fails to do justice to the divergent artistic movements and styles of this era, scholars agree that as a term it nevertheless draws attention to one of these movements' common denominators. Namely, that to a certain extent they all involve a distinct relation to the past and the allegedly monolithic foundations of Western art and culture. Astradur Eysteinsson (8) calls attention to the importance of this affinity with the past and claims that "'Modernism' signals a dialectical opposition to what is not functionally 'modern,' namely 'tradition.'" He carries the argument even further and asserts that this "rage against prevalent traditions is perhaps the principal characteristic of modernism."

This conflictual relationship with the past amounted to a sense of rupture for the Modernist artist, whose cultural pessimism is exemplified by a number of recurrent motifs of anxiety and existential angst. With the breakup of prevalent traditions themes such as alienation, chaos, disintegration as well as disenchantment with western civilisation became characteristic expressions of literary Modernism. As a result, critics have often pointed out that Modernist writing was inclined toward the idea of crisis. While Leo Bersani maintains that the notion of historical crisis illustrates Modernism's "mournful sense of the break itself as unique" (48), Matei Calinescu adds that cultural modernity exhibits not only a negation of the past, it also "turns against itself and, by regarding itself as *decadence*, dramatizes its own deep sense of crisis" (5). The charge of decadence was perhaps most emphatically put by Friedrich Nietzsche, whose reflections on 'modernity' anticipate the Modernist preoccupation with the decline of western culture.[1] In his often-quoted work, *The Case of Wagner*, Nietzsche claims that modernisation fails to provide a meaningful unity and thus undermines a coherent existence. The signs of decadence he recognises to reside in the fact that "life no longer dwells in the whole." He thus contends that literary decadence illustrates the non-unity of the whole, the "anarchy of atoms, [the] disaggregation of will" (qtd. in Calinescu 186-87; original text in Nietzsche 254). Nietzsche's analysis of decadence is

---

[1] Terminologically, the word 'modernity' must here be differentiated from its function as a historical category. In this essay I will use the term interchangeably, accepting Calinescu's (10) definition of "aesthetic modernity [. . .] as a crisis concept," which is "involved in a threefold dialectical opposition to tradition, to the modernity of bourgeois civilization (with its ideals of rationality, utility, progress), and, finally, to itself, insofar as it perceives itself as a new tradition or form of authority."

particularly interesting because his condemnation of modernity as a formless amalgamation of values and ideas appears as a decisive intellectual influence on the Modernist emphasis on fragmentation. Indeed, his attack against modernity was echoed by many Modernists who believed that "modern civilization has brought about the loss of something precious, the dissolution of a great integrative paradigm, the fragmentation of what once was a mighty unity" (Calinescu 265).

This condition of cultural exhaustion culminated in a proliferation of aesthetic experiments, which both absorbed this rupture with a premodern order and reflected the lack of unity. Significantly, it is the fervour with which many Modernists tried to overturn existing modes of representation – or to use Ezra Pound's famous slogan "to make it new" – that aroused the greatest amount of scholarly interest. However, even if the excessive use of artistic experiments is usually considered to suggest bleakness and disintegration, traditional explanations of the Modernist poetics of excess tend to favour aesthetic preoccupations over the despair behind the Modernist confrontation with modernity. Yet the aura of pathology, which becomes manifest in wasteland imagery, the fear of madness and disturbed relations of individuals to their bodies, clearly shows that there is a sense of agony characterising this literary period. I therefore propose that this agony is best understood in terms of a theory about Modernism which interprets the Modernist poetics of excess not as an exclusively aesthetic program, but as a symptom of cultural pathology that can be directly linked to modern decadence.

I am guided in this approach by the work of Jed Rasula. In an immensely suggestive essay entitled "The Pathic Receptacles of Modernity," Rasula draws a parallel between the abundance of aesthetic experiments and the Modernist anxiety about decadence. In contrast to most theories on aesthetic innovations, which according to Rasula (193) make Modernist texts "seem paradoxically comfortable with the agonies they signify, at repose in their distress," he claims that artistic experiments function as desperate illustrations of a collapsing cultural framework. Rasula very efficiently points out the "modernist drama of decomposition of forms" (194) by arguing that the symptoms that emerge are both "amputation and abundance, collapse of a reassuring order and exuberant discovery of new orders" (151). Using images of pathology he asserts that "The question of cultural progress and decline [. . .] is inextricable from the problem of the body" (146). Being registered in trauma, Modernism's problematic confrontation with modernity is therefore primarily reflected by bodily and textual defects. After having tried to locate the significant theme of decadence within the critique of modernity, I now propose to concretise the notion of corporeal damage with regard to the violent gestures of despair and outrage that dominate Lawrence Durrell's *The Black Book* (1938).

Pathological and rhetorical distress are the main elements of Lawrence Durrell's attack against modern culture.[2] At the centre of his first major novel, *The Black Book*, we find the metaphor of "the English Death" whose connotative power can range widely from corporeal damage to cultural decay. While on the one hand, "the English Death" enables Durrell to intensify and dramatise the signs of decadence and the exhaustion of modern life, on the other, it justifies his own need to disrupt and overthrow existing literary and cultural traditions. In other words, decadence here is felt with an intensity unknown before that can only be explained by its literary-historical context. Much of this aggravated sense of crisis derives from the fact that Durrell represents a late Modernist vision of modernity which is based on a complete rupture with both ancient and

---

[2] The issue of rhetorical distress is a complex and important subject, but is emphatically not the subject under discussion here. *The Black Book*'s scandalous content and Durrell's excessive use of obscenity may serve here as an exemplum of this rhetorical symptom of decay.

recently established – i.e. High Modernist – traditions.[3] This becomes clear if we consider that as a late Modernist *Künstlerroman*,
The Black Book's artist figures convey multiple anxieties about cultural decay. Lawrence Lucifer, the book's main narrator, rejects the
historical roots of English culture: "I cannot live because the decomposing bodies of my ancestors dog me at every turn. [. . .] Instead of nourishing us they are the umpires of our defeat, our decline and fall" (157). By utilising Lucifer's struggle to create an authentic – as opposed to a decadent – work of art as a frame of his
narrative, Durrell also problematises his narrator's own relation to
diverse contemporary literary movements. Hence, Durrell's account
of the emergence of the emancipated artist, who tries to "escape
from the chaste seminary of literature in which [he has] been imprisoned too long" (66), can also be read as a rejection of the literary
authority that a number of Modernists had achieved after three decades of mostly formalist experiments.

Indeed, when in its preface Durrell retrospectively describes his
Black Book as "a two-fisted attack on literature by an angry young
man of the thirties" (9), he certainly alludes to his struggle against
antecedent generations of Anglo-American Modernists. From a late
Modernist point of view, their attempts to find new orders that
would put an end to the crisis of modernity failed because the exaggerated aestheticism of writers dedicated to the idea of art for art's
sake produced a life-negating reaction to modernity. Resistance to

---

[3] What is to be noticed here, is that according to traditional definitions of Modernism Durrell's *Black Book* was published several years after Modernism
was said to have faltered and waned. However, most elements of Durrell's response to modernity, such as formal experimentation, the questioning of representational norms, the theme of the alienated artist, cultural pessimism all
exemplify preoccupations of Modernist writing. For commentary on the recent reevaluation of the 1930s as a period that continued to reflect on problems raised by the first generation of Modernists and avant-gardists see Jane
Goldman's *Modernism 1910-1945: Image to Apocalypse.*

this highly aesthetic vision of the world is at the heart of numerous allusions to the desperation and anguish which the various artist figures express as the fear of "a death within life; a life in death" (213). Candace Fertile alludes to this late Modernist scepticism and points out that for Durrell the exclusive focus on art did only "substitute abstract thought for vital energy, dogmatism for experience" (71). Fertile's commentary allows recognition of Durrell's vision of modern decadence. For him the excessive aesthetic experiments of his High Modernist predecessors represent an intensification of cultural decay. Having opposed ideas and abstractions to life, they have produced a form of intellectualism that suffocated any vital experience of life. In contrast to those Modernists who by substituting art for life have actively contributed to the devitalisation of both art and life, Durrell seeks to confront the trauma of modernity by validating vitalism over intellectualism, authenticity over idealism. As Sharon Lee Brown (323-24) observes, "For Durrell both art and life needed renovating. Literature was dead and life in London was 'the English Death'".

With other vitalists of this period,[4] Durrell shares the diagnosis of modernity as a malady that cannot be healed by exclusively concentrating on artistic preoccupations. Approached from such a vitalistic angle, the trauma of modernity is not merely caused by the disintegration of prevalent cultural traditions, but also by the fact that the expanding industrial environments engender a modern way of life that inflicts severe physical damage to the human organism. Indeed, the role of the human body as a victim of modernity is pervasive and not to be ignored. The omnipresence of pathological disfigurations, which are all related to typically modern surroundings, such as the metropolis, reveal that physical distress is one of the main

---

[4] Henry Miller's *Tropic of Cancer*, in particular, has strongly influenced Lawrence Durrell's early work.

symptoms of modern decadence. In conformance with Rasula's thesis that decadence and physical decay are related, Durrell consciously uses physical suffering to invent new forms of crisis. Considering the fact that the collapse of orders, which characterises the crisis of modernity, puts the body in the unique position of active witness and victim of a decaying culture, it is obvious that the healing of the human organism becomes of paramount importance. Even more so if we consider that the body as a healthy organism constitutes a meaningful assemblage, or to use Deleuze and Guattaris' (4) terms "a signifying totality," and therefore offers a powerful symbolic antidote to the fragmentation of modernity.

Yet there remains another reason for the vitalistic assessment of the human body. Against the background of the highly intellectual response that the preceding generation of Anglo-American Modernists offered, vitalists tried to reevaluate embodied experience as a crucial factor of life and art. The philosopher John Dewey helps to focus the premises of this yearning for non-intellectual experience.[5] In *Art as Experience*, Dewey condemns "*theories* which isolate art and its appreciation by placing them in a realm of their own, disconnected from other modes of experience" (10). Genuine experience, Dewey asserts, cannot be based on the isolation of intellectual capacities. Quite to the contrary, it must take into account the various ways in which the human body interacts with its environment: "Experience in the degree in which it *is* experience is heightened vitality" (19). True experience, therefore, should replace a disconnected perception of reality with a total experience that embraces both mental and sensorial capacities. Whereas vitalism has often been interpreted as an attempt to escape from Puritan restrictions,

---

[5] This growing desire to return to the roots of vital experience does by no means originate in the work of Dewey. It can be traced back to Nietzsche's study of Dionysian impulses in an Apollonian world, later reappears as Bergson's *élan vital* or as D. H. Lawrence's celebration of Eros.

Dewey's argument allows us to hazard the claim that it is best understood in terms of the Modernist preoccupation with fragmentation. By opposing the simplicity of natural instincts to the increasingly fragmented structures of modernity such a reevaluation of the human body primarily seeks to overcome the decay of western civilisation by creating a new sense of unity.

Emblematising his endeavour to reaffirm vital experience under machine age duress, the human body appears as a crucial element of Lawrence Durrell's critique of modernity. To begin with, *The Black Book*'s multiple references to corporeal suffering remind us that it is through the body that the trauma of modernity becomes painfully evident. Yet if instead of focusing only on the symptoms of decadence, we recognise the novel's involvement with the loss of unity, the picture begins to change. From this point of view, Durrell's discourse of pathology indicates not only a desire to heal the human body, it also thematises the wish to subjugate the fragmentation of the modern world. The body as both victim and possible source of redemption are therefore foundational to Durrell's attempt to overcome decadence, or to escape from what he calls "the English Death." A further example demonstrating that Durrell's desperate wish to achieve a new unity implies the reevaluation of the human body can be found in Durrell's recurrent allusions to the myth of Osiris, exemplified by desperate exclamations, such as: "Isis where are you?" (171). As Rasula accurately reminds us, the myth of Osiris serves as an allegorical account of the Modernist attempt to assemble the dispersed elements, which "like the dismembered parts of Osiris, are deputized to bear witness to a whole which is inconceivable" (159). However, before looking more closely at Durrell's attempt to overcome the fragmentation of unitary wholes, we should first give some consideration to the way in which he uses a discourse of pathology to intensify a sense of crisis.

In *The Black Book*, the modern city serves as a powerful backdrop for dramatising the diseases of modernity. In Durrell's novel the industrial cityscape and the omnipresent theme of the "the English Death" are complicit. As I noted earlier the use of urban imagery to underline the drama of modern society was a popular device in Modernist literature. This fascination for the metropolis derived partly from Spenglerian theories of decline, in which the city as a "megalopolis" is considered to embody the decay of western culture. In Durrell, however, metropolitan imagery suggests not only decline but also somatic distress:

> The city is beating around me like a foetus, chromium, steel, turbines, rubber, chimneys. The nights are dizzy with fog, and the trains run amok. [. . .] The world is speaking outside me, in the night, luminous with snouts of vomiting steel and chimneys. The new world, whose choice is strangling the fragile flame of the psyche (160).

The threatening aspects of such urban representations express a sense of fragmentation and violence, which insinuate that the narrator experiences his urban habitat as a menacing burden. At the outset we find a heterogeneous list of modern phenomena that perfectly reflects the lack of a unitary whole. The description then represents this fragmented cityscape as a sick environment only to converge the city as a suffering organism with city-dwellers as embodied beings who fail to physically adapt themselves to their deteriorating urban environments.

In Durrell's depiction of London we discover further traditional concepts of decadence, which Calinescu has summarised as follows: "usual associations with such notions as decline, twilight, autumn, senescence, and exhaustion, [. . .] make it inevitable to think of it in terms of natural cycles and biological metaphors" (155-56). But even if Durrell uses seasons to emphasise decline, he takes care to dramatise it through association with images of pathology. Take, for instance, the following excerpt:

> If spring ever breaks in this district it is with an air of sur-
> prised green. A momentous few weeks of fruition in which
> the little unwary things come out in their defenceless, naïve
> way. The soot and the metal paralysis soon eat them. The
> canker of steel rusting slowly in the virginity of the rose.
>
> (109)

The choice of words like "paralysis" and "canker" permits Durrell to intensify his apocalyptic vision, so that the threat of decay is absolute. Here Durrell's discourse of pathology is used to insinuate that when nature's regenerative structures are undermined the process of decay cannot be arrested. For as Calinescu has aptly pointed out, "The true opposite of decadence – as far as biological connotations of the word are concerned – is perhaps regeneration" (156). By creating such a bleak picture of urban environments, Durrell demands his reader to take seriously the menace to which both human and nonhuman life are subjected by the excess of modernity.

Accordingly, Durrell's representations of the various protagonists are laced with images of disease to intensify the trauma of modernity. To emphasise "the English Death" Durrell assembles a group of desperately alienated figures. Most of these protagonists are unsuccessful artists, as for instance Tarquin, who like the two main narrators, Death Gregory and Lawrence Lucifer, is seeking to create a work of art that would create meaning in a meaningless world. Tarquin is introduced to the readers as follows: "Tarquin, for example, six-foot, frost-bound, jack-knifed, yellow with jaundice; Tarquin pinned to a slab of rufous cork, etherized, like a diseased butterfly" (22). Durrell's catalogue of compound words illustrates not only a grotesque disfiguration of the human body, it also points to the disintegration of the human organism into a dissected organism.

What is to be noticed though, is that the monstrosity of this description is grounded on the fact that it fails to represent Tarquin's body as a unitary whole. Here I am touching on a question already adumbrated in an influential study by Elaine Scarry, entitled *The Body in Pain*. Scarry explains that "To conceive of the body as parts, shapes and mechanisms, is to conceive of it from the outside" (285), hereby refuting a vital involvement with one's own body. Similarly, Tarquin's body, which is depicted here as an abstract object of analysis, has been transformed into a dead lump. It thus serves as a denunciation of a devitalised conception of the human body that doubtlessly represses "the felt experience of being a sentient being" (Scarry 285).

An equally disturbing account of embodied experience characterises Death Gregory's attempts of self-analysis:

> The masked face of myself leans down over my body, selects an instrument, and begins. A long bloodless slit in the band of yellow. [. . .] The gutters are slowly, noiselessly brimmed with blood. Discarded livers, kidneys, tracks of coloured guts drop away from under the sheet and plop into an enamel pail. The yellow envelope of flesh which is my belly becomes ever more flaccid, more empty. [. . .] I am thoroughly opened and explored. [. . .] And to no purpose.
>
> (187)

Like the pathological portrayal of Tarquin, Death Gregory's body too is represented as an alienated object: a "yellow envelop of flesh" perceived by the analytical gaze of the observer. Despite the fact that Gregory in this manner tries to explore the depths of his personality, his disembodied and abstract approach does not allow him to reach beyond this "yellow envelop." Just as this metonymy illustrates the fragmented perception of the body, the result of this "introspection" emphasises the extent to which he cannot create a meaningful whole out of this assemblage of organs. We may thus conclude that behind such references to disintegration and corporeal suffering lurks a sense of agony that is directly linked to the theme of decadence.

Yet in order to understand the complex issue of Durrell's fascination for dissected organisms, his critique of modernity needs to be expanded beyond a mere vitalistic preoccupation with embodied experience. Recall that there are several distinct yet related ways to describe the role of "the English Death" in Durrell's *Black Book.* One of its functions is to denounce the historical and philosophical traditions of western civilisation. At the centre of this critique we find the legacy of enlightenment and its celebration of instrumental reason. One of the most intensely debated issues of Modernism's antirationalist and antiscientific reaction to modernity has been enlightenment's model of science and its particular systems of analysis. As a number of scholars have made clear, enlightenment thinkers have developed a model of scientific systematisation that allows modern scientists to work with context-free abstractions. But as Neil Evernden observes, scientific abstractions entail an atomisation of totality. Evernden refers to C. G. Jung in order to exhibit the ensuing implications of scientific abstraction:

> When we abstract 'we take away' or 'withdraw – we remove something from the totality.' Abstraction is not only a noun, [as] we commonly use it, meaning 'the idea of something which has no independent existence' or 'a thing which exists only in idea.' It is also a verb: 'the act or process of separating in thought, of considering a thing independently of its association.' (47-48)

Abstraction, in other words, replaces a holistic perception of the world with a scientific perspective that reduces the world to an object that can be dissected into its fragments. It hereby actively undermines the possibility of a *Ganzheitserlebnis*, to use another term by C. G. Jung, and thus contributes to the sense of decay and fragmentation.

Resistance to this model of scientific systematisation is at issue in Durrell's description of Doctor Bazain. Doctor Bazain's belief in abstract knowledge results in an understanding of the human body as an anatomised corpse: "His universe consists of the frontal lobe, the temporal lobe, and the occipital lobe; not to mention of the parietal lobe, or the medulla. Any phenomenon which exists outside this domain puzzles him. Even simple phenomena like Morgan" (224). Here Durrell uses a catalogue of medical terms to illustrate Doctor Bazain's fragmented conception of the human brain. By describing the medical understanding of the body as an assemblage of isolated elements, Durrell illustrates on a general level, how scientific systematisation produces a vision of the world which reduces it to a hopelessly fragmented totality rather than a unified whole. But Doctor Bazain's failure to grasp "any phenomena" that do not fit his medical frame of reference, such as Morgan the Welshman, hints also at the main problem of abstract knowledge: that the body as a complex organic unity has been replaced by an understanding of the body as an assemblage of fragmented elements. The resulting perception of the individual's body occasions in Durrell's novel multiple references to artificial limbs. The recourse to these medical devices is not merely a grotesque parody of modern decadence. Rather, it accounts for the failure of these alienated characters to experience their bodies as unitary wholes. Once again, Tarquin serves as a nice example. Having turned his body into a manipulable organism, he constructs himself by buying "cheap powders and face creams, had a false tooth put in where the canine was missing, even wonders whether a wig..." Significantly, the ensuing phrase reminds us that this "is the beginning of the disintegration" (167).

While the preceding examples of Durrell's discourse of pathology have demonstrated that the trauma of modernity basically consists of the incapacity of these protagonists to experience their body as an organic unity, the ensuing examples will show that their incapacity to form new wholes has repercussions on other realms, too. Particularly the theme of self-estrangement shows that the symptoms of modern decadence are manifold. As I have suggested above, most of Durrell's protagonists fail to cope with urban life. In fact, their principle activities consist of desperately trying to find meaning in life. As we have already seen, Durrell's portrayal of Tarquin offers a particularly dismal picture of the modern city-dweller. Tarquin's desperate attempts to come to terms with the *malaise* of modern life is enhanced by his favourite occupation: "lying on his back [. . .] catechizing himself" (28). His inability to overcome his increasing sense of self-estrangement, trenchantly described as an "endless game of chess with the psyche" (28), makes him *The Black Book*'s prototype of the modern decadent. For despite his belief that "We must reduce our lives to some sort of order" (53), he eventually sees himself defeated by life-denying "terminologies of theology and psychology running neck and neck, each outdoing the other in vagueness" (40). Taken as a critique of the destructive potential of instrumental reason, this passage additionally alludes to the vitalistic preoccupation with the denial of embodied experience. When Tarquin's "study of himself is so strenuous" that his introspection has "been rapidly making a wreck of him" (40), he certainly respresents the negative effects of a rationalistic, disembodied understanding of the self.

This passage reinforces the necessity to have a closer look at the vitalistic opposition to the enlightenment's heritage of rational humanism. While the discourse of pathology, symbolised by the "English Death," adequately mirrors the protagonists' anxiety about "the disruption of the unity of self" (Briganti 42), it is also important to stress that Durrell's critique of modernity is directed against the overestimation of instrumental reason, or what he ironically calls the "fatal nurse of the ego" (40). As Jürgen Habermas (ix) remarks in his study of modernity, "Interwoven with the critique of reason is a critique of the sovereign rational subject – atomistic and autonomous, disengaged and disembodied, potentially and ideally self-transparent." From a vitalistic point of view, the Cartesian vision of a disembodied mental realm as the true essence of human identity led to the repression of the body and by implication the denial of vital instincts.[6] Retrospectively then, the Cartesian insistence on a disembodied consciousness as the true essence of human identity sustains Durrell's ironic portrayal of Tarquin. Because his search for self is centred on "a vast storehouse of scientific formulae, historical data, hieroglyphs, runes, dogma" (168), Tarquin's introspection intensifies both the sense of fragmentation and the feeling of alienation. As a result, Tarquin's adherence to life-negating principles, eventually transforms him into a lifeless being who "sits all day alone, wrapped in rugs, afraid to walk, his bones are so brittle; afraid to talk, his tongue is so dry" (242).

All these symptoms of decay conspire to produce an accurate sense of the usefulness one has to accredit to Rasula's thesis about the Modernist trauma of modernity as a pathological response to the collapse of a premodern unity when dealing with Durrell's vision of decadence. However, given the fact that Tarquin is an artist, Durrell's portrayal should also help us to understand his endeavour to restore vitality to both life and art. Recall that for Durrell "the Eng-

---

[6] The critique of instrumental reason returns discussion to Nietzsche's aforementioned analysis of modern decadence. According to Calinescu (193), resistance to the life-negating aspects of the definition of the modern human being as a rational subject is also at the heart of Nietzsche's idea that "Decadence turns against life whenever it ascribes to life meanings other than those of life itself."

lish Death" can only be overcome once art and life have been reno-
vated. As an alienated artist, Tarquin therefore additionally illustrates how the denaturalisation of human instincts invalidates him as
an artist. By using Tarquin as an illustration of decadence, Durrell
thematises his anxiety that culture corrupts the artist and his or her
medium, hereby leading to a lack of authenticity in the artist's expression and experience of modern life. It is thus no surprise that
Lawrence Lucifer, the novel's main narrator and artist figure, insists
that the quest for meaning cannot be completed unless false cultural
values have been destroyed. In Lucifer's words, any artistic endeavour to react against the trauma of modernity must be based on "acceptance, the depersonalization of self, of the society one has absorbed. It is not only a question of art, but a question of life" (146).
What this liberation from the repressive structures of western culture implies, can best be analysed in a comparison of Death Gregory
and Lawrence Lucifer. By examining the trajectories of *The Black
Book*'s two main artist figures, it is possible to indicate with some
clarity the general contours of Durrell's antidote to decadence.

Before looking more closely at the divergent achievements of
these two artist figures, we should first give some consideration to
the novel's narrative structure. The narrative flow alternates between
the accounts given by Lawrence Lucifer, the novel's main narrator,
and excerpts from Horace 'Death' Gregory's diary. Whereas Lucifer
reminisces from his new home on Corfu about his past life in the
suburbs of London, Durrell uses the excerpts from Gregory's diary
to provide an alternative account of the gloomy life from which
Lucifer has escaped. Significantly, it is by reading Gregory's diary
that Lucifer is galvanised into trying to escape from "the English
Death." For both protagonists, however, the goal to overcome the
crisis of modernity by trying to find a new authenticity in their lives
and in their artwork is the same. On *The Black Book*'s opening pages
already we perceive that the act of writing is associated both with

the attempt to escape from a decaying literary tradition and the desire to evade the pathology of modern life. Consider for instance Lucifer's opening remarks: "This is the day I have chosen to begin this writing, because today we are dead among the dead; and this is an *agon* for the dead, a chronicle for the living" (20). As Jacques Pelletier confirms, Durrell uses the theme of the quest to dramatise his own understanding of writing as a creative act which, if successful, revitalises the artist and restores literary authenticity.[7]

Just as both Gregory and Lucifer situate their creative endeavours within the context of surmounting the *malaise* of modern life, they also choose the same artistic approach to the fragmentation of modernity. For Gregory and Lucifer alike myth promises to provide a highly effective device for creating a new, distinctively artistic vision of reality. Durrell concurs here with many Modernists who, according to Peter Childs (198), believed that myth offered a "compensat[ion] for the dissatisfying fragmentation of the modern world." The hope that myth might return us to a lost unity is grounded on the belief that it contains structuring principles that antecede rational explanation. Hence, Lucifer, Gregory, as well as Tarquin agree that "The world is crying for it to be restored, but we are offering it only regression – an escape out of the geometrical rat-trap which is really only temporary. It is not only a question of going back to myth. The myth will come back to us" (151). Thus formulated, the revival of a mythical vision of the world might indeed provide an antidote to the trauma of modernity. However, even if myth appears to be a fruitful device for returning to a lost unity, Durrell stresses the difficulty of reclaiming myth when he writes that "the healing mythologies are so etherized that they float away

---

[7] Note also that *The Black Book*'s artist figures bear resemblance to Durrell himself. The use of similar names and the fact that Durrell actually wrote this novel on Corfu should suffice to suggest that there are numerous autobiographical parallels between the author and his artist figures.

elusive, before the mind can grasp them" (150). Here we find exemplified the dilemma behind the recourse to myth. For the modern artist's struggle with a world that he or she perceives to be diseased, debilitating and chaotic, myth in its capacity to create a new visionary unity might indeed sustain the artist's quest for wholeness. Yet precisely because the sense of unity has been lost, the alienated artist can only speak of a mythical reconciliation, while its contents must remain unclear. This becomes painfully evident when Lucifer admits that from "Apes with extosis, and the forty-foot dinosaur with toothache" (158), to the "pyknic from Mars" (159) everything becomes a potentially significant component of this new myth. At the same time the question, "how do I know it is not one of the defunct idealisms" (158) that is thus being revived, must remain unanswered.

Although the passage quoted above insinuates that Lucifer's frantic efforts to create a new myth amidst the scattered fragments of ancient and futuristic phenomena, offers only a feeble hope of redemption, it is nevertheless important to stress that Lucifer and Gregory present two different approaches to myth. Keeping in mind Lucifer's wish to disengage from cultural repressions, it is clear that his search for myth will lead him into new realms. Gregory, by contrast, admits that during his quest for a new myth his "imagination has become a vast lumber room of ideas. There is no dogma which does not find an echo from myself" (181). Gregory's adherence to life-denying principles of rationalisation determines not only his inability to overcome self-estrangement, it also accounts for his artistic failure. That Gregory's sense of alienation arises from his urge to define himself as a purely rational subject is demonstrated by endless nights he spends "in the laboratory which I have made of my ego" (196).

The allusion to the repressive ego is a clue to how Durrell's preoccupation with self-estrangement should be interpreted. For it illus-

trates the influence Georg Groddeck exerted on Durrell's understanding of the trauma of modernity. This direction of interpretation
is supported by several statements in which Durrell expresses his
approbation of Groddeck's theories on disease as a symptom of a
schism between the repressive consciousness and the "It." In *A Key
to Modern British Poetry*, for example, Durrell points out that the
"It" constitutes "The sum total of an individual human being, physical, mental and spiritual, the organism with all its forces, the microcosmos, the universe which is a man" (74). As the "It" is connected
to an affirmation of embodied experience, disease is the symptom of
the growing disequilibrium between body and mind arising from the
repressive intellect, or what Durrell calls "the pretensions of the
ego" (78). Hence, when Gregory deplores that the search for his true
identity is "all filtered, limited, through the wretched instruments of
the self" (41), we may conclude that it is the rational unity of the
ego that disrupts his quest.

It is accurate to say, therefore, that Durrell's representations of
Gregory and Lucifer's relation to corporeality are the most exemplary markers of difference between these two figures. Gregory's
statement, "I am again standing naked in front of the mirror, puzzled
by the obstructing flesh. The great problem is how to get at the organic root of the trouble" (198-99), may serve as a rapid illustration
of Gregory's schismatic perception. For it clearly indicates that his
understanding of the self negates the human body. Even more so, if
we consider that the use of the synecdoche – "obstructing flesh" –
intensifies the disrupted unity of the self which sustains Gregory's
self-estrangement. In contrast Lucifer, whose escape to Corfu sym-
bolises his successful detachment from the debilitating ideologies of
modern England, is determined to bring his quest to an end by rejecting the legacy of rational humanism. Motivated by the belief that
only by overcoming his own sense of alienation a new sense of artistic authenticity may be created, he decides to "go [his] own

bloody way" (233). Instead of accepting the repressive structures of the modern world he admits that "the ravening at the bottom of all this [. . .] is not a thirst for love or money or sex, but a thirst for living" (230). As a reaction to the purely cerebral existence of his fellow artists, Lucifer's thirst for living aims to recover the importance of corporeal existence.

Given the fact that *The Black Book* has a strong vitalistic strand running through it, it is almost unavoidable that the recourse to the human body is centred around the theme of sex. As sex has traditionally been conceived as a purely physical phenomenon, it is little wonder that sexual repression was frequently used to express an accentuated concern about the negative impact of rational humanism. According to Georges Bataille's (242) Nietzschean analysis, modern culture's anxiety about eroticism arises from its radical denial of sensorial experience and its refusal to grant value to the human body as a natural organism. Bataille, therefore, concludes that the problem with this denial is that it leads to a complete ignorance of human nature (95). In like manner, Durrell uses the theme of sex to stress the respective failure of Gregory and Lucifer's successful escape from "the English Death." To the extent that Gregory's previously analysed struggle with the "ego" brings his search for disalienation to a halt, it is obvious that his view of sexuality bears similar traces of repression.

Gregory's subjection to instrumental reason notwithstanding, his relationship with Grace seems to be motivated by a desire to liberate himself from these social restrictions. Indeed, it is only during his relationship with Grace that Gregory finally manages to modify his understanding of himself as a purely rational being. "The cage I inhabited," he writes in his diary, "was broken wide open by our experience" (49). Although through Grace he starts to discover the importance of corporeal existence, her sudden death interrupts this process of self-discovery. As the balance between his intellectual and sensorial experience has not yet been restored, he does not even grieve for her "dissolution, but for [his] own" (187). Resigned, he gets engaged to Kate – "the most ordinary person [he] could find" (209). Instead of renewal, whose inherent "struggle," he decides "is too hideous," he accepts to "suffer the disease to run its course" (209).

His relationship with two different women – Hilda and the enigmatic figure to whom the narrative is addressed – is likewise the crucial factor determining Lucifer's quest for a new unity of identity. However, where Gregory ultimately refuses renunciation of his intellectual judgement of both Grace and Kate, Lucifer does not hesitate to explore sexuality as the purest form of sensorial experience. As his rediscovery of embodied experience must entail a liberation of social norms of repression, his relation to Hilda leads to a gradual effacement of those aspects that define him as a cultural being. Seeking a new "dimension of sensibility I have not hitherto cultivated" (175), Lucifer sees in "Hilda [. . .] the genesis from which I shall be born again on the third day" (98). Hilda is mythologised and becomes the womb to which Lucifer desperately tries to return:

> I am devising in my mind a legend to convey the madness which created us in crookedness, in dislocation, in tort. We are a generation enwombed. [. . .] Like blind puppies we are seeking the way back to the womb, we are trying to wipe away the knowledge of our stillbirth, by a new, a more glorious, more pristine event. (138)

This passage shows that the back-to-the-womb allegory, which functions as the novel's leitmotif, can be linked to two different subjects. On the hand, Durrell's use of the erotic is based on a conversion of the womb into a more complex image of his quest for authenticity. The womb becomes the place where the male artist may recover embodied experience as a vital source and thus restore a new equilibrium between body and mind.

On the other hand, by defining the womb as the place where a new artistic vision of reality can emerge, Durrell reminds us that narratives of creation have traditionally used the womb as the arena for the appearance of world-creation. The philosopher Edward Casey explains that the mastering of original matter constitutes a crucial element of narratives of creation. "To master," Casey (23-24) points out, "is not to bring into being in the first place but to control and shape that which has already been brought into existence." In narratives of creation, therefore, this pregiven "matter connotes *matrix*, which in its literal sense of 'uterus' or 'womb'" becomes "the generatrix of created things". Simply put, while "Creation becomes a matter of mastering matter," the meaning of matrix itself is expanded beyond its "anatomical sense," hereby becoming a "place or medium in which something is bred, produced, or developed, a place or point of origin and growth." I would like to suggest that in several significant ways Casey's account of ancient narratives of creation can be linked to Durrell's use of the womb – that "dark sump of the vagina, brewing vegetable history" (243) – as a potent place, symbolising hope for the creation of a new unity. This interpretation seems justified not only because "both the mythic and the philosophic entities require that creation involve a return to the womb" (Casey 32), but also because it is during sexual intercourse with his unnamed lover that Lucifer comes closest to envisioning a new myth.

Indeed, from the outset, it is only during his meetings with his lover that Lucifer starts to believe in the possibility of vanquishing his despair about modernity. During these encounters he slowly starts to grasp a new vision of unity. "When I am covering you," he insists "my cranium is packed with images, the whole body of the lost worlds is being poured down that narrow slipway to the absolute" (151). Notice the way a sense of wholeness starts to replace precedent references to fragmentation. That his lover's womb is eventually transformed into the arena of a new creation which might yield a new vision of unity, is affirmed by the book's ending. Here Durrell concludes his narrator's quest for authenticity with a sexual act during which Lucifer's Dionysian state of ecstasy leads him to a new vision of the universe. This final sexual scene culminates in a metamorphosis that transforms Lucifer into a tree. On that account Robert Pogue Harrison has advanced the theory that the notion of metamorphosis illustrates a "materialist philosophy of reality, which holds that all embodied substances partake of the same primal matter." Metamorphosis, then, "(from the Greek words *meta* and *morphé*, meaning change of form) is a kind of birth, or rebirth, as one material form returns to its matrix in order assume a new form." For the purpose of examining Durrell's remedy against modern decadence, such an analysis is particularly revealing. For it demonstrates that a concept of metamorphosis premised on the belief that "all things come into being – assume form and appearance – from out of the womb of some primordial, undifferentiated matter" (26-27), indicates that it is during this scene of extreme sensorial experience that Lucifer may finally grasp a new vision of unity.

Hence, I would like to conclude that the womb as a place of creation where primal matter may be moulded into a new form, is employed by Durrell as a powerful symbolical antidote to the fragmentation of modernity. Even more so, since by reading *The Black Book*'s final scene as a narrative of creation, it becomes easier to see how this Dionysian state of ecstasy points to a visionary moment of unity. In order to highlight the gradual building up of this mythical moment, Durrell assembles the fragments that will yield a new vision. Beginning with the observation that this "dancing of fibres along the skin," promises "a new action, a theme as fresh as seed" (241), Lucifer slowly starts to master the undifferentiated images that rise up in his imagination, until finally he perceives "whole universes open silently" (240). The climax of Lucifer's final sexual act, then, is the appropriation of a new condition for artistic creation: "It is not words which grow in me when I see the tendrils of muscle climbing your trunk; [. . .]. Not words but a vocabulary which goes through us both" (240). As a place of creation, however, the womb of his lover provides him not merely with a new vocabulary. Quite to the contrary, it allows the artist to overcome his self-estrangement at the same time as it symbolically yields the foundations for the production of authentic art.

It has frequently been noted that "the ending of *The Black Book* cannot explain [. . .] how the vision of love can be meshed with the new religious/ artistic mythology" (Christensen 32). It seems to me, however, that the promise of both a new vocabulary and a new mythical vision must be interpreted as a healing of the trauma of modernity. The inherent promise of rebirth affirms that the ending is not supposed to afford the contents of a new mythology, but rather the beginning of a new organic unity. The numerous allusions to the notion of chaos, exemplified by Lucifer's statement that "It is on the face of this chaos that I brood" (243), confirm the conclusion that what Durrell attempts to describe here is the first moment of creation. For just as the womb is a basic element of narratives of creation, so chaos, meaning "primal abyss or gap," occur there as a "primordial place within which things can happen." Casey asserts that in this context chaos becomes a "scene of emerging order," and subsequently adds, "To be chaotic [. . .] is not to destroy order but to create it" (9).

Once one grasps the elements of similarity between Lucifer's metamorphosis and traditional narratives of creation, it becomes easier to see that Durrell's use of the womb as a symbolical place from which a new creation – and by implication a new sense of unity – may emerge is presented as a direct response to the crisis of modernity. That the ending of *The Black Book* insinuates a healing of modern decadence is additionally confirmed by the fact that pathological reactions to modernity seem to have been surmounted during the course of Lucifer's vitalistic reacquisition of his sensing body. Unlike most of the novel's disintegrating protagonists, Lucifer does neither suffer from self-estrangement or from any diseases. As we have seen, whereas Gregory's resignation and artistic failure is based on the acceptance of "disease" (209), Lucifer's successful recovery of sensorial experience indicates that he has found the equilibrium necessary both for artistic creation and a vital reevaluation of himself as a healthy human being.

Works Cited

Bataille, Georges. *L'érotisme*. Paris: Éditions de Minuit, 1957.

Begnal, Michael H., ed. *On Miracle Ground: Essays on the Fiction of Lawrence Durrell*. Lewisburg: Bucknell UP, 1990.

Bersani, Leo. *The Culture of Redemption*. Cambridge: Harvard UP, 1990.

Briganti, Chiara. "Lawrence Durrell and the Vanishing Author." Ed. Michael H. Begnal. Lewisburg: Bucknell UP, 1990. 41-51.

Brown, Sharon Lee. "*The Black Book*: A Search for Method." *Modern Fiction Studies* 13.3 (1967): 319-28.

Calinescu, Matei. *Five Faces of Modernism: Modernism, Avant-Garde, Decadence, Kitsch, Postmodernism*. Durham: Duke UP, 1987.

Casey, Edward S. *The Fate of Place: A Philosophical History*. Berkeley and Los Angeles: California UP, 1998.

Childs, Peter. *Modernism*. London: Routledge, 2000.

Christensen, Peter G. "The Achievement and Failure: Durrell's Three Early Novels." *Lawrence Durrell: Comprehending the Whole*. Eds. Julius Rowan Raper, Melody L. Enscore, and Paige Matthey Bynum. Columbia: U of Missouri P, 1995. 22-32.

Deleuze, Gilles, and Félix Guattari. *A Thousand Plateaus: Capitalism and Schizophrenia.* 1980. Trans. Brian Massumi. Minneapolis: Minnesota UP, 1987.

Dewey, John. *Art as Experience.* 1934. New York: Perigee, 1980.

Durrell, Lawrence. *The Black Book.* 1938. London: Faber and Faber, 1977.

---. *A Key to Modern British Poetry.* Norman: Oklahoma UP, 1952.

Evernden, Neil. *The Social Creation of Nature.* Baltimore and London: John Hopkins UP, 1992.

Eysteinsson, Astradur. *The Concept of Modernism.* Ithaca and London: Cornell UP, 1990.

Fertile, Candace. "The Role of the Writer in Lawrence Durrell's Fiction." *On Miracle Ground: Essays on the Fiction of Lawrence Durrell.* Ed. Michael H. Begnal. Lewisburg: Bucknell UP, 1990. 63-78.

Goldman, Jane. *Modernism, 1910-1945: Image to Apocalypse.* Basingstoke: Palgrave Macmillan, 2004.

Habermas, Jürgen. *The Philosophical Discourse of Modernity: TwelveLectures.* Trans. Frederick Lawrence. Cambridge: MIT, 1990.

Nietzsche, Friedrich. "Der Fall Wagner." *Jenseits von Gut und Böse und andere Schriften.* Ed. Rolf Toman. Vol. 3 of *Werke in drei Bänden.* Köln: Könemann Verlag, 1994. 240-77.

Pelletier, Jacques. "Le *Carnet Noir* de Lawrence Durrell et le roman de la transition." *Études Littéraires* 27.2 (1994): 123-33.

Pogue, Robert Harrison. *Forests: The Shadow of Civilization.* Chicago: Chicago UP, 1992.

Raper, Julius Rowan, ed. *Lawrence Durrell: Comprehending the Whole.* Columbia: Missouri UP, 1995.

Rasula, Jed. "The Pathic Receptacles of Modernism." *Ré-inventer le réel. Actes du colloque GRAAT: CERCA, Université de Tours, 26-27 septembre 1997.* Tours: Publications des Groupes de Recherches Anglo-Américaines de l'Université François Rabelais de Tours, 1999. 143-63.

Scarry, Elaine. *The Body in Pain: The Making and Unmaking of the World.* Oxford: Oxford UP, 1985.

The Obscure Camera:
Decadence and Moral Anxiety
in Christopher Isherwood's *Goodbye to Berlin*

Heather Marcovitch
Mount Allison University

Abstract: The legacy of *fin de siècle* conflicts with the rise of Nazism in Christopher Isherwood's *Goodbye to Berlin*. The narrator's fascination with artifice and performance is set against his growing moral outrage against Nazi persecution, raising questions about the moral value of decadence in late-Weimar Berlin.

"I am a camera with its shutter open, quite passive, recording, not thinking." This statement at the beginning of *Goodbye to Berlin* (1) is the most famous sentence in all of Christopher Isherwood's writings and has therefore received considerable attention from critics. Originally, the statement was seen as reason to include Isherwood in the group of "documentary" writers of the 1930s, but the recent critical consensus has been to see it rather as a disingenuous claim.[1] The sentence leads critics to assert that the narrator's so-called camera-like perspective is an unsuccessful pose, serving only to emphasize the crucial role the narrator plays in influencing the events as they unfold and in shaping them in his retelling. By his own admission, Christopher the narrator concedes that "Some day, all this will have to be developed, carefully printed, fixed" (1).

Although "I am a camera" is traditionally used as the point from which to examine the complicated relationship in the stories be-

---

[1] Martin Green (285), for instance, sees Isherwood as a "faux-naïf, using naïve tones to say subtle and sardonic things". David P. Thomas (47) pointedly notes that the statement and the passage that follows it are "the revelation of personality and not the exposition of theory. It is, indeed, entirely misleading as a description of Isherwood's narrative method".

tween fiction and autobiography – a relationship impossible to ignore with a narrator named Christopher Isherwood and with the added knowledge that the characters in the stories are fictionalized representations of the people Isherwood actually befriended in Berlin – it is also indicative of another set of tensions working in the stories, namely the moral and intellectual tensions that arise by being both observer and participant in the narrated events.[2] With "I am a camera," Christopher[3] announces the particular narrative persona he is adopting: the distanced observer, neutral in perspective, whose presence does not affect in the least the actions of the characters whom he encounters. That this persona is essentially a sham is suggested throughout the stories where, despite his intentions, Christopher *does* engage in relationships with other characters and even influences their actions. An argument with Sally Bowles, for example, in which his feelings are wounded, leads him to select her as underage con artist's Paul Rakowski's next mark. Likewise, his visit to Frau Nowak in a sanatorium leads to an odd, endearing moment of human connection between himself, Otto, and the women patients. But, clinging to the pose of the camera, and beginning most of the stories with a panoramic description of the setting, the narrator maintains a position for himself as an outsider, isolated in an exis-

---

[2] The relationship between Isherwood's fiction and autobiography is already well-documented in criticism and will only be discussed here tangentially. For representative discussions of this aspect of Isherwood's writing, see Brian Finney's *Christopher Isherwood: A Critical Biography*, Paul Piazza's *Christopher Isherwood: Myth and Anti-Myth*, and Jonathan H. Fryer's "Sexuality in Isherwood."

[3] The identical names of narrator and author here will inevitably lead to some confusion when considering them as distinct from one another. In keeping with the method Isherwood uses when referring to himself as a character in his works, the author will be referred to by his surname and the narrator by his first name.

tential sense from the inhabitants of Berlin.[4] He remarks, for instance, in the first "Berlin Diary," that the young men whistling to their girlfriends discomfort him. "But soon a call is sure to sound," he writes, "so piercing, so insistent, so despairingly human, that at last I have to get up and peep through the slats of the venetian blind to make quite sure that it is not – as I know very well it could not possibly be – for me" (1-2). Christopher takes a certain amount of pleasure in his loneliness; by peeking out at the young lovers, his identity as outsider, and therefore as the one capable of making sense of these events, is confirmed. But another identity, that of voyeur, is also introduced in this passage and, with it, Christopher, despite his pose as an outsider, begins to participate in the decadence of late-Weimar Berlin, the undisclosed reason he came to the city.

Christopher's identification with a camera and, more importantly, his adoption of this artificial pose throughout the stories, points to a more widespread anxiety about Berlin's decadence. *Goodbye to Berlin* is a fictionalized chronicle of Isherwood's residency in the city between the years 1930 and 1933. The interconnected stories trace the emerging tensions between the decadence of late-Weimar Berlin and the rise of the Nazi Party, and Isherwood uses the changing political situation in Germany to question the decadence that originally drew him to Berlin. Specifically, decadence is portrayed in the stories in two ways: the decadent milieu of the Berlin demimonde and the legacy of *fin de siècle* decadence that finds its way into the narrator's anxieties. For Isherwood, as for his precursors from the *fin de siècle*, decadence's pleasure lies as much in the moral anxieties it raises as in the sensual hedonism it promises. As Charles Bernheimer (3) notes, "To judge decadence as bad would not assure one's immunity from its seductions since such judgment seemed to

---

[4] Norman Page (149) claims that Isherwood, drawing on his experiences writing for film, was influenced heavily by cinematography.

be a part of what defined the phenomenon." Decadence is not simply an immersion in corruption; it is also the act of wondering about the implications of such corruption on the self and, for some authors, a polemic against a repressive moral culture that would label alternative sensual and sexual experiences as corrupt.

For Isherwood, as well as for his narrator, Berlin is one of the last sites of decadence accessible to a young Englishman. In his autobiography, *Christopher and His Kind*, Isherwood asks, "Wasn't Berlin's famous 'decadence' largely a commercial 'line' which the Berliners had instinctively developed in their competition with Paris? Paris had long since cornered the straight girl-market, so what was left for Berlin to offer its visitors but a masquerade of perversions?" (29). More pointedly, Isherwood writes, "To Christopher, Berlin meant Boys" (2). Christopher's perceived asexuality in *Goodbye to Berlin* is the result of Isherwood not wanting to write a novel in the 1930s with an openly-gay narrator/protagonist; instead, Isherwood allows the city's nightlife to signify the sexuality that he represses in his narrator.[5] The atmospheres of the Salomé, with its "young men with plucked eyebrows" (192), the Troika, and the Alexander Casino, populated by gay, bisexual, and cross-dressing hustlers, are

---

[5] Considering the narrator's emotional distance within the story becomes complicated by the later knowledge that Isherwood regretted not depicting Christopher as openly gay, especially since his own experiences in Berlin revolved around the homosexual nightclubs. Isherwood defended this choice in a lecture given to the Modern Language Association in 1974 by saying that he didn't want his narrator's sexuality to overwhelm other aspects of the book (Fryer 348). Earlier, though, Isherwood admitted in a 1961 *London Magazine* interview that his caginess about his narrators' sexuality led to his unwillingness to reveal too much about their characters, thus causing their emotional distance from other characters and "a kind of void in the books" (qtd. in Finney 111). Isherwood's closeted attitude in the 1930s, understandable though it may be, is but one explanation for the isolation of his narrator; Isherwood is too nuanced a writer to have it be the definitive one.

what often draw Christopher out of his lonely room, out of his isolation, and into direct engagement with others.

Embedded within Berlin's display of hedonism, however, is the very fretfulness that also characterizes Isherwood's narrator. Peter Gay, in his study of culture in the Weimar Republic, notes, "The excitement that characterized Weimar culture stemmed in part from exuberant creativity and experimentation; but much of it was anxiety, fear, a rising sense of doom" (xiv). While Gay here is discussing more licit aspects of German culture, this anxiety is manifested in Isherwood's depiction of the underworld as well. For example, two of the nightclubs the characters frequent, the Lady Windermere and the Salomé, directly reference Oscar Wilde, and Herr Landauer's remarks about Wilde as the exceptional man brought to ruin by a repressive society suggest that the intermittent evocations of Wilde foreshadow the fall of decadence in Berlin.[6] In another instance, Otto Nowak, the bisexual gold digger, has a recurring dream of a hand ominously looming over him. "One day," Otto says, "I shall see the Hand again. And then I shall die" (113).

The demimonde of Berlin, however, accounts for only one part of the decadence which concerns Isherwood and his narrator. Isherwood also implicitly asks the question whether a decadent narrator is feasible, even ethical, in a city about to see a dictator come to power. The source of this question lies in the literary heritage with which Isherwood must come to terms, specifically the legacy bequeathed by the English Decadent writers of the *fin de siècle*. In *Children of the Sun*, his study of literary dandyism in the 1920s and 30s, Martin Green (14) identifies Isherwood as one of the writers who "were, and saw themselves as, originators of a new 'aesthetic'

---

[6] The use of Wilde as a decadent touchstone is something Isherwood found in Berlin upon his arrival; both the Lady Windermere and the Salomé were actual nightclubs.

phase in English high culture, to be characterized by ornament and brilliancy, playfulness and youthfulness, and by a turning back on the old forms of seriousness and power." Isherwood, according to Green, is too much the "naïf" in his literary persona to be an unqualified dandy, but the debt to 1880s aestheticism and 1890s decadence is present in the narrator's willingness, if not to experience hedonism himself, then to watch and record other characters' experiences of it. Moreover, as Richard Gilman suggests, the term 'Decadence' in and of itself is slippery, its meaning changing depending on the perspective of the subject using it. Decadence's meaning, Gilman (11) argues, lies rather in its effect, particularly a "quality of languor, of debility, a suggestion of repletion but also of continual striving toward pleasure of a bizarre, peripheral kind." Isherwood's decadence relies specifically on the achievement of such an effect; the disengaged narrator suggests that languor while his curiosity about the other characters suggest a desire for and at the same time a fear of immersing himself completely in pleasurable experiences. Christopher takes care to divide his time between the denizens of the underworld, such as Sally Bowles and Otto Nowak, and the momentarily more respectable citizens of Berlin, such as the Landauers and the Bernsteins. The atmosphere of the Troika, as well, is an indicative description of the decadent ennui that seems to permeate Isherwood's Berlin demimonde. While the Troika saxophonist sings

> with a knowing leer, including us all in his conspiracy, changing his voice with innuendo, rolling his eyes in an epileptic pantomime of extreme joy [. . .], the two flaccid gentlemen chatted to each other, probably about business, without a glance at the night-life they had called into being; while their women sat silent, looking neglected, puzzled, uncomfortable and very bored. (14)

The ethos that privileges the artificial over the natural is one which Isherwood inherits from the *fin de siècle* Decadent writers (who, in turn, trace their fascination with the artificial to the French Decadent writers of the mid-nineteenth century).[7] Isherwood is by no means the first English writer to depict an underworld where an individual's performative qualities supersede the natural self. Arthur Symons's 1892 poem "Maquillage," for instance, speaks of "The charm of rouge on fragile cheeks, / Pearl-powder, and, about the eyes, / The dark and lustrous eastern dyes" (152), while his 1895 poem "Prologue: Before the Curtain" depicts individuals so inured to their artificial performances that the performances have become monotonous, unconscious, and, in a negative sense, naturalized:

We pass, and have our gesture; love and pain
And hope and apprehension and regret
Weave ordered lines into a pattern set

---

[7] In particular, the English Decadents idolized Charles Baudelaire, who conceives of art as a dynamic relationship between the eternal and the temporal. In "The Painter of Modern Life" (1859), Baudelaire writes,

An artist with a perfect sense of form but one accustomed to relying above all on his memory and his imagination will find himself at the mercy of a riot of details all clamouring for justice with the fury of a mob in love with absolute equality. All justice is trampled under foot, all harmony sacrificed and destroyed; many a trifle assumes vast proportions; many a triviality usurps the attention. The more our artist turns an impartial eye on detail, the greater is the state of anarchy. (16)

According to Baudelaire, then, the artist must impose artificial constraints upon reality in order to organize and highlight the interplay between the eternal and the temporal that he sees as being the aspect that defines beauty. Oscar Wilde continues this thought in "The Decay of Lying" (1889) when he writes, "What Art really reveals to us is Nature's lack of design, her curious crudities, her extraordinary monotony, her absolutely unfinished condition. [. . .] Art is our spirited protest, our gallant attempt to teach Nature her proper place" (970).

Not for our pleasure, and for us in vain.
The gesture is eternal; we who pass
Pass on the gesture; we, who pass, pass on

One after one into oblivion,
As shadows dim and vanish from a glass. (153)

The note of despair in Symons's poem, which suggests that individuals are creatures compelled to reduce their essential human traits to a series of repetitive, thoughtless performances, is echoed in *Goodbye to Berlin*, particularly in Isherwood's description of Sally Bowles who, as Norman Page (195) argues, is a pale imitation of the late nineteenth-century trope of the femme fatale. Symons is working within a cultural atmosphere which is at once fascinated and repelled by the notion that individuals are performing beings, ones who have always operated within the parameters of artifice. The recognizably decadent sense of ennui is, in part, a result of the writers' ambivalence towards artificiality and performance. Ernest Dowson's (89) narrator in "Non Sum Qualis Eram Bonae Sub Regno Cynarae" (1891) replaces his beloved with a prostitute, and his ambivalence about this act operates as a refrain throughout the poem: "Surely the kisses of her bought red mouth were sweet; / But I was desolate and sick of an old passion." Even Oscar Wilde, who in his critical essays champions the triumph of art over nature, reveals a conflicted view of artifice in *The Picture of Dorian Gray* (1891), where the perfection of the protagonist's artificial self is achieved at the expense of his humanity.

Like Symons, Dowson, and Wilde, Isherwood is both fascinated with and slightly repelled by the prevalent artifice he discovers in Berlin. From his initial description of her green fingernails, which evokes the *fin de siècle* trope of the green carnation as the artistic revaluation of nature, Sally Bowles appears to be the epitome of the self as performance, where, as Philip Auslander (30) notes, "the actorly self is, in fact, produced by the performance it supposedly grounds." Moreover, Sally's performative nature, like Gilman's definition of Decadence, lies in its effect rather than in any intrinsic meaning. Christopher cannot help but see Sally in theatrical terms, from her dress which produces "a kind of theatrically chaste effect, like a nun in a grand opera" to her being "absurdly conscious" of her beauty (27). Sally's performance extends to her everyday speech; Christopher remarks that "Sally's German was not merely incorrect; it was all her own" (26-27). Alan Wilde, elaborating on Sally's theatrical manner of speaking, writes, "Substituting emphasis for politeness, her conversationally vivid but imprecise language, a fluid succession of terribly's, marvelous's, and interminable, hollow superlatives, amounts to a kind of italic prose, directed, again in aesthetic terms, essentially at performance rather than meaning" (483). Sally's artifice succeeds in rousing Christopher's critical spirit; in fact, Christopher tends in this story to conflate criticism with emotional closeness. This is not necessarily a mistaken identification on Christopher's part – rather, Sally's artifice, which Christopher believes hides an anxiety about her conventional middle-class roots, creates Christopher's own performance as an aesthetic snob, obscuring his insecurities about his own character weaknesses. "I only meant," he says to Sally, "that when you talk like that it's really just nervousness. You're naturally rather shy with strangers, I think: so you've got into this trick of trying to bounce them into approving or disapproving of you, violently. I know, because I try it myself, sometimes" (33). The "Sally Bowles" story is, in fact, one of the few occurrences (save for "The Landauers") where we find Christopher both so critical and so engaged. In Sally's case, her performance offers Christopher a safe space to develop his own performance and, in so doing, break away from the detached pose he claims at the beginning of the book.

It is commonplace to view decadence as the repressed element of the norm, a subversion of conventional beliefs in progress and morality. What Isherwood brings to light in "Sally Bowles" is how much conventionality, in turn, acts as decadence's repressed or, in Sally and Christopher's case, its unfulfilled desire. Charles Bernheimer (2-3) points out that "[t]he notion of decadence seemed to elicit at once a desire to subvert the traditional moral code and a need to affirm the values of that code." David Weir (18), referring to the French Decadents of the mid-nineteenth century, claims that while these writers claim to feel no affinity with the world of the middle class, they are in fact bourgeois at heart. In Isherwood's story, the desire for conventionality and the shame of acknowledging this desire manifest themselves in a sense of profound isolation, experienced in different degrees by both Sally and Christopher.

The ideal of the decadents is the notion of a community of outsiders, bound together by their unwillingness to subscribe to conventional mores. For Isherwood, though, this community is fragile precisely because it relies on the sense of oneself as outside the larger, more mainstream community. During their brief acquaintanceship with the debauched American Clive, for example, Sally and Christopher witness the funeral procession of Hermann Müller, the former Chancellor of the Weimar Republic. Christopher, witnessing both the sombre procession and Sally's ignorance of and indifference to Müller's political significance, confronts his own sense of isolation. "She was quite right," he admits,

> We had nothing to do with those Germans down there, marching, or with the dead man in the coffin, or with the words on the banners. In a few days, I thought, we shall have forfeited all kinship with ninety-nine per cent. of the population of the world, with the men and women who earn their living, who insure their lives, who are anxious about the future of their children. Perhaps in the Middle Ages

people felt like this, when they believed themselves to have sold their souls to the Devil. It was a curious, exhilarating, not unpleasant sensation: but, at the same time, I felt slightly scared. Yes, I said to myself, I've done it, now. I am lost. (49)

The sense of isolation and the anxiety of having lost touch with the world is an important part of Christopher's experience in Berlin, as it provides him with pleasures and fears that are inextricable from one another. Life in the decadent underworld causes one to crave community with the mainstream (indeed, the unfulfilled desire provides one with no small amount of pleasure), but isolation is too integral a part of the underworld. The feeling of emotional closeness, then, becomes a matter of performance, of playacting at relationships, since any attempt at genuine closeness runs contrary to the decadents' way of being.

Sally's performance of the femme fatale *manquée*, coupled with Christopher's avuncular, albeit slightly crotchety, performance, leads the two to play at conventionality as another form of artifice. Although their relationship is prefaced by Sally's insightful remark, "But I'm glad you're not in love with me, because, somehow, I couldn't possibly be in love with you – so, if you had been, everything would have been spoilt" (34), the two occasionally gesture towards courtship. It is conventionality, however, rather than romance, which intrigues them. While recuperating from her abortion, Sally fabricates a romance with Christopher in part to mollify the nurses and in part to perform a scenario straight out of the films popular in the 1920s, in which "we were most terribly in love but fearfully hard up, so that we couldn't afford to marry, and how we dreamed of the time when we'd both be rich and famous and then we'd have a family of ten, just to make up for this one" (53-54). Sally's clichéd fantasy allows her to avoid having to acknowledge that no amount of performance can transform the emotionally traumatic experience into a theatrical or cinematic effect. In contrast to Brian Finney's (149) argument that Sally's abortion leaves her "virtually untouched," the abortion and the threat of scandal that accompanies it force both Sally and Christopher to confront the conventional mores that their underworld activities are, in part, a spirited protest against. Sally rejects Christopher by insisting that he is not typically masculine enough to suit her, while Christopher briefly wonders, with no small amount of trepidation, whether all this playacting has given him genuine romantic feelings for Sally. The two only reconcile in the wake of a con-artist's ruse, when artificiality once again becomes the accepted method of being in this world.

The struggle between subversion and conventionality in "Sally Bowles," or between artifice and authenticity, takes place on a relatively abstract, comfortable level for Christopher. The termination of his relationship with Sally merely leaves him with a slightly wistful sensation, rather than with any lasting regrets. Only as *Goodbye to Berlin* begins to chart the transformation of the Nazi party from a fringe group of hoodlums to the eventual ruling party of Germany does the dynamic between the decadent and the norm take on a new urgency. Specifically, Christopher's relationship with the Landauers, a well-to-do Jewish family, highlights the way in which Nazi ideology exploits this dynamic. The Landauers, in almost every sense, are conventional bourgeoisie, yet they are being labelled by the Nazis as not only decadent but as degenerate threats to the moral health of the nation. The hidden desire for conventionality, then, becomes tainted by Nazi ideology. Likewise, Weimar-era decadence loses much of its meaning when prostitutes, demimondaines, and Jewish businessmen are all categorized with the same noxiously crude brushstrokes. "The Landauers" force Christopher to confront his initial stance as voyeur by putting him in a situation where his sense of moral obligation trumps his previous intellectual fascination with decadence.

As the stories progress, then, decadence becomes less appealing for Isherwood and more a source of anxiety, especially in its failure to resist the shifting ideology in Germany. With "The Landauers," Isherwood confronts the question of decadence and morality by exploring the similarities between the demimonde and the bourgeoisie. Like Sally Bowles, who is modelled after Isherwood's close friend Jean Ross, Natalia is based upon Gisa Soloweitschik, who was once involved with Isherwood's friend Stephen Spender, while his friend Wilfrid Israel is the model for Bernhard. In *Christopher and His Kind*, Isherwood (68) acknowledges that his fictionalization of Gisa and Wilfrid portrays them in an unfairly harsh light. Natalia, he claims, lacks Gisa's considerable warmth and attractiveness, and Bernhard never displays any of Wilfrid Israel's activism.[8] His apologetic explanation in the autobiography suggests that he conceived of the Landauers as respectable versions of his more overtly decadent characters. Neither Natalia nor Bernhard Landauer are members of the Berlin underworld (although Bernhard's character suggests a familiarity with it), yet they embody an aspect that Isherwood previously explored in minor characters such as Pieps and Kurt, the young hustlers in the Alexander Casino, namely a belief in the artificial as a panacea for social ills.

Isherwood is aware, however, that the Landauers' precarious position as Jews sets them apart from the hustlers and performers he depicts elsewhere in the stories. Isherwood begins "The Landauers"

---

[8] Wilfrid Israel, like Bernhard Landauer, helped to run his family's department store in Berlin. Defying Nazi pressure, he refused to fire his Jewish employees, nor would he fly the swastika in front of the department store building. Until the Nazis confiscated the store in 1939, Wilfrid helped as many Jews as he could emigrate from Germany. He escaped to England just before the war broke out but, in 1943, on a return trip from Portugal where he was helping Jewish refugees emigrate to Palestine, his plane was shot down by German fighters (*Christopher and His Kind* 68-72).

with an account of an anti-Jewish demonstration in October 1930, which he calls his "first introduction to Berlin politics" (139). From there, politics keep intruding into the story, colouring his accounts of Natalia and Bernhard in a way that suggests that the Jewish characters can never be separated from their political context. It is this revaluation of individuals according to Nazi ideology that profoundly discomforts Isherwood and, as a result, his narrator becomes both increasingly distanced and morally outraged. While the Nazi presence is felt from the first story, and Christopher clearly loathes the odious Nazi doctor in "On Ruegen Island," only in "The Landauers" does Christopher make a small gesture of defiance against the Nazis – he purchases an item from the Landauers' boycotted department store.[9]

Yet his association with the Landauers leads Isherwood to question whether his narrator's decadent tendencies have compromised his moral integrity. As harshly as he may portray Natalia and Bernhard, Isherwood is even more unforgiving in his depiction of his narrator. Christopher is impatient, pretentious, and cruel to Natalia. He utters pompous remarks such as "No Englishman ever laughs when he's amused" (144), becomes petulant when a concert hall does not meet his aesthetic standards, and purposely arranges a meeting between Natalia and Sally, even though he knows that Sally's sexual openness and casual anti-Semitism will offend Natalia. Despite Isherwood's later admission in *Christopher and His Kind* (64) that he portrays Natalia as a "bossy bluestocking, desperately enthusiastic about culture, sexually frigid and prudish," Natalia still comes across as innocent and patient in her friendship with Christopher. Her love of culture is inseparable from her adoration of her family and of the intellectual discussions she often has with them. Despite her growing insecurity about being Jewish in Berlin,

---

[9]   Norman Page (58) points out that this scene is autobiographical.

Natalia demonstrates, within her middle-class boundaries, an essential pragmatism about her future, planning to study art in Paris so that she may provide for herself should her father lose his fortune (145). Christopher is irritated by her attitude, but this reaction arises from the fear that, in the face of the growing threat against the Jews, the decadents' sense of themselves as marginalized becomes less meaningful.[10]

But while Natalia's optimism runs counter to Christopher's sensibility, Bernhard's apathy and ennui attracts him. Bernhard, in fact, exhibits the character traits of a stereotypical *fin de siècle* decadent. Often gloomy and morose, he shuns the company of the mainstream despite his status as the bourgeois businessman, preferring to dwell on his physical and mental hardships for his own pleasure. Christopher remarks on their first meeting, "He was soft, negative, I thought, yet curiously potent, with the static potency of a carved ivory figure in a shrine" (154). More so than Natalia, Bernhard is sensitive, despite his success, about the pejorative attitudes often held by Gentiles towards his Jewishness; at one point, he remarks to Christopher, "It disgusts your English public-school training, a little – this Jewish emotionalism" (171). For Bernhard, though, his differences, resulting from his Jewish upbringing, define him less than his decadent tendencies, and this sense of himself leads him to treat the death threats made against him with disturbing nonchalance. "My existence," he says, "is not of such vital importance to myself or to others that the forces of the Law should be called upon to protect me" (179).

---

[10] In this instance, Isherwood's decision to erase his, and by extension his narrator's, homosexuality from the stories causes Christopher to remain distanced from the Nazis' persecution of so-called degenerate threats to German moral integrity. Because he keeps silent about his homosexuality, he cannot identify himself as another victim of Nazi ideology.

Bernhard's subsequent description of himself as unhealthy, lacking mental proportion, morbid, and unbalanced bears an eerie similarity to the Nazi doctor's pronouncements on Ruegen Island about Communism being a mental disease, homosexuality a reversion to atavism, and the need for discipline as a cure for degeneration. Yvonne Holbeche (40) points out Bernhard's "decadent inertia which marks him as representative Jewish victim," in that he ascribes to the very ideology that is bent upon his destruction. Bernhard takes pleasure in wilfully disregarding the death threats. Yet, at the same time, he cannot quite believe that, given his prominent position in Berlin's business world, he is in any real danger. Christopher, unable to empathize with Bernhard's situation, fails to understand the ambivalent position experienced by Bernhard and, indeed, by many of Berlin's respected Jewish citizens. Therefore, Christopher ultimately fails Bernhard in much the same way he fails Natalia, by withdrawing from the sense of real danger that surrounds him. When Bernhard obliquely asks Christopher to leave Germany with him, Christopher interprets the request as a joke. Only later, when he overhears two men discussing Bernhard's death in a concentration camp, does he realize his mistake.

Bernhard, then, despite his position as eventual victim of the Nazis, contributes to the moral apathy that Isherwood locates in the general population. What is a chilling thought in the story is Christopher's realization that the German Jews, in the given political climate, are being turned into bad performers. In this case, their performance is based on being full and accepted German citizens – at a party held on the night of the 1930 elections, which saw the Nazis increase their government seats from twelve to one hundred seven, they seem more concerned about a Communist takeover of the government. But Christopher realizes that the performance is hollow. "However often the decision must be delayed," he notes, "all these people are ultimately doomed. The evening is the dress-rehearsal of a disaster. It is like the last night of an epoch" (177). Bernhard's own performance rings false as well because his own dramatics pale in light of his changed circumstances. Individual performances and attempts at artifice become meaningless when external events impose on one a drama that is beyond one's control. Christopher, already sensitive to the hidden desire for conventionality inherent in decadence, turns away from the notion that, as far as the Nazis' anti-Semitic ideology is concerned, conventionality and decadence collapse into one another, with disastrous results.

While Christopher throughout *Goodbye to Berlin* has been plagued with a moral anxiety that at times has affected his narrative pose, in the second "Berlin Diary" he suffers, if not a moral breakdown, then a disintegration of his narrative persona. He has abandoned the conceit of the camera in favour of the mirror, as if, as Alan Wilde (485) argues, "to bear witness to the failure of an intended objectivity, a failure that is, above all, moral." No longer isolated from Berlin as he was in the first "Berlin Diary," Christopher identifies with a city on the edge of its own moral demise. "Berlin," he writes, "is a skeleton which aches in the cold: it is my own skeleton aching" (186). Whereas in the beginning of the book, Christopher catalogues the decadent landscape of seedy cabarets and pick-up bars with a naïf's wide-eyed wonder, in this final story his descriptions reflect the moral guilt he has accumulated witnessing the end of decadent Berlin.

Indeed, Isherwood's Berlin at the end of the book is an apocalyptic Vanity Fair, where an S.A. officer is recognized as one of the hustlers at the Alexander Casino and where the middle-class housewife Frau Krampf is forced to satisfy a butcher's perversions in order to receive meat for her family. Furthermore, the character of Berlin itself has changed from a nurturer of sexuality and decadence to a femme fatale, luring newcomers in order to destroy them:

> But the real heart of Berlin is a small damp black wood – the Tiergarten. At this time of the year, the cold begins to drive the peasant boys out of their tiny unprotected villages into the city, to look for food, and work. But the city, which glowed so brilliantly and invitingly in the night sky above the plains, is cold and cruel and dead. Its warmth is an illusion, a mirage of the winter desert. It will not receive these boys. It has nothing to give. The cold drives them out of its streets, into the wood which is its cruel heart. (187)

As Christopher describes this altered Berlin, he identifies its core as being the dark, primitive aspect of nature that the city is built to obscure. But Berlin no longer succeeds at artifice; instead of being a consolation against nature, artifice becomes the device by which people are ruthlessly flung back into nature's darkest elements.

Even the decadent places of Berlin cannot sustain their artifice. Christopher's final visit to the Salomé reveals the customers' futile attempt to maintain their decadent appeal: "A few stage lesbians and some young men with plucked eyebrows lounged at the bar, uttering occasional raucous guffaws or treble hoots – supposed, apparently, to represent the laughter of the damned" (192). The "apparently" that Christopher inserts in his description indicates a failure in the Salomé's decadence. Like its namesake in Oscar Wilde's tragedy that became the libretto for Richard Strauss's opera, the Salomé's decadent ethos is doomed – only, instead of clearing the way for the coming of Christ, its demise heralds the triumph of Hitler. Isherwood notes that at this point the police have begun to raid the underworld with increasing frequency and the Salomé itself now numbers American homophobes among its guests. Yet the sense of doom in the club is calculated for effect; the club's regulars seem to have no interest in presaging their future. Berlin's decadence, Isherwood implies, has forgotten that artifice is a critical tool, borne out of serious intent rather than frivolity. As Holbeche (36) notes, it becomes "increasingly apparent that passive detachment comes to mean something very close to moral failure." Decadence's failure, according to Isherwood, is not only that it is no longer a means of criticizing the dominant mores, but that it has allowed itself to be absorbed in its enemy's ideology. The Nazis, he notes, do not recognize ironic distance or detachment; in their earnestness, they will treat the decadent as a serious threat to the moral health of the state.

Despite the ominous overtones in his final description of Berlin, Isherwood is aware that the city's transformation will be subtle, a matter of adaptation rather than a sudden shock. His former landlady, Frl. Schroeder, is emblematic of such a transformation. Commenting on her new reverence for Hitler, Christopher notes,

> She is merely acclimatizing herself, in accordance with a natural law, like an animal that changes its coat for the winter. Thousands of people like Frl. Schroeder are acclimatizing themselves. After all, whatever government is in power, they are doomed to live in this town. (207)

Nature rears its ugly head yet again in this story as an oppressive agent and as an annihilator of individual differences. Yet it is not only the fallen bourgeoise Frl. Schroeder who is victim to this oppression; Christopher remarks about the underworld, "The political moral is certainly depressing: these people could be made to believe in anybody or anything" (190).

Throughout the book, Christopher is compelled to negotiate his sense of himself as an outsider in Germany, his immersion in the decadent milieu of Berlin, and his growing moral outrage against Nazism, particularly its anti-Communism and anti-Semitism. Decadence is usually seen as an amoral, or even an anti-moral, movement. Its underlying mandate, in many instances, has been that morality is a form of oppression that marginalizes individuals who explore the vast range of physical and emotional experiences so crucial to being in the world. Christopher's detached pose is in this sense Isherwood's abstaining from a morality in which, as a gay man sympathetic to Communism, he cannot participate. But the increasing power of the Nazis leads to moments of tension in Christopher's detachment and begs the question whether the decadence of Weimar-era Berlin is not only outdated but, in its anti-morality, a silent abettor of the growing Fascism of the era. While anti-morality presupposes an alternative moral position, the pervading fear throughout the book is that, in light of the Nazis' ideology, anti-morality could slip easily into immorality. Neutrality could turn into apathy, and the denizens of the underworld, committed to the free existence of sexual, social, and political differences, will, in order to protect their subculture, watch a dictator assume power and do nothing.

The question implicit in Christopher's observations about Berlin under Hitler's rule is to what extent, given his newfound identification with the city, is he involved in this form of adaptation? David Thomas (51) argues that *Goodbye to Berlin* "attempts to cure the neurotic hero by tapping springs of human sympathy, substituting people for the artificial sanctuary of art, religion, or politics. The hero is still impelled to flight, but has found a new honesty and self-knowledge." Yet Christopher's newly-acquired self-knowledge is tinged with the awareness that he, too, is capable of shutting his eyes to Berlin's fate. The final lines of the book describe an image of Christopher smiling as he watches the people of Berlin, noting that "they have an air of curious familiarity, of striking resemblance to something one remembers as normal and pleasant in the past – like a very good photograph" (207). Isherwood ends the book, as he begins it, with the trope of the camera. Yet the anxiety of the narrator has transformed this trope from one of neutral observation to one of distortion, a turning away from the harsh realities that, despite his moral objections, he is unable to alter.

Works Cited

Auslander, Philip. *From Acting to Performance: Essays in Modernism and Postmodernism.* New York: Routledge, 1997.

Baudelaire, Charles. "The Painter of Modern Life." *The Painter of Modern Life and Other Essays.* Ed. and trans. Jonathan Mayne. London: Phaidon, 1964. 1-40.

Bernheimer, Charles. *Decadent Subjects: The Idea of Decadence in Art, Literature, Philosophy, and Culture of the Fin de Siècle in Europe.* Ed. T. Jefferson Kline and Naomi Schor. Baltimore, Maryland: Johns Hopkins UP, 2002.

Dowson, Ernest. "Non Sum Qualis Eram Bonae Sub Regno Cynarae." *Aesthetes and Decadents of the 1890's.* Ed. Karl Beckson. Chicago: Academy Chicago, 1993. 88-89.

Finney, Brian. *Christopher Isherwood: A Critical Biography.* London: Faber and Faber, 1979.

Fryer, Jonathan H. "Sexuality in Isherwood." *Twentieth Century Literature* 22.3 (1976): 343-53.

Gay, Peter. *Weimar Culture: The Outsider as Insider.* New York: Harper and Row, 1968.

Gilman, Richard. *Decadence: The Strange Life of an Epithet.* London: Secker and Warburg, 1979.

Green, Martin. *Children of the Sun: A Narrative of "Decadence" in England After 1918.* New York: Basic, 1976.

Holbeche, Yvonne. "Goodbye to Berlin: Erich Kästner and Christopher Isherwood." *AUMLA* 94 (2000): 35-54.

Isherwood, Christopher. *The Berlin Stories: The Last of Mr. Norris, Goodbye to Berlin.* New York: New Directions, 1988.

---. *Christopher and His Kind 1929-1939.* New York: North Point, 1996.

Page, Norman. *Auden and Isherwood: The Berlin Years*. London: Macmillan, 1998.

Piazza, Paul. *Christopher Isherwood: Myth and Anti-Myth*. New York: Columbia UP, 1978.

Symons, Arthur. "Maquillage." *Aesthetes and Decadents of the 1890's*. Ed. Karl Beckson. Chicago: Academy Chicago, 1993. 152.

---. "Prologue: Before the Curtain." *Aesthetes and Decadents of the 1890's*. Ed. Karl Beckson. Chicago: Academy Chicago, 1993. 153.

Thomas, David P. "'Goodbye to Berlin': Refocusing Isherwood's Camera." *Contemporary Literature* 13.1 (1972): 44-52.

Weir, David. *Decadence and the Making of Modernism*. Amherst, Massachusetts: U of Massachusetts P, 1995.

Wilde, Alan. "Language and Surface: Isherwood in the Thirties." *Contemporary Literature* 16.4 (1975): 478-91.

Wilde, Oscar. "The Decay of Lying." *The Complete Works of Oscar Wilde*. New York: Barnes and Noble, 1994. 970-92.

Permissive Paradise:
The Fiction of Swinging London

Nick Freeman
University of the West of England

Abstract: This essay examines the representation of decadence in British popular fiction of the 1960s, with particular reference to works set in "Swinging London." It argues that London was widely perceived as a decadent site, but that opinion was strongly divided about both the nature of this "decadence" and its consequences. One strand viewed decadence as positive, a move away from suffocating archaic conventions. A second was completely opposed to such developments, while a third, in many ways the most interesting, assumed a more ambivalent stance. Certain writers and film directors relished describing what ultimately they chose to condemn, particularly "permissive" behaviour involving sex and/or drugs.

"They're selling hippie wigs in Woolworth's, man. The greatest decade in the history of mankind is over," mourns the drug-addled Danny in Bruce Robinson's film *Withnail and I* (1987), set in September 1969. Yet for the neo-conservative folk singer in Tim Robbins' *Bob Roberts* (1992), the 1960s mark a moral and political nadir, setting in motion social changes from which America is still reeling. The legacy of the decade remains hotly contested in the liberal democracies of the twenty-first century. Did it see the beginnings of a new society distinguished by growing social equality, or did it encourage instead dangerous radicalism and unthinking self-indulgence that irrevocably rotted the body politic?

Such polarised perspectives are characteristic of discussions of decadence as well as of the 1960s. "[T]he notion of decadence is inhabited by a doubleness that puts fundamental moral and social values in question," Charles Bernheimer observes:

There is an implicit appeal to a norm that sustains society's assumptions about what is natural, good, right, life-sustaining, progressive and so forth. But there is also the suggestion that this appeal constricts human potential, denies opportunities for pleasure, and discredits the attraction of the perverse and destructive. (Bernheimer 51)

This essay will examine how such "doubleness" manifested itself in British popular culture of the 1960s, specifically in the representation of "Swinging London" between 1964 and 1971. Novelists, and indeed, journalists and film makers of the time, found various forms of "decadent" behaviour to be provocative and, on occasion, remunerative subject matter, but their attitudes towards it were often ambivalent, even troubled.

When in April 1966 Piri Halasz hailed the English capital as "Swinging London" in her article "You Can Walk Across It On The Grass," readers of *Time* were, she recalls, "mostly horrified. They were conservative for the most part and it struck them as sinful and decadent," though others "thought it was perfectly marvellous and loved every bit of it" (qtd. in Levy 227-28). While one might ponder how "sinful and decadent" are configured here, the article proved extremely influential for American tourists who headed for a remarkably selective version of the English capital. Its colour photographs and a map showing the most fashionable shops, restaurants, galleries and casinos painted a bewitching, if thoroughly misleading picture of the metropolis as a place of uninterrupted frivolity and thrills. Halasz's prose conveyed a breathless excitement in its relish for what seems a brave new world:

This spring, as never before in modern times, London is switched on. Ancient elegance and new opulence are all tangled up in a dazzling blur of op and pop. The city is alive with birds (girls) and beatles, buzzing with minicars and telly stars, pulsing with half-a-dozen separate veins of excitement. The guards now change at Buckingham Palace to a Lennon and McCartney tune, and Prince Charles is firmly in the long-hair set. (Halasz 32)

Such absurdities did not go unchallenged. Robert Murphy notes how the article was "important in crystalising an image" (Murphy 140), but points out that Halasz was far from the first writer to celebrate the "swinging" city. The *Weekend Telegraph*'s feature, "London – The Most Exciting City," and David Bailey's collection of glamorous celebrity portraits, *Box of Pin-Ups*, had both appeared in 1965, as had the first issue of the magazine *London Life*. By the time Halasz had "discovered" the capital, British commentators were becoming markedly cool towards "a fantasy world far beyond the means of most Londoners," and as Nik Cohn remarked, scarcely appreciated an American visitor colluding in "a media myth" (Levy 230). The unapologetic Halasz published *A Swinger's Guide to London* the following year, though as George Melly noted, the image of "the pop dandy and dolly frugging in an 'in' discotheque" was about to be killed "stone dead" by the hippies of the Summer of Love (154).

Melly overstates the case a little, for although the "real" Swinging London may have disappeared in 1967, its media after-image lasted for several more years: American tourists explore a cynically commercialised Carnaby Street in *If It's Tuesday, This Must Be Belgium* (1969). Nevertheless, the pace of change was such that the insistently topical Swinging London film had virtually died out by 1970. It had become increasingly obvious to all but the most optimistic or naïve that Cohn's "media myth" had seriously misrepresented London life, and the cinema of the early 1970s was markedly less sympathetic to "cloud-cuckoo land" (Rhode 203).

However, both its celebrants and its critics needed Swinging London to exist. For those in the vanguard of social change, it was a powerful symbol of a new Britain that was supposedly classless, dynamic, *fun*. "Hipness, decadence and exquisite tailoring," were keynotes of "mid-sixties swinging London" for the singer, Marianne Faithfull:

> We were young, rich and beautiful, and the tide was turning in our favour. We were going to change everything, of course, but mostly we were going to change the rules. Unlike our parents, we would never have to renounce our youthful hedonism in favour of the insane world of adulthood. (Faithfull 59)

For those alarmed by such words however, and inclined to see decadence in a less positive light, the city was an equally convenient and memorable image of decline. Whether or not there actually was a Swinging London is less important than what it might represent, and this was invariably a nebulous "permissive society" that licensed sexual and narcotic experiment and rejected traditional social and moral constraints. What Faithfull saw as youthful exuberance casting off archaic conventions and poisonous inhibition was for others a decadent preoccupation with personal pleasure at the expense of social responsibility, tradition and "decency." The battle lines between the two camps were firmly drawn, even before Halasz's article appeared, and grew ever more distinct as the decade progressed.

The result was the emergence of works that located themselves within a nominally permissive framework only to resort to more established moral standpoints, treating "swingers" much as the Spartans had their Helots centuries before. Pete Walker's exploitation film, *Cool it Carol!* (1970), is especially culpable here in its story of provincial teenagers drawn to London in search of the experiences they have been promised in films such as *Smashing Time* (1967) and *The Jokers* (1967), works which were themselves parodies of the London created by films such as *The Knack* (1965). Carol (Janet Lynn) and Joe (Robin Askwith) seek the simulacrum with dogged enthusiasm – "this is what I thought it would be like," cries a delighted Carol as she is almost squashed by a passing bus – only to be entrapped in "the vice-ridden London of sexploitation" (Hunt 101). The couple manage to escape back to the provinces, "disillusioned" but "neither damaged nor chastened" (Hunt 102) by their misadventures, as Walker revels in the conditions that have made his film possible while simultaneously reviling many of those who are equally keen to profit from them.

It was film and popular fiction that constructed and dramatised Swinging London with the greatest enthusiasm. To put it crudely, older established writers and journalists were usually too old and too established – too openly affiliated to "high" culture and historic universities – to be sympathetic towards the increasingly youth-driven world of the swinging city. This did not stop some of them; Kingsley Amis for example, eyeing it from a position of mockery and longing, or others from pepping up characterisations and plot lines with the trappings of fashionable morality in the manner of Iris Murdoch. Amis' *I Want It Now* (1968) was still being marketed as firing "some deadly accurate shots" at the "clichés of the so-called permissive society" (back cover) in 1976, but its techniques are essentially those of *Lucky Jim* (1954) with updated cultural references. Murdoch was more ambitious, not to say pretentious in her approach, but like Amis used the various forms of "decadence" – sexual, intellectual, moral – as a backdrop to her fiction. The leisured navel-gazers of her novels live beyond the confines of Swinging London, inhabiting instead a parallel universe of adultery, pseudo-science, and unlikely nomenclature. The British literary scene of the late 1950s to the mid-1960s was anything but moribund, but as Patricia Waugh observes, its senior novelists had little interest in "swing or utopianism" (Waugh 10). Anthony Burgess, Doris Less-ing and Angus Wilson, to use three of her examples, might have been interested in broadening the imaginative and even the moral compass of the English novel, but their experiments were usually conducted at a marked distance from the din and glitter of Carnaby Street. Much "significant" English fiction of the 1960s attempted to explore and negotiate the effect and boundaries of "permissiveness" within the bourgeois intelligentsia, but it rarely engaged with Halasz's Technicolor world of "op and pop."

Popular fiction, particularly mass market paperback fiction, was much more willing to explore such terrain, but seemed uncertain of its own stance or role in the swinging decade. Writing in 1970, George Melly appreciated the popular poetry and "new" journalism of the 1960s, and applauded Colin MacInnes' *Absolute Beginners* (1959), yet saw little merit in the efforts of subsequent "pop fiction" to provide "vicarious kicks for straights" (Melly 217). On one hand, its rapid composition and swift production schedules allowed it to be topical and address immediate social concerns from the "front line." On the other, the speed of change in popular culture was so rapid that novels dated quickly and were in many cases never reprinted.

The fiction published by New English Library, Corgi, Pan and others tended to view the supposed excesses of Swinging London through the smoked glass of the cautionary tale. Provocatively packaged works such as Simon Cooper's *The Rag Dolls* (1968) and its follow-up, *The Pretty Boys* (1970), Jackie Collins' *The Stud* (1970), and Mariella Novotny's *King's Road* (1971) walked a line between celebration and denunciation. Each combined hysterical descriptions of wild parties, exclusive night spots, trendy boutiques and what Novotny's cover blurb called "the high-life and low-life" of "London's turned-on beautiful people," with a notably didactic streak. These novels luxuriate in accounts of "permissive" behaviour just as *Cool it Carol!* does, only to denounce such activity in a final

reversion to older mores. "Decadence" is usually allowed to be be-
guiling in the first half of the book, but its transgressive appeal must
be discounted, usually through the ruin of those who embody it. It is
no surprise to see the resolutely unglamorous Georgy win out over
the heartless sophisticate Meredith in Margaret Forster's *Georgy
Girl* (1965), still less to see her cinematic incarnation, Lynn
Redgrave, triumph over the beautiful yet callous Charlotte Ram-
pling in the film version of the following year.

Sex was a major component of the Swinging London "scene"
fermented in the British media, often overlapping with drugs in a
double assault on established social norms. As Elizabeth Wilson has
observed in a discussion of the social change of the late 1960s,
"there was a compulsion to be sexual" but "by an impossible sleight
of hand, sexuality was both to expand and flower in liberated fashion *and* to be organised within marriage" (Wilson 110, qtd. in Murphy 142-43). The contraceptive pill was not yet in widespread use,
and indeed, was initially only prescribed for married women, but
sex seemed nonetheless omnipresent, with its profile in youth-
orientated popular culture particularly high. In his 1969 *cri de
coeur, The Neophiliacs*, Christopher Booker noted how the fashionable clothes of the mid-1960s, particularly ever skimpier miniskirts,
"grabbed at the attention" with "exhibitionist violence" (273). The
result was what he saw as sexual immorality and the disappearance
of individual identity. Such "hard looking uniforms" were, he said,
"curiously impersonal, like the expressionless stare that so often
went with them or the throwaway generic terms – 'birds' or 'dollies'
– that were used to describe their wearers." For Booker, an admit-
tedly extreme commentator, London was fast becoming a City of
the Plain, a morally and linguistically degenerate metropolis where
the rise of slang and the cult of celebrity, particularly where it concerned working class actors and photographers, were symptoms of a
far greater cultural malaise. "London is like a vast central nerve, and

if the nerve goes rotten, then sooner or later the tooth goes rotten too," warned Robert Bruce in the same year. "It was in London that the New Morality first took root" (Habicht xiii). "What a freak show. Long hair, beatniks, druggers, free love, foreigners," snarls James Fox's Chas Devlin, the East End gangster caught up in the psychedelic confusion of *Performance* (1970).

While some were condemnatory, others recognised that they stood to profit from aspects of the sexual revolution. One result of this was a series of leering estimations of women in the capital. "Young English girls take to sex as if it's candy and delicious," wrote American journalist John Crosby in "London – The Most Exciting City" in April 1965 (qtd. in Levy 229). The following year, another sexually voracious American, Ted Mark's Steve Victor, "The Man From ORGY," titillated his readers with a vision of "bar-hopping in the part of town known for London britches falling down. Sort of a bust-man's holiday, you might say"[1] (Mark 1). Geoffrey Gorer's *Sex and Marriage in England Today* (1971) found that 63% of women and 26% of men were virgins when they married, and that default assumptions of promiscuity in young women were largely mistaken. Despite such surveys however, the male fantasy of an edibly pretty nymphet on every street corner became increasingly insistent.

Considering "lads and loungers" in the popular culture of the early 1970s, Leon Hunt identifies a "middle aged but fashion conscious" figure he terms "Hair Spray Man" (63). Hair Spray Man is "too old or 'straight' to be inserted unproblematically into 'the permissive society,'" Hunt observes, "but dips a cautious toe in its waters, through longer hair, terylene flares, or the spectacular floral shirts offered by Double Two International's That Shirt!" He seeks the sexual free-

---

[1] The acronym "ORGY" represents the "Organisation for the Rational Guidance of Youth"!

dom of the mythic metropolis without the responsibility attendant upon it, and dreams of what Kurt Muller and Kidge Wurdak's 1969 folio terms *Pussies in Boots*. A sub-section of the publishing industry sprang to his aid in works such as *The London Spy* (1971), a guide to London's "treasures and pleasures." In a section entitled "Sex: Women for Men: Pulling," it offered the following advice to potential swingers desperate for a piece of the action:

> The traditional place to get your eye in is down the King's Road. Arm yourself with a pint or a Pimms or a Pernod and position yourself on the pavement outside the *Chelsea Potter* or the *Markham Arms* [. . .] You know what you're there for; they know what you're there for. King's Road birds are used to being accosted every thirty yards they walk [. . .] Not that all King's Road birds are groupies (girls passed around like a joint between members of a pop group). But they are very wary. So have a few shapes by all means to get your chat flowing. But don't be discouraged if you only draw blanks. (Allen and Guirdham 135)

"Chelsea Girl" was footloose, fancy-free, and gifted with perfect skin and willowy physique. Like Swinging London itself, she was best regarded as semi-mythical. There were certainly young women in the city's south-western districts who embodied the media image and made the King's Road the "traditional" haunt of the Chelsea Girl: the actress Imogen Hassall recalled that "Chelsea was very 'in' [. . .] one was known as a jet set girl – and with this jet set girl you slept around" (qtd. in Leigh 86). Few however could live the dream offered by fashion magazines, colour supplements and films such as *Billy Liar* (1963), *Darling* (1965), and *Kaleidoscope* (1966), where Susannah York owns a Hampstead boutique and designs "kinky clothes for baby-faced Chelsea girls who like to show off their pretty little knees." Aptly enough, Chelsea Girl was soon to become the name of a high street clothing outlet that, like the similar Kensington Freak, kept the associations of Swinging London alive into the 1980s and beyond, even as its fashions faded from view.

Subsequent commentators, notably Julie Burchill in her 1986 book *Girls on Film*, have ridiculed the ideal of the Chelsea Girl, but the archetypal dolly was very much part of Swinging London's landscape of sexual opportunity, at least where Hair Spray Man was concerned. Charles Bronson in *Twinky* (1969), and bizarrely, Norman Wisdom, reinventing himself as a romantic lead in *What's Good for the Goose* (1969), both found themselves smitten with such creatures. "The relationship between a materially rich, emotionally impoverished middle-aged man and a spontaneous, sexually willing young woman is a common theme in 60s British cinema," Robert Murphy observes, citing six examples from 1969 alone (154-55). Chelsea Girls were beautiful, "liberated" (that is to say, submissive, and willing to have sex with men considerably older and less attractive than themselves), and, most importantly, available, at least in fantasy, to precisely these individuals. One might "draw a blank" with the perfect physical specimens frequenting the Chelsea Potter, but there was always their fictional alternative. Popular fiction consequently found the Chelsea Girl irresistible.

Were Chelsea Girl and Hair Spray Man "decadent," or merely a symptom of decadence? One could hardly see the inter-generational relationships of late 1960s British cinema as groundbreaking in many respects, especially when those with older women either in heterosexual unions such as *Tam Lin* (1971) or lesbian ones such as that between Beryl Reid and Susannah York in the film version of *The Killing of Sister George* (1969) were typically portrayed as unnatural or tragic. What was perhaps different about the media image of the King's Road dolly was her apparent insistence on disregarding traditionally "acceptable" behaviour. "She's free, she doesn't care about convention," insists an interviewee in Peter Whitehead's

1967 "pop concerto," *Tonite, Let's All Make Love in London*. "She's free, she does what she likes . . . How else can you describe a dolly girl?" Any feminism that she might have practised was accommodatory rather than revolutionary, but she certainly had little desire to follow the rules of a previous generation, at least in the short term.

Chelsea Girl's "liberated" ethics made her a more than suitable consort for Philip McAlpine, the swinging spy hero of a quartet of novels by Adam Diment that appeared between 1967 and 1970. Diment's descriptions of her combined a pinch of truth with the transparent wish-fulfilment of Hair Spray Man, amalgamating experiences promoted by the media as typical of the swinging world with satirically exaggerated archetypes. The description of the twenty-two year old Veronica in *The Dolly Dolly Spy* (1967) relishes casual daring in reference to taboo behaviour, once more suggesting a deliberate break from previously dominant standards of behaviour:

> Her experience, which includes a large number of love affairs, modelling jobs, minor television appearances, two abortions and a wide range of kinky and interesting episodes, hangs around her like a halo. There, you would say on seeing her, is a girl who has seen life. Paddington pot parties, a hundred odd secretarial jobs like her present one [. . .] a film part which curled up and died on the cutting room floor. Following the flotsam of the Jet Set across Europe, Paris, Cannes, St Tropez, Venice, Sardinia, Baden Baden, Rome and back to Paris. (Diment, *Dolly* 33)

Diment's treatment of sex relished the incestuous idiolects of the era, switching effortlessly from spy romp to journalistic cliché. *The Great Spy Race* (1968) saw his hero describe himself as "gay man about Swinging London, Philip McAlpine," and allude self-consciously to "The New Morality." Most memorably, McAlpine offered sideswipes at earlier rebels, celebrating commitment and consequence-free "fun" sex over what he termed D. H. Lawrence's "deadly earnest copulation" (Diment, *Spy Race* 38).

At such moments, for all the anti-erotic incompetence of its sexual descriptions – "slipping slowly into her plump, warm clingingness" is an especially choice example (*Spy Race* 38) – Diment's fiction is self-aware and slyly parodic, biting the hand that feeds it with considerable élan. Comments reprinted on the paperback edition show reviewers joining the game just as eagerly as Diment himself, with the *Times Literary Supplement* calling the book "a real gas," and the *Northern Echo* savouring its "totally with-it sex-elation." Maurice Richardson even found the novel "orgiastic" when reviewing it for the *Observer* (*Spy Race*, back cover), innocuous though it seems today. McAlpine pursues dolly birds with priapic enthusiasm and sometimes smokes marijuana, but he could hardly be considered "decadent." References to the occasional joint were a world away from the accounts of heroin addiction in "underground" fiction by William Burroughs and Alexander Trocchi, since in Diment's work, drugs were merely an entertainment, not a transgressive destiny. As there were only 3071 convictions for cannabis possession in the UK in 1968, one wonders how many of Diment's readers could have had the chance to compare their experiences with those of McAlpine:

> "Philip, Philip," she said, trying to tear off my jeans. Making love when you're stoned is like jumping off the edge of the world. Great heats, enormous pressures, weird textures and an orgasm like a silent super-Nova. You feel as though you are coming for hours – It just goes on and on.
>
> (*Spy Race* 118)

Such recreations do not compromise McAlpine's ability to serve the state's political purposes, even if, in a nod to the times, and fiction

such as Len Deighton's *The Ipcress File* (1962), he frequently pro-
tests at having to do so.

Diment's publisher promoted the twenty-three year old novelist as
the embodiment of the swinging city. The paperback of *The Dolly
Dolly Spy* carried a comment from Atticus of the *Sunday Times* announcing that Diment's hero "is based on himself. That is to say he's
tall, good-looking, with a taste for fast cars, planes, girls and pot"
(back cover). Such marketing, and the author's identification with
his characters that was encouraged by first person narration, trans-
planted the dandified young protagonist of a film such as *Blow-Up*
(1966) into a world that combined the realistic detail of Deighton
with the more outlandish elements of the cinematic James Bond.
Their swinging trappings, the party he attends in *The Great Spy
Race*, which is held "in a large studio flat over a boutique doing a
strong line in old Wehrmacht uniforms" and filled with beautiful
women, dope smoke and the noise of "the very latest Stones' LP"
(*Spy Race* 29-30), are just that: trappings. Superficially if pleasura-
bly shocking to the strait-laced, McAlpine's adventures are in fact
perfectly tailored to the fantasies of his readership, those who, like
the speaker of Philip Larkin's "Annus Mirabilis" (1967) fear that the
beginning of sexual intercourse in 1963 was "rather late for me"
(167).

The "wild" party was a stock feature of a number of Swinging
London novels. An excuse for a pause in narrative and lashings of
facile exoticism, it allowed novelists to describe would be "outra-
geous" events, such as the arrival of a black girl in a topless dress at
The Stud's Hobo club (Collins 12). It was the profusion of such incidents in literature and film of the time that prompted their parody in
Michael Moorcock's *The Final Programme* (1965-66, revised

1969).[2] Here the seemingly endless list of guests suggests not only London's bewildering heterogeneity but also the fondness for "people collecting" displayed by an emerging generation of society hosts and hostesses eager to expand their social horizons. In-jokes abound in a scene that serves as Swinging London's answer to Trimalchio's feast in the *Satyricon*, a parallel reinforced by the appearance of Fellini's film version of Petronius in the same year as Moorcock's novel:

> The Man and a couple of friends were the first arrivals. "I thought I'd avail myself of the facilities," said The Man, taking off his heavy raincoat. He wore a high-collared green corduroy jacket and Hamlet tights. He looked a wow.
>
> The flood was on, and half-suspicious guests got the mood of the place before they let themselves relax. There were Turkish and Persian lesbians with huge houri eyes like those of sad, neutered cats; French tailors, German musicians; Jewish martyrs; a fire-eater from Suffolk; a barbershop quartet from Britain's remaining American air-base – the Columbia Club in Lancaster Gate; two fat prudes; Hans Smith of Hampstead, Last of the Leftwing Intellectuals – the Microfilm Mind; Shades; fourteen dealers in the same antique from Portobello Road, their faces sagging under the weight of their own self-deception; a jobless Polish frenchpolisher brought by one of the dealers; a pop group called the Deep Fix; a pop group called Les Coques Sucrés; a tall Negro; a hunch-backed veterinarian named Marcus; the Swedish girl and a juicy youngster; three journalists, who had just finished spending their golden handshakes; Little

---

[2] *The Final Programme* was serialised in the science fiction magazine *New Worlds* from 1965 to 1966, and was heavily revised before appearing as a novel in 1969.

Miss Dazzle, whom one of them had discovered in El
Vino's; an Irishman called Poodles; the literary editor of the
Oxford Mail and his sister; twenty-seven members of the
Special Branch; a heterosexual; two small children; the late
great Charlie Parker, just in from Mexico under his alias
Alan Bird – he had been cleaning up for years; a morose
psychiatrist from Regent's Park named Harper; a great
many physicists, astrologers, geographers, mathematicians,
monks from disbanded monasteries, warlocks, out-of-work
whores, students, Greeks, solicitors; a self-pitying albino;
an architect; most of the pupils from the local comprehensive school who had heard the noise and come in; most of
their teachers; Jerry's mum; a market gardener; less than
one New Zealander; two hundred Hungarians who had
Chosen Freedom and the chance to make a fast buck; the
father of one of the children from the comprehensive
school, though he didn't know it; a butcher; another Man; a
Displaced Person; a small painter; and several hundred
other individuals not immediately identifiable.

(Moorcock 98)

At such moments, Swinging London is both decadent and absurd,
its penchant for self-indulgence and aimless hedonism emphasised
in the context of its deliberate fictionality. Moorcock's cosmopolitan
guest list is a satirical one, but only just. The party lasts for months,
"Guests died or left and new ones came" (102), while its excesses
are remarked upon in passing and without sensationalism. While
Diment insists on the outrageousness and modishness of events that
now seem relatively unexceptional, Moorcock is blasé though wise
to the exploitative undercurrent of the sexual revolution. "The four-
teen antique dealers from the Portobello Road were enjoying the
Polish french-polisher in a gang bang," we learn, while the warlocks

seek a virgin for a "symbolic sacrifice [. . .] Only symbolic, you understand." (101)

Working in the cultural margins of avant-garde science fiction, Moorcock attracted little mainstream attention with such *jeux d'esprit*. Elsewhere however, what was perceived as sexual excess became an ambiguous facet of outwardly salacious paperbacks. The sexual revolution posed awkward questions for the more politically aware women writers of the time, since it was certainly possible to see "liberation" as a subtler form of slavery. "I think the only thing women's emancipation has meant is the freedom to get laid," Cas (Christian Doermer) tells the heroine of Mike Sarne's *Joanna* (1968). Sandra Shulman, later secretary of the feminist Fawcett Society, published *The Daughters of Satan* (1969) and *The Degenerates* (1970), novels that combine lurid description with moral condemnation in stories where sexual excess, occultism, and drug use play leading roles. *The Daughters of Satan* quotes a fictitious "scandal sheet" as reporting, "Top Civil Servant photographed nude at teenage orgy [. . .] naked nymphs and LSD supplied for his pleasure," and notes that "Yet another dope-peddling ring had been uncovered" (*Daughters* 8). From such asides, one might expect the book to be a denunciation of debauched activities, yet its provocative cover and the tag-line, "their beautiful bodies belonged to the devil," encouraged quite the opposite assumption.

The Degenerates, a title that at once condemns and intrigues, repeated this approach. Nominally a no-holds barred account of Satanism in the swinging metropolis, "the horrifying story of an evil and depraved cult" (front cover), it is exactly the type of fiction that Melly scorned as providing "vicarious kicks for straights." Like many New English Library publications, the book was strikingly presented – the front features a blindfolded naked "dolly." the back a magic circle – but these images promise a very different novel from the one Shulman delivers, perhaps suggesting that the writer and the publicity department were at odds. The novel begins in arch, cod-fairy tale form in identifying the typical Chelsea setting: "'Once upon a not very distant time it was Chelsea on a Saturday night" before describing a Black Mass and Satanic initiation (1).

Unfortunately, it seems torn between modern Gothic and rehashing the Profumo affair in the style of a middlebrow novelist such as Andrea Newman. Various socially influential Hair Spray Men share the favours of a young model, who is inevitably a Chelsea Girl though one given a touch of exoticism through being of mixed race. Blackmail, gonorrhoea, and guilt seem the inevitable wages of sin, before the Satanists murder the girl for threatening to betray their secrets. Shulman later claimed to have written her sex scenes as a "shopping list of perversions" and apparently did not know the meaning of the sexual slang she employed (Hunt 76). However, despite her exuberant descriptions of it, she misses no chance to denounce promiscuity, and often blurs the line between the narrator and the utterances of various characters. She is similarly condemnatory towards the occult, and her combination of the two allows a doubly powerful assault on "decadence" as a destroyer of innocence and tradition alike.

Ironically, some would see the publication of novels such as *The Degenerates*, like films of the order of *Cool it Carol!*, a work denounced by Dilys Powell as "a patch of untreated effluent," (*Sunday Times*, 22 November 1970, qtd. in Hunt 99) as itself symptomatic of cultural decline. As the novel winds wearily to its conclusion, we are told:

> If the 1963 scandal [i.e. the Profumo affair] had been the signal for a new freedom, then [this one] produced a backlash. Various radical groups began hitting out at permissiveness. Many upholders of complete liberty demanded a new order. (186)

Sharing exploitation cinema's mixture of titillation and moral rebuke, *The Degenerates* offered a curious amalgam of quasi-feminist
critique, sleaze, tabloid outrage and fashionable occult paraphernalia, beneath which lurked a scepticism about the "freedoms" of the
permissive society that became increasingly savage as the novel
progressed. Swinging London was passing, it seemed, from euphoria into its "hangover" period, and as Alexander Walker observed,
the question underlying it had changed from "What's it all about?"
to "What will you settle for?" (16). Unsurprisingly, the book cannot
suspend these diverse ingredients in workable equilibrium, being
too sensational for moralistic readers, yet too moralistic for sensa-
tionalists, the youth market that was New English Library's target
audience (Hunt 76).

The capital's bewildering social diversity and pace of life proclaimed its aggressively modern self-fashioning. In one of the intro-
ductory essays to Frank Habicht's photographic collection, *Young
London: Permissive Paradise* (1969), Heather Cremonesi argued
that London offered "the promise of the long, sweet daisy-open-free
life for all," blending the best of the past with optimism for the future (Habicht x). For Robert Bruce however, London had become "a
vision of hell," in which "The relaxation of the old rules and
boundaries has left many people feeling insecure, and some of us
actually frightened" (Habicht xiii-xiv). Christopher Booker agreed.
The Neophiliacs imagined a time traveller from 1955 being disturbed by young people "now in many cases sharply divided from
the rest of the population by their clothes and appearance." The
"number of men wearing hair down to their shoulders, and the number of girls with their hair cropped boyishly close" was similarly appalling (Booker 273). Androgyny and sexual experiment were an
emetic combination for conservatives, yet, predictably, they fascinated a reading and film-going public often denied such experiences. The trial of Mick Jagger and Keith Richards for drugs of-

fences in June 1967 enthralled the nation, offering as it did a confrontation between youthful revolt and traditional authority typified by the famous exchange between the guitarist and the prosecution concerning the unconventional sexual attitudes of Marianne Faithfull:

> *Prosecutor*: Would you agree, in the ordinary course of events, you would expect a young woman to be embarrassed if she had nothing on but a rug in the presence of eight men, two of whom were hangers-on and the third a Moroccan servant?
> *Richards*: Not at all.
> *Prosecutor*: You regard that, do you, as quite normal?
> *Richards*: We are not old men. We are not worried about petty morals. (Qtd. in Levy 284-85)

Transgressive sexuality manifested itself in a variety of ways in Swinging London fiction, though it rarely reached the shocking heights of Turner's menage in Roeg and Cammell's *Performance*, where Mick Jagger's possibly bi-sexual rock star lives in retirement with two young women who are themselves lovers. In the wake of the limited legalisation of homosexuality in the Sexual Offences Act (1967), some writers approached topics such as bisexuality with sympathy and insight. Penelope Gilliatt's script for John Schlesinger's *Sunday, Bloody Sunday* (1971), though occasionally melodramatic, displayed an emotional honesty that produced absorbing human drama rather than a sexual circus. "Surprisingly, perhaps," writes Alexander Walker:

> what motivates these characters isn't sexual jealousy [. . .] The man and woman in the film are almost maddeningly sensible about sharing their mutual boy-friend in their respective beds. What comes between them is an intangible

discontent with life rather than any competitive tussle for love. (18)

The setting is hardly Swinging London, being disillusioned and uncertain rather than suggestive of carnival, but Murray Head's bisexual sculptor is from the same world as the Chelsea Girl, one where the sexual and moral norms of a previous generation of the English bourgeoisie have little meaning. Some might argue that the film cynically configures bisexuality in such a way as to make it palatable to a heterosexual audience, but it would be fairer to say that, a mere decade after Dirk Bogarde's anguished barrister had fought homosexual blackmail in *Victim* (1961), the sexual orientation of the film's protagonists was no longer its primary issue. For liberals, this represented enlightened attitudes, for conservatives, the last word in moral pollution. Tellingly however, the film fared poorly at the box-office: perhaps, as Walker suggests, returns would have been better if "sex had played a more decisive role" (18).

Elsewhere however, bisexuality and even incest became symptoms of everything that was "wrong" with Swinging London and, by extension, the permissive society. In Jenni Hall's *Ask Agamemnon* (1964), twin siblings Jacki and Julian Dewar, whose oddly ritualised relationship revolves around the title's childhood teddy bear, find themselves lost and exploited in the big city, eventually becoming caught up in murder. By the time the novel was adapted for the screen as *Goodbye Gemini* in 1970, though, the relationships it dramatised had become altogether more sensational at the hands of screenwriter Edmund Ward. Chelsea Girl Jacki (Judy Geeson) resists Julian's advances, but still finds herself enmeshed in a blackmail plot, while Julian is lured into a threesome with a pair of drag queens he believes to be female prostitutes. After this "lengthy set up," says Kim Newman, one of *Goodbye Gemini*'s few critical commentators, "the film detours into outright looniness," with its plot increasingly incoherent (29). The effect is to denounce the "anything goes" immorality of the Chelsea Set while openly admitting its fascination. Unlike the teenage couple of *Cool it Carol!* however, there can be no muted return to provincial life. London has drained and discarded the Dewar twins, and the film offers the same conclusions as the Victorian journalist W. T. Stead had made during his investigation of child prostitution, "Maiden Tribute of Modern Babylon" in 1885: "the maw of the London Minotaur is insatiable" (qtd. in Ledger and Luckhurst 34).

The Rag Dolls shares this exhibitionistic yet ultimately downbeat atmosphere. The briefly popular paperback edition, which went through four impressions in 1970, boasted that it "took five years to live and two years to write," and claimed to lay bare "the men-women and women-men who cater to the kinky tastes of the boutique set." Its striking cover, a staging of Christopher Booker's worst nightmare in which a booted dolly bird in a mini dress is pawed by an androgynous youth, suggests the dynamic narrative and sexual promise expected from pulp fiction. Cooper also claimed "honesty and frankness" for his treatment of the "fashion revolution." Blurring fact and fiction through his "first-hand experience of the fashion world, both in London and New York" (inside cover), Cooper teased his readers in the same way as *The Degenerates*. The novel feeds off contemporary preoccupations, but whereas Diment had played the permissive society for laughs, and Shulman had condemned its effects on women, albeit in a rather confused way, Cooper openly favoured titillation over analysis. A cynical morality tale of the road to ruin, *The Rag Dolls* gleefully served up a bisexual pop star and a too close for comfort relationship between beautiful siblings Rupert and Caroline. It spiced the mixture further with drugs and homilies on the fickleness of fame and the emptiness of a popular cultural establishment that sees "love [as] a four letter word; sex just another way to pass the time" (back cover). The result was a piece of myth making that both gloated over and condemned the

"New Morality," while at the same time suggesting that such behaviour was largely confined to elite boutiques of Chelsea and Kensington. Realistically speaking, very few Romans could have experiences like those recounted in the *Satyricon*: two thousand years later, the horizons of Swinging London seemed similarly circumscribed. As the actor Michael Caine ruefully observed in March 1971:

> blokes come over here and talk about the permissive society, but I think it's all a bit of a myth. They're just balling the same couple of hundred girls that everybody else has been having. I'm sure the whole thing is kept going by a couple of hundred ravers. (Qtd in Connolly 131)

J. A. Cuddon's (208) definition of decadence suggests that "the term usually describes a period of art or literature which, as compared to the excellence of a former age, is in decline." Its characteristics typically include:

> The autonomy of art, the need for sensationalism and melodrama, egocentricity, the bizarre, the artificial, art for art's sake and the superior "outsider" position of the artist *vis-à-vis* society – particularly middle-class or bourgeois society. Much "decadent" poetry was preoccupied with personal experience, self-analysis, perversity, elaborate and exotic sensations.

If one takes the view of Bruce or Booker, then London was undoubtedly in decline, hard though it may be to feel nostalgia for the material conditions of 1955. The cultural upheavals of the twentieth century had eroded the certainties on which their view of the world had been based, replacing them with Marianne Faithfulls and Philip McAlpines who have little respect or sympathy for the old ways. For conservative commentators, novels such as *The Rag Dolls* or

The Degenerates, and indeed, the publishing industry that promoted
them, might thus be regarded as complicit in the degradation of taste
and morals, even if the selfish hedonism of their protagonists is ultimately punished.

One can identify too most of Cuddon's elements in the fiction and
film that fabricated the mythic Swinging London, especially if
"straight" becomes a synonym for bourgeois. The "decadent" urge
to catalogue material possessions, taken to such an extreme by J. K.
Huysmans in *À rebours* (1884) here finds expression in the detailed
attention paid to description of clothes and décor. The quest for sensation and the constant battle against ennui that had underlain the
same novelist's *Là-bas* (1891) recurs in the fashionable Satanism of
Shulman's jaded swingers. Behind this lay a limited revival of interest in late nineteenth-century decadent writing and art, with a major
exhibition of Aubrey Beardsley's work at the Victoria and Albert
Museum in 1966, and an unexpurgated translation of *À rebours* being published by Penguin in 1959. Faithfull later remarked that "if
you asked someone if they had read Huysmans [. . .] and they said
yes, you'd immediately hop in the sack" (qtd. in Lachman 295).

However, despite popularity of this novel in bohemian circles,
there is little suggestion of decadent literature's fondness for formal
experiment in the fiction considered here, which parades its demotic
affiliations or else teases suburban and provincial readers with hints
of inside knowledge. *The Rag Dolls* promised to take "the lid off the
'swinging London' myth" (Cooper, inside cover) but it merely replaced one set of clichés with another, maintaining that "it was in
the interest of people [. . .] to keep London swinging, in legend if
not in fact" (Cooper 13). Though there were occasionally innovative
touches, notably the multiple narrators of *The Stud*, there was nothing as overtly radical as the *avant-garde* style of *Performance*, or
the cut-ups of Moorcock's Cornelius stories.

Such a pessimistic reading of the Swinging London phenomenon is, though, at odds with the type of enthusiastic promotion found in Halasz and Cremonesi, or the exuberant image it has enjoyed in its many revivals, most recently the Austin Powers films of Mike Myers. Here, Swinging London is a beginning, not an end: if it is "decadent" then it is so only in the sense of being harmlessly irresponsible in its devotion to pleasure. There is little hint of any more cynical or exploitative element to London life or to the "permissive society," and many memoirists of the period look back with perhaps rose-tinted spectacles at a time when, as Angela Carter wrote, "truly it seemed like Year One, when everything holy was in the process of being profaned" (qtd. in Maitland 1). The opposition of these views is irreconcilable, depending, like the assessment of decadence itself, on the principles and positioning of the commentator.

Works Cited

Allen, Robert & Quentin Guirdham, ed. *The London Spy: A Discreet Guide to the City's Pleasures.* London: Anthony Blond, 1971.

Amis, Kingsley. *Lucky Jim.* London: Gollancz, 1954.

---. *I Want It Now.* 1968. London: Panther, 1976.

Austin Powers: International Man of Mystery. Dir. Jay Roach. Guild/New Line, 1997.

Berheimer, Charles. "Unknowing Decadence." *Perennial Decay: On the Aesthetics and Politics of Decadence.* Ed. Liz Constable, Denis Denisoff, and Matthew Potolsky. Philadelphia: U of Pennsylvania P, 1999. 50-64.

Billy Liar. Dir. John Schlesinger. Vic Films, 1963.

Blow-Up. Dir. Michelangelo Antonioni. MGM, 1966.

Bob Roberts. Dir. Tim Robbins. Rank/Polygram/Working Title, 1992.

Booker, Christopher. *The Neophiliacs: A study of the Revolution in English Life in the Fifties and Sixties.* 1969. London: Fontana, 1970.

Burchill, Julie. *Girls on Film.* New York: Pantheon, 1986.

Collins, Jackie, *The Stud.* 1970. London: Pan, 1984.

Connolly, Ray. *Stardust Memories.* London: Pavilion, 1983.

Cool it Carol! Dir. Pete Walker. Pete Walker Productions, 1970.

Cooper, Simon [Harold Carlton]. *The Rag Dolls.* 1968. London: Corgi, 1970.

---. *The Pretty Boys.* London: Souvenir, 1970.

Cuddon, J. A. "Decadence." *The Penguin Dictionary of Literary Terms and Literary Theory.* London: Penguin, 1998. 208-09.

Darling. Dir. John Schlesinger. Anglo-Amalgamated, 1965.

Deighton, Len. *The Ipcress File.* London: Hodder, 1962.

Diment, Adam. *The Dolly Dolly Spy.* 1967. London: Pan, 1968.

---. *The Great Spy Race.* 1968. London: Pan, 1969.

Faithfull, Marianne, with David Dalton. *Faithfull.* London: Penguin, 1994.

Forster, Margaret. *Georgy Girl.* London: Secker and Warburg, 1965.

Georgy Girl. Dir. Silvio Narrizano. Columbia, 1966.

Goodbye Gemini. Dir. Alan Gibson. Cinerama, 1970.

Gorer, Geoffrey. *Sex and Marriage in England Today: A Study of the Views and Experiences of the Under-45s.* London: Nelson, 1971.

Habicht, Frank. *Young London: Permissive Paradise.* London: Harrap, 1969.

Halasz, Piri. "You Can Walk Across It On The Grass." *Time.* 15 April 1966: 32-42.

---. *A Swinger's Guide to London.* New York: Coward, McCann, 1967.

Hall, Jenni. *Ask Agammemnon.* London: Cassell, 1964.

Hunt, Leon. *British Low Culture: From Safari Suits to Sexploitation.* London: Routledge, 1998.

Huysmans, J. K. *À rebours.* 1884. Trans. as *Against Nature* by Robert Baldick. Harmondsworth: Penguin, 1959.

---. *Là-bas.* 1891. Trans. as *Down There* by Keene Wallis. New York: Boni, 1924.

If It's Tuesday, This Must Be Belgium. Dir. Mel Stuart. United Artists, 1969.

Joanna. Dir. Mike Sarne. TCF/Laughlin, 1968.

The Jokers. Dir. Michael Winner. Universal, 1967.

Kaleidoscope. Dir. Jack Smight. Warner/Winkast, 1966.

The Killing of Sister George. Dir. Robert Aldrich. Palomar, 1969.

The Knack. Dir. Richard Lester. United Artists, 1965.

Lachman, Gary Valentine. *Turn Off Your Mind: The Mystic Sixties and the Dark Side of the Age of Aquarius.* London: Sidgwick and Jackson, 2001.

Larkin, Philip. *Collected Poems.* Ed. Anthony Thwaite. London: Faber, 1988.

Ledger, Sally & Roger Luckhurst, eds. *The Fin de Siècle: A Reader in Cultural History c.1880-1900.* Oxford: Oxford UP, 2000.

Leigh, Wendy. *What Makes a Woman Good in Bed?* London: Mayflower, 1979.

Levy, Shawn. *Ready, Steady, Go!: Swinging London and the Invention of Cool.* London: Fourth Estate, 2002.

MacInnes, Colin. *Absolute Beginners.* London: Allison and Busby, 1959.

Maitland, Sara, ed. *Very Heaven: Looking Back at the 1960s.* London: Virago, 1990.

Mark, Ted. *Dr Nyet.* New York: Lancer, 1966.

Melly, George. *Revolt into Style: The Pop Arts in Britain.* London: Penguin, 1970.

Moorcock, Michael. *The Final Programme.* 1969. Rpt. *The Cornelius Quartet.* London: Phoenix House, 1993.

Muller, Kurt & Kidge Wurdak. *Pussies in Boots.* London: Luxor Press, 1969.

Murphy, Robert. *Sixties British Cinema.* London: British Film Institute, 1992.

Newman, Kim. "*Goodbye Gemini.*" *Ten Years of Terror: British Horror Films of the 1970s.* Ed. Harvey Fenton and David Flint. Guildford: FAB Press, 2001. 28-30.

Novotny, Mariella. *King's Road.* London: Leslie Frewin, 1971.

Performance. Dir. Nicolas Roeg and Donald Cammell. Warner, 1970.

Petronius. *Satyricon.* c.65CE. Trans. Paul Gillette. London: Sphere, 1970.

Rhode, Eric. "The British Cinema in the Seventies." *The Listener,* 14 August 1969: 201-03.

Satyricon. Dir. Frederico Fellini. United Artists, 1969.

Shulman, Sandra. *Daughters of Astaroth.* 1968. Rpt. as *The Daughters of Satan.* London: New English Library, 1969.

---. *The Degenerates.* London: New English Library, 1970.

Smashing Time. Dir. Desmond Davis. Paramount, 1967.

Sunday, Bloody Sunday. Dir. John Schlesinger. United Artists, 1971.

Tam-Lin. Dir. Roddy McDowall. Winkast, 1971.

Tonite, Let's All Make Love in London. Dir. Peter Whitehead. Lorrimer Films, 1967.

Twinky. Dir. Richard Donner. Rank, 1969.

Up the Junction. Dir. Peter Collinson. Paramount, 1967.

Victim. Dir. Basil Dearden. Rank, 1961.

Walker, Alexander. *National Heroes: British Cinema in the Seventies and Eighties.* London: Harrap, 1985.

Waugh, Patricia. *Harvest of the Sixties: English Literature and its Background 1960 to 1990.* Oxford: Oxford UP, 1995.

What's Good for the Goose. Dir. Menahem Golan. Tigon, 1969.

Wilson, Elizabeth. *Only Halfway to Paradise.* London: Tavistock, 1980.

Withnail and I. Dir. Bruce Robinson. Handmade Films, 1987.

Derek Mahon: "A decadent who lived to tell the story"

Brian Burton
The Open University

Abstract: This essay examines some of the primary methods employed by the Northern Irish poet Derek Mahon in his critique of modern-day cultural decadence. He shows that while decadence has become a dominant attitude among Northern Irish Protestants as a direct outcome of the province's strained political situation, his own attitude towards it is fundamentally paradoxical.

The suburbs of Belfast have long provided Derek Mahon with a fruitful source of inspiration for charting the decay and degeneration of Northern Irish cultural life. Even before the onset of the Troubles in 1969, Mahon was casting an ironic eye over Ulster's political and social institutions, keeping watch for their supposedly imminent collapse. This cod-apocalyptic vision has its roots in Mahon's apprehension of decadent tendencies in a society determined by a difficult history where the tensions of the past continue to influence the present. Decadence, especially as practised by the French Symbolists and the (predominantly) English poets of the 1890s, operates from a position of novelty and rebellion against an established order, yet Mahon views it as a cyclical phenomenon that repeatedly reasserts itself either as *fin de siècle* revolt or, in the case of his 1998 collection, *The Yellow Book*, as millenarian insecurity and fear. *The Yellow Book* repeatedly alludes to significant eras in Irish cultural and political history: 1690, when the defeat of Irish Catholics under James II at the Battle of the Boyne paved the way for the rise of the Protestant Ascendancy and the petty-bourgeois values Mahon sets out to, by turn, lambaste or lampoon; the 1890s, the scene of Wilde and "Yeats's 'tragic' generation" (Mahon, *Collected Poems* 239), who sought to emulate the decadent behaviour of their French precursors; Dublin in the 1960s; and the late-twentieth century, which has witnessed the first stages of technology's usurpation of the book. Other decadent eras, too, are referenced, including Juvenal's "modern Rome" (243) and the 1930s London of Cyril Connolly, whose pithy apothegm, "To live in a decadence need not make us despair; it is but one more problem the artist has to solve" (Mahon, *The Yellow Book* 10), provides *The Yellow Book* with not only an epigraph but also an aesthetic agenda.[1]

Mahon's fascination with decadence and late nineteenth-century aestheticism permeates his first collection, *Night-Crossing*, which pre-dates *The Yellow Book* by almost thirty years. These early poems embody Mahon's double-edged response to the *fin de siècle*, and have provoked Edna Longley to remark, "The belief that art has its own ends, independent of the social order, can be radical as well as escapist" (Longley 31). While "The Forger" embraces faith in art as "A light to transform the world" (*Collected Poems* 21) and "Van Gogh among the Miners" makes a religion of art, Mahon's paean to the poets of the Nineties, "Dowson and Company," is less overt in its praise of aestheticism. The poem ostensibly pokes fun at "important carelessness," the hallmark of dandyism and the Decadent movement, while questioning the lasting historical significance of these poets and their own self-important, self-deluding aspirations: "Perhaps you found that you had to *queue* / For a ticket into hell, / Despite your sprays of laurel" (Mahon, *Night-Crossing* 4). Along with Yeats, Richard Le Gallienne, Lionel Johnson, and Arthur Symons, Ernest Dowson was a member of the Rhymers Club, a group of London-based poets which might be seen as a distant forerunner of Philip Hobsbaum's Group of 1960s Belfast. Although friendly with many of the latter's number, Mahon was never a paid-up mem-

---

[1] The Connolly quote has been omitted from the revised version of *The Yellow Book* as found in *Collected Poems*.

ber of the Group, and his natural aversion to such coteries hovers quietly behind the poem, a fact emphasised by Longley's comment on Mahon's commitment to personal autonomy, which manifests itself in his poetry as ironic detachment from his tribe.

At first glance "Dowson and Company" strikes a derisory pose towards the tenets of orthodox religious faith, asking, "Did death and its transitions disappoint you, / And the worms you so looked forward to?" (4), while simultaneously demanding that Dowson and his cohorts "ask no favour of reincarnation." For the Nineties poets, poetry itself became a form of religion that relied for its truth not on strict moral rectitude but on life lived in accordance with the self's authentic quest for emotion-driven experience. Mahon characterises these artists as asserting their individuality by retiring weary from a world that refused or was unable to see beyond their self-constructed, self-alienating façades. The dandyism they wholeheartedly embraced had, since Baudelaire, been an affectation of aloof insensitivity towards the world, taking sartorial elegance and personal grooming as ways of setting them apart from the general run of men in order to reinforce their cult of the self. The Nineties poets inherited from the French Symbolists the desire to expose, articulate, and even embody a consciousness of rupture and separation, as well as a desire to challenge accepted social and cultural norms. Dandyism's pose of excessive refinement represented a backlash against a civilisation with which the Nineties poets were bored, and these outward signs of sophisticated extravagance concealed an unprecedented tolerance toward suffering. Indeed, a significant proportion of their number died young, mainly through alcoholism. Mahon describes their eyes as being "Bleak from discoveries" (4), although this characterisation is later modulated by an ascription of naïve innocence, described in paradoxical terms that are both compassionate and scathing: "You were all children in your helpless wisdom" (4). Here, Mahon suggests the intrinsic disorder and lack of control exhibited by the Nineties poets, an attitude exemplified by Dowson's predisposition towards self-pity: "I was not sorrowful, but only tired / Of everything that I ever desired" ("Spleen").[2]

Mahon himself is not predisposed to self-pity – he is far too ironic for that – and in "The Sea in Winter" he documents his own slide into and recovery from alcoholism with typical self-mocking detachment:

> Back on the grim, arthritic coasts
> Of the cold north, where I found myself
> Unnerved, my talents on the shelf,
> Slumped in a deckchair, full of pills,
> While light died on the choral hills –
> On antabuse and mogadon
> Recovering, crying out for the sun.
>
> (Mahon, *Poems 1962-1978* 111)[3]

Mahon here makes explicit the relationship between his own decadence and its atrophying effects, and the North of Ireland. The desire for the oblivion alcohol can bring represents a desire to escape the guilt Mahon feels for what Elmer Kennedy-Andrews has referred to as an "ambiguous relationship with his people, who still expect his 'ministry'" (Kennedy-Andrews 15). Mahon's subsequent loss of personal vitality (he only published one full collection and one pamphlet of original poetry between 1977 and 1995) resulted in a cathartic retreat from Ulster's troubled society as a way of renegotiating his own place in the world. Despairing of the North of Ireland's retreat into cultural barbarism, Mahon acknowledges his own

---

[2] This original poem should not be confused with Dowson's translation of Verlaine's poem of the same name.

[3] This version of 'The Sea in Winter' is taken from *Poems 1962-1978* as the version contained in *Collected Poems* has been wholly revised with the excision of eight stanzas.

tenuous position, describing it as "*Un beau pays mal habité*, / Policed by rednecks in dark cloth / And roving gangs of tartan youth" (*Poems 1962-1978* 110). And so we discern the dual sense of Mahon's alienation: although trapped in society, intuitively feeling "disgust / At their pathetic animation," he remains isolated from it, asking, "Why am I always staring out / Of windows, preferably from a height?" (112). Consequently, many of his poems are addressed to and identify with the outsiders, the oppressed, and the damned of historical contingency (Knut Hamsun, Thomas de Quincey, and van Gogh, for example), rather than to his own community. Moreover, the weight of his Ulster Protestant heritage brings the additional fear of rejecting Christianity, and its associated values, outright. Patrick Crotty (283) has claimed that "the Ireland of the 1960s genuinely represented the dying phase of a theocratic but in some respects comfortable and homely political order," and this observation certainly chimes with Mahon's own perception of Belfast as a city enduring the painful throes of unshackling itself from "The cold gaze of a sanctimonious God" (*Collected Poems* 13). Yet in "Glengormley," another of his earlier poems, Mahon satirises this "homely political order" as little more than the blithe acceptance by Ulster Protestants of prevailing social conditions.

Named after the Belfast suburb where Mahon grew up, "Glengormley" gives expression to the deep-seated fear that old religious superstitions have not been usurped entirely, despite the claims offered by modernity for civilised behaviour and rational superiority. Mahon seems to celebrate the triumph of modernity, stating "Now we are safe from monsters," but then voices his concern that there are no longer any saints or heroes who might offer some protection against the new era's "dangerous tokens" (14). The terrier-taming, hedge-trimming inhabitants of Glengormley occupy a world of conformity and bourgeois banality that is both the very antithesis of decadent revolt and the exemplification of sterile, decadent absurdity. Behind the poem's opening line, "Wonders are many and none is more wonderful than man" (14), lies a heavy irony that both condemns and feels sympathy for these suburban citizens who have chosen to conceal themselves from the reality of sectarian violence by continuing with their everyday lives. The Protestants of suburban Belfast have, for Mahon, grown complacent thanks in part to the wealth generated by the city's industrial past, and we can detect in the poem a suggestion that violence in Ulster is both a symptom and a consequence of the affluence on which Belfast's decadence is founded. Mahon seems to be saying that ever since the usurpation of Catholics, to whom a major portion of Ireland's dramatic myths truly belong, the Protestants have brought violence upon themselves since decadence is one of the consequences of the transition from one set of religious loyalties to another He also reminds us, through the trope of the "conspiring seas" (14), that the North of Ireland is not only bounded but also marginal, and therefore contingent on its own historical, political and cultural processes. And it is through this contingency, and the concomitant dread of retribution, that Mahon's sense of guilt manifests itself.

A further consequence of Belfast's affluence is found in its people's fetishisation of material objects, which Mahon considers a sure sign of cultural decadence that has its roots in Protestant suburbia. "A Bangor Requiem," section XVIII of *The Yellow Book,* is a less than sentimental meditation on the life of the poet's (then) recently deceased mother. Mahon brands the poem "a cold epitaph from your only son" (261) while relating his mother's fondness for "'Dresden' figurines" and "junk chinoiserie" to her concern for the "appearances" that ruled her life (260). Yet Mahon does not simply condemn his mother for a fascination with a form of artifice that provides a rebuke to aestheticism and its concomitant illusion of value. He also sees in her collection of domestic kitsch a typically decadent glorification of the unnatural and non-utilitarian that has emerged from bourgeois pretensions, the siege mentality of wartime accumulation (he refers to "a bombing raid glimpsed from your bedroom window"), and a culture controlled partly by a Protestant church determined to maintain its own position of power:

> Shall we say the patience of an angel? No,
> not unless angels be thought anxious too
> and God knows you had reason to be; for yours
> was an anxious time of nylon and bakelite,
> market-driven hysteria on every radio,
> your frantic kitsch décor designed for you
> by thick industrialists and twisted ministers. (260)

His mother's bungalow is thus transformed into a metaphor for Ulster: each is a place to which the poet feels drawn because of its relationship to his strained conception of home ("By / Necessity, if not choice, I live here too," he writes in "Glengormley" [14]), yet ultimately neither can sustain his refined aesthetic sensibilities, and he is driven to "travel south" where he might feel more at ease beneath the "blue skies of the republic" (261).

The Yellow Book takes its title from the famous literary journal of the 1890s, which itself became a by-word for the Decadent movement of Wilde, Dowson and Symons, and as a whole the collection "dramatise[s] the sense of the cyclical recurrence of eras of decadence" (Crotty 274). Writing at the tail-end of the 1990s, Mahon repeatedly relates the contemporary world to those of the late seventeenth and the late nineteenth centuries. By juxtaposing these three *fins de siècle*, he conveys both the impact of religious sectarianism on Ulster and the Protestant population's *laisser-faire* response to it:

> I thought of the plain Protestant fatalism of home.
> *Remember 1690; prepare to meet thy God* –
> I grew up among washing-lines and grey skies,
> pictures of Brookeborough on the gable-ends,

revolvers, RUC, 'B' Specials, law-'n'-order,
a hum of drums above the summer glens
shattering the twilight over lough water
in a violent post-industrial sunset blaze
while you innocently hummed 'South of the Border',
'On a Slow Boat to China', 'Beyond the Blue Horizon'.

(Collected Poems 261)

By looking towards increasingly distant elsewheres, the geographi-
cal allusions contained in these song titles foreground the "withdrawal *from* others, [and the] withdrawal *of* others" that Edna Longley (35) has identified as being characteristic of Decadence. Mahon
effectively attacks unionist culture through objects of popular culture, which act as poetic springboards from which to launch his own
escape away from Ulster's cloying domestic Protestant world and
into what he hopes will be a brighter, more optimistic future in the
Irish Republic. Such escape is merely one aspect of Mahon's acceptance of personal responsibility and his desire for authenticity,
which springs not only from his fascination with existentialism, but
also from his conscious adoption of the individualism and aestheticism that David Weir (2-3) recognises as decadent responses to cultural barbarism or collective social upheaval. During Mahon's life-
time cultural barbarism has, in Northern Ireland, degenerated into
sectarian violence and a taste for the artificial; hence Mahon's
mother's obsession with "ornaments and other breakable stuff" (*Collected Poems* 260) and the implication that an unbridgeable gulf exists between high aestheticism and what he perceives as base popular art forms. Yet he also credits his love of art to the influence of
his mother as he states, "all artifice stripped away, we give you back
to nature / but something of you, perhaps the incurable ache / of art,
goes with me as I travel south" (261). This comment contains an
echo of Pater's remark on the "incurable thirst for the sense of escape, which no actual form of life satisfies, no poetry even" (Pater

213-14). Yet it also points towards both Mahon's appreciation of art as being a matter of inheritance and the recognition that his mother taught him to strive to be an autonomous, authentic individual. Indeed, the phrase "all artifice stripped away" appears designed to poke fun at the Symbolists and Nineties poets who felt compelled to draw attention to themselves by living behind cosmetic masks, while indulging their feckless taste for "celibacy or satyriasis" (*Collected Poems* 240).

Mahon's curious description of his love of art as an "incurable ache" suggests not only that his aesthetic sensibility is a form of sickness leading inexorably towards death and decay, but also that the appreciation of art is itself a manifestation of decadence. "A Bangor Requiem" raises the questions of where the appreciation of art comes from and what end it serves. Such questions have, however, been partially answered earlier in *The Yellow Book*. Section V, "Schopenhauer's Day," establishes the idea that the world of nature is in constant opposition to that of the mind, and that this conflict can only be resolved tenuously (if at all). "The only solution," Mahon writes with tongue firmly in cheek, "lies in *art for its own sake*" (233), a stance which, in true Decadent fashion, seeks to replace the constancy of personal responsibility with the transience of aesthetic egocentricity. Yet his quest for "redemption through the aesthetic," by shunning dependence on the irrelevant religious dogma similarly denied by "Spring in Belfast," must ultimately rely for its resolution on an encounter with nature: "birds in spring / sing for their own delight, even if they also sing / from physical need" (233). The poem therefore negotiates a position halfway between compulsion and desire that has its roots in pain and guilt. The supreme fiction of art is in constant struggle with the often violent historical conditions that form identity; while Mahon can ask "Has art, like life itself, its source in agony?" (231), art also "suggests alternatives to the world we know / and is to that extent consoling" (254).

Part of this consolation comes from the desire to order the world into something meaningful and comprehensible. Describing his mother as "a rage-for-order freak" (260) serves to remind us of the poem "Rage for Order," where Mahon identifies with the "Grandiloquent and / Deprecating" poet who is "far / From his people" (47). The poet is once more poised between compulsion and desire as he views the shattered remnants of his home environment:

Somewhere beyond
The scorched gable end
And the burnt-out
Buses there is a poet indulging his

Wretched rage for order –
Or not as the case
May be, for his
Is a dying art,
An eddy of semantic scruple
In an unstructurable sea. (47)

Edna Longley (33) has described the language and register of Mahon's most famous poem, "A Disused Shed in Co. Wexford," as "dandyism, high style, high camp, aesthetic display," and "Rage for Order" exhibits the same traits. As with "A Bangor Requiem," the poem brings aestheticism and religion into contact through its depiction of apocalyptic retribution, and the loss of order violence has wrought on Belfast is itself a symptom of the decadence that has engendered Mahon's pessimistic response to the historical reality of national decline.

In other poems he is even more explicit in depositing blame for the socio-political situation in Ulster at the doors of complacent Protestant households – such as his mother's – through a recognition of Catholic insurgence, both real and potential. In "The Last of the Fire Kings" Mahon strikes a pose as the decadent aesthete "Perfect-

ing my cold dream / Of a place out of time, / A palace of porcelain,"
while claiming to be "Through with history" (*Collected Poems* 65).
The irony, of course, is that history continues unabated and cannot
be avoided since even the aesthete cannot evade historical processes. Mahon's position as Fire King, as bringer of order, is destined
to be short-lived as he confronts the "barbarous cycle" of usurpation
and the community that demands "that I inhabit, / Like them, a word
of / Sirens, bin-lids / And bricked-up windows" (65). Baudelaire
(33) once noted the distinction between the free-thinking individual
and the superstitious majority – "The masses are born fire-
worshippers" – and the poem turns on the conflict between the collective desires of the many and the self-determining needs of the individual. Decadent civilisations are always at the mercy of barbarism, whereby the barbarian becomes the agent of history, and in the
case of Mahon's Ulster, decadence is construed both as a historical
category and as a form of moral approbation designed to shock the
Protestant community out of their complacency.

In an interview with Eamon Grennan (166), Mahon describes
himself as "an out-and-out traditionalist" who adheres to "the Coleridgean sense of formal necessity," although he playfully satirises
this attitude in Section XI of *The Yellow Book*, "At the Chelsea Arts
Club," stating, "Maybe I'm finally turning into an old fart / but I do
prefer the traditional kinds of art" (*Collected Poems* 245). Even his
earliest work, and its reliance on traditional forms, displays a maturity that shows that Mahon has always had something of the "old
fart" about him. The combination of wit and passion in the above-
quoted lines, the switch from self-derision to heart-felt sincerity, is
inherited from a tradition in English poetry that stretches back to at
least the sixteenth century, and it marks *The Yellow Book* as an hon-
est, if somewhat ambitious, project designed to lament the passing
of an idealised past while deriding a far from ideal present: "Not
many / in the trade now can decently impersonate / the great ones of

the tragic repertoire" (241). Mahon sees this as his own condition, reduced to invoking and parodying those writers of the past whose depictions of the human predicament he considers exemplary. He populates *The Yellow Book* with many such writers, including Wilde, Huysmans, and Austin Clarke, each of whom exercised a reaction against society by pitting the individual imagination against established social mores. Mahon repeatedly invokes the presence of Decadent artists throughout *The Yellow Book* as a way of exposing the degenerative slide from *fin de siècle* aestheticism towards contemporary cultural barbarism. "Hangover Square," which casts the Nineties poets in a starker light than "Dowson and Company," is a catalogue of allusions, both explicit and implicit, to many of the main figures involved with French symbolism and the English Aesthetic movement. Yeats, Dowson, Lionel Johnson, Richard Le Gallienne, and Arthur Symons are all named directly, while Dowson's poem, "Non Sum Qualis Eram Bonae Sub Regno Cynarae" provides a central reference. We can detect in this poem a certain admiration for the rejection by Decadent artists of political and psycho-sexual conventions when Mahon writes,

> I remember London twilights blue with gin
> *sub regno Cynarae*, the wine and roses
> where 'she-who-must-be-obeyed', furs next the skin,
> drove us to celibacy or satyriasis. (240)[4]

Vowing to "keep alive the cold candle of decadence," Mahon allies himself with those poets who chose to shun the stifling values of Victorian society as a way of maintaining his desire to outlive short-lived cultural fads and "surviv[e] even beyond the age of irony / to

---

[4] In the original version of the poem, which has been dramatically revised for inclusion in *Collected Poems*, this section was followed by the line "forgive me, love, for my apostasies" (*The Yellow Book* 29).

the point where the old stuff comes round again" (*Collected Poems* 240).

Yet there is no such approval to be found in "At the Chelsea Arts Club," which describes the tabloid sensationalism, "instant celebrity," and immediate gratification of late twentieth-century youth culture as having replaced the aesthetics of individualism with a more violent and tawdry way of life:

> Everywhere aspires to the condition of pop music,
> the white noise of late-century consumerism –
> besieged by Shit, Sperm, Garbage, Gristle, Scum
> and other raucous trivia, we take refuge
> from fan migrations, police presence, road rage,
> spy cameras, radio heads, McDonald's, rowdytum,
> laser louts and bouncers, chat shows, paparazzi,
> stand-up comedian and thug journalist,
> TOP TORIES USED ME AS THEIR SEX TOY
> and Union-jacquerie at its most basic. (245)

What Mahon perceives as the "trash aesthetics" (245) of the postmodern age is of a piece with the culturally decadent fetishisation of material objects. The contemporary world's fascination with "video nasties and shock computer graphics" (245), the transient values of "a junk-film outfit or an advertising agency" (227), and the detritus of "Christmas rubbish" (265) serves to compound the bourgeois obsession with utilitarian objects, establishing a tense opposition with what Mahon considers more civilised *fin de siècle* ideas. Mahon's preference for art that serves no immediate purpose, such as "the heartfelt calculus of Bach and Mozart / or the calm light of Dutch interior art," is based on his faith in the Coleridgean aesthetic principles that characterise the struggle to perfect the work in the hope of perfecting the life.

In this sense, Mahon identifies with Baudelaire who, writes Richard Gilman (82), "spoke of the good bourgeois as 'an enemy of art, of perfume, a fanatic of utensils'. By this invective he was defending the nonutilitarian in an age that seemed to worship only the immediately useful". However, Mahon's outrage at the post-modern world's reliance on (to him) alien and alienating technology, where "computer talks to computer, machine to answering machine" (*Collected Poems* 227), seems to stem from his own tendency towards fetishisation. One of the main themes voiced in *The Yellow Book* is Mahon's concern with the imminent death of the book. Significantly, he chooses to glorify his love of the printed word by citing three texts – one erotic, two from the Nineties – which he reads in isolation from suburbia and, again typical of the decadent writer, from the world of business and finance:

> Commuters hustle home to Terenure and Foxrock
> while I sit in the inner city with my book
> – *Fanny Hill, À Rebours, The Picture of Dorian Gray* –
> the pleasures of the text, periphrasis and paradox,
> some languorous prose at odds with phone and fax. (226)

Mahon's mission is to document and, in his own way, combat what he perceives as a contemporary form of social evil, that of cultural "dumbing down." He is both fascinated and appalled by this manifestation of human irrationality and cultural entropy, and is consequently nostalgic for a former age, a time when the world was not in thrall to the products of "progress" and the global domination of technology. Yet while Mahon is sceptical not only of the lasting value of the Nineties poets' work but also of his own, he is also concerned that poetry, and indeed all literary art, will be killed off by the unfeeling forces of science and materialism. In "Remembering the '90s," the unrevised version of "Hangover Square," he writes,

The most of what we did and wrote was artifice,
rhyme-sculpture against the entangling vines of nature –
a futile project since, in the known future,
new books will be rarities in techno-culture,
a forest of intertextuality like this,
each one a rare book and what few we have
written for prize-money and not for love,
while the *real* books like vintage wines survive
among the antiquities, each yellowing page
known only to astrologer and mage
where blind librarians study as on a keyboard
gnomic encryptions, secrets of the word,
a lost knowledge; and all the rest is lit(t)erature.

(*Yellow Book* 29)

In the revised version, the last six lines have been replaced with
the following:

No doubt I should invest in a computer
but I'm sticking with my old electric typewriter,
its thick click, black ink on white pages,
one letter at a time, fur round the edges.

(*Collected Poems* 240)

Taken together, these very different versions of the poem divulge
Mahon's fear not only for the future of poetry, but also for the manner in which it is produced. His reluctance to embrace modern technology exposes his own fetishisation of what many would now consider an outmoded means of writing. Just as contemporary culture
places value on fashionable clothes and the products of technology,
and just as Mahon's mother considered decorative – if ultimately
useless – objects beautiful, so Mahon himself exhibits a decadent
tendency to revolt against "the new world order" (225). More important, however, is the way the poem dramatises Mahon's apoca-

lyptic fear for the future of literature itself. As Patrick Crotty (284)
notes, "our millennial dilemma is presented as more serious than
any other period of deliquescence in that literature itself, which survived previous cultural breakdowns to bequeathe [sic] us an invalu-
able record of decay, seems threatened with extinction." Yet the
poem also reveals Mahon's adherence to traditional – if not archaic
– methods of composing (there is something monastic about producing works "one letter at a time"), as well as his reliance on craftsmanship. Condemning the financial impetus behind much contemporary writing, Mahon portrays art, its artefacts, and indeed its artifice as having to confront the threat of a utilitarian world governed
by technology and hell-bent on mass-production.

   In his most recent collection, *Harbour Lights*, Mahon returns to
the theme of decadence in a number of its poems, but there is a far
stronger sense of optimism here than in *The Yellow Book*. The title
poem locates the poet in a twilit, liminal environment – a coastal
town in Co. Cork – where he meditates on a new day and the fresh
promise it brings: "in the morning when the sun comes up / there
will be snail-mail with its pearly gleam" (62). The bright future
Mahon imagines is far removed from the technological age of com-
puters ("snail-mail" suggests its electronic antithesis), "structural
electricity" (66), and the "lies and nonsense" (61) told on television,
although his reverie also distances him from "the global shit-storm"
(64) of continual worldwide violence. Such a retreat into a more pacific world permits him the mental freedom to reconsider the pessimism of *The Yellow Book*, and Mahon luxuriates in the possibility
that "some immigrant teenager / will write the unknown poetry of
the future" (62). Yet the intellectual liberty offered by aesthetic
decadence must still confront the descent into material decadence
where there can be no guarantee of a known future: "for ours is a
crude culture dazed with money, / a flighty future that would ditch
its granny" (63). Nevertheless, Mahon's fear of impending cultural

collapse is now tempered by the knowledge that youth culture is not altogether corrupt, and that elsewhere there may be, like Mahon himself, another "strange child with a taste for verse" (*Collected Poems* 106).

The same idea is expressed in "Lapis Lazuli," a poem dominated by the presence of Yeats. Not only are the title and dedication – (for Harry Clifton) – borrowed wholesale, but the poem's theme of tragic joy, its dedication to linguistic and syntactic play, and even Mahon's questing sense of wonder all pay homage to Yeats's powerful, abiding influence. Indeed, busts of Yeats and Buddha "supervise" (*Harbour* 24) the writing of the poem, exerting a joyous, zen-like tranquillity over one of its most disquieting moments:

> While planes that consume deserts of gasoline
> darken the sun in another rapacious war
> a young woman reads alone in a lighted train,
> scratches her scalp and shoves specs in her hair,
> skipping the obvious for the rich and rare.
> Hope lies with her as it always does really. (25)

Thirty years ago, Mahon opened "A Disused Shed in Co. Wexford" with the line, "Even now there are places where a thought might grow" (*Collected Poems* 89), and that sense of amazement at the lingering power of the human imagination remains, even if it means that taking pleasure in the written word must reflect a decadent urge to shut out the realities of war and violence in briefly-snatched moments of quiet contemplation. "Lapis Lazuli" posits introspection as a decadent indulgence that forms "the raw material from which art is born," yet is necessary if, as Yeats's poem claims, the poet is to sing of his joyful insights into art's redemptive potentiality: "Do we die laughing or are we among those / for whom a spectre, some discredited ghost / still haunts the misty windows of old hopes?" (*Harbour* 24, 25).

"The Seaside Cemetery," the closing poem of *Harbour Lights*, is a version of Valéry's "Le cimetière marin." The poem is a powerful discourse on transience, death, the futility of art, and the "confrontation between universality and individuality" (Crow 24). Valéry's early poetic career was aligned with the Decadent Symbolist movement, but he gradually turned away from it in order to accommodate in his work the unpredictable and uncontrollable forces of nature that had previously proved alien to both intellect and consciousness. Mahon, however, has never been a full-blown Decadent or Symbolist, and he has always appreciated and valued the noumenal qualities of the natural world. Yet Valéry's poem has provided him with an ideal vehicle for launching his own investigation into the idea that, in spite of relentless human violence, the world can still offer "depths beyond the reach of art" (*Harbour* 72). By adapting Valéry's poem and revealing its relevance to a post-modern world, Mahon establishes a trans-historical discourse with an important nineteenth-century precursor and in the process subjects his own affiliation with the values of the Decadent movement to close scrutiny. "The Seaside Cemetery" deals with what is attainable both in poetry and in life. Mediating between presence and absence, the poet ascertains the field of the possible as belonging to the world and within mortal bounds: the derangement of the senses created by the world's "diversity" (73) can only be comprehended once the mind has achieved clarity. But this is not to say that clarity leads to poetic purity, since purity ends only in disillusionment and detachment from life, so the poet wants the "sun-dazzled pages" (75) of his notebook to fly away so that he might escape the compulsion to perfect the work and focus instead on the life.

Mahon describes himself as "a decadent who lived to tell the story" (*Collected Poems* 239), a self-mocking statement that seems to allude to his battle with alcoholism during the 1980s. With survival, however, has come a shift in poetic purpose. In 1995, following a 13-year hiatus when he produced little original work, Mahon published *The Hudson Letter*, whose title poem adopted a more casual and conversational voice which would, in *The Yellow Book* and *Harbour Lights*, develop into his predominant style. Looser and more conversational than his readers had come to expect, *The Hudson Letter*, and more especially *The Yellow Book*, were vilified by some critics for what was perceived as Mahon's betrayal of his usual lyric brevity. In a 1981 interview Mahon declared: "I enjoy the sense of struggling against a form, and that provides the creative tension that tells me that this is a real poem that I'm writing" (Kelly 10). In a later interview he stated that his formal sense had previously been "too polished," and that future collections would become "more conversational, floppier, looser" (Battersby 26). Indeed, the eclogue-like structures of *The Yellow Book* seem deliberately designed to poke fun at the Decadents' creed of brevity. But despite the presence in *Harbour Lights* of the Valéry translation/adaptation and the lengthy "Resistance Days," Mahon has to some extent returned to his earlier, more concise style; "Bashō in Kinsale," for example, even revisits the compact three-line stanza – short in length, long in syllable count – so often deployed by Mahon ("The Dawn Chorus," "A Lighthouse in Maine," "The Woods," and "The Joycentenary Ode" are just a few examples that spring to mind). Although it may cast an eye towards William Carlos Williams, this attenuated form has become such an indispensable weapon in Mahon's armoury that it is now difficult to dissociate him from it. This struggle with form is consistent with what Edna Longley (31) has called "Mahon's powerful feelings of attraction-repulsion towards the *fin-de-siècle*." Yet Mahon's constant desire to perfect the work, "by translating aesthetic principles into formal practice" (31), conflicts with the realities of the life. Describing this condition as "the Decadent dilemma," R. K. R. Thornton (26) writes:

> The Decadent is a man caught between two opposite and apparently incompatible pulls: on the one hand he is drawn by the world, its necessities, and the attractive impressions he receives from it, while on the other hand he yearns towards the eternal, the ideal, and the unworldly [. . .] and the incompatibility of the two poles gives rise to the characteristic Decadent notes of disillusion, frustration and lassitude at the same time as the equally characteristic self-mockery.

Mahon is torn between the life of art and the practical life. Alienation, exile and isolation are central themes of Mahon's poetry, suggesting that he is attracted more to solitude than to sociability, and his work frequently retreats into the Decadent, if not elitist, world of philosophical ideas and ivory towers. But it is just as likely to eulogise the natural world or lament the loss of community, as in "Glengormley." Mahon's is thus a poetry of paradox, with the poet refusing to be neither completely alone nor completely integrated into society, completely devoted either to art or to artifice, completely enamoured of the drive towards perfection or completely divorced from it. And perhaps it is thanks to this paradox that he has survived to "tell the story" while so many of his nineteenth-century precursors fell victim to decadent excess.

Works Cited

Battersby, Eileen. "Made in Belfast." *Sunday Tribune* 26 Aug. 1990: 26.

Baudelaire, Charles. *Intimate Journals.* Trans. Christopher Isherwood. Introd. W. H. Auden. 1930. London: Panther, 1969.

Crotty, Patrick. "Apocalypse Now and Then: *The Yellow Book.*" Kennedy-Andrews 273-96.

Crow, Christine M. *Paul Valéry: Consciousness and Nature.* Cambridge: Cambridge UP, 1972.

Ernest Dowson, "Spleen," *The Symbolist Poem: The Development of the English Tradition*. Ed. Edward Engleberg. New York: Dutton, 1967. 218.

Gilman, Richard. *Decadence: The Strange Life of an Epithet*. New York: Farrar, 1979.

Grennan, Eamon. "Derek Mahon: The Art of Poetry LXXXII." *Paris Review* 154 (2000): 151-78.

Kelly, Willie. "Each Poem for me is a New Beginning." *Cork Review* 2.3 (1981): 10-12.

Kennedy-Andrews, Elmer, ed. *The Poetry of Derek Mahon*. Ulster Editions and Monographs 11. Gerrards Cross: Smythe, 2002.

---. "Introduction: The Critical Context." Kennedy-Andrews 1-28.

Longley, Edna. "Looking back from *The Yellow Book*." Kennedy-Andrews 29-48.

Mahon, Derek. *Night-Crossing*. London: Oxford UP, 1968.

---. *Poems 1962-1975*. Oxford: Oxford UP, 1979.

---. *The Yellow Book*. Oldcastle: Gallery, 1997.

---. *Collected Poems*. Oldcastle: Gallery, 1999.

---. *Harbour Lights*. Oldcastle: Gallery, 2005.

Pater, Walter. "Aesthetic Poetry." *Appreciations with an Essay on Style*. London: Macmillan, 1889. *The Victorian Prose Archive*. Ed. Alfred J. Drake. June 2002. 25 Aug. 2005 <http://www.victorianprose.org>.

Thornton, R. K. R. "'Decadence' in Later Nineteenth-Century England." *Decadence and the 1890s*. Ed. Ian Fletcher. Stratford-upon-Avon Studies 17. London: Arnold, 1979.

Weir, David. *Decadence and the Making of Modernism*. Amherst, Massachusetts: U of Massachusetts P, 1995.

Yeats, W. B. *The Collected Poems of W. B. Yeats*. London: Papermac-Macmillan, 1982.

Contributors

Brian Burton completed his Ph.D. thesis on the poetry of Derek Mahon in 2004. He has taught English at the University of Durham, and is currently an Associate Lecturer with the Open University. His publications include essays on Mahon, Samuel Beckett, and Gérard de Nerval. He is presently conducting research on the poetry of North East England.

Michael R. Catanzaro is a lecturer at the University of Toledo in Toledo, Ohio where he received his Ph.D. in English literature and where he has worked for the past twelve years. Born and raised in Ambler, Pennsylvania, he received a double-major undergraduate degree in English and Spanish literature from Temple University in Philadelphia, Pennsylvania. He received a master's degree in English from Northeast Louisiana University in Monroe, Louisiana.

Peter G. Christensen is Associate Professor of English at Cardinal Stritch University in Milwaukee, Wisconsin, USA. He received a Ph.D. in Comparative Literature from the State University of New York at Binghamton. His specialty is in nineteenth- and twentieth-century comparative literature, and he has published two other articles on Vernon Lee.

Petra Dierkes-Thrun (Ph.D. University of Pittsburgh, 2003) is a Lecturer in the English Department at Santa Clara University, California. Her interests include interdisciplinary approaches to British, European, and transatlantic literature, art, and philosophical aesthetics of the 1850-1939 period; women's and gender studies; critical and queer theory; and Victorian and Modernist visual rhetoric and culture, including film and popular culture. She is currently working on a book manuscript dealing with adaptations and transformations of the Salome theme in 19th- and 20th-century literature, dance, opera, and film, and has published articles on Oscar Wilde, Richard Strauss, and George Bernard Shaw.

Paul Fox (Ph.D. University of Georgia) is an Assistant Professor at Zayed University in the United Arab Emirates. He has published articles upon *fin de siècle* aesthetics, Walter Pater, Oscar Wilde and J. M. Barrie. He is currently completing a book-length study of Decadence and aesthetic time.

Nick Freeman received his Ph.D. from Bristol University and teaches English at the University of the West of England. He has published widely on 19th and 20th century literature, and also has a strong interest in post-war British film and television.

Eric Langley teaches and lectures in Shakespeare at the University of St Andrews. Forthcoming publications include work on eye-beams, Renaissance suicide-notes, and the rhetoric of anti-suicide polemic. A book length study on narcissism and self-murder is under publisher's consideration, and on-going research considers the literary representation of drunkenness and the rhetorical features of inebriation.

Deborah Lutz received her Ph.D. in 2004 from the Graduate Center of the City University of New York. She has taught English literature at Hunter College since 1998 and is a visiting Assistant Professor at Montclair State University. Her forthcoming book, *The Dangerous Lover: Gothic Villains, Byronism, and the Nineteenth-Century Seduction Narrative* (Ohio State UP), traces a literary-historical itinerary of the lover whose eroticism comes from his remorseful and rebellious exile, from his tormented and secret interiority. She has two forthcoming publications, one on the origins of the eroticism of the pirate and the second on the revivified interest in the gothic romance: "The Eroticism of the Nineteenth-Century Pirate Poet: Byron, Scott, and Trollope" in *Pirates and Mutineers* and "The Dark Brooder and the Haunted Mansion: the Revival of the Gothic Romance in the 21ˢᵗ Century" in *Empowerment versus Oppression: 21ˢᵗ Century Views of Popular Romance Novels*. Two of her recent publications include "The Secret Rooms in My Secret Life," *English Studies in Canada* 31 and "Love as Homesickness: Longing for a Transcendental Home in Byron and the Dangerous Lover Narrative," *The Midwest Quarterly* 36. She has also recently annotated numerous Modern Library editions of nineteenth- and twentieth-century classics. She is currently working on a book on Victorian pornography.

Ewa Macura teaches English literature at the Warsaw School of Social Psychology. She has recently completed her doctoral dissertation on New Women and the rhetoric of Decadence and degeneration at the *fin de siècle*. Her research interests include feminist theory, Victorian literature and cultural studies.

Sarah Maier, Associate Professor, completed her doctoral research at the University of Alberta with *Dionysian Dominatrices: the Nineteenth-Century Decadents/ce of Alcott, Egerton, D'Arcy and Rachilde* (now with Manchester UP), and she is also a graduate of The School of Criticism and Theory at Darmouth College (New Hampshire). She has published two editions of Hardy's *Tess of the D'Urbervilles*, as well as articles in areas of nineteenth- and twentieth-century literature, decadents/ce, images of women, literary theory, and children's literature. She is currently working on an edition of Wilkie Collins's *Basil* for Broadview Press; her other current research projects are on the subjects of *Millennial Madnesses: Cultural Paradigms at the Fin(s) de Siècle(s)*, fictional representations of serial killers and on Marie Corelli. Dr. Maier is also the recipient of the Dr. Allan P. Stuart Award for Excellence in Teaching.

Heather Marcovitch is a Lecturer in the Department of English Literatures at Mount Allison University, New Brunswick, Canada. She works on aestheticism and decadence in the nineteenth- and twentieth-century. She has written on Oscar Wilde, Ella D'Arcy, and Christopher Isherwood.

Ann-Catherine Nabholz received her Ph.D. from the University of Basel (Switzerland) and the University of Orléans (France) in 2004. She is currently working on the publication of her dissertation, entitled *The Crisis of Modernity: Culture, Nature, and the Modernist Yearning for Authenticity.*

Bonnie J. Robinson is an Associate Professor of English at North Georgia College & State University. She has published articles on creative writing and Victorian literature, including guest editing a special issue of *Victorian Poetry* on turn of the century British women poets. She is also the founder and faculty adviser of the literary e-zine *Unfettered Muse* (www.unfetteredmuse.com).

Shafquat Towheed, educated at University College London (B.A., M.A.) and Corpus Christi College, Cambridge (Ph.D.), was until recently a Postdoctoral Fellow in English at the University of Nottingham, and now teaches at the Institute of English Studies, University of London. He researches widely in late nineteenth- and early twentieth-century English and American literature and is the author of scholarly articles on Charlotte Brontë, Hubert Crackanthorpe, Rudyard Kipling, Vernon Lee, J. Sheridan Le Fanu, R. L. Stevenson, Mrs Humphry Ward, and Edith Wharton amongst others. Current work in progress includes a monograph that examines the interaction between copyright law, creativity and the definitive text in the period c. 1880-1930; an edition of Edith Wharton's correspondence with her London publisher; editing a collection of essays on Edith Wharton and the material culture of the book, and more articles on Vernon Lee and the history of ideas, c. 1875-1935. He is also currently co-editing (with Mary Hammond) a collection of essays on publishing in the First World War.

James Whitlark, author of *Illuminated Fantasy: From Blake's Visions to Recent Graphic Fiction* and *Behind the Great Wall: A Post-Jungian Approach to Kafkaesque Fiction*, wrote sections of twenty-five other books and has published numerous journal articles. He is Professor of English at Texas Tech University, where he has won several teaching awards.